ROANE COUNTY, West Virginia Families

By William H. Bishop

Excerpted from
*History of Roane County
West Virginia*

CLEARFIELD

*O*riginally published as pp. 431-704
of *History of Roane County, West Virginia* (1927).

Reprinted for
Clearfield Company, Inc. by
Genealogical Publishing Co., Inc.
Baltimore, Maryland
1995

International Standard Book Number: 0-8063-4586-1

Made in the United States of America

CHAPTER X.

HISTORY OF FAMILIES OF PIONEERS OF ROANE COUNTY; THEIR MARRIAGES AND MANY NAMES OF THEIR DESCENDANTS WITH ANECDOTES ILLUSTRATIVE OF THEIR CAREERS AND CONTRIBUTIONS TO PUBLIC WEAL.

The sources of the author's information for this chapter are in most cases an interview with a member of the family mentioned; biographs in Hardesty's History, being a book containing an outline of United States history, of Virginia, West Virginia, and a group of counties including Roane, Jackson, Calhoun and Wirt, in which is written a dictate dbiograph of each subscriber, of date 1883.

Also from records of conveyances in Roane and adjoining counties out of which Roane was made.

Dates of marriages in quotation marks are taken from marriage records; these records made prior to year 1882 do not give ages of the parties.

ADAMS:

Andrew Jackson Adams, later Captain Adams, came with the Bishops and Harpers to Pocatalico, "about the year" 1843; he was one year older than the John Bishop, father of the author of this book. I can state correctly that Andrew J. Adams was born in Pike County, Kentucky, in the year 1829, son of a highly respected young Virginian and his wife, both of whom died there in Kentucky. We have no information as to the given names of his parents or of the events that left him an orphan, too young to preserve the history of his parents. He was fourteen years of age when he came to this Pocatalico country and made his home among the Bishops or Harpers as he choose; always received at the fireside or dining table with the other boys of the family; when the jeans or linen in the loom was having yard after yard added day by day as women of the household worked and sang "Andy's share was always counted among the necessary yards to weave; so with the tanner and the shoemaker of the family." Andy's shoes or boots were counted with the rest.

After the breaking up of the Bishop family, elsewhere related, Andy went with the larger Bishop boys to Ripley, in the adjoining county, there he and the Bishop boys worked for a short time carrying brick on the brickyard; next we know to relate is that at the age of twenty-three, Andy has a contract to build a certain section of the Glenville, Ripley and Ohio turnpike, through Cassville (later Spencer); again about the year 1853, he is a construction contractor building parts of the Ravenswood and New California turnpike in Jackson County; here he courted and married his wife, Eliza Pickens, daughter of John and Mary A. (Lawrence) Pickens, of Mason and Jackson Counties; one son was born to Andrew and Liza (Pickens) Adams, his name Phillip Curry Adams; he is the same P. C. Adams so often mentioned in the history of the business of the City of Spencer.

On the outbreak of the War of the Secessions "Andy" Adams enlisted as a private November 26, 1862; in Co. H, Third Regiment, W. Va. Volunteer Cavalry. Promoted 2nd lieutenant Feb. 19, 1863; 1st lieutenant Feb. 15, 1865; in place of A. W. Adams, who was transferred; promoted to captain April 20, 1865; mustered out June 30, 1865. In this war service he steadily rose from subalteran ranks to that of captain, with which commission he was mustered out of service at the end of the war. He at once went into business of divers kinds, at Ravenswood, West Virginia, the main one of which was that of a hardware store; about the year 1875, he came back to Roane County with his wife and son, Phillip C., transferring also all his business to Spencer, and as shown by reports of committees of the county court, was an active participant in the county's public business for some seven to ten years, during which time he returned to the haunts of his boyhood days and bought some three hundred acres of land, part of the old Bishop-Josiah Hughes place, and there built the best farm house of the time in the district and tried to become a farmer; cleared many acres of the then still untouched forest, employing more workmen than the natives there had ever seen in one gang; the wife and son liked it all, and settled themselves, keeping up the farm and raising the best herds of cattle of the district for some fifteen years. Captain Adams' business in town kept him there; from whence he finally went to Minnesota and never returned; died and was buried there about the year 1912.

Phillip Curry Adams, son of the Captain A. J. Adams above mentioned, married Mollie J., daughter of Hezekiah and Jemima Miller, of Lower Spring Creek, on the 27th of June, 1886, his age 28. To Phillip C. and Mollie J. Adams were born and by them reared in the Town of Spencer the following named children: Ernest E., Ruth, Harry Rudolph, Hubert S. and Phillip C. junior.

ADKINSON: Of Reedy.

James Adkinson and his wife Margaret (Templeton), whom he had married in Marietta, Ohio, she a daughter of an early settler on the Little Muskingum River, with some of their first children, acquired a large tract of forest land on Čolt Run of Left Reedy Creek, about the first of the decade, 1850; made here the average sufficient farm for the times. And here brought up their family of four sons and four daughters, their names, Sarah, Eliza, Nancy, Mary Ann, Charles, George, James Jr., and Leander Loch.

Marriages of some of the above sons and daughters:

Sarah married Thomas McGraw, December 12, 1864.

Eliza married Bert Dalrymple, see name Dalrymple.

Nancy and Mary Ann's marriages we do not find.

Charles, son of James and Margaret Adkinson, married Miss Sarah Evilsizer, in Roane County, May 10, 1879.

George and James's marriages not found.

Leander Loch Adkinson, son of James and Margaret, his wife, was born in the year 1858; on November 12, 1880, married Miss Elizabeth Nester, of Tanners Run of Spring Creek.

Leander L., in recent years has become wealthy from petroleum oil income; has acquired the old Roach farm on Middle Reedy, or nearly all of it; where he yet lives, holds stock in the banks of Reedy Town and does his part as a good citizen. To Leander and Elizabeth Jane (Nester) his wife, have been born and by them brought up three sons and three daughters, all or most of them have married and have families.

ANDERSON: Of Reedy.

Ezra D. Anderson, veteran of the Civil War was born on Sandy, Jackson County, West Virginia, 1847, died at Reedy, year 1926; was one of the family Anderson, pioneers of the middle Ohio River valley; he was a son of John and Betsy Ann (Boice) Anderson; enlisted as a soldier in the Union forces and served through the Civil War.

At once on return from the war in the year 1865, he united in marriage with Mary Jane Powers—his blue uniform his wedding suit. Mary Jane was a daughter of Elihu Powers, a noted man of his times in Jackson County.

These newlyweds made their home on Sandy not far from Sandyville for the first eight years of their wedded lives; purchased a tract of forest land on Staats Run of Middle Reedy and moved themselves and family on it in the year 1873. There brought up their family of seven sons and two daughters whose names given in order of respective births are as follows:

William Hezekiah, born 1866; John D., Remus E., Denzil, Charles B., Edward Hayes, Randolph D., Irene Jane and Ida May. The first wife having died, Ezra married Miss Lummie Starcher, of Spencer, West Virginia; of this marriage one child, the daughter, Icy, was born.

Of this family, William Hezekiah, is an ordained minister of the Gospel, and Remus E. has been for many years the popular baggage master of the B. & O. train on its run between Spencer, his home and Parkersburg or other points on the Ohio River division.

ANDERSON: Of Western Reedy District.

Ezra Engle Anderson was born and brouht up in Wetzel County, West Virginia; there united in marriage with Miss Elizabeth Masters, born in Green County, Pennsylvania. Lived the first eighteen years of their married lives in Wetzel County; came to Roane County in the year 1893, their family, two sons and two daughters, with them; the eldest then about seventeen years of age. They purchased a farm near the head of Longs Run and Buffalo Fork of Mill Creek, and settled there for their permanent home.

The names of their sons and daughters are as follows: Daniel Harvey, born in the year 1876; Florence, born in the year 1882, married here, John Tatterson; Cynthia Bell, born 1884, married Albert B. Payne, son of Ebenezer Payne; Richard Ezra Anderson was born in the year 1886.

Of this family the son Daniel Harvey, now referred to as the Rev. Dan Anderson, is most widely known. He studied for the ministry and was ordained and admitted a member of the West Virginia M. E. Conference, in the year 1916, and placed in charge of the Mount Union circuit on head waters of Reedy. Has ever since continued in the ministry. He is married and has a family.

ARGABRITE:

Isaac and Betsy (Swope) Argabrite, both Virginians, married in Greenbrier County, western Virginia, came to these parts and settled on upper Middle Fork of Reedy about the year 1844; with them or born soon after their arrival were their three sons and three daughters: George, Jacob H., Floyd, Amanda, Elvira and Rebecca, all of which children grew up, married near and raised families, of which read on:

George Argabrite, son of Isaac and Betsy, married Emily (Hardman), then widow of John Ingraham, with three children: Hugh, Alice and Lycurgus, the last born December 26, year 1853; the names of the children born to George and Emily Argabrite are Ella, wife of Thomas Snow; Fannie, wife of E. Swazy Ball; Rebecca, wife of Dempsy Parsons; Mary J., wife of John Roberts; and two sons, Romeo and William Argabrite.

Jacob H. Argabrite, son of Isaac and Betsy, married Alice, daughter of John and Emily (Hardman) Ingraham; the names of the children of Jacob H. and Alice Argabrite, in order of their ages are Fleetwood, eldest, born April 20, 1865; Homer Elliott; Ida, wife of Oscar Hunt; Benjamin D. ,a graduate physician now of DePoy, Kentucky; Merit French, now a merchant and restauranteur of Spencer, and Emma, wife of Homer Thompson, of Spencer, electric engineer of the Spencer Water & Ice Company.

Floyd, son of Isaac and Betsy Argabrite, died some years ago leaving two sons, William and Cola, both now of the City of Spencer.

The three daughters of Isaac and Betsy are, Amanda, wife of Thomas Simmons; Elvira became the wife of Henry Greathouse, and Rebecca married John Erran Greathouse.

Martin Argabrite, born in Greenbrier County, came to these parts with his brother Isaac, in the eighteen-and-forties; he was a pensioner of the war of 1812; he married.

Of the children of Martin Argabrite we can name here Diana, who married William Burdette; Kellis, who married Jinnie Hardman; they have left one son, Okey Argabrite, who now (1926) lives at the old home place above Peniel with his wife, a daughter of Miles Board, of Jackson County; and Wiley W. Argabrite, who married Mary Showen; this is the Wiley W. Argabrite mentioned in the history of the City of Spencer, in which he appears to have owned a tavern about the time of the Civil War.

ARMSTEAD: Pioneers of Hurricane Creek.

James Miller Armstead and his wife, Jeanette (Davis) Armstead, both of Fluvana County, Virginia, with four first born of their children, came to Hurricane Creek, of Big Sandy waters, about the year 1846, having purchased, or soon acquired a tract of five hundred and fifty acres of forest lands lying on Hurricane; attacked the forest in the way of all other pioneers, had health and good sense, and theirs was the noted place for thirty years; a part of this tract remains the property of a descendant of theirs.

The names of the sons and daughters of James Miller Armstead and his wife, Jeanette (Davis), given in order of their births, are as follows:

James Alfred, never married, died a bachelor at eighty.

Susan, married John H. Campbell; he died leaving one child, a daughter named Irene.

Sarah A., married Robert Wright.

John, Mathew and Joseph, three sons enlisted as soldiers in the Confederate service, 1862 to 1865, all died leaving no posterity.

Thomas J., also served through that Civil War and married Cynthia Prudence Parker, May 13, 1868.

Benjamin F., born on Hurricane in the year, 1848, married Miss Frances Ellen Naylor, daughter of John M. Naylor, year 1872; they settled on Hurricane and there reared the following sons and daughters: John R., Benjamin H., the person giving the writer this information; he married a Miss Lola B. Ashley. The daughters of Benjamin F. and Frances E., his wife, are Nort E., wife of James Carpenter; Jeanette Ellen, wife of Benjamin H. Ashley; Bessie Evans, and Mrs. Ruby Ethel Myers.

Elisha Norton was twice married, first to Isabel E. Oxier, 1874; she died leaving some children; Frances A. ("Sis"), wife of Milton I. Oxier, married year 1874. Jeanette married Van Patten.

ARMSTRONG:

Hon. Matthias Benson Armstrong, born in Lewis County, western Virginia, February 10, 1820, a son of John J. P. and Margaret (Jones) Armstrong, who settled in this part of Reedy country in the year 1843. Matthias B. Armstrong's name is seen conected with much of the earlier business of the village later becoming the City of Spencer. He appears to have been a resident of the villages New California and Reedyville; when the County of Roane was formed; the first county court convened in his residence; he was thrice married, the second wife died childless; the names of the children of Matthias B. and first wife, Nancy (Rader), in order of their births, are William H., 1844; next Newton B., John Wesley Chapman, lawyer, mentioned in the chapter of this work: History of the City of Spencer, in list of lawyers of the town; and Florence M. Armstrong. For his third wife Matthias B. married Louisa, daughter of Elijah and Nancy (Lewis) Flesher, formerly of Lewis County, but of Jackson County at time of marriage of Matthias B. and Louisa; he held the office of county surveyor of Roane County, four years, and served one term, year 1872, as State Senator for Fifth Senatorial District, at which time his residence was Reedyville.

Newton B., son of Matthias B. Armstrong, married Miss Almeda McCarty, November 2, 1869; Newton B. Armstrong was prominent in the county for some fifteen years, 1875 to 1890; dealt in timber; served as assessor of the county one term. To Newton B. and Almeda, his wife, were born and reared one son, Chapman and several daughters, whose names we do not know.

ARNOTT: Of Spencer and Spencer District.

William Arnott and Adaline (Lowe) Arnott, his wife, with a large family of children came here to Roane County in the year 1854, from Monroe County, where both had been born and were married.

He was a son of a Henry Arnott, a Scotch settler in eastern Virginia. For ancestry of Adaline see Lowe.

The names of their children stated in order of births, "to the best of recollection" of Henry M., a son, are as follows:

Elizabeth, William Thomas, Henry Mathew, Ellen, Cornelius Pendleton, Virginia, Rebecca, Clark and Eliza.

Their marriages and residences at sometime:

Elizabeth married William German, lived at Long Bottom, Meigs County, Ohio.

William Thomas, married Isabelle Danalson, in Roane County, May 12, 1866; made their home on Spring Creek; reared the following named children: Dr. Ulysses G., of Point Pleasant; Reverend Forest Arnott; Romeo F.; Ess; a daughter, Otie, wife of Ernest West of Spring Creek; John, a business man of Spencer; and Orville, teacher awhile in Roane County, clerk in store Charleston; died there, year 1927.

Henry Mathew Arnott, son of William and Adaline, married Matilda McMullen of Spencer, August 28, 1868; they lived many years in

HISTORY OF ROANE COUNTY 437

Spencer; he was a wagon maker and proprietor of a shop at intersection of Main Street and Ripley turnpike, now Rex Arnott's garage site. To Henry Mathew and Matilda, his wife, were born and by them reared the following named sons and daughters:
Estey Cole, resident of Clay County.
Roxie, who is wife of John W. L. Kyer, of Ravenswood.
Belle, wife of Nathan Cunningham, Moundsville, W. Va.
Hayes E., married Miss Starkey, always residents of Spencer.
Melissa, wife of J. Otis Summers, native of Roane County, now resident of Charleston.
H. Rex R., married Mida Cleavenger, May 14, 1903; he is propriettor of the Arnott "Chevrolet" Garage, Spencer.
Jeannette, married Leonard Schnoffer, resides at Marietta, Ohio.
Dorothea, married John Hall, their residence Akron, Ohio.
The other six children of William and Adeline (Lowe) Arnott, all married and made their homes in Meigs County Ohio; their names as follows:
Ellen, married Levi Wagoner of Long Bottom.
Cornelius Pendleton, lives at Racine.
Virginia, married Benjamin Hamilton, Meigs County, Ohio.
Rebecca, married George Allison, of Antiquity, Ohio.
Clark, married and made his home at Antiquity, Ohio.
Eliza, married a Mr. Jackson Lack, of Antiquity, Ohio.
AYERS:
Buenos Ayers, one time resident of Reedy, grew up on eastern head of Mill Creek, was born in Ritchie County, western Virginia, April 30, 1848, son of Jeremiah and Eleanor (Campbell) Ayers. Jeremiah Ayers was an old time schoolmaster, sagacious, a little impatient with old illiterates of those he met; by this lost much of his due as a citizen; for his son, Buenos, he hoped for high attainments in his ancestral profession and encouraged him in every way. Buenos attended Marshall College at Huntington, came forth to Roane County about the year 1873, and organized a "Subscription School," a kind popular at that time. Professor Nash, author of "Nash's School Grammar," was in Roane at the same time, taught at Walton and at Spencer. Buenos taught several such schools at Reedy Town, and two on Middle Fork; on Middle Fork for a reason that will appear presently; he was an enthusiast and did much to make popular the advantages of good education, even college education. June 18, 1874, at her home on Middle Fork, Buenos Ayers married Minerva Jane, daughter of Andrew B. and Mary (Stewart) Chancey; Andrew B. Chancey owned a big farm of some three hundred acres, in fine condition, well stocked, and his was a popular family; had been deputy sheriff and was an active citizen. On her marriage the father, Andrew B., gave and conveyed to his daughter Minerva Jane the upper end of his farm, with the usual "horse, saddle and bridle," a cow and calves; this land lay near the home of the author of this work, only one small farm between. On his wife's lands Buenos built the first pre-

tentious frame house on the Middle Fork, rivaling that of his father-inlaw. Soon was elected superintendent of schools of Roane County, which office he filled with ability and satisfaction years 1875-1877; many of what is now "Roane County's first crop of teachers" trace their inspiration to the work of Buenos Ayers. While in this official school work he studied law at home under direction and tutelage of old lawyers at Spencer and was soon after admitted to practice, but did little of it; about the year 1880, he with his family removed from Reedy and became residents of Ripley, West Virginia, where he practiced law some, was a commissioner in chancery of the circuit court; was elected as a justice of the peace and served that office one or more terms of four years; died there as also—possibly—did Minerva Jane, his wife. Buenos had some brothers and sisters, the names of these we can give from recollection—long years—in order of their recollected ages, are, Jefferson, a Confederate soldier; Elizabeth ("Lizzie"), a school teacher, who became the wife of Robert E. Lee, and resided at Shirtsville, Wirt County, many years; Ballard, of whom we venture no recollection, and Gelia, the youngest, who united in marriage with Rex Roland Rohr, in Spencer, the 28th day of January, 1885; his age 28, her age 23; he was editor and proprietor of the Weekly Bulletin, the county's leading newspaper at that time. This couple resided in Oakland, California, the last we knew of them, to which State they went from Spencer many years ago.

Of the marriage of Buenos and Minerva Jane Ayers were born three children: Minnie L., December 10, 1876; Nora F., September 18, 1881; and A. J., July 14, 1875.

BAKER: Of Curtis District.

Aaron Baker, born in the State of Maine, March 17, 1812, son of Aaron and Hannah (Smith) Baker, both of Maine; in Noble County, Ohio, 7th day of April, 1842, he and Sarah Jennings of that county were married; of this, five children were born: Hanna, David N., Elizabeth Jane, Ruth and Gamaliel. For a second wife Aaron Baker married Emily Jane McMun in Sharon, Noble County, Ohio, February 28, 1858, she being a daughter of Isaac and Maria (Moore) McMun; of this marriage, ten children were born, five sons and five daughters, all in Noble County, Ohio. Their names in order of dates of their births are: Aaron W., Lydia M., Cordelia A., Elmer Ellsworth, James Grant, Isaac A., Martha F., Mary Viola, died at two years, Margaret Luella, and Henry Clarence Baker. H. Clarence yet resides on the old farm just above the post office Clarence in Curtis District. Aaron Baker, the father above mentioned, came to this part of Roane County in the year 1881; he was a devout member of the Methodist Episcopal Church; gave of his time and means to building and support of his church, while clearing away the heavy forest and making the farm and home. But for a short mention of the above facts of his life found in Hardesty's History to which he or some member of his family subscribed, name and memory of this good citizen would have been lost to the public; he has been dead so long, only two or three of the oldest citizens remember him. His children seek no public mention.

BAKER: Of Reedy, Spencer, Jackson County.

The first person of this family name to pioneer in these parts was John Baker, who came to the lower Reedy Creek about four miles below "Three Forks' 'in the early part of the decade, 1840's, having with him his wife, whom he had married in Randolph County, western Virginia, to whom was born at Horseshoe Bend in Randolph County, Elijah, of whom we can authoritatively say further, as follows:

Elijah Baker was born October 4, 1815, at Horseshoe Bend, Randolph County, Virginia; married Miss Nancy Wolfe. Elijah dealt in real estate; bought, moved on, and sold and moved off; thus he and Nancy had first homes at divers places on Reedy, Mill Creek and lastly on Big Sand Creek, flowing into the Ohio at Ravenswood.

While living on Reedy two miles above "Three Forks" their son, Dallas Monroe, was born September 19, 1846; sometime after this Elijah and family moved over on Big Sand Creek, above mentioned, settling on a large tract of land, near the half-way between Ravenswood and "Three Forks of Reedy" through which lands ran the Ravenswood and Spencer turnpike, skirting a wide flat knoll on which he built the family residence, having a cross-roads store on the opposite side of the pike. Here for several years his was the best farm between Reedy and Ravenswood, until younger men, the Dawkins and Hutchinsons outstripped him.

During the Civil War Elijah Baker counseled all to keep in the paths of honor and chivalry, whether an enlisted soldier or guerrilla, Union or Secesh, and risked his life in that service as often perhaps as any who bore arms at the front.

A service he performed in that line for the mother of the author of this book, her name Sarah (Roach) Bishop, of her we write here, as an instance of the war-times service of Elijah Baker; a kind we only read of in stories of times "When Knighthood was in Flower;" this is it in part:

It was near the close of that internecine war, late in the year 1864; the strife in Roane County waxed to such heights that reprisals and avengements were being resorted to; the Confederate armies in Virginia were in dire need of the very necessaries of life. Every soldier on furlough or "A. W. O. L." from that naked and hungry army came with letters for the folks at home, and braving all vigilance of Union scouts and home guards with which the county at that time was well covered, made his way, usually at night, to the home of the parents of his comrade at the moment yonder in Virginia or faraway South, gazing on the pitiless stars and praying that "mother will receive and feed my distressed and hungry comrade."

Orders from Union authorities had been given to home-guards to destroy all residences in which aid and comfort was habitually given "Rebels."

A few farm houses had been destroyed under that order. The farm home of Delilah Roach was designated next; she being a widow, of whose family three sons were obnoxious,—one, Jesse, with Lee's army, two others at home, garrulous and vindictive; receiving and feeding continually "skulking Rebels;" a term of imprisonment in Camp Chase had not cured nor detered. That home was the house in which mother was born, her only home, her husband, John Bishop, at the time trudging in the ranks on the Potomac, a volunteer of the Union army. It must not be done! It shall not be done, said Sarah (Roach) Bishop, as she waited at the boat landing at Longbottom, for the next packet for Ravenswood. At Ravenswood, some friends carried us—I was then approaching five years old and with mother—out to William Flesher's, then the owner of the big water mill at what is now Silverton. The next morning we were taken into Elijah Baker's wagon and carried to his home,—half the distance of the whole journey,—cared for there until the next morning, when Elijah again brought out his wagon and carried us to Reedy, delivering us there into the care of old William Stewart, a kindred spirit in war philosophy. From Three Forks two miles further, and we were at grandma's.

The family home was saved. But there was tragedy. (See paragraph in the Chapter, "The County In the Civil War.")

A further word and the reader will more fully appreciate how unusually chivalrous was the service of Elijah Baker. Something of what others were doing:

Just a day or so before we arrived at William Flesher's, a child had been killed while playing on the little veranda of a house near Flesher's, by a shot fired from the top of a nearby hill; "mistook the child for the dog," was the opinion of some. Only a few days before, a shot from the woods of a near hillside on Elijah's own farm sped so close him, under such circumstances, that the action of the shooter bore no other interpretation that that murder was intended. Elijah was a large man, broad and erect with a large beard and pink cheeks; deep, low pitched, strong voice and serene countenance; his beard was full, heavy and gray, when I last saw him, which was about the year 1884.

Elijah and Nancy (Wolfe) Baker reared only one son; his name, Dallas Monroe Baker, born on Reedy, September 19, 1846; married Mary E. Johnson, near Sandyville in Jackson County, West Virginia.

Mary E. was daughter of John Johnson, born in Ramsy Parish, Essex County, England, December 14, 1814, and came by way of Canada to New York, stopping for awhile at Chestrfield in that State; there he married Miss Barbara Carr, born at that place. John and Barbara, his wife, with Mary E., came to Sandyville, Jackson County, in the year 1854 or 1855.

HISTORY OF ROANE COUNTY 441

To Dallas Monroe Baker (and wife, Mary E.) were born and by them brought up the following named children:

First, John Maurice Baker, Esq., November 22, 1872; married Jessie Riley of Jackson County, West Virginia, September 19, 1899; commenced married life in that county and served one term (4 years) as prosecuting attorney of Jackson County, then moved to Spencer (see Chapter, this book, "City of Spencer"). To John M. and Jessie, his wife, were born and by them brought up one son and one daughter; their names, Clay Baker and Mary Baker. Both have married and gone forth.

Second, child of D. M. and Mary E. Baker, is Della, who married Captain Lee Knotts, in Jackson County, West Virginia. He was raised to his captaincy in the World War, 1917-1918, and is at this date abroad in the military service of the United States.

Third, child of D. M. and Mary E. Baker, married Mr. Robert LeBlanc.

Fourth, Mary G., married Reverend H. A. Spencer.

Fifth, James Elijah, married Anita, daughter of Doctor W. L. Craig.

Sixth, Ida B., married Anderson Johnson.

Seventh, Charles Edgar Baker, born at Sandyville, Jackson County, West Virginia, November 20th, 1886; married Ninera, daughter of Daniel and (............ Riley) Dawkins of Jackson County, West Virginia. Charles Edgar was elected sheriff of Jackson County, 1924, for the term commencing next following, and is now, 1926, serving his county as its sheriff.

BALL: Of Curtis District.

James Alfred and Elizabeth (Elliott) Ball,—he, born in Washington County, Pennsylvania, December 11, 1837; she, in the same state and county, June 1, 1835,—came from there to Curtis District, year 1874, purchased lands on the Spencer and Ripley turnpike where it crosses the divide between Reedy and Mill Creeks. With J. Alfred and Elizabeth came their three sons: Elroy S., Orville P., and Hudson O., the last of whom died in 1878. This family soon made a good farm and entered into the citizenship of the district and county. J. Alfred was most active in Curtis and Reedy Districts, serving one term as a constable of Curtis District; and did his part as a promoter of interest in churches and schools.

Elroy S. Ball, son of J. Alfred and Elizabeth above mentioned, was born in East Finley Township, Washington County, Pennsylvania, October 24, 1863; married Fannie, daughter of George Argabrite of this district and have a large family; taught school in his younger days; has been elected and served five terms as a justice of the peace of Curtis District, and owns and lives on the old "home place."

Orville P. Ball, son of J. Alfred and Elizabeth, was born in Washington County, Pennsylvania, September 4, 1870, married Anna Fouty— a neighbor girl—they have three daughters and one son. Russell Ball, born in Curtis District, May 16, 1905, is now linotype man in the work of the *Times Record*, a newspaper of City of Spencer.

BALL: Of Left Fork of Reedy.

About the year 1873, the two brothers, Major William Ball and Samuel Benton Ball came to Reedy. Major was tall, finely proportioned; S. B., inclined to the shorter and more rugged; both blonds of the brown hair and beard. They were born in Gilmer County, West Virginia, sons of Robert and Lucretia (Martina) Ball, descendants of colonial families of those names, early settlers in the Monongahela Valley.

William, the elder, served with Lee's armies in Virginia during the Civil War, when he was advanced to the rank of major; hence "Major Ball." These brothers engaged in the timber business on the Little Kanawha and its tributaries. Their business brought them to Reedy, where Major William united in marriage with a Miss Sallie Conrad. He became owner of the better part of the Mordecai Thomasson-Ben Riddle farm on Left Reedy; was prominent for fifteen years, 1875 to 1890; no children were born to Major Ball and his wife.

Samuel Benton Ball, son of Robert and Lucretia, his wife, married twice; first, on April 17, 1873, to Miss Victoria Armstrong, daughter of Lenox Armstrong of Jackson County, West Virginia, one time sheriff when Reedy was part of Jackson County. Acquired a large farm on Left Reedy, his home; was elected and served one term as member of the County Court of Roane. To S. B. and Victoria (Armstrong), his wife), were born in Roane County, two daughters and one son. Their names in order of their respective ages are: Minnie, Frank Lenox and Ida.

Minnie is the expert court stenographer in Spencer; Frank L. married Miss Blanche Tallman, 6th April, 1910; his age 30, hers 24. She was a daughter of Samuel and Rosa (Seaman) Tallman of Right Reedy.

Ida united in marriage with Holly H. Burke—neighbor—29th July, 1905; her age 21; his age 24. They live at Parkersburg.

Victoria, the first wife of Samuel Benton Ball having died, he united in marriage with Miss Myrtle Armstrong, on 4th day of October, 1888; his age 47, her age 30. She was a sister of the first wife. The farm at this time comprised nearly four hundred acres, well furnished home and much live stock. He died in the year 1908. The family yet holds the farm.

Of the marriage of S. Benton and Myrtle (Armstrong) Ball, were born and became citizens, four children whose names respectively, are Beulah A., Brooks, Eugene and Nina. Beulah A. and Brooks are still single; Nina married Mr. Paul Lukens, born in Pendleton County, West Virginia, and Eugene was killed in service in France in the World War.

BARNES:

Edgar W. Barnes was born in Harrison County, Western Virginia, October 3, 1833, the son of John and Frances (Vincent) Barnes, Virginians by birth. Edgar W. Barnes, now an M. D. and a graduate of one of the Eastern schools of medicine and surgery, came to Roane County about the year 1856 or 1857, for it is observed that on May 28, 1857, he and Eleanor, daughter of Josiah and Elizabeth Hughes, were wedded. She was born in Marion County, Western Virginia, April 8, 1838. Two young people these were. He twenty-four and she nineteen. Dr. Edgar W. Barnes so far as we can learn was the first regular practitioner of medicine to locate in Harper District. He enlisted and served through the Civil War as a Confederate soldier. In the year 1880, in an interview, he mentioned with some pride his farm on which he resided and from which he attended to the duties of his profession. He and Eleanor raised only the child; Leslie D., born January 1, 1862; Married M. Starcher June 11, 1883.

BARR:

Dr. Thomas Barr, son of Thomas and Elizabeth (O'Connor) Barr; the father, Thomas, was born in Edinburg, Scotland; the mother, in Dublin, Ireland. Both died in Lynchburg, Virginia, he in 1851, she 1853, Thomas, Jr., subject of this sketch, being nine years old when his mother died. Dr. Thomas Barr was born in Amherst County, Virginia, March 15, 1844; he does not tell how or where he grew up in his biography dictated to Hardesty's about the year 1883. Enlisted in the Confederate army, 1862, Co. K, 14th Va. cavalry; as observed, he was only twenty years old when he enlisted. As the Virginia cavalry furnished its own mounts, he must have been a young man of promise. He served through this war, coming out unscathed. In Greenbrier County, August 22, 1866, he married Allie F., daughter of John and Mary (Hyde) Kincaid; three years later they arrived in Roane County, their first born with them; they made their first home at Peniel on upper Reedy; from which point the doctor went out plying his profession, soon gaining a good reputation as an efficient and kindly physician.

He makes no mention in his biography where or when he obtained his medical knowledge; he was liked and succeeded. After a few years at Peniel he moved his family to Reedy where he lived for some years in the neatest and best kept residence of the village, the leading physician for nearly ten years. About the year 1884, the family moved to the State of Colorado.

To Dr. Thomas Barr and Allie F. (Kincaid), his wife, were born in years prior to their departure for Colorado the following children: Harry W., September 14, 1868; Charles C., February 4, 1870; Otey H., December 11, 1872; Willy G., October 24, 1877; Walter B., August 21, 1880; Emma G., December 21, 1882. Though there is not one of this estimable man's family in this State, and maybe not one will ever see this, oblivion shall not claim them.

BATES:

Franklin E. and Elizabeth (Kesler) Bates, his wife, came from Fayette County, West Virginia, about the year 1857, and settled on a tract of forest land on lower Reedy not far from "Three Forks" in the same year. He was a veteran of the War of 1812; enlisted and met his death in the Civil War. They had some sons and daughters, the first two or three of whom were born in Fayette County, Western Virginia. A daughter, Margaret A., married Jacob M. Leasher, December 6, 1867. A son, John H. Bates, married Miss Fluvana McClung in Roane County, March 4, 1872; she a daughter of Mortimor M. McClung and wife, of near Reedy. A daughter Fannie married and made her home "back in Fayette County."

The children of Margaret A. and Jacob M. Leasher were several sons and daughters; of these are remembered George, Roland and Cyrus. There were some daughters, but we fail to get their names.

BATTEN: First of Spring Creek.

The first of this family name "Batten," was William J. Batten, his wife, nine sons and one daughter came from Hackers Creek, Lewis County, West Virginia, and settled first on what is now the high school grounds. William J. Batten was a blacksmith or day laborer. His wife who came here with him died, and soon afterward he married Catherine Runnion, March 12, 1857. Of this marriage were born six sons and five daughters; of the above twenty-one Battens we have much general, but little sufficiently specific information to write here. All married and settled in Roane County. The son of the family best known in the Town of Spencer, was William H. Batten who married Rachel Harper, daughter of Henderson Harper of Poca. These were the parents of a William, Jr.; Joseph; Pery; Lee, and Louis, the youngest.

BECKLEY:

The first of this family name residents of Roane County were the Rev. Neville Craig Beckley, his wife, who before marriage was Miss Elizabeth Lore of Raleigh County, and their three children, Alfred C., Emma J. and Robert H. The family arrived here from Fayette County, in the year 1874, the Rev. Neville C. having been sent here by the Methodist Episcopal Conference to take charge of the work here in Roane.

The Methodist Episcopal's strongest locality at that date was upper Middle Fork of Reedy in Curtis District. Here Reverend Beckley located his family and made their home, from which he went out in the surrounding country and preached his regilious faith and for years urged on communities the value of Christian religion; during which time he laid the foundation for a strong church in the county, the full fruition of which occurred under his successor, the Rev. C. H. Lakin, who saw an increase in church buildings from one, that at Reedy, known as "Fleshers Chapel," to a dozen or more scattered about the county, including one in the Town of Spencer. Reverend Neville C. Beckley died at Charleston, where he was taken suddenly ill while on his way to a new appointment in Fayette County.

The history of the Beckley family is an illustrious one; a National history of no small import, and of the State of West Virginia none more important. Lewis' History of West Virginia devotes a little more than four pages to General Alfred Beckley, founder of Raleigh County, the county seat of which is "Beckley," that perpetuates his name. He was the father of Neville Beckley, our citizen preacher above mentioned.

We have room here for only an outline of the history of the Beckley family, and we reduce that outline to the following facts:

The first of the name gaining public notice was a John Beckley, clerk of the national House of Representatives during the presidency of Washington, the elder Adams and Thomas Jefferson; Mayor of the City of Richmond, 1783; member of the Board of Aldermen; Secretary of the Virginia Constitutional Convention, 1788, and the first Librarian of Congress: died April 8, 1807. Of the family John Beckley left, we will write here of one only, General Alfred Beckley. He was born on Capitol Hill, City of Washington, 26th of May, 1802; and, as observed, was a fatherless child at five years of age. He says, "My mother removed to the City of Philadelphia with myself, a boy of five, her only child; she lived in Philadelphia till some time in May, 1814." "While in Philadelphia I was sent to several schools of repute." "We removed to Frankfort, Kentucky, in May, 1814."

"In 1819, Mr. Monroe, then president, and a warm friend of my father, on application of my mother, through Gen. William Henry Harrison, gave me the warrant of cadet of the United States Military Academy at West Point, N. Y." "On General Harrison's invitation I became an inmate in his family at North Bend for six months, availing myself of the instruction of General Harrison's private instructor to his children."

"I graduated on the 1st day of July, 1823, number nine in a class of thirty-five." * * * "I served thirteen years honorably in the United States army; two years of which was in Florida, 1824-1826." This was in the Seminole War; six years arsenal duty near Pittsburgh; two years at Fort Hamilton Narrows, N. Y.

In the year 1836, General Alfred Beckley married Miss Amelia Neville Craig, daughted of Neville Craig, Esq., editor of the *Pittsburgh Gazette,* and at once resigned his commission as an officer of the army.

After this marriage and resignation he set out with his wife and mother for Fayette County, Western Virginia, for the purpose, as he says, "To improve a body of unsettled stony lands for my widowed mother and myself lying in the southern part of Fayette (now Raleigh) County." (There were several hundred thousand acres of this land, we are told.) In the volume "History of Fayette County," by Peters &

Garden, 1926, the value of this Beckley land is mentioned on page 546. "Sold for $3,000; now worth $150,000." "In 1849, the General Assembly of Virginia, elected me as Brigadier General of Militia, creating for me a new district."

When the Civil War broke out General Beckley was ordered out, and had to go, as we must surmise, against his sentiments, for he later resigned his commission and General Floyd disbanded the Virginia militia. General Beckley became a prisoner with the other citizens of Raleigh Court House when Colonel Hays took the place in 1862. General Beckley was paroled. The son, Neville, subject of this sketch, enlisted and served in the Union army.

To General Alfred Beckley and Amelia Neville (Craig), his wife, were born several children there in Raleigh, the new county formed by his enterprise, in the year 1850; its county seat, "Beckley."

The names of these children were: John Isaac, William, Henry, Alfred, Jr., and Neville Craig, the Reverend Nevil C., who became the citizen preacher of Roane. The old General after the death of Amelia N. C., married a second wife whose name we do not have, and of this marriage were born: Webster, Stewart and Mariah.

Of the children of the Rev. Neville C. Beckley we should here say: Alfred Craig married Leona A. Sleeth, of Middle Reedy, 14th August, 1877, "of age." We do not have the record of the miarriage of Emma J. Robert Henry married Mary Wine, daughter of Richard Wine of Spencer, April 4, 1881, "consent of parents."

Robert H. and Mary, his wife, made their life's home here in Spencer. For many years he plied the trade of house and sign painter; of later years he has kept a store of general supplies for such work, including paintings, pictures, wallpaper, etc. To Robert H. and Mary (Wine), his wife, were born: J. Walter, James, Melissa, Neville, William B. and Howard.

BELT: Of Upper Spring Creek.

In a "History of Our Western Border" by Lucius C. McWhorter, which deals mainly with the early settlements of Marrison County, it is stated that the "Belts" of the pioneer people were descendants of a certain Captain "Broadbelt" of the Revolution, and one branch of these descendants dropped the first syllable and called themselves just plain "Belt," and another branch of the family tree used the name in the form, "Bent,' 'and in those names conveyed lands, married and signed papers.

Hedgmon Belt and his wife Sarah Ann (Nichols) Belt were the first of the name to settle in Roane County, and came here from Lewis County, Western Virginia, where Hedgman was born, March 16, 1833, son of Delana and Hester (Golden) Belt, natives of Fauquier County, Virginia, who settled in the Monongahela Valley, Delana having served in the War of 1812. Sarah Ann, the wife of Hedgmon, was born in Lewis County, Western Virginia, May 16, 1833, married Hedgmon there January 15, 1856. She was a daughter of John and Nancy

(Bailey) Nichols, born in Harrison County (the part later Lewis County); the former, 1807; the latter, 1812. Both the Belts and Nicholas were in Roane as early as 1865. The Belts made their home farm on head of Charles Fork, Spring Creek.

To Hedgmon and Sarah Ann (Nichols), his wife, were born and by them reared the following named children.

Challenge F., born 1856, married Miss Gay Arnold; D. Scott, 1860; John Christoy, 1862; Sheridan P., 1866; Emma A., 1867, married John C. Tuttle; Jacob M., born 1870; Henry W., 1872; Della A., 1874; Hedgman David, September 30, 1876; and Cammie, 1878. Cammie married Rossel Garrett Thompson, son of F. Marrion Thompson of upper Spring Creek, 24th April, 1900; her age, 21; his, 24. Hedgman D., of above, married Miss Blanche Eva Hinzman, March 1, 1905.

BENT: Of Head of Spring Creek.

George Bent and his wife Elizabeth (Mitchell) Bent, who had united in marriage in Lewis County, Western Virginia, came to these parts with several of their first born children about the year 1849; acquired a large tract of forest land on the head of Spring Creek, next the divide, and through which State Route No. 14 now passes; there made their home, brought up their family, and completed their span of life.

Their children were nine sons and four daughters whose names are, John, Eli, Vanburen, Jerome, Archelleus, Tarleton, Columbus, Arista S., Dempsey and James A.; Susan, Melissa, Elizabeth, and Amanda.

Of these we have the further information.

Jerome and Archeleus were soldiers in the Civil War, Confederate volunteers ,and killed in battle near Richmond.

James A. Bent, born in 1855, and for twenty years has been a resident lawyer of Elkins, Randolph County. He is author of "Bent's Digest," the first digest of decisions of the Supreme Court of West Virginia.

Eli V. Bent, son of George and Elizabeth Bent, his wife, was born in Lewis County, Western Virginia, January 9, 1839; stayed with the old farm in Roane; was prominent in public affairs of the county for twenty-five years; elected and served one or more terms as a justice of the peace of Spencer District, some time in the 1880's; spoken of as "Squire Bent;" was ever a devout attendant of his church, the Methodist Protestant. His body lies in the cemetery of Hebron Church where he attended through many years of his life. He was twice married. First to Miss Catherine Cox, November 15, 1859, she a daughter of the early settlers, Isaac and Sarah (Nisely) Cox. We do not have the names of their children, if any. Carterine having died, Eli V. united in marriage with Miss Julia Smith, September 28, 1890. She was then 23 years of age and a daughter of James J. and Emma (Rogers) Smith of Big Sandy. The joint labor of Eli V. and Julia built the new frame farm dwelling and improved many fields. There they brought up their family, one daughter and two sons, whose names are Melissa, Kenna M., and Claud S.

Melissa married Pat A. Engle, of Geary District. (See family name, "Engle.")

Kenna M. Bent married Miss Ruby Snodgrass, 25th October, 1916; his age then 22, her's 20. They, with their children, have their home in the City of Spencer, in which he is one of the club men and business men.

Claud S. Bent married a Miss Moss; he also lives in Spencer, being an engineer at the Spencer Water and Ice Company plant, now the West Penn Electric Company.

BISHOP: Among pioneers of Pocatalico, later Reedy.

This is the family of the author of this book. Each of the Colonies had an ancestor of a notable of this name as appears in American Biographies.

We can trace our ancestry no further back than to the country on the head waters of the Roanoke River, Virginia. There, in a section then Montgomery County, George Bishop married Miss Ann Boothe, about the year 1776. George and Ann made their first home where married; later passed further westward and lived in what later was Russell County, Virginia, in which place the younger ones of their children were born and reared. The names of all—Rachel, Nancy, Margaret Pauline "Polly", Sarah Ann, John, James and two daughters whose names are lost to us, they being she who married a Mr. Lester, and was mother of that James Lester, popular horseman of near Ripley, years 1850 to 1870, the other of unremembered name, she who became the wife of Moses Hunt and lived in Russell County, Virginia, some years before and after the year 1830. Further of these:

Rachel Bishop married Armstead Harper in Russell County, and came to the Pocatalico country among its first settlers.

Nancy married David Keen in Russell County, about the year 1825. These are the parents of that James Keen, early settlers in Geary District.

Sarah Ann married Charles Drake, in Russell County, about the year 1830. They came soon to Big Sandy and their spent their lives and reared a family. See name, "Drake."

John Bishop, son of George and Ann (Boothe) Bishop, married in Russell County, Virginia, Miss Elizabeth (Mutter), born "in Virginia," father said; yet from the name Mutter and possession by the Bishops of an old leather bound Bible printed in Low Dutch, in which are recorded in English, names and births of "Mutters," we are persuaded this great-grandmother was of the settlements of the Shenandoah Valley, a daughter of a German or Flemish family, they were weavers of fine fabrics. However, the Bishops were of dark complexion, the women handsome brunettes. In the Bishop family was handed down a special knowledge of fine metal working, such as excellency of tempering tool steel, alloying, welding and chasing; knowledge, which if properly commercialized would have netted a fortune. An incident in point:

when the Huffmans or McGrews of Parkersburg and Elizabeth mill fame, invented the band-saw about the year 1868, the great ribbon of steel on striking a hard knot, would break or sever itself where it had been joined; they had heard of John Bishop's skill in metals and came to Long Bottom, Ohio, where he (John Bishop II) then had a barrel factory, and got him to go with them to their mill and join or weld their refractory band saw.

He did this for them and handed them the formula for the mere recompense of twenty dollars. In the meantime Pittsburgh men who had visited and admired the bits, planes and edged tools of his factory, all of which he had made and tempered with his own hand, had obtained and carried away to their steel works at Pittsburgh all John Bishop knew of working of steel; not having paid a cent for it. His notions of the "cavalier bountiful" overrode the more practical.

Returning to the family tree:

John and Elizabeth Bishop, his wife, lived most of their married career on Big Sandy about where Pikeville is now; to them were born there the following sons and daughters: Aaron, Ann, George, John, Moses, Rachel and Cydnie, born respectively, within the years 1822 to 1842.

In the year 1843, John and Elizabeth, with their family migrated to this Pocatalico River; she fell sick here and died in a short time after arrival. The older girls kept the pioneer cabin home a few years, marrying and leaving one at a time. The pioneer home was sold and John with his younger two boys and two daughters next have their home at Minersvill, Ohio; in the meantime John has united in marriage with Miss Susan Utt; of this marriage, were born one daughter and two sons; their names: Caroline, Wilburn and Melvin D., now (1927) of Ravenswood, W. Va. For marriages of the older members of this family of John Bishop I, see Chapter IV of this book.

Rachel Bishop married John Blackburn in Jackson County; lived during the Civil War in Ravenswood and were of the first home builders and home owners in the City of Huntington, where both died leaving some grandchildren: Blackburns. Cydnie married Lewis Anderson, son of "Andy" on Strait Fork Sandy, three miles east of Ravenswood, spent their lives there.

Moses Bishop married Eliza Lester on Reedy, daughter of John Lester (first) and .... (King) his wife, about the year 1853; they made their first home at Pomeroy, Ohio, where the wife and mother Eliza died about 1868, leaving the following named children: Mary, Harvey, Isaiah, Jeremiah, and Wilk or Wilkin W. Moses then and there made another marriage; this time to a Miss Martha Campbell; this was right after the close of the Civil War, and the family made their residence for some years following at Long Bottom, Ohio, where the family grew up and scattered. The last we heard of Wilk, he was a resident and established hardware dealer in Los Angeles, California. Of Moses's second marriage a daughter named Nora was born at Long Bottom.

HISTORY OF ROANE COUNTY

John Bishop, son of John and Elizabeth Bishop, father of the author of this compilation and book, was born in Pike County, Kentucky, on the 19th day of February, 1830; married on Reedy, year 1854, Sarah Roach, daughter of William and Delilah (Carney) Roach, pioneers on Middle Fork of Reedy, at that time. They made their home first at Murraysville, where John was the blacksmith for the great Jack Flesher board yard there. He enlisted as a volunteer in the Union Army and served through it—up the Kanawha and over into Virginia, through most of the battles and was of the western wing of the Army of the Potomac when General Lee surrendered. He returned; his family in the meantime having moved over into Long Bottom Village. Lived here until 1870, then brought us all to Middle Reedy where, on mother's inheritance of the Roach farm we became farmers all; John bought adjoining pieces of lands and made a good farm. The sons and daughters of John and Sarah (Roach) Bishop, named in order of their births are as follows: Charles Remington, Frances Roxana, William Henry, Elizabeth "Libbie," Jesse Edmond and Ettie May. Their marriages: Charles Remington married Miss Palmira Jane Candler of Reedy, January 16, 1875, she a daughter of John W. Candler of Right Reedy. Remington and Jane's residence now (1927) is Cottageville, West Virginia, where he has been railway station agent for fifteen years; they have reared two daughters whose names are Nannie (Mrs. Jesse Straight now), and Pearl (wife of Reverend Nida).

The daughters, Frances Roxana and "Libbie," died in youth; their tombstones mark their burial places in the cemetery at Long Bottob, Ohio.

William Henry Bishop, son of John and Sarah (Roach) Bishop, was born at Murrayville, December 14, 1860; had first primer lessons in Ohio schools at Long Bottom; was sent to subscription schools at Reedy; became a school teacher in Roane's corps; principal of the Town of Spencer schools, 1884-1885, studied law at Spencer under John G. Schilling and J. W. C. Armstrong, was admitted to the bar 1885; attended Peabody Normal at Nashville, Tennessee, 1886-7; was three and three-fourth years instructor of civilization to the Jicarilla Apaches of New Mexico; returned 1890; resumed practice of law in Spencer, here married Miss Gertrude Duling, July 7, 1892 (see family Duling); was elected and served one term as prasecuting attorney for the county; one term, 1924-26 as delegate for Roane County in the State Legislature; is author of two books on State Municipal Law; and is author of this county history.

The children of William H. and Gertrude (Duling) Bishop are Monad A., born in Spencer, June 19, 1893; graduated from Marshall College, Huntington; taught school; married Mr. Raymond A. Lee, October 3, 1914; he served overseas in the World War; was mustered out a second lieutenant; is now captain in the reserves. Sarah Christine, born May 10, 1900; graduated from Spencer high school; took courses in music and art at Cincinnati Conservatory; taught in the public schools; married Mr. Cecil O. Snyder, of Bedford County, Pennsylvania, at home in Spencer, August 6, 1924.

Ettie May Bishop, daughter and youngest child of John and Sarah (Roach) Bishop, was born on Reedy, 1871; was sent to Marshall College, Huntington, West Virginia, became a teacher; married James A. Criss, of Harrison County, West Virginia, in Spencer, on the 22nd day of March, 1893; her age 22, his 27; they made their home in Sutton, Braxton County, West Virginia, where she was a teacher for some terms, and there died, 1909, leaving an only child, his name Harry Bishop Criss; he served overseas in the World War; returned carrying some small pieces of shrapnel in the thick of his thigh, yet not adjudged a cripple or invalid.

Jesse Edmond Bishop, youngest son of John and Sarah (Roach) Bishop, was born at Long Bottom, Ohio, 1869; was a "store keeper" at Reedy a short time; married Miss Martha Curfman, June 15, 1893; his age then 25, her's 18; she was born on Lower Reedy, daughter of Samuel and Mary (Cain) Curfman, Mary being a daughter of Rev. Thomas H. Cain the pioneer preacher of Reedy history. J. Edmond and Martha have resided in Pittsburgh, Pennsylvania, the last fifteen years; they have brought up one child, a son, Carl Bishop.

BLOSSER: Of Reedy pioneers.

Henry Blosser, son of a colonial family who settled in Pennsylvania prior to the Revolution, is first known as a frontier soldier in defense of the fort at Wheeling; at that place he married Miss Isabell Stewart in what is now Green County, Pennsylvania; she was a sister of William and Charles Stewart also stationed at or near Wheeling; all these with their wives and children came to "Three Forks" of Reedy, arriving about the year 1816, acquired lands adjoining that of the Stewarts, and there lived out their allotted years.

To Henry and Isabelle (Stewart) Blosser, his wife, were born and reared two sons and two daughters, whose names and marriages are as follows:

Robert, who married Susan Murray, 1857, he then thirty-five years of age.

Isaac, whose marriage we do not know.

Matilda became the wife of Neddie Greathouse of the pioneer family of that name near "Tanners Crossroads."

Jane married Peter Conrad, Sr., of lower Reedy.

Isabelle married Arnold Starcher of Henry Fork country.

Robert Blosser of the above family is the man who lost his life in the tragic mill explosion, related in the History of Reedy District: Chapter V.

To Robert and Susan (Murray) Blosser, his wife, were born the following children:

John H. married Miss P. Jane Straight, daughter of James A. Straight, of Spring Creek country, May 1, 1884; his age 26, her's 18;

he lived many years at Reedy; was partner with S. B. Seaman, Jr., in erection and running the first steam flouring mill at Reedy.

Peter married Miss Olive L. Board, 7th August 1887; his age 25, her's 23; "At Good Hope Baptist Church."

Robert C. married Mary Wyatt October 14, 1894; he then 31, she 23 years of age. "At the bride's parents home."

Susan C. married Charles F. Gough of Reedy, September 1, 1882.

BOARD: Of Curtis District.

Board, William M., 1830-1914, son of John Board an early settler of the adjoining county, Jackson, married for a first wife Susan Waybright; they made their home for the first several years in Jackson County; the names of the children of William and Susan, mentioned in the order of their ages, are Emma Jane, who married Hugh Ingram, son of John Ingram of the same neighborhood.

Ernestine, who married Sase Hardman; Hon. Michael Thomas, married for first wife Elenora Curry, of this marriage three daughters were born: Minnie Bell, Sadie and Myrtle; for a second wife Michael T. married Dora Winter, of this marriage no children are living. Michael Thomas Board lived many years on upper Reedy; was elected and served as a member of the House of Delegates of the State Legislature, thirty-second session, year 1915.

We do not have the names of all of this family.

For a second wife William Board married Mary Hess; of this marriage seven children were born, whose names in order of their births are Thomas James Board.

Second child: Reverend Benjamin T. Board, he married Annie, daughter of C. Columbus Kelley, of Curtis District. Reverend Benjamin T. Board has for several years been a highly respected member of the West Virginia Methodist Episcopal Conference.

Fourth child of William and Mary (Hess) Board is Viola, she married Asbury Reed. Sixth child, Nora, who became wife of William S. Roberts. Seventh, Lakin Board, married Mary, daughter of Frank Wolfe; Lakin became owner of the old William Board home farm, where he now is living and prospering.

All these Boards were public spirited and influential in their neighborhood; William Board settled there about the year 1872; soon a neighborhood M. E. Church was built, next a parsonage on lands donated by William, and that became the center of the M. E. Church business of the whole district and so remained for twenty-five years.

BOARD: Among first settlers of "Three Forks" of Reedy, 1816.

Patrick Board, this pioneer, came to "Three Forks" 1816, with his wife, whom he had married in Green County, Pennsylvania, about the year 1804; this is inferred from a biograph of Joseph Stewart of Reedy, which states he, Joseph, was born in the year 1820, son of William and Mary (Board) Stewart, she a daughter of Patrick Board.

The names of the children of Patrick Board and wife were: Mary, William K., Alexander Sandy, and Gamaliel. We have not definite knowledge that Gamaliel was a son of Patrick and wife. Of Patrick's family we say further:

Mary, the daughter, as above said, became the wife of William Stewart.

William K. Board, was twice married; his first wife a Miss Smith. The wife I knew of was born Nancy Flesher, daughter of Dempsy P. Flesher and wife, the early settlers at mouth of Cains Run. William K. Board was a born cavalier of the religious turn; was a preacher of some ability; but he depended on his farm which he made on Folly Run, a mile from Three Forks. He had given great attention to the best language; and in this he was so nearly alone, his doffing his hat, his bowings, gesticulations and especially his I-N-G endings in pronunciation of words, was mimicked by the waggish for merriment.

The sons and daughters of William K. Board and his wives were Jefferson, Sarah R., wife of Alfred Berry; Nancy Elizabeth, wife of Albert G. Gough; Julia Ann, "Tip" and Dempsy; these all married and reared families. W. Dempsy Board married Miss Margaret Staats on the 27th of March, 1878, she a daughter of John and Margaret "Peggy" (Carney) Staatts, earliest settlers on Staats Run of Middle Fork of Reedy.

Alexander Sandy Board, son of Patrick Board and wife, was born on Reedy, December 12, 1816, died there May 22, 1880. He united in marriage with Miss Rebecca Stutler, born in Harrison County, March 15, 1822, daughter of John and .... (Carder) Stutler, his wife. See name Stutler.

Alexander Sandy and Rebecca Board made their best and last home on Right Fork of Reedy, on a good farm lying across the Revenswood and Spencer turnpike, one-half mile west of "Three Forks." He was an enthusiastic Methodist and noted as a best singer; we hear excellent voices of his grandchildren and their children, resident now (1927) in Spencer. His was rated the best farm of that Right Reedy for twenty years.

To Alexander Sandy and Rebecca, his wife, were born and by them brought up the following children:

Thomas, Margaret, wife of Daniel Roberts; Christopher C., Josiah Nelson, Lemuel H., Colonel Pogue, Marietta, wife of Silas B. Seaman, Jr.; and Marshall Alexander C.

Their marriages other than above given:

Christopher C. Board, son of A. S. and Rebecca, above, was born on Reedy, September 21, 1848, married Miss Susan C. Seaman in Marietta, Ohio, on November 27, 1866; she was born February 14, 1848, daughter of Silas B. and Margaret (Burdette) Seamon, of Right Reedy. Christopher C. Board was ordained a preacher of the M. E. South Conference, and served several circuits in adjoining counties for some years.

To Christopher C. and Susan B. Board, his wife, were born and by them brought up the following children: Joseph S., December 8, 1867; William D., August 1, 1869; Margaret R., October 1, 1871; Jennetta C., February 14, 1874; Alexander F., December 17, 1875; Lake B., April 19, 1878, and Marvin A., December 1, 1880. These have married and also have families; Joseph S. was first a school teacher, then a carpenter; had his home in Spencer many years where he married Miss May Dulin and they have brought up a family; their names, from memory are Lakie, now Mrs. Munson; Lena, Willa, Brooks, Dulin, Albert, Edwin, Bruce and James.

Josiah Nelson Board, son of A. Sandy and Rebecca, his wife, was a school teacher, one of the first under the free school system; a good one; the author of this was one of his pupils at one term; an excellent teacher of vocal music of great tenor range; he married Miss Flora Ann Stewart, January 25, 1881, she a daughter of William P. and Annie, of Reedy Town. See Stewart. Josiah N. and Flora, his wife, acquired the Board senior farm and he ran it some years, then removed self and family to the State of Ohio; on the Sciota or Muskingum. We do not have the names of their children.

Lemuel H. Board, son of A. S. and Rebecca Board, married Miss Isabelle Samantha Chancey, March 5, 1875, she the daughter of Squire Roswell R. Chancey, of Middle Reedy. I have not the names of their children of whom I know there were three or four.

Colonel Pogue Board, son of A. S. and Rebecca, married Miss Emma Paine, in Jackson County; they made their home on a part of the parental lands for some few years, then sold and went elsewhere.

Marshall Alexander C. Board, son of A. S. and Rebecca Board, married Miss Ella M. Hardman, December 3, 1886; he then 21, she 21. He engaged in farming; later sold his patrimony and went to Calhoun County and engaged in farming; they reside there yet; he has been elected and served at least one term as sheriff of Calhoun County.

BOGGS. James, John, Pioneers.

BOGGS: Of Geary District.

Henry Clay Boggs, son of James A. and Susan (Cutlip) Boggs, was born in Braxton County, western Virginia, on the 23d of January, 1845, descendant of the old Virginia family of Boggs's, of which we have only meager information; he had at least one brother, James M. Boggs, a lieutenant in the Confederate service of the Civil War, 1861-65.

Henry C. Boggs married Sarah Ann Elizabeth, daughter of John S. and Nancy A. (Hayhurst Garee) Boggs, in Marion County, western Virginia, May 18, 1865; they came to this county and settled on upper Big Sandy in the year 1868; later in their lives this family acquired and made a farm out of woodlands in Smithfield District of Roane. Henry Clay Boggs sought no public office, just worked and reared his family, striving to make each a respectable citizen. Of this marriage were born eight sons and four daughters as follows: James C., 1866; Susan E., 1867; Mary A.,

1868; Luther S., 1870; Joseph J., 1872; Robert E., 1873; Nancy A., 1875; Isaac E., 1877; Margaret A., and Charles M., twins, 1879; Clarence C., 1882, and Garee, 1884. Garee Boggs was a prominent young school teacher, 1910 to 1915; and Isaac B. Boggs was county superintendent of schools, term 1915 to 1919.

BOGGS: Of Smithfield.

James R. Boggs was born in Greenbrier County, western Virginia, May 22, 1800, son of John, born in Ireland, and Susan (Drinnen) Boggs, his wife, a Virginian lady; John claims to have had five brothers in the battle of Point Pleasant. James R. was twice married; first wife, Harriet Walkup, and their children were Susan, John Nathaniel and Mary J.

James R. Boggs's second wife was Lacy Ann O'Brien, whom he married in Gilmer County, western Virginia, year 1845, and with his family came in the next year and settled on Middle Henry Fork, then a part of Gilmer County.

To James R. and Lacy Ann (O'Brien) Boggs were born, on Henrys Fork, Walter D., 1847; Sarah, 1849; Melinda, 1852; Caroline, 1854; and Mary J., 1858.

Of this James R. and Lacy Ann Boggs family we write further:

Thaddeus Boggs, the son, succeeded to the home lands on Henrys Fork, and was long a well known man of the county; he was born "on Easter Sunday," 1835; on outbreak of the "Civil" war he enlisted in the 34th Virginia Infantry, transferred to the cavalry of the Confederate forces; was two months a prisoner at Wheeling; four months at Fort Delaware, and two months at Point Lookout—captured each time; returned unhurt.

In the same year of his return, 1866, Thaddeus Boggs married Susan Webb, of his own neighborhood, yet born in Washington County, Virginia, in 1840; to Thaddeus and Susan were born five children as follows: Melissa, 1866; Alice, 1867; Anderson, March 22, 1868; George W., October 17, 1872; Rebecca, 1877.

Melissa became the wife of Rev. Wilbur Spencer; Anderson married and lives in Smithfield District; George W. has been a resident of Columbus, Ohio, for several years.

Later in their lives this family acquired and made a farm out of woodlands in Smithfield District of Roane.

BONNETT: Of upper Pocatalico and Spring Creek. Descendants of Jesse Hughes, the famous Indian scout of "Border Warfare."

Jacob Bonnett, son of a Jacob Bonnett of the Bonnett family figuring in Indian atrocities committed on the intrepid settleds of the Monongahel aValley, was born in that valley, and there united in marriage with Martha Hughes, daughter of the famous Jesse Hughes.

Soon after marriage they came "West" and settled near Uriah Gandee's about the divide between the Kanawhas, within the years 1824 to 1830; there made their life time's home, and there brought up the following sons and daughters:
Mansfield, Perry, WilliamGandee, Harriett, Elizabeth, and Nathan. All we know of these several children of Jacob and Martha (Hughes) Bonnett is that all grew up and made homes—the average substantial farm home of their time, and were all industrious and respected citizens; all married here in what is now Roane, except Perry Bonnet, who was killed when a young man in the battle at Cloyds Mountain in the Civil War.

These marriages were before the formation of Roane County and will be found recorded in the marriage books of Jackson or Kanawha County. But we are told that William Gandee Bonnett married Miss Missouri Ellis. Harriett Bonnett married Laban Shouldis of Flat Fork. Elizabeth Bonnett married William Shouldis and Nathan Smith Bonnett married Miss Minerva Hopkins on September 15, 1871.

BOOTHE: In western Harper District.
Matthias Boothe, farmer, whose farm and home is in that part of Harper District extending over and including head waters of Mill Creek, is the more extensively known member of this family at the present (1927).

Ancestry:
Two brothers, James Boothe and Charles Boothe, both born in Russell County, Virginia, sons of Joseph and Susanna Boothe, his wife, came into the country of the Pocatalico at what is now Lower Harper District, about the year 1836; one of these passed on to Mason County, on the Ohio, in a short time. Both these have some descendants in Jackson, Mason and Roane.

Matthias Boothe is married and has brought up a family of several children. He probably married in Jackson County. I do not have the names of these children.

We are informed that Matthias is the youngest of the family and that he had two brothers whose names were Julian and Joseph N. Boothe. Joseph married Matilda Cunningham, 1869.

Of women of this family we get the following names from the Roane County marriage records:
Rebecca Boothe to Moses R. Whited, December 22, 1858.
And the following whom we do not know:
Mary Ann Boothe to James Wilson, year 1856.
Mary Ann Boothe to Eli Jackson, January 2, 1857.
Margaret M. Boothe to John C. Lockhart, June 1, 1859.

BOWYER: Of Curtis District. One son spells the name "Boyer."
The father, mother and six or seven children of this name Bowyer or Boyer, came from Roanoke, Virginia, and settled in Curtis District about

the first of the decade, 1850; the names of these sons and daughters of this family are:

Sarah, who married Henry (Fuzzy) Parsons and were the parents of a Travis and a Ballard Parsons, juniors.

Malinda, married John Coast, of Jackson County.

Andrew —. "Bowyer" married Malinda, daughter of Joseph Carpenter of Reedy; this is the Andrew J. Bowyer of the History of the County and City of Spencer; once a justice of the peace in Spencer; also was a deputy sheriff of the county; these: A. J. and Malinda were the parents of James E. Bowyer, who married .... Rawlins.

James married a Miss McGraw.

Rebecca, wife of a Mr. Cain, of Reedy.

Martha, who married "Dick" 'Stutler, of Reedy.

George W. was born year 1852, on Reedy, married August 31, 1872, Emizette, daughter of Josiah Miller of Reedy, whose father was Samuel Miller, the pioneer; this George W. was the youngest of this Roanoke family.

To George W. and Emizette (Miller) Boyer were born five sons and two daughters:

Okey N. Boyer, married 1870, Melissa F. Roberts of Upper Reedy; he 31, she 27, and daughter of Daniel Roberts.

William A. Boyer married Angeline, daughter of Jeremiah Miller, 9th October 1892; his age 19, her age 21.

Jonathan Alonzo Boyer, married Stella Conley, 1903; his age 29, her age 24; she the daughter of Benjamin Conley, of Flat Fork.

Nellie married Charles E. Rader, son of Martin Rader, on Left Reedy, 9th February, 1896; Charles E.'s age 20, Nellie's age 18.

Clark W. married Miss Flesher, of Reedy.

Robert Fleet married Mary J. Wilson, 17th July, 1907; his age 26, her age 21; she was a daughter of Abram Wilson, of upper Spring Creek.

Lelia A. married Nester Anderson Whited, 17th July, 1912; his age 27, her age 25. He was a son of Ransom Whited.

BRADLEY: Of Upper Spring Creek and Smithfield. Member of the County Court of Roane.

Early Benjamin Bradley, son of Charles Lewis and Ruhama (Greenleaf) Bradley, was born on upper Mill Creek near Gay—United States post office—May 13, 1899.

Ancestry:

James Bradley settled in Jackson County, possibly before the year 1845, coming there from Rockbridge County, Virginia. He married Miss Nancy Rhodes in Jackson County, she a sister of Peter Rhodes, pioneer miller of Harper District. These, James and Nancy (Rhodes) Bradley, are the parents of the Charles Lewis Bradley, first mentioned.

Charles Lewis and Ruhama (Greenleaf), his wife, brought up the following named six sons and seven daughters: Frederick O., Early

Benjamin, Thomas, John, Kenney, Homer, Erney and daughters, Dora, Emma, Lydia, Mary, Vada, Rhoda and Merlie.

Early Benjamin Bradley, son of Charles L. and Ruhama (Greenleaf), his wife, married in Roane County, Miss Dora Walsh on the 13th day of May, 1899; his age then 25, her's 17; she a daughter of John Mac Walsh and wife, of upper Pocatalico, below Looneyville. Early B. and his wife acquired lands near the place of marriage and made them into a good farm on which he and his family have lived ever since. He was elected by the people as a commissioner of the County Court of Roane County in 1924, commenced his duties January 1, 1925, is now serving the public. The family of Early B. and Dora, his wife, consist of five sons and four daughters.

BUCHANAN: Of Spencer District.

Joshua Buchanan born on Fishing Creek in Ohio County, West Virginia, about the year 1831, came with his parents, William and wife to Wood County, West Virginia, when a young man; while a resident of Wood County Joshua Buchanan married Elvilda Buchanan, who was born in Noble County, Ohio, about 1832, daughter of a Buchanan family of no known relation to that of William Buchanan, father of Joshua.

Joshua and Elvilda made their home in Wood County for many years during which time all their five sons and three daughters were born.

This family all came to Roane County about the year ....

The names and marriages of these Buchanan sons and daughters are as follows:

Lazarus "Elias," married Lillie Victoria, daughter of Lee Chambers, of Smithfield, the 7th of April, 1901; his age 41, her age 41.

William Henry died in youth.

Uriah Lytle married Emma, daughter of Thomas R. Conley, of upper Spring Creek.

Alexander L. married Gertrude Kieffer, daughter of Andrew Kieffer, of Smithfield, March 23, 1902, his age 32, her age 22.

Alexander L. was elected and served one term as a justice of the peace of Spencer District.

To Alexander L. and Gertrude (Kieffer), his wife, were born in Roane County, eight sons and two daughters; their home farm is in Smithfield District.

John S. and Sarah A., son and daughter of Joshua, first named, died, neither having married.

Elizabeth Ann, daughter of Joshua and Elvilda, married William Whetzel Short, of Spencer District. Rebecca Viola of this first family was thrice married; first two husbands died, her last being Ruben Reynolds, of Spencer District.

BURDETTE: Of Left Reedy in Curtis.

Ellison Burdette, pioneer of above locality, was born in Monroe County, West Virginia, and came to these parts when a young man in the first of the 1830's; married Annie H. Thomasson, January 4, 1838, daughter of John P. and Nancy Thomasson, of county history; settled on lands at the forks of the roads half mile below Reedyville; the Gilmer, Ripley and Ohio turnpike later built through his lands and past his dooryard; was for twenty years a prominent personage as owner of a good farm and first class citizen.

To Ellison and Virginia (Thomasson) Burdettte were born and reared there on the farm the following children:

Nancy C., who married Fletcher S. Riddle, year 1856, with whom she made her home in Ritchie County.

Mary, who married a Mr. Boyd and went to Ohio.

Matilda married Joseph Hardman; they went West.

Virginia (in name "Dinia") married George Hardman, the 23rd of October, 1867; they made their home in Calhoun County.

Rebecca became wife of Abram McCoy.

Pleasant Hyder Burdette, the only son of Ellison and Virginia (Thomasson) Burdette, succeeded to the home farm; married Violina Bennett, March 19, 1873, to them were born and reared two sons and three daughters:

John E., whose career we do not know.

Abram, who married Lummie Chapman, the 20th of February, 1910; his age, 24, her age 22; they moved to Ohio.

Martha Ellen.

Vernah, who became the wife of Cyrus Andrew Leasher, on the 16th of August, 1905, her age 19, his age 25.

Mattie, yet single.

ELIJAH BURDETTE, of Middle Reedy in Curtis District located on lands and made the farm now the County Poor Farm; he was prominent from years 1845 to 1868, or thereabout; we have no data as to whence he came or of his wife's family name; but at that home they reared several daughters, and two sons named Morgan and William C., the latter married Josephene Kyger March 1, 1869; now long a farmer and stock man on Right Fork Sand Creek, in Reedy District.

BURDETTE: Of Middle Fork in Curtis District.

Two brothers of this name appear to have come here about the same time; their names, Richard and Elijah. Of their marriages and families we have little information. Next following we give such as we have:

Richard, "Old Dick," as pioneers usually called him because of a grandson being known as "Dick Burdette," was a sporting man and particularly a horse fancier, bought, sold, traded and raced in any settlement that had a horse it cared to match against his; attended the horse races regularly at New Orleans; his career ended, he left in that neighborhood a son whose name was Thompson Burdette. Information of Thompson's career is more meager than that of his father; yet he left a son on the ancestral lands whose name is Perry Dixon Burdette, born about the year 1850; he married in Curtis District Miss Mary Ellen Miller; they made their home on the Spencer and Ripley turnpike near Peniel some twenty-five years, farming and trading.

To Perry D. Burdette and Mary E. (Miller), his wife, were born and grew up five sons and three daughters. Their names in order of births are as follows:

Camden Josiah, Lycurgus C., Thornton Cadmus, Georgia, Roy Teddy, Clyde, Flossie and Eupha.

Of these we can write further as follows:

Georgia married Kenna Ivens, residents now of Gay, West Virginia. Flossie married Charles S. Knopp, of Liverpool, West Virginia.

Eupha became wife of V. L. Douglass, they reside in Spencer District.

Lycurgus C., while but a boy enlisted in the United States Army, became Sergeant of Battery C, First U. S. Artillery, and was one of the few of that battery who survived the historic Galveston Flood, of September 8, 1900. His story of the awful night, and of his clinging to a square of flooring of some wrecked building which he seized as it passed, and on which he was washed ashore, would be a small volume of itself; he is now a resident of the City of Spencer with his wife and family; he got a broken shoulder and crushed collar bone, permanent injuries, in that Galveston catastrophe; a generous government gives him a United States pension of twenty-five dollars a month.

BURDETTE: Of Spencer.

St. Clair Burdette, born in Monroe County, Virginia, about the year 1824, married Octavia Kincaid in Meadow Bluff, Greenbrier County, West Virginia, in first years of decade, 1840; moved to Fayette County, next to Grass Lick, Jackson County, 1862, then came to Roane, settling on upper Flat Fork of Poca in Harper District. To St. Clair and Octavia Burdette were born nine children. Of these, five were born in Fayette County, and the four younger were born in Jackson County. The names of these given in order of their ages (by Jiles N. Burdette, a son) are as follows:

Charles, who married Jane Gandee, daughter of George Gandee, son of Uriah, of Gandeeville.

Mary, who married Henderson, son of Geo. Gandee, son of Uriah Gandee.

Sarah married Jonathan R. Reed, of Flat Fork.
John Asher, died in youth.
Jiles Numern, see further at end of this.
Martha, married Crittenden Coon, of Higby.
Ellen, died in youth.
Alice, married Joseph Fields, of Flat Fork.

HISTORY OF ROANE COUNTY 461

George, married Julia Suck, daughter of the feed and mill merchant at Silverton, Jackson County, West Virginia.

George entered the Christian ministry in his early manhood, choosing his place with the United Brethren; he has long been spoken of as the Reverend Burdette; has been president or moderator of their General Conference; he is now (1926) resident minister of a United Brethren Church in Huntington, West Virginia.

Of Jiles N. Burdette, of the City of Spencer, we write further: He was the fifth child and third son, as observed above; born about 1859; married Martha Ellen Hildreth, of Spring Creek, October 30, 1882, at the home of the bride's parents, William Harrison and Sallie (Hickman) Hildreth. Jiles was ordained a ministed of the Baptist Church in the year, 1886; preached to churches of his charges in Jackson, Roane, Wirt and Calhoun Counties for a period of about ten years, then returned to his trade—house carpenter; was long a prominent A. F. and A. M. and became a permanent resident of Spencer about 1902.

To Jiles N. and Martha Ellen, his wife, were born the following named children, in order of their ages:

Maud, married Harvey J. Simmons, of Spencer, on November 14, 1904.

May, married Earl Simmons, garage and auto dealer of Spencer at this time (1926).

Sallie, married Frank Turnbull, of Colorado.

Clyde L., married Katherine Arnett, 5th June, 1919, his age 28, her age 19; she is a daughter of Hayes Arnott.

Otho and Hugh, both unmarried young men of Spencer.

Abby, married Lyle Chapman, of Huntington, West Virginia.

BURDETTE: First of the name in Reedy.

Willis Burdette and his wife, born Miss Boon, "a direct descendant of the famous Indian scout, Daniel Boon," says Mrs. Isabell R. (Burdette) Hardman, her granddaughter, were both born in what is now Monroe County, of Virginian parents; were married in Monroe County and several of their oldest children were also born there. Lived in Greenbrier County in 1817, then came to the "Kanawha Licks," Malden; lived in Kanawha County a while, and are settlers on Middle Fork of Reedy shortly before the 11th day of January, 1829. I am able to be thus specific, because on that date Silas B. Seaman and Margaret Burdette, a daughter of Willis Burdette, were united in marriage on the Middle Fork of Reedy, then in the jurisdiction of Wood County. Margaret J. was born in Monroe County, December 19, 1809, says Moses Seaman, her grandson; in his biograph in Hardesty's History; the same is given by Chris C. Board in his biograph in the same book.

Willis Burdette and wife spent all the remainder of their lives on Reedy. Their children must have all been born before they came to Reedy, for as observed Margaret J. was married there at twenty years of age. The names of these children of Willis and wife were as follows:

Elihu, Lovel, Parkson, John, William and Margaret J.—Seaman. Further:

Elihu and Lovel each married while that part of Reedy was under jurisdiction of Wood, Wirt or Jackson; we do not have their records here; each made a home and farm, and reared a family. As to Parkson and John, we know nothing at all.

William Burdette, son of Willis and (Boon), his wife, was born in Greenbrier County, West Virginia, September 7, 1817; worked at the Kanawha "Licks"; there married Miss Elizabeth Doolittle, about 1822; moved with his family to "Cassville"—Spencer—1849; lived here until 1869, when he with all his family, two sons and nine daughters, except two, Sallie and Elizabeth R., removed to Clay County, Missouri. Sallie had married Jeff or "Jeffrey" Simmons, Elizabeth R. had married Cassett Hardman: See family name Hardman.

BURKE:

Robert Peter Burke and his wife, who before marriage was Miss Amos, both natives of Culpepper County, Virginia, arrived in the Town of Spencer about the year 1860, having with them one son, the son's name Lewis Hamilton, and two daughters, and soon, 1861, purchased a lot and erected on it their home on the northwest corner of Market and Beauty Streets.

He was a first-class carpenter and builder and a man needed; he was also a devout Baptist. They lived here many years ,during which time two sons and two daughters were born, their names James, Roberta, Elizabeth and William E.

The wife and mother died and sometime afterward R. Peter, returned to Virginia and united in marriage with Miss Elton Rebecca Amos, a sister of his first wife; she was at once a devoted mother to her sister's children.

Later Robert Peter purchased a farm far up on the Charles Fork of Spring Creek, mostly still in the virgin forest, and there with his family made his abode for the remainder of his lifetime. He went out from here on his missions of Sabbath school and church work to which he was so greatly devoted. When he died he bequeathed to the church five hundred dollars to be paid out of his savings or personal property, the real estate he left to his wife and children.

To R. P. and Elton Rebecca (Amos) Burke was born and reared only one child, a son named Lemuel Judson.

Lewis Hamilton, eldest son of this family, became a young school teacher—at a very youthful age. The blood of the cavalier surged swift and hotly through him; in February, 1880, he was united in marriage with Miss Julia A. Riddle; to them was born one son, Holly H. Burke. He married Miss Ida Ball, of Reedy, July 29, 1905.

All the other sons and daughters of Robert Peter Burke married and established homes and families in this county.

BUTCHER: Of Smithfield District.

James A. Butcher and Martha (Smith) Butcher, his wife, arrived here from Ritchie County, West Virginia, in the year 1875; a deed to James A. Btucher for 114 acres of land lying on Hays of Henrys Fork bears date 1875. In this year these Butchers with some children settled on this branch of Henrys Fork and soon cleared away the forest and made a good farm. Of their family born in Ritchie or in Roane after coming here, we can give names as follows: Mary C. and Floyd, both died; Isaac B. married Myrtle Boice, died leaving five children—their names, Fannie F., Annie and Ella Florence, each married in Ohio and make their homes there; Hoyt R. married Anna, daughter of Samuel Starcher, of Henrys Fork, and continues the family name here on the paternal lands.

James A. Butcher, ancestor above, is remembered as an enthusiastic attendant on all communications of the Masonic Lodges.

BUTCHER: Of Reedy and near Spencer, 1858. Ancestry:

Joseph Butcher and Eunice Fisher, descendants of early settlers in the Monongahela Valley, were married in Lewis County, near Weston, about the year 1830. Inferring from recorded ages of their oldest children, began their wedded life there as farmers; they were parents of three sons and three daughters, whose names were Wilson, Margaret, Lucinda, Matilda, John Webster and Joseph A.

The father, Joseph, having died in Lewis County, the widow, Eunice, married a Mr. Badget; of this union one son and one daughter were born; names, George Bollin and Elizabeth, "Bettie."

All this family—married and single ones—came to Roane County and established their respective homes in the year 1858 or 1859. Wilson Butcher, not married, died of wounds received as a Confederate soldier.

Marriages of the others of the family:

Margaret Butcher, born in Lewis County, January 1, 1839; in the same county married John Flesher about the year 1859; he was a son of George Flesher, who made his home on Left Reedy, one mile above "Three Forks." Of this union two sons are remembered, Andrew L. and William Flesher. See Flesher.

Lucinda, married Peter Bush about 1854; they made their first home on Tucker Run of Left Reedy, next on Main Left Reedy, three miles above "Three Forks." Their children—remembered—were William, George and a daughter. This is the Peter Bush mentioned in Chapter V. as the distiller of brandies.

Matilda married Harrison Rexroad of Lewis County.

John Webster Butcher, son of Joseph and Eunice, his wife, married in Lewis County, Miss Eliza Glaze.—See name Glaze. John W. and Eliza made their home on the Ravenswood and Spencer turnpike about three miles north of Spencer; there made out of the forest a farm of comfortable production, and there reared their family of three daughters and three sons, whose names and somewhat further are:

Mary Lucinda, who became a popular teacher, married Napoleon B. Hoff. See name Hoff.

Sophia Eunice, married Charles Thomas Mitchell 1878. See the name.

Charles Henry, yet at the old homestead, or near it, was born in 1859; married Miss Gillie Elizabeth Barr, a neighbor's daughter, on November 9, 1881; they have reared two sons and three daughters.

James Madison Butcher, son of John W. and Eliza (Glaze), married Miss Mary Esta Looney, on December 17, 1882; she a daughter of Lewis W. Looney, of Walton District. See Looney. He was a good carpenter and worked here several of his first years; and a find of petroleum oil on his lands, about 1915 ,made further labor unnecessary; their home now is Kent, near Akron, Ohio. We are told they are parents of seven sons and seven daughters. Success to them all.

Everett, youngest son of John W. and Eliza, married at 23, Miss Martha Argabrite, 21, on November 25, 1896. Died, leaving one son and one daughter.

Joseph A. Butcher, son of Joseph and Eunice, his wife, was born in Lewis County, "1845, died 1887." (From his grave stone in Roach Cemetery) Married Miss Phoebe Buckby, likely in Jackson County. Her parents lived near the Jackson boundary line at the time. Their children were Lewis and Sarah. The home of their married lives was on Middle Fork of Reedy.

BUTCHER: Of Middle Forks of Reedy, 1882 to 1919.

Nicholas F. Butcher, was born in Lewis County, West Virginia, in the year 1835. We have no information as to his parentage. He was a recognized brother of the James Addison Butcher mentioned in Chapter VI: Smithfield District, as husband of Mary Ferrell, sister of State Senator Thomas Ferrell, and who served as a Confederate soldier through the Civil War, while Nicholas F. served through that same war a volunteer in the Federal Army.

After that war Nicholas F. tarried in Greenbrier County, married there the wife who came with him to Reedy, and died there, childless. Afterward, on May 22, 1888, Nicholas F. Butcher, age 45, united in marriage with Phoebe S. (Buckby) Butcher, age 29, she the widow of Joseph A. Butcher, deceased. He sold his lands and thenceforth was father of the household and liked by his step-children.

To Nicholas F. and Phoebe S. (Buckby-Butcher), his wife, were born and reared two sons and one daughter; their names Paul, Walter and Lotis.

Paul lives at the old home place and has been a teacher in the primary schools of the State for some years.

CAIN: Among the first settlers of Reedy.

Thomas Cain was born in New Jersey, son of a colonial family that arrived there from Wales. He gave one of his sons the name "Teign," suggesting Devonshire, England. Thomas grew to manhood in New Jersey and there married a Miss Hary Horner, and he and this wife came farther west and settled and lived for a short time in Green County, Pennsylvania, and from Green County came to Reedy in the year 1817, settling a mile or so below the "Thee Forks" on or at the mouth of the small branch of main Reedy Creek ever after called "Cain's Run."

Thomas was a man of some education and was the first school teacher to assemble and teach the youth of the "Three Forks."

To Thomas Cain and Mary (Horner) Cain, his wife, were born and by them reared there on Reedy, seven sons and four daughters, whose names in order of their births, sons and daughters separately, are: Alfred, Thomas H., Teign, Gamaliel, John W., James and Dr. Daniel; Mary, Rachel, Margaret and Nicie. We are told further of this family by S. J. "Dutch" Cain, son of Thomas H. and grandson of the pioneer Thomas Cain, that: Alfred Cain, son of the pioneer Thomas, married Mary Corbet, for further see their family names last of this Cain article.

Thomas H. Cain, son of Thomas and Mary (Horner) Cain, began preaching in the two or three social centers of Reedy country when he was only seventeen years old; in Hardesty's History of Roane County, it is said that Thomas H. Cain, a baptist minister organized a congregation at Reedyville in the year 1840. He was an active minister of the gospel as shown by Roane County marriage records down to the eighteen hundred and eighties. When a young man Rev. Thomas H. Cain married Miss Elizabeth Dye, of Reedy country; to them were born and by them reared five sons and four daughters; their names as follows: Dissoway (Duisossoway if same as his material grandfather Dye), Thomas, Jr., Elijah, Samuel, who married Rebecca Bowyer, Alfred Jr., who married Lizzie Ann Bates; Delphia Jane, at 17 married David Enoch, 21, January 8, 1857; Mary Ann, married Samuel Curfman, December 27, 1858, and Elizabeth who married James Curfman, August 18, 1865. The mother, Elizabeth (Dye), having died, Rev. Thomas H. Cain, for second wife, married Miss Sarah Morris, daughter of Isaac Morris, then resident of Wirt County; of this marriage were born and reared two sons, their names George and Stonewall Jackson; the latter being nicknamed "Dutch." I do not know the career of George, but S. J. "Dutch" on the 3rd day of November, 1889, married Marietta Doolittle, of the Doolittle family of Reedy, the marriage record having it: "Dutch Cain and Etta Doolittle, his age 22, her age 19;" they settled first on a farm below Reedy and lived there until the year 1900, at which time they became residents of the Town of Reedy, where "Dutch" keeps a watch and clock repair place with a barber shop in connection with it; he also owns and rents some residence properties in Reedy. To "Dutch" and "Etta" (Doolittle) Cain, his wife, have been born, and yet with them one son, now about twenty-one years of age, and three daughters all younger than the son.

Teign Cain, son of Thomas, the pioneer, leaves no record of himself in Roane County; also Gamaliel and James Cain leave us no information; Daniel leaves a record of himself in Wirt County history, as "Daniel Cain, M. D., born January 22, 1828, son of Thomas and Mary (Horner) Cain;" married Lettia Sheppard September 7, 1851; made their home at Zackville, Wirt County, West Virginia.

John W. Cain, son of Thomas and Mary (Horner) Cain, married Miss Eliza Conrad; they reared no son or daughter, but he was the most active business man of this pioneer family of Cains; he is the John W. Cain, partner of Albert G. Ingraham, as builders of the first court house of the county; he and Louisa Ann, his wife conveyed as a gift, the church lot near Reedy "on Cain's Run," to the Baptist Church of Christ called Good Hope, party of the second part, to have and to hold as long as they maintain on it a house of worship; done August 8th, 1859.

Of the daughters of the pioneers Thomas and Mary (Horner) Cain, we are told that Rachel married a Batten; Mary married Thomas Lee; Margaret married Wilson Sheppard and Nicia became the wife of Johnathan Sheppard of Wirt County.

Returning to the first name:

Alfred Cain, born about the year 1815, son of Thomas and Mary, pioneers, married Miss Mary Corbet, of the Reedy country. Alfred was popular and prominent in county affairs for fifteen or twenty years; studied law, practiced some, especially in the courts of justices of the peace; was one time sheriff of the county, sometime in the 1870's. To Alfred and Mary (Corbet), his wife, were born, at Reedy, three sons and six daughters, their names: William, killed in mill explosion.

George R. married Mary J. Simmons, August 29, 1870, died soon afterward, leaving a son and daughter: Trace and Ethel Cain.

John W. married Sarah Eliza McCarty, of Reedy, July 26, 1860; they made their home in Spencer for some years; Louanna, a daughter, and William, a son, are remembered of their four or five children.

Rachel married Henry Knopp; Margaret L. married Hampden Parrish, of Jackson County, November, 1873.

Mary Jane married Staats Parsons, of Jackson County, West Virginia, made their home for awhile in Spencer, later in Jackson County. To them were born four sons and one daughter; her name Lora Catherine, 1878, married G. M. Sergent, of Spring Creek, later of Spencer, in year 1900; they have one son, Ewel Sergent. Their home and business is in Spencer. See Chapter IX of this book, City of Spencer. Of the other two daughters of Alfred Cain: Harriett and Elizabeth, I have no information, but we see on the marriage records of Roane County, "Gamaliel Board to Sarah I. Cain, September 2, 1868."

CALDWELL:

The Harper District farm which had most distinction for a decade next following the Civil War, was that of Joseph F. Caldwell, situated between the mouth of Trace Fork and Big Creek, containing 359½ acres; a great acreage of this was cleared of its heavy timber and brought into a high state of cultivation; about the year 1880 it had made its owner, Joseph F. Caldwell, spoken of as one of the county's wealthy men; this farm was long known as the "Caldwell Place," and by recitals in a Deed of Release, by Andrew Board of Greenbrier County, West Virginia, "To Joseph F. Caldwell and his mother Matilda, and three sisters: Janett, 'Caroline and Frances," dated 1867, we are informed that about the year 1844, William Hanford Caldwell, whose wife was Matilda Crawford Caldwell, died in Greenbrier County, West Virginia, and had apportioned his real estate among his children, placing this 359½ acres on Poca then Kanawha County, in the care of Andrew Board, Trustee, "until all said children should become twenty-one years of age," about the year Joseph F. Caldwell reached the age of twenty-one, the above mentioned Release of this patrimony was made and all the beneficiaries arrived here; Janett soon married Daniel Stover Looney; Caroline married W. Parrott Ferrell and Frances married, first Z. C. Ellis and on his decease she married James Hammond; this we get from a chancery suit in which Joseph F. Caldwell becomes the owner of Frances' share of the old Caldwell "place."

The children of Joseph F. Caldwell and Rosanna (daughter of Robert Cleek) Caldwell, his wife, whom we can name here are William R., Clinton H., Joseph E., Perry W., and Dr. Mark Caldwell; the names of the daughters are Annie, who married Irven F. Conley; Matilda, who married Dr. D. William Shirkey, and Martha who became the wife of John Hively.

CALLOW:

John R. Callow and Elizabeth (Hitt) Callow, his wife, came to Reedy in the year 1883. He was born in the Isle of Man, April 18, 1784, son of Robert Callow, and arrived in the United States in time to serve and did serve as a soldier in the War of 1812. Elizabeth (Hitt) was born in Fauquier County, Virginia, April 2, 1790; there she and John R. Callow were married about the year 1820. Of this marriage two sons were born and came with their parents to Reedy. Their names, George W. and Elijah; of these we write as next follows:

George W. Callow was born in Fauquier County, October 26, 1822; on April 2, 1846, he married Sarah M. Flesher, born in Lewis County, western Virginia, July 5, 1826, the daughter of George A. and Sallie (Connolly) Flesher, of the old families of Fleshers and Connollys of the Monongahela Valley; George and Sarah M., his wife, commenced their wedded life on Reedy and soon made a substantial home for themselves on Left Hand Fork about a mile from Three Forks. To George W. and Sarah A. were born five sons and six daughters, named as follows: Mary E., born 1847, died in youth; Melissa J., 1848; Mahala, 1854; Sarah C., died in youth; Emily S., 1863, and Ruann, a twin with the son Albert, born 1866. The names of five sons are William A., born

1849; Charles W., 1852, lived in Cass County, Missouri, about 1880; Elijah Jr., 1856; Henry F., 1861, and Albert twin of Ruanna, 1866.

Elijah Callow, son of John R. and Elizabeth Callow, above mentioned, was born in Fauquier County, Virginia, 1825, came to Reedy with his parents as stated, 1833; married July 15, 1852, Mary C., daughter of Jacob C., and Sarah (Walker) Smith, born in Kanawha County, western Virginia, 1833, Jacob Smith having settled on Reedy on his lands adjoining the Callow lands about the year 1852, this being then a part of Wirt County.

Elijah and Mary C. Callow, his wife, began their wedded life on part of the paternal lands and proved skillful farmers and good citizens; of this wedded life six sons and four daughters were born, named, George A., born 1854; William V., 1857; Jacob C., 1862; Jefferson H., 1866; Andrew C., 1873, and John R., 1875; the daughters' names were Elizabeth A., 1853; Mary P., 1860; Charity Ann, 1868, and Magnolia, 1870.

George W. Callow and Elijah Callow both served as volunteers in the Confederate Army of the Civil War, and both endured imprisonments and hardships of that awful war. At home again they enjoyed prosperity, contributed to church and schools, and had the unstinted respect of all their neighbors to time when they were gathered to their fathers.

CAMPBELL: Of Spencer.

John Chambers Campbell, Sr., and his wife, Anna, natives of Franklin County, Virginia, with their family of three sons and three daughters, were the first of this name resident of Spencer. John C. Campbell and his wife were married and lived for a time in Franklin County, Virginia. We infer from a statement of a grandson, Mr. Cork, that Rebecca, his mother, a daughter of John C. Campbell, was born in that county.

They, John C. and wife, came to Clarksburg, West Virginia, where they resided for a time, from there to Glenville, West Virginia, thence to Spencer, shortly after the "Civil War"—about the year 1868. This date we infer from a marriage record, a daughter, Annie B. to Henry Depue. John C. Campbell was a lawyer, but in failing strength of limbs, he acquired the large old frame hotel situate on the corner of Main and Market Streets, the principal hostelry of the town then, conveyed to the wife and family by John G. Duval and others, 2nd April, 1869, and carried it on for some years; was elected and served a term or two as a justice of the peace. They educated one son as a physician and one as a lawyer. They were Presbyterians in religious sentiments. As the name indicates, they were of Scotch descent; the men all blonds.

The names of the children of John C. Campbell, Sr., and his wife are as follows:

Mary Louise, wife of Milton Norris, Glenville.

Anna Belle, married Henry Depue of Spring Creek, September 26, 1872. See name Depue, Chapter VI, this work.

Rebecca Lupton, married James Cork in Clarksburg. See name Cork. After his death, she married Capt. M. W. Kidd.

William C., physician, married Miss Prudentia Lewis (See name, Lewis), January 10, 1882; they made their home on Long Ridge beyond Walton; reared several children.

John C., Jr., married Miss America Simmons, December 30, 1872.

Benjamin W. We have nothing of his career.

Augustus M., as a gay young lawyer, was Roane's first resident prosecuting attorney; married first, Miss Annie Wilson, 1882, he about twenty years of age then; he made a second marriage here, and was parent of some children; on expiration of his office he went to California.

Of the children of John C. and America (Simmons) Campbell, we recall the following: Mary, who married J. Claud Bartlett (widower, age 44) on September 4, 1898; her age then 24 years. They made their home in Spencer several years and to them were born one son and one daughter.

Ashby, wedded somewhere in the State of Ohio, a Miss of Swedish extraction; he acquired the John C., jr. and America's home farm and live here yet, 1926.

Rebecca, daughter of John C. Jr., and America, his wife, wedded William Wyley Schwender, at her home, on November 2, 1904; her age then given as 24, his 25; they resided here some years then moved to Ripley. They have several children.

CANDLER: Of Reedy District.

John W. Candler was born near "Three Forks" of Reedy, about the year 1828, son of William Candler and his wife, Elizabeth Seaman Candler, who was a daughter of David Seaman first of the name among pioneers of Reedy, sister of Silas B. Seaman. This William Candler, father of John W., was a trader in produce on the Ohio River, and was accidently drowned in that river on one of his trips about the time of the birth of John W., the only child of himself and Elizabeth (Seaman), his wife, who also did not live to old age. John W.'s home was always with or near his uncle, Silas B. Seaman, on Right Reedy.

He married Miss Elizabeth J. Napp, daughter of a family of that name of Mason County, about the year 1850. They made their home on a tract of five hundred acres of land lying one mile from "Three Forks" up on Right Fork; attacking the then unbroken forest, they made and maintained a good home, from whence they went forth into the neighborhood affairs, he always performing a conspicuous part. He was a large man and convincing talker, a rare humorist at times; ever a tetotal abstainer from use of intoxicants, in a time when drinking it, even to excess was popular, even with his uncle and relatives. He was devoted to the Methodist Episcopal Church and liberal to it with his time and earnings.

To John W. and Elizabeth (Napp) Candler were born two sons and five daughters. Their names and marriages as follows: Palmira Jane married Charles Remington Bishop, of Reedy, February 16, 1875, her age 23 or 24, his 20. Albert, next child, died.

Susan Victoria, married William Leary, of Reedy, January 10, 1883.

Martha M. married Lafayette W. Headley, December 5, 1908; his age then 53, born in Pennsylvania; her age 45.

Thomas A. married Esther Leary, on Middle Fork, March 22, 1891; his age given 23, her's 20. These now (1927) reside in the State of Missouri.

Delilah Elizabeth, married Benj. Franklin Riddle, of Middle Reedy, August 7, 1892, her age 24, his 33.

Sarah Candler was the youngest of the family.

CANTERBURY: Of Walton District.

Zadoc Canterbury, first of the name here, was born in Monroe County, Virginia. There he married Miss Marcina Snow, about year 1840; to them were born one son and one daughter, their names, Caroline and John D.

Zadoc, with his wife, Marcina and their two children above named, came to McKowns Creek of Pocataligo about the year 1859, acquired a tract of land and made a good home half mile east of Walton. The daughter, Caroline, born in Monroe County, Virginia, September 25, 1843, married Frederick Gandee, of Gandeeville. See name Gandee.

John D. Canterbury, son of Zadoc and Marcena, married Miss Martha Jane Hively, on 29th day of August, 1870. They made their permanent home on or near the old Canterbury land.

There were other Canterburys, but I do not know their antecedents, nor family relations.

Eli Canterbury, married Kate Chapman, March 5, 1873.

James Canterbury married Darthalia Thompson on March 31, 1880. There was a Henry, Sr., and Henry, Jr.

Calvin Canterbury married Miss Mary Jane Ellison, a daughter of Samuel Ellison; made a home here and brought up the following children:

Ohley, "Oley," who married Bertha, daughter of Elijah Igo, of Geary District; Ohley and Bertha have their farm home on Cotton Tree.

Ballard Canterbury, son of Calvin and wife, lives in Kentucky, and another son, John Canterbury, lives in Logan County, West Virginia.

CARPER:

Nicholas Carper and Sarah (Nida) Carper were the first of this family who came to this country; arrived here in the year 1858, both descendants of old colonial families of Virginia; they appear to have began wedded life in Giles County, in which county their eight sons and two daughters were born, all of whom came with them to Roane County.

Nicholas soon purchased a tract of three hundred and ten acres of land lying on Shaver Fork, which Beverly J. Taylor conveyed to him in fee simple by deed, dated 28th July, 1868. Over their heads and all about them, a heavy forest "its mighty branches tossed"; an ideal place for such a family of boys: Alkanah, the eldest, then a lad of ten years. The dominating impulses of this parental pair of pioneers were to make a best home and contribute to making a most moral neighborhood, the latter to be accomplished by support of the Baptist Church, both lived to see full fruition of their hopes.

The names of these children of Nicholas and Sarah mentioned are Alkanah W., Clifton H., Calahan C., Miles M., Shelton V., Charles W., James Ballard, Harvey R., Almira and Martha.

Alkanah W. Carper was born October 15, 1839; on November 22, 1865, he married Mary J., daughter of John and Frances (Cochran) Smith ,a pioneer preacher, having come here from Nicholas County, western Virginia, in which county Mary J. was born (see Smith); of this marriage three daughters and four sons were born, all in Roane County, Sarah F., September 22, 1866 ;Orpha M., October 30, 1868; John N., June 24, 1871; Stella A., August 25, 1873; Joseph N., August 8, 1875; William I., May 3, 1873; James G., August 30, 1880. Alkanah W., familiarly called "Kane,' 'served with the Union soldiers three years of the Civil War, Company B, 9th W. Va. Infantry.

The foregoing names of children is copied from Hardesty's History, and its correctness must be doubted as to names of children. A marriage record in county clerk's office has this: "Nelson J. Carper to Ocie Osborne, March 30, 1904; his age 27, her age 22."

Clifton H. Carper, son of Nicholas and Sarah (Nida) Carper, was born in Giles County, Virginia, year 1843. In Roane County, December 9, 1867, he married Prussia, daughter of Mordicai and Margaret (Greathouse) Stackhouse, who came here from Jackson County, western Virginia; of this marriage were born three sons and three daughters: Woodville G., July 7, 1869; Shelton R., January 4, 1871, died in youth; George A., April 3, 1873; Mary G., February 12, 1876; Prussia E., June 22, 1878, and Lillie O., June 24, 1881. Clifton H. Carper was a Union soldier, Co. B., 9th W. Va. Infantry; taken prisoner at Cloyd Mountain, escaped soon and joined his company; his hardships of this is the thrilling episode of his life.

Miles M. Carper, son of Nicholas and Sarah (Nida) Carper, born December 14, 1846; married Jane D., daughter of William and Priscilla (Samples) Paxton, in Clay County, December 28, 1871. To this union were born five sons and one daughter: Walter V., January 6, 1873; James M., June 2, 1875; Christopher C., April 2, 1877; Wm. H., died in infancy; Freddie, born June 9, 1881, and the daughter, Lillie B., September 17, 1883.

Shelton V. Carper, son of Nicholas and Sarah his wife, was born Jan. 8, 1851; in Roane County, June 17, 1877, he married Susan J., daughter of Dusossoway and Mary A. (Patton) Ledsom, in this district. Their children are Ocia B., born Oct. 13, 1878; Rama D., Dec. 13, 1880, and Oka

P., April 18, 1882. Sallie married Josiah King; Pruda married Geo. W. King; Robert F. married Lizzie Hively and Roy married Bertha Nida; both these sons live on the old home farm.

Shelton V. Carper was above the average of citizens in common sense; was elected and served one term as Delegate for Roane County in the State Legislature, twenty-ninth session, 1909.

Calahan C. Carper ("Cal"), son of Nicholas and Sarah (Nida) Carper, was born in Giles County, Virginia—one of the older sons of the family—and came to Big Sandy, now Geary District, with the family; for wife he married Rachel C. Taylor, daughter of "Henty" Taylor, March 29, 1869—name of wife and date of marriage taken from the county marriage records.

Of this marriage we can name the following four sons and four daughters:

Charles, Ephraim, Waitman, George, Cynthia, Dora, Mollie and Stella.

Further:

We do not have the names of wives of Charles and Ephraim Carper of above family.

George married a daughter of William Knight.

Waitman married Charity Drake, daughter of Newton Drake of the Drake family of Geary District.

Mollie became the wife of Jackson Knight, son of William P. Knight, of Left Hand of Sandy.

Stella married George W. McCrosky, son of William C. McCrosky of Big Sandy of Geary District.

James Ballard Carper was born in Giles County, Virginia, August 13, 1855, son of the Nicholas and Sarah (Nida) Carper, first of the Carpers in Roane; came to this county with his parents in 1858; married in Roane County Rebecca, daughter of Alexander Justice and his wife of a Russel County, Virginia, family of the name Justice.

Harvey R. Carper, born in Giles County, Virginia, year 1857, son of Nicholas and Sarah Carper, first of the name in Sandy country, married Savanah Cook, born in Roane County, April 11, 1873, daughter of Barnabas S. and Sarah J. (Truman) Cook, at the home of B. S. Cook, her father, at mouth of Left Hand, August 15, 1888. Of this wedded life of Harvey R. and Savannah were born the following named sons and daughters: Otis Gay, 1889; Clara Ethel, 1891; Molta Ray, 1895; Anna and Amma, twins, 1900; Romie Carl, 1902; Hazel died in infancy, and John Edward, born in 1912.

Soon after marriage, Harvey R. and Savannah made their home on a farm adjoining the B. S. Cook farm, and have lived there ever since, and their children were born there.

We find no record of the Almira, daughter of Nicholas and Sarah Carper. But we find in marriage record that a Martha E. Carper married James H. Goad, September 14, 1868. Marriage records of that date do not show births, age or parentage of the parties to the wedding.

HISTORY OF ROANE COUNTY   473

CASTO: Of Harper and Walton Districts.
These are descendants of Johnathan Casto of the pioneers of Jackson County, in the ramifications of whose family tree we find no one sufficiently interested to help us. However, we find by Roane County marriage records that Captain William Gandee, born in 1813, when a young man married a Miss Margaret Casto, and they continued their part of the Gandee family at Gandeeville; and this accounts for other early settlement of Castos on the waters of the Pocatalicos. We note other marriages such as: John B. Casto to Eliza Lowe, January 15, 1868; and John B. Casto to Phoebe Taylor, March 19, 1871; the information for the marriage licenses given by Alex Taylor.
There were in this locality several brothers and sisters of above named John B. Casto, all of whom married and made homes and reared families, scattered from the Town of Spencer, in which are descendants, clear across the country to Mason and Jackson Counties.
Some of the older of these Castos served as enlisted Union soldiers throughout the Civil War. See the rosters of enlistments given in Chapter I of this book.
The sons of Levi and James served in the Confederate Armies, enlisting from Jackson County.

CASTO:Of Spencer—City. Descendants of pioneers of Jackson County.
Definite information of this family commences with the careers of three brothers all born on the Buckhannon River of the Monongahela, in the decade, 1785 to 1795; their names Levi, Johnathan and James, the latter two of the brothers were soldiers of the war of 1812.
Levi while an unmarried young man came to Mill Creek in what was afterward Jackson County, West Virginia, "in the year 1812," says his son, Dr. Absalom in his biograph in Hardesty's, and married about 1816, Miss Hannah Carney of the same place and they settled on Mill Creek.
The other two brothers, Johnathan and James, on return from the 1812 war, "settled in Jackson County," says Benjamin Franklin Casto, a son of Johnathan and Magdalene (Westerholt) Casto, "in the year 1816."
James Casto, the third brother, married in Jackson County, Miss ...., and settled on Grass Lick, made a large farm there and he and his wife there reared ten children, whose names, as our informant, Jennings B. Casto, gives us them are as follows:
Elmore, William, Nathan, Mary, Minerva, Riley, Nicholas, George, Charles Carney and Robert Casto. Of these:
Charles Carney Casto, son of James Casto and wife, married in Jackson County, Miss Martha Stewart, in 1859; she was a daughter of George Stewart, son of a pioneer Stewart of Jackson County. Charles C. and Martha, his wife, acquired a tract of 312 acres of land ,in forest then, lying on upper Mill Creek near the mouth of Frozen Camp Creek; here they prospered and reared six sons and four daughters whose names are as follows: Jennings Bell, Rosie Catherine, Thomas L., Minnie B.,

Robert A., Holly Lee, Perry Asbury, John Riley, Maud and Fannie. These are named in order of their respective ages; their respective marriages are as follows:

Jennings B. Casto married Miss Sallie Smith, daughter of Clay C. and Margaret (Goff) Smith, of Spencer, 1899. To Jennings B. and Sallie, his wife, were born one son and two daughters, whose names are Vora, Corinne and Clay Clayton, now a physician in Columbus, Ohio. Always made their home in Spencer, where J. B. conducted for some years a mercantile business. He was elected and served one term, four years, as a justice of the peace; also served one term as mayor of the town.

Rosie Casto, daughter of C. C. and Martha, married in Jackson County, West Virginia, Dr. Alexander R. Parsons, later many years a citizen of Spencer; they had no child.

Thomas L., son of Charles C. and Martha Casto, married Miss Drusilla Brown, born in Harrison County, at her parents' home on Middle Reedy, June 3, 1886; his age 22, her's 20; they later made their home in Spencer, where they reared two sons and two daughters whose names are Coy, John, Rosie and Drusilla.

Minnie B., daughter of Charles C. and Margaret Casto, at her home in Jackson County, married Martin K. Goff, of Spencer, date we do not have. They made their home in Spencer District; we can name of their children, Rosa, married and lives in Pittsburgh, Pennsylvania, and Erline, wife of Wilbur T. Lowe, of City of Spencer, married August 15, 1919.

Robert A. Casto, son of C. C. and Martha, commenced business as a young man in Spencer, married Miss Margaret Smith, in Spencer, March 30, 1894; his age 23, her's 35; she was born in Barbour County, West Virginia, a sister of Joseph M. Smith, long a jeweler in Spencer. To Robert A. and Margaret ("Maggie") his wife were born and reared in Spencer, one son and one daughter, their names, Ralph W. and Aubra E., now wife of J. Chris Looney.

Holly Lee, son of Chas. C. and Margaret Casto, became a graduate physician and surgeon, settled in Spencer, married Mary McMahon (then widow O'Brien), August 12, 1906; his age 32, her's 28; she and her first husband were parents of a daughter, her name May, now wife of Frederick McIntosh, jr., hardware merchant of City of Spencer.

Maud M. Casto, daughter of Charles C. and Martha, his wife, married in Spencer, Dayton Rhodes. (See Rhodes.)

Fannie Casto, youngest of the foregoing C. C. Casto family, married in Jackson County, Charles Conner, they have two children, Perry and John R. Casto died not having married.

After death of the first wife, Margaret, Charles C. Casto married Minnie Moss of Reedy (she then a widow of .... Callow), daughter of Robert and Eliza (Rhodes) Moss; the record date of marriage, September 17, 1891; his age 52, her's 22. One child was born of this marriage, a son named Kenna Casto.

CHANCEY:

Hiram and Elvira Chancey, young husband and wife settled on Middle Fork of Reedy about the year 1820. Died, she about 1854, he 1858.

Where and when either was born we have not been told. From recollections of remarks made by their children, they came from New England or Pennsylvania, by way of Marietta and Ravenswood on the Ohio River.

He was a steadfast Wesleyan in religious notions and a preacher of that creed.

They came with a title or at once acquired a title to a tract of three or four hundred acres of forest land adjoining Willis Burdette and William Roache's lands on the Middle Fork of Reedy; they visited and kept up acquaintance with people of Ravenswood and upper Mill Creek countries of Jackson County. He was a man of an education a little better than the average pioneer, and was influential there for forty years.

They reared a large family of children; of these we can give the following names:

James, Elvira, Calvary, Roswell R., Irene, Andrew B. and William Alexander. Marriages and families of these:

James married in Mill Creek country and made his home there and reared a family.

Elvira married a James Hartman; went West.

Calvary married a Miss Westfall, prior to formation of Roane County, and they made their home and reared a family on the Middle Fork of Reedy; they had one child, his name Andrew; this wife having died, Calvary married Rebecca Hall about the year 1850, and brought her to his home; their children's names are Samantha Jane, David H. Alexander, Alice, Millie Catherine, Clifton, Calvary Mede and Isaac.

Roswell R. Chancey, son of Hiram and Elvira, pioneers, married Miss Violetta Meadows, daughter of Rev. Meadows, and sister of Andy Meadows, resident many years on Steer Creek Gilmer County, West Virginia.

They made their home on part of the ancestral lands on Middle Fork of Reedy. He "took to learning" and was prominent in his neighborhood and the county for a space of twenty years, 1855 to 1875. Was scrivner for his neighborhood, a justice of the peace of Reedy District one or more terms; member of the County Court of Roane County; active and liberal in contributions to his church, Methodist Episcopal.

They reared three sons and two daughters whose names in order of respective ages are, Jacob Tichnell, Rose (died), Samantha Bell, Hiram Irven and William Hannibal. Of these we write further:

Jacob Tichnell married Miss Sarah Alcinda Graham, on September 8, 1874; she a daughter of Joseph Graham. (See Graham.) They made their home near; and to Jacob T. and Sarah A., his wife, were born and reared Nina, wife of Elisha McCutchen, married August 28, 1802; Nevil Lakin and Joseph.

Nevil Lakin Chancey, son of J. T. and S. Alcinda, became a young school teacher; married Miss Roxie McClung of Reedy, May 29, 1897, ages 21 and 20; was elected and served two terms as county superintendent of schools of Roane County, 1902-1910. Has for several years last past been superintendent of schools in Mingo County, West Virginia.

Samantha Belle, daughter of Roswell R., married Lemuel H. Board, of Reedy. (See "Board.")

Hiram Irven, son of Roswell R. and Violetta, married Miss Mary Florence McGraw, December 23, 1887, his age 27, her age 17.

William Hannibal married Mary Delana, October 19, 1883, his age 23.

Turn back to Hiram, pioneer:

Irena, daughter of Hiram and Elvira, married George W. Fore. (See "Fore.")

Andrew B. Chancey, son of Hiram and Elvia, his wife, was born 1830; about 1850 married Mary Stewart, daughter of William, pioneer at Reedy. They made their large farm second one above "Three Forks" on Middle Fork. He was prominent in affairs of the county twenty years; deputy sheriff, stock man and good farmer. The children of Andrew B. and Mary (Stewart) his wife, were Minerva Jane (see Ayers), Harvey and Susan; Susan married William G. Ayers, November 9, 1884, her age 20, his age then 22; they made their home in Gallopolis, Ohio.

Wm. Alexander Chancey, son of Hiram and Elvira, pioneers, married Miss Sarah Ann Rhodes, October 6, 1856, she the daughter of Samuel and Parthena Rhodes of Middle Fork of Reedy; William A. was killed by accident at a "Barn Raising" at about middle life.

The children of Wm. A. and Sarah Ann Chancey, named in order of ages, are: Cora Lelia, Jane and Martha. Cora Lelia married Leroy M. Eagle, February 26, 1877.

Martha and Jane Chancey married, and went away.

CHAPMAN: Of Smithfield.

Henry and Nancy (Williams) Chapman came from Putnam County, western Virginia, and settled on Henrys Fork, near where Linden now is, in the year 1855; of their family we here can name only the one son, Sylvanus G.

Sylvanus G. Chapman, son of Henry and Nancy (Williams) Chapman, was born February 29, 1854, in Putnam County, West Virginia; he was a volunteer soldier of the Confederate armies for two years, commencing 1862; at home again, on July 12, 1867, Sylvanus united in marriage with Henrietta B. Young, born in Kanawha County, June 17, 1850, she being the daughter of Benjamin Strader and Lucinda (Huffman) Young, who came to this part of Henrys Fork in 1853. Charles F., the father of Benjamin S. Young, was a noted Indian spy of "Fort Jones."

To Sylvanus and Henrietta B. (Young) Chapman, were born eleven children on the farm on Henrys Fork, their names: Mary Alice, 1868; Martha J., 1869; Benjamin F., 1870; Fannie E., 1872; Carry B., 1874; William S., 1875; Lucy D., 1876; Lotta V., 1878; Henry N., 1879; John G., 1881, and Henrietta D., December 29, 1882. Of this family we write further:

Mary Alice, married Charles McMillan of Henrys Fork.

Martha J. married W. Mac Samples, of Geary.

Benjamin F. married Mina, daughter of John J. Board, of Tariff; to Benjamin and Mina (Board) Chapman was born one daughter, Lena B., December 11, 1898; she graduated from Spencer High School Normal Department and took one year in Mountain State Business College at Parkersburg, West Virginia. She is now (1926) bookkeeper and stenographer for Time Record, newspaper, Spencer, West Virginia.

Benjamin F. Chapman died March 20, 1900.

Ella, daughter of Sylvanus G. and Henrietta B. Chapman, married Edward Goodwin of Ravenswood.

Bell married Samuel F. Sarver, son of Hon. John Sarver, of Smithfield District.

William S. Chapman, served two years in the Spanish-American War; married Rhoda Wright.

Lucy Chapman married William S. Rishel, farmer and merchant of Linden.

Lottie Chapman married George Sarver, later Hon. George Sarver, he having served a term in the State Legislature.

Henry Nelson Chapman, married Jennie, daughter of W. Scott Simmons.

John Gideon Chapman, married Mary Simmons.

Dottie Chapman married Mr. O. Hutchinson.

CHENOWITH: Of Reedy.

Ira S. Chenowith with his wife and possibly the first born of their children, made their farm home near the head of Right Fork of Reedy, on the Ravenswood and Spencer turnpike, three and a half miles west of the village of Reedy; here attacked the forest and made their home, possibly before the Civil War.

He was, may be, relative by marriage to John Stalnaker, who had his home at the head of the other fork of Right Reedy; Mrs. Stalnaker being a Chenowith by birth. Ira S. Chenowith was the first farmer of that creek to abandon the log house and build a new frame dwelling. "Lives in a white house," was an expression tinged a little with envy in those days—about 1875. He was an active man of good judgment, successful for that time and environment. He encouraged me, the writer of this, by assuring me it was worth while to get an education. On the pike, among a number traveling to the county seat, Spencer, where on that day was a mass convention to nominate candidates for county offices, the company selected me to make a nominating speech, placing the name of Ira S. Chenowith, of Reedy, as a candidate for commissioner of the county court. I made the speech, he was nominated, and won in the general election; was president of the court for one year; his name appears on the records of the court for the years 1885 to 1889, with those of William D. Kelley and Almarine B. Jackson.

At the farm on Reedy, above mentioned, Ira S. Chenowith and his wife ended their course of life.

To them were born and by them brought up the following children, named in order of ages: Martha J., James O., Mary A., Job, George M., Bertram ("Bert"), and Clay.

Martha A. married Albert Hutchinson September 17, 1867.

James O. married Miss Alice Lance September 7, 1876.

Mary A. married Gallatin J. Hamrick December 15, 1885.

George M. married Nora McClung December 13, 1891; his age 24, her's 24, she a daughter of M. A. McClung, of Reedy.

We do not have the marriages of Job, "Bert" or Clay.

CLEAVENGER: Of Reedy and Spencer.

Bailey Cleavenger and his wife Lydia (McDonald) with one or two of their first born children were the first of this family name here.

Bailey was born—maybe—in Barbour County, western Virginia, in the year 1821 ,son of a William Cleavenger, one of three brothers— William, Samuel and Edmond—who came to Barbour County from Pennsylvania; William having died in Barbour County leaving one daughter and this son Bailey. The daughter grew up there and married a Mr. Cole; the son, Bailey, was reared by his uncle, Samuel Cleavenger. He married Miss Lydia A. McDonald in Harrison County, she a daughter of the family McDonald, pioneers of Harrison County, a sister of Judson McDonald, long a well-known citizen of Lewis and Harrison Counties.

Bailey and Lydia A., his wife made their first home in Barbour County, and came to Reedy in the year 1853, acquired a large tract of land on the Ravenswood and Spencer turnpike four miles from Spencer toward "Three Forks"; spent their lives there, and reared their family there.

He was one of the first of Union soldiers, volunteers from these parts; was killed near his home the next year. See chapters of this book first above referred to.

The sons and daughters of Bailey and Lydia A. (McDonald) Cleavenger are the following, named in order of their respective births:

Moses, Sarah Jane, James M., Tabitha A., Charles C., John C., and William H. Their marriages and something further:

Moses Cleavenger, son of Bailey and Lydia A., his wife was twice married; first wife, Miss Mary Elizabeth McKinley, whom he married on March 11, 1875, she was born November 30, 1853, a daughter of

HISTORY OF ROANE COUNTY 479

Thomas and Catherine (Neal, of Wood County) McKinley, settlers on Bear Run Spring Creek, soon after this marriage.

Moses and Mary Elizabeth made their home on part of the family lands on Ravenswood and Spencer turnpike, lived out their live's spans there, changed many acres of heavy forest into fertile fields; maintained a substantial home and there reared their several children whose names are as follows: Ada, Catherine, Mida and Clyde C. Ada remains single, the others married. Catherine ("Kate") married Henry C. Taylor, of Roane, on September 6, 1917, her age 35, his age 35.

Mida married Rex Arnett, of Spencer, May 14, 1903; her age 19, his age 21.

Clyde C., became a resident of Spencer, while yet a young man, clerk of a bank; was elected and served a term as clerk of the circuit court, and re-elected to the same office for the term commencing 1923, and is yet serving; he united in marriage with Miss Faye Lawson, of Gandeeville, October 22, 1921; his age then given 31, her age 23.

The mother, Mary Elizabeth (McKinley) having died, Moses married Mrs. Verna ("Louverna") Riley (widow Sinnet), September 6, 1894, his age 47, her age 34; of this marriage came a daughter named Anna, who married a Mr. Chaney.

Sarah Jane, daughter of Bailey and Elizabeth Cleavenger, married Isaac M. Glaze. See Glaze.

Tabitha A. married Nicholas Simmons, December 1, 1875. See Chapter VII.

James M. Cleavenger, son of Bailey and Elizabeth A., his wife, was born in Barbour County, western Virginia, July 1, 1849; was accepted as a volunteer soldier in the Union service, Co. D, 7th W. Va. cavalry, not quite fifteen years of age at time of enlistment; served in the Virginian battle fields until the close of the war, escaped unscathed. He married in Barbour County, West Virginia, on November 18, 1874, Miss Elizabeth Dorcus Hamrick, born in Augusta County, Virginia, March 26, 1847, daughter of Dr. Graham and Margaret (Whitner) Hamrick, residents of Barbour at time of this marriage.

James M. and Elizabeth Dorcus, his wife, made their home in Spencer, where he, through his long years of activities carried on various business and held public offices; here they brought up their family, and here this wife and mother died; James M. is yet a citizen often seen on the streets. The names of their children in order of births are: Estella, died not married; Elsie, yet single, and George Girty.

George Girty married a Miss Bessie Heck, on April 7, 1904, his age given 22, her's 22; she was born in Jackson County, West Virginia, a daughter of Henry Heck—third Henry of that family name, later and at this time a resident of Spencer. George Girty died a few years after this marriage, leaving one child, the daughter, Dorcus Cleavenger.

Charles C. Cleavenger. son of Bailey and Lydia A., his wife, was reared on Reedy; taught school, was elected by the people and served one term as clerk of the County Court of Roane County; his term is distinguished by the beauty and legibility of his pen-and-ink records. He united in marriage with Miss Nancy ("Nannie") C. Mitchell, of Spencer, November 29, 1876—ages not given then. (See family name "Mitchell.") They made their home in Spencer. After expiration of his office he became a large dealer and shipper of live stock; he died after birth of their sixth child; the names of these: Robert Charles, Mason, May, Bertha and Carrie "Dock" and Nell. These all married except Mason and Bertha, who are yet single; the others made their homes elsewhere.

John C. Cleavenger, son of Bailey and Elizabeth A., stuck to the farm on the turnpike; married on March 5, 1877, Miss Flora J. McKinley, of Reedy District then, born October 28, 1855. daughter of Thomas M. and Catherine M. (Neal) McKinley. John C. died in early middle life. Of the marriage of John C. and Flora J., were born and reared the following sons and daughters: Blanche, Bessie, Alma, Rosie, Winnie, Brice and Paul.

William H. Cleavenger, son of Bailey and Elizabeth A., was twice married: First to Savena Crislip, daughter of Asby Crislip of Reedy, on October 9, 1882, he then 21, she younger. Of this marriage a son was born, his name Ernest; went to Colorado. His second marriage was with Miss Maggie Miller of Spring Creek, on March 27, 1887, his age 26, her's 18; several children were born of this marriage. We have not their names. They all have chosen homes elsewhere.

COMBS: Of Henrys Fork and Spencer.

The first of this family name making a home here were Sallie (Sergent) Combs—widow—with her six sons and six daughters; this widow was a sister of J. Madison Sergent of Spring Creek and David, Jr. and Henry D. Sergent of Johnson Creek of Pocatalico.

Cullen Combs, of old Virginia parentage, in Russell County, met and married Miss Sallie Sergent, daughter of David Sergent and wife. Cullen and Sallie acquired and made a large farm situate on the River Clinch, well stocked and highly productive at time of outbreak of the Civil War, but at the close of that war denuded, desolate and in debt. Cullen sold it and moved to a place in Kentucky; there discouragement and ill health drove him back to Russell, where he died in the year 1866, leaving surviving him the wife, Sallie, and the sons and daughters first mentioned. She with all these came to Roane for a home near her brothers; in the year 1870, purchased lands on upper Henrys Fork, made her home and ended her days in peace and comfort.

The names of the Combs, sons and daughters, given here in order of ages, as near as William David, one of them remembers, are as follows:

Eliza, who married George McFarlan; William David (see at end of paragraph); Frederick, married a Miss Christian, of Kentucky; Thomas, married Miss Helmick in Roane; Julia Ann, married Presley E. Vineyard (see Vineyard); Virginia, married in Morgan County, Kentucky;

HISTORY OF ROANE COUNTY 481

John Miller, married Miss Julia Tallman, February 2, 1878 (see name Tallman); Mary married John Jones of Cotton Tree,˙Walton District; Angeline married James Perry, went to Kentucky; Beverly married thrice, lived in Fayette County, West Virginia; Fielding ("Fied") married Miss Snodgrass.

William David Combs, now (1927) of Spencer, son of Cullen and Sallie (Sergent) Combs, his wife, born on the Clinch River in Russell County, Virginia, November 20, 1844, came to Roane County in the year 1870; on February 8, 1872, united in marriage with Miss Mary Jane Trout, who was born May 12, 1854; they made their home on head waters of Henrys Fork in Smithfield District, and there made and maintained a comfortable farm home, and brought up and gave to the citizenry of Roane County, seven sons and five daughters, whose names, given in order of ages are as follows:

Ferdinand, L. Dondine, Jeanette, who united in marriage with "Flem" Steber in the year 1903, at Parkersburg; Board, Roy D., Oscar, Frederick F.; Eliza and Harry each died before marriage. About the year 1915, William D. and his wife Mary J., purchased a home in Spencer, where they live in ease, their hard-earned lands being in the oil field yields ample income for their declining days.

CONLEY: Of Harper District.

Jeremiah Conley and his wife, Delilah (Davis) Conley, whom he had married in Harrison County, came here in the year, 1859, and made their home in a good part of upper Flat Fork Valley, next that of Stephen Starcher. The Conleys continued to beat back the forest and buy more lands near or adjoining, until at one time they owned some five hundred acres, the half of which was in cleared fields. The children of Jeremiah and Delilah Conley whom we can name here, are Irven F., John Marshall, and Benj. F. Conley, and Esta M., who married John B. Wright, September 10, 1896, his age 27, her's 27.

Irven Fletcher Conley, born in the year 1859, married Annie, daughter of Joseph F. and Rosanna Caldwell, of the Caldwell place above the mouth of Flat Fork, on the 15th day of January, 1896; Irven F. and Annie C. have brought up two daughters, Gladys and Reva. Gladys married Dr. Cloyd E. Cox, a practicing physician now located in McDowell County, West Virginia; Reva became the wife of Orville Reed, and they now reside in Charleston, West Virginia. Irven F. yet owns a large part of the old home place.

John Marshall Conley, son of Jeremiah and Delilah Davis Conley, sold his possession here some fifteen years ago, 1910, or thereabout, and went to Boulder, Colorado, where he now resides.

Benjamin F. Conley, son of Jeremiah and Delilah (Davis) Conley, married Annie, daughter of William Riley, pioneer, of Flat Fork; Benjamin F. died about the year 1896, leaving surviving him nine children, all yet living though the lapse of time since the father's death is now thirty years; their names are James W., residing near Reedy; George Ferdinand, Elsie, wife of Louis O. Steinbeck, of Charleston; John Isaac, who married Icy, a daughter of Dr. L. A. Rader, of Gandeeville; Robert, a farmer near Cincinnati; Stella, wife of Alonzo Bowyer, of Harper District; Okey Columbus, not yet married; Ord, married a daughter of Jacob Gandee; Coy Calvin, married Velma, daughter of John M. Looney, of Johnson Creek, Walton; and Hetty. wife of Rex Key, of Countsville, Harper District.

COOK: Of Geary District.

Barnabas Snow Cook was first of this family name who made a home in this county; he came shortly before the Civil War. He was born in Kanawha County, western Virginia, June 10, 1832, son of Rev. Barnabas Cook and Christianna (McCune) Cook, his wife, he was a pioneer of Kanawha County, coming to Kanawha from New England. Barnabas Cook, Sr., served as a justice of the peace of Kanawha County, one term as its sheriff, and used much time preaching the Christian gospel over a period of twenty-five years; the marriage records of Kanawha of that period are strewn with his name and reports of marriages. The History of Calhoun County shows that he and Lorenzo Dow preached at Arnoldsburg in the year 1820. He reared five sons: Barnabas Snow, Peter M., Simeon, Timothy and Saul; all served as soldiers on the side of the Union in the War of the Secessions; only Barnabas Snow and Peter M. Cook, of this family ever made their homes in Roane.

Barnabas Snow Cook united in marriage with Sarah J. Truman, September 7, 1851; she was also born in Kanawha County; they lived first in Calhoun County, later in the Town of Spencer, where he plied his trade of shoe and boot maker; at that time owned an acre lot lying on the west side of Market Street, cornering on Market and Beauty Streets, thence southward, and included the part now the Presbyterian Church lot. To Barnabas Snow and Sarah J., his wife were born ten children; their names: Caroline, 1853; Ellen, 1855; Bennett, 1857; Columbus, 1860; Barnabas (III); Ulysses G., 1866; Edwin M., 1868; Everett, 1871; Savannah, 1873 and George W.

Caroline married Ephraim Sergent, 1878.
Bennett married Sarah Sergent, 1880.
Columbus married Melissa Sergent, 1883.
George W. married Rachel J. Kiser, July 23, 1883.

Savannah married Harvey R. Carper, May 16, 1888, her age 16, his age 30; Barnabas married Mary J. Nida, January 6, 1887, his age 24, her age 18; Ulysses G. married Alice J. Nida, July 12, 1888, his age 30, her age 17; Edwin M. married Elizabeth Shamlin, May 8, 1892, his age 25, her age 17. All these have reared families, some of them large ones.

COOPER: Dr. Francis W. Cooper, of Reedy, its first resident physician, 1887.

Dr. Francis W. Cooper came to "Three Forks" about the year 1867, from upper Meigs County, Ohio, near Athens. He was a graduate of one of the National Schools of Medicine; tall, straight, blond with a flowing, almost red beard, which parted and streamed back past the sides of his elegant body as he rode against the wind. He was a familiar figure on all Reedy's roads for nearly twenty years. He served rich and poor with the same promptness, skill and care. An eight-mile ride on a winter night by him was expected, and I never head of an expression of dissatisfaction from him or from those he served. He was the family physician at our home—home of the parents of the author of this book.

He was addicted to over indulgence in drinking of intoxicating liquors when at public gatherings of a business or political purpose; he had many enemies made by his biting retorts—often in epigram—to those keepers of morals (of others than themselves) with which all communities ever were harrassed and ever will be. He had an impolitic impatience with ignorance in that strange intellectual who succeeds financially, and seldom hesitated in showing such a one his ignorance and making of him an enemy of the kind who mopes away and nurses revenge. He was thrice married. First to a Miss Spicer, who died, next with Miss Melissa J. Stewart, at Reedy, July 14, 1869, she a daughter of Joseph Stewart, son of the pioneer William Stewart. One child was born of this first marriage, her name Oheplia; she grew up here, went to her father's people in Ohio and was lost to recollection. The wife Melissa having died, Francis W. soon united in marriage with Miss Pruda Boice, daughter of a family of the name, residents of Seaman Fork of Reedy.

They made their home at a crossroads at the head of upper Left Reedy, which the doctor facetiously named "Windyville." He practiced from this home for some fifteen years.

Of this third marriage some children were born; two are remembered here as young men about the year 1894. Their names, "Fritz" and "Don."

CORDER:

John Corder was born in Barbour or Lewis County, western Virginia, 1821, son of Joseph and Jane Corder, grew up there and married Miss Rebecca Thompson; they came to Sand Creek and settled not far east of Sandyville, where Joseph A., the son, was born on July 4, 1854. At the same time or within a few months at least Rebecca died.

In the year 1856, for a second wife, John Corder, 35, married Miss Mary Roach, 26, daughter of William and Delilah (Carney) Roach of Reedy; they acquired a tract of land on head waters of Elk Fork of Mill Creek about what is now the boundary line between Jackson and Roane Counties, and felled the forest trees and made a home in which were born their following named five children: Charles, Edward, born November 16, 1859 (of City of Spencer later), Malinda ("Linnie"), born

1861; Eliza, married Albert Parsons of Spencer, and Delilah usually called "Lilah." The wife, Mary (Roach) Corder, died on November 5, 1868. On January 16, 1874, John Corder, for a third wife, married Mrs. Sarah Ann Chancey (nee Rhodes) at that time widow of Alexander Chancey, deceased, of Reedy. John Corder died in the month of December following. Of this marriage a daughter was born but we do not have her name; she was brought up by her mother or her half-sister, Mrs. Leroy Eagle, long a resident of Parkersburg.

CORK:

Jacob Frank Cork, lawyer and business man of Charleston, West Virginia, now, was the first and only of this family name in Roane County; was born in Clarksburg, W. Va., April 2, 1857, son of Captain John James Cork and Rebecca Lupton Campbell. (See Campbell, ante). Captain John James Cork was born in Lewiston, Va., November 9, 1831, died December 2, 1864. Rebecca Lupton Campbell was born 1830, in Franklin County, Virginia, daughter of John C. and .... Campbell, died in Charleston, West Virginia, 1922. Rebecca L. and her son, J. Frank's residence in the Town of Spencer, commenced when John C. Campbell and his family became residents here. On June 9, 1882, Rebecca L. Cork and Captain Martin W. Kidd, of Spencer, were united in marriage, and made their residence here until the death of Captain Kidd.

The "Kidd" memorial window in the Spencer Presbyterian Church was donated to the church by Rebecca L. and her son, Jacob Frank Cork at the time of erection of that church, of which church they had long been members. Though residents of Charleston at the time, their religious sentiments were still with the village church; the bodies of Captain and Rebecca Kidd lie buried in the Spencer cemetery, Rebecca having died in November, 1922.

Jacob Frank Cork, of above paragraphs, graduated from Glenville Normal School, 1874; taught school in Roane County; attended Fairmont Normal; entered West Virginia University 1879; had its B. A. degree 1883, LL.B. 1884, M. A. degree 1884, admitted to the bar at Spencer 1884, where he first practiced law; chief clerk of State Department of Free Schools with B. S. Morgan, superintendent, appointed to the post by Governor Flemming; did much in construction of the then infant free-school system. Miss Harriett Adelaid Chevalier became the wife of Jacob Franklin Cork in the year 1880; she was born April 25, 1857, daughter of Major Arthur H. and Susan V. Chevalier, residents of Parkersburg at the time of the daughter's marriage with Mr. Cork. They took up their residence in Charleston when Mr. Cork became part of the State's Free School force; where they have lived ever since, Mr. Cork resuming practice of the law after his term of office as school man expired. He is reputed to have prospered as such a city pioneer should, and is one of Charleston's wealthiest men at time of this writing.

To Jacob Frank and Harriett A. (Chevalier) Cork, have been born and by them brought up three sons and two daughters: John Rolfe April or August 6, 1882; Virginia Chevalier, May 19, 1886; Helen W. and Donald Lupton (twins), September 12, 1891, and Edward Chevalier, March 21, 1896.

COTTLE: Of Curtis and Reedy Districts:
First of this family name here, were seven sons and two daughters, children of William and Abbie (Rader) Cottle of Greenbrier or other southeastern county of western Virginia; they came, two or three of the older sons first, about the year 1854 or 1855; their names in order of respective ages are:

Charles, Davis S., Michael, Allen M., Samuel Price, Richard ("Dick"), Nancy ("Nann"), Margaret and W. Scott.

Their respective marriages and so much as we know of each follows:
Charles Cottle, married Miss Minerva Stewart, a daughter of William and Mary (Board) Stewart, at Reedy, at that time a part of Wirt County; they made their home at Reedy, Charles being a farmer and carpenter. The names of their children in order of births are:

Safrona, Mina, Fannie, Major J., Harry C., and Ollie.

Safrona married John Watson, November 12, 1880.

Mina married George Burgess, July 6, 1892, her age 26, his age 26; one child was born, her name Beulah.

Fannie married Andrew Alderman, February 3, 1889, her age 19, his age 22.

Major J. married.

Harry C. married Miss Stella ("Estella") Buck, then of upper Reedy, May 6, 1900, his age 26, her's 26.

Ollie married J. H. Craig, November 27, 1900, her age 24, his age 23.

Davis S. Cottle, second son of William and Abbie (Rader) Cottle, married Miss Emily J. Armstrong, August 5, 1867, she a daughter of Matthias B. Armstrong, of upper Reedy.

They made their life-time home on lands on Middle Fork of Reedy at and near Peniel, where they carried on a crossroads store for sometime in connection with their farm.

To Davis S. and Emily J., his wife, were born and by them reared the following sons and daughters:

Homer H., Clarence V., William B., Paul Festus, Newman, Louise, Davis Smith and Grace. Their respective marriages so far as we find on the county records are as follows:

Homer H., age 26, to May Taylor, 25, June 2, 1895.

Clarence V. married Fannie Vandevender, daughter of Allen Vandenvender.

William B., we have no record.

Paul Festus married Miss Maggie Fetty, September 14, 1899, his age 22, her age 18, she a daughter of Middian Fetty of Reedy.

Newman, not married.

Louise, married Wm. Park Smith, of Reedy, May 21, 1905, his age 25, her age 21.

Davis S., Jr., and Grace are yet young·persons not married.

Michael Cottle, third son of William and Abbie, married a Miss Jane Parker; we have nothing of their careers.

Allen M., fourth son of William and Abbie, married Miss Nancy E. Board, February 23, 1870, she a daughter of A. Sandy Board and wife of near "Three Forks of Reedy." Allen M. was the efficient blacksmith many years in the village, where he and Nancy E. made their life's home. To them were born and by them reared three sons and three daughters whose names in order of ages are as follows: Camden L., Cadmus G., Allie, Vaught, Icy and Lucy. The marriages of these appear:

Camden L. to Fannie Seaman, April 16, 1899, his age 24, her age 21. Cadmus G. to Ethel Lester, October 18, 1911. Allie, 19, to Robert Coe, 21, March 1, 1896. Vaught, no marriage. Icy, no marriage. Lucy, we hear, married some gentleman in the State of Ohio, and lives in that State now.

Samuel Price Cottle, son of William and Abbie (Rader), while a young man married Miss Florence D. O'Hara, of Reedy, daughter of James O'Hara, on February 5, 1871. S. Price and Florence, his wife, made their home on the upper Middle Fork of Reedy and farming was their life's work; to them were born and by them reared the following named children: Charles Clinton, Thomas Camden, Pauline and Jessie L. Of these:

Charles Clinton married Miss Flora Ferrell, then of Roxalana, Roane County, on the 11th day of February, 1897; he was a traveling salesman, but died while yet young. To Charles Clinton and Flora (Ferrell) his wife were born and by them reared two children, sons, their names E. Brooks and Samuel Price Cottle. The last home of this as a united family was at Spencer; here the boys graduated from the Spencer High School, and went to the State University; we hear that one is now a practicing physician in Morgantown, West Virginia. Thomas C., above named, married Miss Olive Scott, of upper Reedy.

Richard ("Dick") Cottle, sixth child of William and Abbie Cottle married a Miss Thorn in Wirt County; we do not have their career.

W. Scott Cottle, seventh of the family of William and Abbie (Rader) Cottle, his wife, became a blacksmith and had a shop for sometime at Reedy; he married Miss Flora A. Seaman, November 9, 1884, his age 31, her's 21; she was a daughter of David Seaman. W. Scott also in later years became a farmer. We do not know whether or not they have a child or children.

Nancy ("Nannie") Cottle, one of the two daughters of William and Abbie (Rader) Cottle, married Charles Fouty, October 1, 1880; she was killed on Market Street, Spencer, 1926, by an automobile; she left some children we are told.

Of Margaret Cottle, daughter of William and Abbie, we have no record.

HISTORY OF ROANE COUNTY 487

COX: Of Smithfield and Walton.

Isaac Cox and Mary (Nicely or Knisely) Cox, his wife, were natives of the Monongahela Valley, married in Lewis County, and came to upper Flat Fork of Pocatalico in what later was west Smithfield District about the year 1844; to them were born in Lewis County two sons and seven, eight, maybe ten daughters, of whom Lucinda became the wife of Samuel M. Tallman, May 23, 1851; other names we do not have, but some or all of them came to Roane County.

The names of the two sons were Isaac, Jr., and Washington.

Isaac Cox, son of Isaac and Mary (Nicely) Cox, married in Roane County, Phoebe Frances Daugherty, January 10, 1856; we have no record of their daughters, if any; their sons were Washington, James Madison and Charles Lewis Cox. Further:

Washington Cox, son of above family, married Rachel V. Wilson, January 24, 1859; she was the only daughter of William R .and Elizabeth (Wolfe) Wilson, resident at the time of marriage, on upper Spring Creek. Washington and Rachel V. settled on the head of Rush Creek of Poca; he acquired there some eight hundred or more acres of land, and in his twenty-five years of industrious life they cleared and made into grassy fields about five hundred acres; for this twenty-five years— 1880 to 1905—"Wash" was a devoted Mason communicant of Moriah Lodge of Spencer, and never missed. He was an extensive stock raiser. To Washington and Rachel were born five or six daughters and only one son, his name Jacob; he married a Roane County Miss, and they have left some children.

Of the daughters of Washington and Rachel V., we can name, Myrtle, who married Walter J. Falkner of Spencer, and Julia who became the wife of William H. Harlow, now of Spencer.

James Madison Cox, son of Isaac Sr., and Mary (Nicely) Cox, has been twice married; the first, February 15, 1882, to Miss Cerilda Summerfield; of this marriage several sons and daughters were born. His second marriage was with Josephine Fisher, April 21st, 1900, his age 38, her age 34; to them were born two sons and one daughter. The home of this family is on upper waters of Poca, next the Kanawhas divide and Spencer District.

Charles Louis Cox, son of Isaac Cox, Jr., and wife Frances (Daugherty) Cox, was born in Roane County, and has been twice married; his first wife, Dorinda Jane Cutright, with whom he married, March 8, 1880; she was a daughter of Elmore Cutright of upper Spring Creek; to Chas. Louis and Dorinda Jane, were born one child, his name Curtis Cox, now married and resides on upper Spring Creek. The second marriage of Chas. Louis was with Angie Frances Hughes, then widow of Robert Hughes, deceased, to whom she had been married as Miss Angie Frances Ferrell. This last marriage was on January 22, 1922, his age 62, her age 60.

COX: Pioneers of Reedy, Flat Fork, Charleston, Spencer.

We have not searched out the relationship of Isaac Cox pioneer of upper Spring Creek and Phillip Cox subject of this sketch; both, however, came from the Monongahela Valley about the same time.

Phillip D. Cox was the first "crossroads" regular merchant at "Three Forks" of Reedy. (See Chapter V of this book.) He is said to have cut out the bridle path across the divide between Middle Reedy and Pocatalico, thence down one branch, yet known as "Cox's Fork." He is said to have visited Reedy often as an itinerant trader from Lewis or Harrison County, several years before establishing his store and bringing his wife, Catherine, and their children there. He died there about the year 1855.

John Greenleaf (see name Greenleaf) married the widow Catherine, and he was administrator of Phillip D. Cox's estate, and guardian of his heirs.

The names of the sons and daughters of Phillip and Catherine Cox, his wife were: David, Sarah, Mark, Sr., and Mariah; most of these married and made their homes in Roane County.

David Cox, son of Phillip and Catherine, married Rachel A. Raines, on January 24, 1870; she a daughter of .... Raines of Coxs Fork of Poca. Their children were Florence, Mark, Jr., Joseph, Perry, Thomas Floyd, Ezra Monroe, Otto Jennings, Nathan Dennis, William Ray, and Nellie May.

Perry Cox, son of David and Catherine (Raines) Cox, married Miss Martha Anderson, on October 9, 1903, his age 25, her's 21, she a daughter of Alexander Anderson and .... (Harper) Harper, his wife. Perry is the popular automobile merchant of Spencer at this time (1927).

Sarah Cox, daughter of Phillip D. and Catherine, married Isaiah Boggs.

Mark Cox, son of Phillip D. and Catherine, married Miss Annie Bradley, in Jackson County. Mark was a popular teacher for some years. Their children are Howard, who married Martha Westfall; Artemius W. Cox, proprietor of A. W. Cox Department Store, Charleston, West Virginia, 1915 to now, 1927; Ayward Cox, who married a Miss Shuldis, and Nellie Cox, who married Kinney Gandee.

COUNTS:

Silas B. Counts, the son of Isaac Counts and his wife who came from Russell County, Virginia, and settled in Jackson County near the head of Higly country sometime in the "early forties," having married Lavinia Hughes, daughter of Josiah Hughes, Sr., therefore a sister of John and Thomas Hughes, Sr., purchased from his father-in-law, Josiah, Sr., a large tract of land covering the head of Trace Fork, 1870, a year later he obtained a part of the "Slaughter land" on the head of Big Creek, later a small tract from A. J. Adams adjoining his other lands; within ten years he was spoken of as having one of the best farms of that part of Harper District; "a stock man and a money lender." "The Counts with the great beard." In later life he kept his beard clipped. Lavinia having died, he married for a second wife Josie Ferrell, daughter of William Parrot Ferrell, Rev. John H. Smith, officiating clergyman, as shown by his certificate of record dated 7th day of October, 1896. About .... they sold all their holdings here in Roane County and took up their residence in Parkersburg, West Virginia. Silas B. Counts had two brothers: Cain and Wade, who were frequently mentioned in business and gossip of this part of the county.

CRAIG: Of North Spencer District.

Winfield Scott Craig was born in Noble County, Ohio, in the year 1846; married in that State, Elizabeth Jane Ward, who was born in Washington County, Ohio. These two came to Roane County in the year 1876; purchased a tract of 326 acres of land, all in the forest except about three acres; this lay between Little Creek and Main Spring Creek about two miles north of Spencer, and on this land he made his home at once and there set an example of industry and frugality of great value to his neighborhood.

He worked early and late; made and used the last old-time solid wooden-wheeled wagon seen in Spencer; on this, drawn by the last ox team of the country used for the purpose he brought his produce to town for sale, about each week for twelve years. Within ten years his was a good farm; fields had been cleared and fencing done; in the year 1900 he erected a commodious farm dwelling, and was deemed prosperous and progressive; was a member of the Board of Education of Spencer District for some successive term along about 1892 to 1912.

Oil and gas was found on his farm about the year, 1913, small producers but encouraging so that the Craig field is considered a substantial one; he died in the year 1925, and was buried in the cemetery on the farm at this date showing about two hundred acres of cleared and cultivated fields, done by this industrious family.

To W. Scott and Elizabth Jane Craig were born and here grew up the following sons and daughters: Henry Wilbert, 1876; Florence, 1898, married Mac Hiex; Fred E., 1879, he is founder, owner and publisher of the Reedy News, a weekly newspaper; James Andrew, 1882; Lydia, 1884, married Clay Goff, son of Geo. F. Goff; and Addie, born 1886, married Robert C. Hall, farmer of Pennsylvania.

CRISLIP: . Of Reedy and Spencer.

Jacob Crislip and Elizabeth, his wife with several children born to them while residents of Harrison County, on the Monongahela River, were the first of this family name here; they had acquired a large tract of land on upper Left Reedy Creek in what later was included in Curtis Magisterial District. The date of this must have been in the first of the decade, 1850.

It is seen on records of conveyances that Jacob and Elizabeth, his wife under date, May 31, 1862, conveyed unto A. West, Jr., 315-acre tract of land on Left Reedy in exchange for the Mill property of A. West, Jr., being three and a half acres "on Spring Creek adjoining Jesse Tanner's survey," on the south side of the "base line." How long he ran the mill or whether Jacob and family came to reside here at the mill, we do not know; if they did, they soon returned, for there on the upper Reedy was the Crislip home and neighborhood for forty years; from there their sons and daughters were married; two sons, Lemuel and Asby carved larger farms out of the paternal lands, and continued the Crislip prestige there for twenty-five more years and there both died and were buried. They were loyal to the Union through the Civil War, and devout Methodist Episcopals in church affiliations.

Lemuel Crislip, son of Jacob and Elizabeth, his wife, was born in Harrison County, western Virginia, October 16, 1822; married Miss Salina Peck, born March 11, 1825; of this marriage several sons and one daughter was born; however, we are able to name two only: Cyrus A. and Olive. Of these further:

Cyrus A. Crislip, son of Lemuel and wife, married and made his home many years on part of the old home farm; later moved to Spencer; was elected by the people and served one term as delegate for Roane County in the State Legislature, twenty-second session, 1895; served as United States postmaster at Spencer a term of four years, later moved to Upper Meigs County, Ohio, and died there.

Cyrus A. Crislip and wife brought up two children, a daughter and a son, their names, Sallie O., who married John H. Kincaid, on April 10, 1908, her age then 22, his age 33; he was born in Fayette County, West Virginia; of this marriage two children were born; they have their home at or near Coolville, Ohio. Romeo R. Crislip, son of Cyrus A., and wife, was twice married first to Miss Ocie Morford; of this union a daughter was born; his second marriage was with a Miss Wine.

Olive Crislip, daughter of Lemuel and Salina Crislip, was wife of John A. A. Vandale, attorney of Spencer, West Virginia. They brought up three children in their home in Spencer, Earl, Laura and Geneva; all long ago gone elsewhere.

Asby Crislip, son of Jacob and Elizabeth, his wife, was in age next to the brother Lemuel; he married Miss Mary Timel, or Timmel, daughter of Frank Timel and wife, the German teacher and musician mentioned in Chapter IX of this book.

Asby and wife made their home on the broad good lands at the mouth of Stover on Left Reedy; on account of their fine farm and home, and contributions to their church, they were popular for twenty-five years; they brought up and sent out a successful family; their names in order of births as remembered by the writer, Savena, Alonzo L., Estella, Addie, and Maud, whose marriages and somewhat further we give:

Savena, when quite young united in marriage with William H. Cleavenger, October 9, 1882; of this union is the son, Ernest Crislip, a business man of Colorado. Savena's second husband was David A. Brown, with whom she married on June 10, 1886; her age then 20, "his age 31, a widower;" of this marriake two have been brought up, Charles and Nell.

Alonzo L. Crislip, son of Asby and Mary, his wife, became a dentist; made his home and business in Spencer; married Miss Katie L. Bond, December 23, 1901, his age given 33, her's 18; they brought up two daughters, Frankie and Mary K. (See Chapter IX, History of The City of Spencer.)

Addie Crislip, daughter of Asby and Mary, united in marriage with William Huddleston, of Spencer, May 1, 1898, her age 25, his age 30, made their home in the Town of Spencer; his career is shown in Chapter IX. They brought up two daughters, Ophelia and Pauline.

Alice Crislip, daughter of Asby and Mary, married Okey J. Chambers, Esq., February 16, 1896; she then 20 and he 25 years old. (See List of Attorneys, Chapter IX and Chapter VI.)

Estella Crislip united in marriage with Albert S. Heck, June 15, 1898, her age 24, his age 25; he was born in Jackson County, West Virginia. (See Chapter IX.) They have brought up, in Spencer, three daughters and one son; their names, Ardis, wife of Byron Morford; Estel, wife of Dewey Perkins. (See family names, Morford, Perkins). The son's name is Henry Heck; a daughter, now nine years of age, called Carrol.

Names and marriages of other crislips well known residents of the upper left Reedy whose family connections the writer does not venture to give:

Luther Crislip to Melissa Riddle, September 21, 1870.
Daniel W. Crislip to Mollie Cummings, August 20, 1881.
J. M. Crislip to Florence Armstrong, February 8, 1879.
Daniel W. Crislip to Myrtle Peck, widow, December 9, 1906, his age, 33, her age 23.

NOTE: Ages were not entered on marriage records in Roane County prior to 1882.

CROSS: Of Spencer since year 1870.

Elmer Elsworth Cross and his family first of the name here. Their ancestry:

Waid Cross was a son of a family of Crosses, colonists of Connecticut, having married in Connecticut and lived there for sometime, he with his family came to the Ohio about the year 1802, and settled as pioneers on the Little Muskingum River about two miles above Marietta, then a neighborhood center of several families all from New England.

Waid Cross and his wife reared only one son, his name, Lucius Cross; he grew up at the pioneer home there and married Miss Thirza Stanley, in the year 1822, she a daughter of Timothy Stanley of Revolutionary fame.

Lucius and Thirza soon disposed of the farm on the Little Muskingum and removed down the Ohio to Racine, acquired a large tract of forest lands lying about two miles back from the river, and on it began an ancestral home; cleared many acres and made them into fertile fields; a notable farm by the year 1832; in which year they built a ten-room frame dwelling, at that time deemed the best home in Meigs County. There Lucius and Thirza, his wife, reared their family—five sons and four daughters— and completed their spans of life. The names of their children given in order of births are:

Abigail, born about 1823, married William Curtis.

Eliza, born about 1825, married William Carson.

Murial, born about 1827, married Wesley Hayman.

Lucius, Jr., born about 1830, married Elizabeth Reynolds.

Timothy, born about 1833, married Miss .... Jones.

Waid, born about 1835, married Addie Miles.

Davis Barker, born about 1837, was thrice married: Miss .... Carpenter; Miss .... Becknell; Miss .... Amanda Batey.

Edwin, M. D., born about 1839, located in Chicago.

Lydia, born about 1841, married Thornton Mallory.

All the above marriages were in Meigns County, Ohio.

Lucius Cross, Jr., son of Lucius and Thirza (Stanley), his wife, grew up there on the farm described, and in the year 1858 married Miss Elizabeth Reynolds in the village of Racine. He acquired a part of the home-farm and on it, on Bowman's Run, built the "Cross" water grist mill, with improvements and equipments for making fine bread stuffs deemed "up to date" really in advance of the times.

Lucius and Elizabeth there reared their family and finished their careers. Their children were five sons and two daughters whose names are:

Elmer Elsworth, Edwin Lucius, Alban Benton, Oscar Groo, Hayman Joy, Jessie Floy and Julia Bessie. Of these:

Elmer Elsworth Cross, son of Lucius, Jr., and Elizabeth (Reynolds) Cross, his wife, was born on the farm described, January 24, 1861. Educated in the schools there and Normal at Syracuse. Grew to manhood there, learned the miller's trade, as well as quality of, and dealing in live stock.

"Striking out" for himself, he acquired the St. Dennis Flour Mill at Ravenswood and ran it for some years. In the meantime he united in marriage with Miss Emma M. Gould, at Ravenswood, October 19th, 1891. She was born at Mannington, West Virginia, December 10th, 1870, daughter of William H. Gould and his wife, at time of marriage of the daughter, residents of Ravenswood, West Virginia.

In the year 1911, Elmer E. Cross sold the St. Dennis Mill and purchased a stock farm of four hundred and twenty-five acres in Roane County, lying two and a half miles north of Spencer on the Spencer and Ravenswood turnpike—now State Road No. 14. Settled the family there and all are yet there.

To Elmer E. and Elizabeth M., his wife, were born and by them reared the following three sons and two daughters:
Chester, Zana Merle, Charles Gordon, Lucius Stanley and Madeline Elizabeth.

CUMMINGS: Of Walton District.

Hugh Cummings and Catherine (Armentrout) Cummings, his wife, both of old Virginia families, with some children, came from Monroe County, Virginia, and settled in the Pocatalico country in the year 1854. Hugh Cummings, Sr., the father of the above named Hugh, the pioneer, was born in England, came to America and served in the Continental Army of the Revolution.

We have no information of any (except the one son) of children of Hugh and Catherine (Armentrout) Cummings, that son was Hiram Cummings, born in Monroe County, Virginia, August 7, 1824; on September 11, 1845, he was united in marriage with Emaline Dodd, in Monroe County; she was born in Botetourt County, Virginia in 1824, the daughter of John and Sarah (Stone) Dodd, his wife, who also came and made their home in Roane County, in 1871.

Hiram Cummings and his wife, Emeline (Dodd) Cummings, first made their home for nine years in Craig County, Virginia, where Hiram served as a Justice of the Peace for nine years before coming to Roane County, and served as a Justice in Roane County for twelve years of his life. To Hiram and his wife, Emeline, were born ten children, eight of whom grew up, married and made homes for themselves in Walton District; their names in order of their births are:

Martha, March 5, 1850; Clifton B., December 17, 1851; John H. W., March 15, 1853; Thomas H., July 8, 1856; David T., January 24, 1859; Mary L., February 16, 1861; Edward L., August 17, 1863, and Lawson L., February 16, 1866.

Further of the family:

John H. married Sarah Jane Summers, December 23, 1873, and their children—as told me by a neighbor of the family—are James, Ida, Mary Florence, wife of Webster W. Lee; Benjamin H. married Della Jones, 1913; his age 24, her's 20. She was a daughter of Daniel Jones.

Thomas H. Cummings, son of Hiram and Emeline (Dodd), and others we cannot be sure of distinguishing on the marriage record, but we give here what we find as follows:

David T. Cummings to Sarah S. Summers, January 17, 1881; Lee L. Cummings to Laura Gibson, February 16, 1888; William Cummings to Malinda A. Harper, November 7, 1876; Samuel E. Cummings to Eliza J. Dougherty, January 9, 1884; Thomas P. Cummings to Samantha J. Hill, September 15, 1892, his age 21, her age 17; David T. Cummings (widower) to Lucinda Summers, November 5, 1891, his age 32, her age 22, "at the resident of Martin Summers."

CUNNINGHAM: Of Spring Creek, Spencer, Walton.

These are descendants of the Cunninghams of the Monongahela Valley, mentioned in the "Border Warfare" and other books recounting settlement of the "Western Border and Indian Atrocities."

George Cunningham and his wife, Catherine (Smith), born in Harrison and Lewis County, Virginia, with some children born while residing in that county, came to this Spring Creek country about the time of building of the Glenville, Ripley and Ohio turnpike—1850— bought a large tract of land on that pike, a mile west of "New California" and extending to the head of Tanners Run, there they soon made such a farm as gave them standing and respect among all who came or went. The names of their children, (possibly all born in Lewis County, W. Va.,) were: Pery Green, Marshall, Julia Ann and George Porter.

Perygrine, or (Pery Green), usually mentioned as P. G., married in Lewis County, Miss Eliza Allman; they made their home, first on the home lands on Tanners Run, then awhile in New California; next— about 1868—at Walton, where they died and are buried. Pery G. entered into a partnership with James T. Ward, of Spencer, and they moved to Walton and there opened a general store, for the purpose of handling the marketing of the vast forest of timber then just coming into demand; they traded largely. Pery G. became the owner of large acreages of land.

To Pery G. and his wife, Eliza (Allman), were born, and brought up, three daughter, whose names are Safronia, married Beniah Depue (then Jr.) March 6, 1878; Madora, married Jarrett H. Depue October 1, 1885; Laura, married Dr. Ed Jones, May 11, 1898, she then 21, he, 23.

Marshall Cunningham, son of George and Catherine, his wife, married in Lewis County, W. Va., Elizabeth Bonnett, about the year 1851, made their home on the paternal lands on Tanners Run. To them were born two daughters and a son. Their names: Nancy C., born in 1852, married Mathew Hively, of Walton District; Columbia, wife of George Dougherty, of Walton, and George Franklin Cunningham, who, on growing up, became a lawyer, was one term Prosecuting Attorney of Roane County; was twice married, first wife Miss Belle Thompson, second Miss Clara Allen. Of the first marriage one daughter named Ethel was born; of the second marriage one son and two daughters. George F. and his wife and son moved their homes to Oklahoma about the year 1920. Marshall Cunningham was killed by a political enemy during the Civil War broils, leaving above three children to care of their relatives. Julia Ann, daughter of the pioneers, George and Mary Cunningham, married Russell Alvis and they made their lifetime's home on Tanners Run and there reared a large family.

George Porter Cunningham, son of George and Catherine (Smith), his wife, was born in Lewis County about the year 1846; came to this country with his parents; married Sarah Jane Ward, daughter of Aquilla Ward, of in or near Spencer, February 7, 1867; being the youngest of the family he succeeded to the ancestral home on Tanners

Run, then yet containing a large acreage; he conveyed to the public a cemetery lot for that neighborhood, also gave a lot for the first school house for the nighborhood and saw the public gratitude give its name to the Hoff family, the place ever since being known as "Hoff Town."

To George Porter and Sarah Jane (Ward) the wife of his youth and his old age, were born Dora, Viola, Irven Ward, Emma O., Arthur, Okey Blaine and Verna; two or three children died in youth.

Viola married Charles Overholt; Irvin Ward married Mary Miller, then widow Huffman, they have two sons and six daughters. Arthur married Viola Criner; Verna married Charles Carroll and Okey Blaine married Florence Greathouse, daughter of Benjamin R. Greathouse, they live near the City of Spencer and have a large family of children.

CUNNINGHAM:

Nathan Cunningham, son of Joel and Mary (Casto) Cunningham, born in Jackson County, August 9, 1839, enlisted in the Union Army, 1861, advanced to place of Second Lieutenant. Married Permelia, daughter of William and Mary E. (Strain) Ray. Made a farm on the Millcreek side just beyond the head of Higly. Nathan was prominent in public affairs for some years next following the Civil War; was a Justice of the Peace eight years; Assessor for the county one term of four years; was assaulted and killed on the public road, in or about the Kanawha County line, by persons whose identity has never been established in any court. His widow, with her eight or nine children, managed the farm for many years after the death of Nathan.

CURFMAN: Of Reedy. Two brothers, James and Samuel.

These we are told came from Greenbrier County to Reedy in the first of the decade of 1850.

Samuel Curfman united in marriage with Miss Mary A. Cain on December 27, 1858, she a daughter of Rev. Thomas H. Cain—see "Cain." Samuel and Mary A., his wife, made their home on Cain's Run. Farmers; they brought up one son and two daughters. The son, Thomas, married Mattie Beach. Mary married James Bee Lester—see Lester. Martha married J. Edmond Bishop—see Bishop.

James Curfman, the other of the Curfman brothers, married Miss Elizabeth Cain, August 18, 1865, she a daughter of the Rev. Thomas H. Cain—see "Cain." James and his wife made their home on Cain's Run. We do not have the names of the children—if any—of James and Elizabeth Curfman. Both Samuel and James enlisted in the Confederate army and served through all the campaigns of the Civil War—1862 to 1865.

CURTIS: Of Curtis District.

William Walker Curtis, later Captain William W. Curtis, was born in Lewis County, W. Va., August 29, 1832, son of John and Prudence (Cutright) Curtis. In Lewis County, July 18, 1850, William W. Curtis and Rebecca Wetzel were married. She was born in Lewis County, June 4, 1830, daughter of David and Regina (Fultz) Wetzel, both born in Shennanadoah County, Virginia, and were pioneer settlers in the Monongahela Valley, Rebecca being a near relative of Lewis Wetzel, or "Whetzel," as sometimes spelled, of "Border Warfare" fame, as also are the Cutrights, of the Monongahela settlements.

William W. and Rebecca Curtis made their home in Lewis County for the first six or seven years after marriage, coming to the upper Reedy country in the year 1857.

William W. and Rebecca acquired a large farm on upper Reedy Creek and soon made a home of ample repose for those days. The names of their several sons and daughters who grew up are as follows:

Francis M., born May 7, 1851, made his first home at Alkiers Mills, Lewis County.

Rulina, June 19, 1853, married Thomas J. Hardman, October 13, 1869, made their first home at Peniel, Roane County.

Albert Lee, December 10, 1854, first home at Wolfe Summit, Harrison County.

Martha, lived at Spencer in 1882.

Nathan, born June 7, 1858, married Miss Samantha Elizabeth Lucas, November 14, 1878. She is a native of Noble County, Ohio. Two brothers of her's resided in Curtis District for a time. See at end of these Curtis paragraphs.

A. J. Lyda Curtis, son of Captain W. W. and Rebecca, was born March 14, 1861; married Miss Sarah R. Parks May 7, 1891. His age 30, her's 28.

Albert Lee and A. J. Lyda both became popular preachers of the Methodist Episcopal conference. A. J. L. returns to Roane occasionally on business or to visit his relatives.

L. Ordway Curtis, born September 7, 1879, son of Nathan and his wife, Samantha E., grew up in Roane, a fair product of good ancestry and the free schools; taught school a few terms; was elected by the people and served one term as Clerk of the Circuit Court of Roane; at close of his term launched into the general Auditor's office at Charleston, year 1924, and removed himself and family to the capital city and is yet there.

L. Ordway Curtis and Virginia Ingram, daughter of Lycurgus Ingram, were united in marriage "at the M. E. Parsonage" in Spencer, W. Va. on August 21, 1905. His age 25, her age 20. To this union were born some children, the names of two of whom are Hal and Helen Virginia, both youths yet.

The career of Captain Curtis can be gathered from Chapters I, II and IX of this book, showing how his appreciative contemporaries named a magisterial district of this county in his honor. He was in the Battle of New Creek, August 4, 1864, received his mortal wound there and died on the way home. Some two years later the widow married James Riddle. See "Riddle, James."

CUTRIGHT: Of Upper Spring Creek.

Elmore Cutright, with some of the younger members of his family, were the first of this family name here.

He was born in Upshur County, or on Hackers Creek of the Monongahela, within the years 1815 to 1820.

In a book entitled "Our Border Settlers," or words of that import, by L. C. McWorther, its material based on excrepts from "Border Warfare" and pioneer traditions gathered for him by Judges Henry C. and Marcellus McWorther, and largely the story of Hackers Creek and vicinity, they say this name, now "Cutright," is the pioneer "Cartright," scribes catering to pronunciation suppressed the "r."

Elmore Cutright married Miss Nancy Wolfe on Hackers Creek, she a daughter of a brother of James R. Wolfe. See name Wolfe.

Elmore and his wife made their home for the first twenty-odd years after marriage in Upshur County, where their family of eight sons and three daughters were born. Leaving there and coming to Roane County about the year 1870, most of the older sons of the family having married in Harrison, Lewis or Upshur Counties, never came here. Elmore was soon known as a breeder and raiser of large cattle. He enjoyed this distinction for some fifteen or twenty years.

The names of all the sons and daughters of Elmore and Nancy (Wolfe), his wife, are as follows: Nicholas, Granville, Jacob, Asa, Lemuel, Alonzo, Columbus C., James Andrew and Jane, Ellen and Indiana.

Of these the following ones married or made homes here: Indiana married Jonathan T. Wolfe in Roane, June 3, 1878. Ellen had married George P. Lawson and came here. See name Lawson. Jane, married in Roane, Charles Lewis Cox, see his name in its alphebetical place.

Columbus C. married Miss Cynthia Carpenter here, February 19, 1880, they brought up one son and three daughters. Their names: Herbert E. Cutright. The daughters by marriage are Mrs. Howard West and Mrs. J. Rosco Lawrence. See family name, and Mrs. Albert Stephens. See family West, Nancy Lawrence.

James Andrew Cutright, son of Elmore and his wife, came heer with his father and the father's family, likely a married man at the time. His wife was Mary Izabelle Wolfe. They were farmers and made their home in this upper Spring Creek neighborhood. They brought up only one son and one daughter, Elliott D. and Minnie, she married David Dixon.

Elliott Downtain, only son of James A. and Mary Isabelle (Wolfe) Cutright, was born April 10, 1881, on Spring Creek; married, May 9,

1904, Miss Lora Hersman. He then 23, she 21, and a daughter of Jacob and Elton (Camp) Hersman.
Elliott D. Cutright is a stock raiser and farmer.

DALRYMPLE:
This name is a compound Celt-Scotch word meaning a rimpled or uneven plain or valley.

The first of this name in Roane County was Jeremiah Dalrymple and his wife, Elizabeth Jane (Snow), both born in Warren County, Pennsylvania, descendant of one of those numerous Scotchmen granted lands for services in the French and Indian War, 1755.

They came here from Pennsylvania, where their five children were born, by way of Ohio, where they lived for a few years, thence by way of Jackson County, and to Reedy, in the years 1875; at that time they were poor, not landowners, but honest, industrious, intelligent to highest degree possible in persons uneducated and without "book larnen," all of quiet and unobtrusive manners. The names of the three sons and two daughters of Jeremiah and Elizabth Dalrymple are, Andrew J., William, Herbert C., Jane, who married John Stutler of Reedy, son of Christopher Stutler; and Alice, died unmarried.

Andrew J. and William Dalrymple went to Jackson County while young men and we have nothing of their future thereafter.

Herbert Clarence ("Bert") Dalrymple married Eliza Ellen Atkinson, daughter of James Atkinson of Reedy, year 1877, settled first on Left Reedy; and about the year 1883, bought the 100 acres of forest lands on head of a branch of Left Hand, in Walton District; there he worked twenty years paying for this tract of land in small installments, by labor, having agreed to clear for cultivation five acres of land, at twenty dollars per acre, each year until his debt was paid; he paid all. The names of the children of "Bert" and Eliza, are George, Sherman H., Robert Lawrence, Margaret, and Ethel. "Bert" was born in Warren County, Pennsylvania, November 17, 1851; now seventy-five years old, in business in Spencer, 1926, erect, hale and strong; the type of the tall Scotchman, lean, his once red hair now gray, his skin florid and freckled.

DALTON:
The first of this family name who settled here was John Daltton and his second wife Katie, both born in Carroll County, Virginia, and arrived here about the year 1856, with them some sons and daughters. These were children of a first and the second marriage of John Dalton, the name of the children of the first marriage were Joseph and possibly Lyn, the daughter; Serena, who married Isaac P. Taylor, August 8, 1865, and Lyn (Lynn) married Susan Payne, August 20, 1869. We are not sure these last two named were a son and a daughter of John Dalton, but their names appear on the marriage records of the county, and no other Dalton family resided in Roane at that date. Of John Dalton's second

marriage (and Katie) were born one son and one daughter; their names, Peter and Mary. Of these children of John Dalton, pioneer, we write further:

Joseph Dalton, son of John and his first wife, was born in Carroll County, Virginia, about the year 1848; came with the family here to the Upper Pocatalico country about 1856; married Miss Mary Lesher and they made their home on upper Spring Creek; to Joseph and Mary (Lesher) Dalton were born and grew up two sons and four daughters whose names are: Henry J., Mary Jane, who married a Thomas Jennings; Kate, wife of Homer West; Annie, wife of Lucius Hersman; Hattie, wife of Holbert Hersman, both these Hersmans being sons of Hon. John M. Hersman; and John Robert Dalton married Blanche, daughter of Jacob Hersman of upper Spring Creek.

Henry J. Dalton, first of the family of Joseph, married November 1, 1887, Lizzie Burke, her age 22, his age 22; she was a daughter of Peter Burke, early settler of Charles Fork of Spring Creek. To Henry J. and Lizzie were born one daughter and three sons: Leota, Homer, Orville and Clyde. Lizzie died some year ago, and Henry J.'s present wife was Miss Larena Giles of Taylor County, West Virginia.

DANIELL: Of upper Spring Creek.

The first of this family name "Daniell" to settle here was James A. and Sophia (Weatherilt) Daniell, his wife, and three of their first-born children; both parents having been born in London ,England. On coming to the United States they landed in Massachusetts and lived a year or two in that Commonwealth, and came on here in the year 1843, settling on upper Spring Creek about one mile from "Cassville" as then called, now (1926) City of Spencer, the place is yet known as "Daniells Run. Sophia, the wife and mother, died here, in the year 1865.

Henry Daniell, a brother of James A. came to Massachusetts with him; thence here; thence to Mason County, West Virginia, where he married, lived and died, no child of his having been born; thus perished the name in his line.

James A. Daniells was a man of somewhat better education than his neighbors here; we do not have his age, but there are those yet living who have heard him relate his experiences as a drummer boy on the field of Waterloo (1815).

He erected on Spring Creek near Daniells Run and maintained for some years a small water grist mill which served his neighborhood for several years.

The children of James A. and Sophia (Weatherilt) Daniell, given me by Okey J. Daniell in part, and in part gathered from the biograph of James W. Daniell found in "Hardesty's" and from Roane County marriage records, are as follows:

Charles A., James W., Frank G., Mary, wife of George Springston, Nellie, who married Millard Filmore Simmons, February 16, 1878, and

Susan married Francis Marion Thompson, of the same neighborhood in which her parents lived, September 25, 1866.

Each of the foregoing have established homes and reared families here or elsewhere. Of these we write further, so far as informed: Charles A. Daniell, son of James A. and Sophia (Weatherilt) Daniell, married here, at Spencer, Edith Wees, daughter of Elijah Wees, member of the first county court, therefore "Squire Wees."

Charles A. and Edith, his wife, made their first home on upper Spring Creek on part of the "home place," where they lived until the year 1880, when they with their family moved to their good farm on Lower Reedy, in Wirt County, West Virginia. Their children reared to adult age, are five sons and one daughter, their names:

Fleet F., who married Amanda Graham, daughter of Richard ("Dick") Graham, of Wirt County.

John K. married Margaret Stutler, daughter of Squire Joseph and Rebecca (Board) Stutler, of Reedy, May , 1894, his age 30, her age 23.

Charles A. Jr., married Mary J. Hildreth, daughter of Harrison Hildreth, of Little Creek, September 6, 1887, his age 21 ,her age 18.

James M. married Dora Fought, daughter of Alfred Fought, of Wirt County.

Okey J. married Ottie Burdette, daughter of Reverend George and Belle (Lee) Burdette, of Wirt County. Okey J. is back at Spencer now, proprietor of a bus line—Spencer to Elizabeth and Parkersburg.

Nettie B. married John Duke, large farmer and stock raiser of Mill Creek, Jackson County. His parents, Michael Duke, Sr., and wife, were long residents of Reedy. Their marriage record must be in Wirt, the county of the bride's residence at time of marriage. And this is all the family of Charles A. Daniells first mentioned.

James W. Daniell, son of James A. and Sophia (Weatherilt) Daniell, was born in Massachusetts, September 18, 1842; came with his parents to Spring Creek country when about one year old—so he says in his biograph in Hardesty's History; married Elizabeth C. Wolfe, a neighbor's daughter, being a daughter of Joseph B. and Elizabeth (Alkire) Wolfe, of upper Spring Creek; here Elizabeth C. was born, March 20, 1845, and married James W., March 24, 1868. They made their home-farm from part of their ancestral lands, and there the following children were born and grew up:

Flora B., December 21, 1868, married Birdsey N. Hughes, June 2, 1901, his age 30 ,her age 32.

Ella M., October 25, 1871; no marriage record here.

Juno Bird, March 9, 1875; no record.

Zona S., July 20, 1877, married Gilmer C. Sleeth, his age 24, her age 22.

Clyde, born August 4, 1881, married Mary Jane Hildreth, of Little Creek, September 3, 1887, his age 21, her's 18.

Frank G. Daniell, son of James A. and Sophia (Weatherilt) was born on the Spring Creek farm home April 13, 1851, grew up here, educated such as given in subscription schools and home; settled in Charleston, W. Va., year 1872, married Miss Sarah T. Hodges, age about 22, year 1878, she born in Monroe County, Va., a daughter of William L. Hodges and his wife, residents of Charleston, W. Va. at time of this marriage.

Franklin G. some time after marriage engaged in the mercantile business in Charleston, in which business he has continued unto date of this writing.

To Franklin G. and Sarah F. (Hodges) his wife have been born and brought up one daughter and two sons, their names:

Bessie B., born about 1880, married Albert Young of Charleston. They now live in Chicago.

Carl F., born about year 1882, and William born 1884, died at age of nine years.

DAVIS: Of Geary District.

William H. Davis, old William, long a resident and the miller at Osbornes Mills, was born in Rockingham County, Virginia, in the year 1816, son of Mathew S. Davis, soldier of 1812; was there apprenticed to a millwright, and learned that trade; went from there south, from place to place at mill work; came up the Mississippi, Ohio, Great Kanawha, and settled in Kanawha County about the year 1846. There about the year 1853 or 1854 united in marriage with Mary Catherine Hill, born in Kanawha County, 1828. Of this marriage four sons and three daughters grew up; their names, Mathew H., born about the year 1858; Albert Gallatin, 1856; John R., 1865, and William Willis, 1867. The names of the daughters: Adelaid, wife of Fred M. Hinzman; Susan died, and Lucy, who became the wife of J. P. Myers. William H., first named, became proprietor and manager of Osbornes Mills, December 25, 1866.

Mathew H. Davis, above named, married twice, first Ida E. Carder, of Kanawha County. Of this, four children were born. His second marriage was with Sarah E. Rogers, of Clay County, daughter of Levi and Naomi (Skidmore) Rogers. We have no record of Albert G. Davis.

John R. Davis, son of William H. and Mary Catherine (Hill), above mentioned, for several years, taught school and assisted in running the mill—Osbornes Mills.

William Willis Davis, son of William H. and Catherine (Hill) Davis, above, also did his first work as helper about the mill; taught several terms of free schools of Roane County; was conspicuous in the first of the "Teacher's Institutes" of the county at Spencer; married Ella, daughter of Benjamin Hickle, of upper Spring Creek, Aug. 29, 1891, his age, 22, her's 22; of this marriage were born four daughters and one son; their names: Bly, Pansy, Gypsy, wife of Harry Vance of Spencer; Faustine, a Miss at home; and the son, Glenn, now (1926) a young man at home.

Willis W. Davis and wife Ella have a nice farm home on the State road, Spencer to Clay. Willis was Democratic nominee, 1924 campaign, for the office of sheriff.

DAWSON:
Albert G. and Villa M. (Reed) Dawson, were born in Harrison County, Western Virginia, he on October 24, 1833, she, November 24, 1833, made their home on upper Middle Reedy in what later became Curtis District, September, 1856; he enlisted in the Confederate service of the Civil War. He is remembered by the oldest citizens yet as the largest man of all the country, though never corpulent; tall and gigantic, he was usually designated as "Big Bert Dawson." Whether "Bert" and Villa M. raised more than one child we can not say. We have a record of one, Columbus Albert, who had the foresight to subscribe for a book, 1882, in which a short biography of subscribers is given. In this is seen "Columbus Albert Dawson, born in Roane County, September 26, 1856, and in this county his wedded life began, Dora B. Wade becoming his wife on the 14th day of March, 1880." Dora B. was a daughter of Otho and Sarah (Wright) Wade, he born in Monongalia County, 1833; she, in Green County, Pennsylvania, 1836. They came as residents of Roane County in the year 1873. To C. Albert and Dora Wade Dawson were born in Roane County, West Virginia, two daughters: Ella Maud, 1883, and Lillie May, 1881. C. Albert Dawson was one of Roane County's first crop of school teachers that came out of the free school system; he taught seven years and was seen at all the first "Teachers' Institutes" of the county.

DEARMAN: Of Harper and Curtis Districts.
The paternal ancestors of the Dearman families of Roane County, were for one generation residents of Loudon County, Virginia (there known as deArman). A more immediate ancestor, Peter Dearman, settled in Harrison County, western Virginia, and died there—at Hackers Creek—about the year 1840; he was twice married. Of his first marriage were born Andrew and Nancy; of the second marriage were Alfred, Elliott, killed in war; Allen, died unmarried; Hannah, and Matilda Jane. These all came to Roane County, the first of them as early as the year 1841. Their marriages and descendants:

Andrew married ....; of their children we can name two, Romeo Dearman and Gibson Dearman, the latter long a respected farmer of the head of lower Flat Fork of Poca.

Nancy became the wife of Samuel Romine, of Harper District. Hannah married, first, Wm. H. Raines; second, James Lowe, of Harper, 1857.

Alfred Dearman, son of Peter Dearman of Harrison County, was twice married. We have no names of any children of his first marriage; for a second wife he married Rebecca, daughter of James Riddle of the chapter of this work: "The County." Rebecca was at the time of her marriage with Alfred Dearman, the widow of Jonathan, son of Leonard

Simmons, having two children named Margaret ("Polly"), later the wife of L. S. Goff, of Spencer, and Joseph Simmons.

To Alfred Dearman and Rebecca (Riddle-Simmons) were born two sons, named Ulysses Lincoln Dearman, now (1926) a practicing graduate physician, with his home and principal office, a hospital, at Town of Reedy; his wife being Jerushia, a daughter of the Mount family of near Reedyville. See name "Mount."

Lonzo Dearman, of this family, is a plumber in the City of Spencer, not married at this time, 1926.

DEPUE: Of Reedy and Spencer.

Marshall Depue was born January 23, 1833, son of Beniah and Evaline Belmont (Boggs) Depue, at their home on Spring Creek near Spencer. Beniah Depue and the father-in-law, John Boggs, owned about the time of birth of Marshall, several thousands of acres of forest lands on Spring Creek and Reedy. Marshall's education was that of the average alert student of the pioneer subscription schools aided by an occasional private tutor.

At about 26 years of age he met and married Miss Elizabeth E. Jarrett, born February 24, 1841, daughter of Eli and Nancy (Newhouse) Jarrett, then of Jarretts Ford, on the Elk of the Great Kanawha.

Marshall and Elizabeth, his wife, soon made their home on the Ravenswood and Spencer turnpike at about the half-way between the "Three Forks" and Town of Spencer. There he owned about twelve hundred acres of forest lands to the clearing of which and making it into agricultural fields, he gave all his well-directed energies for twenty-five years, at the end of which time about a thousand acres were blue grass pasture fields well stocked with the "Big Roane Durham" breed of cattle. He built the commodious farm dwelling on his farm about the year 1881, at that time the largest and best between Spencer and Ravenswood.

He was never a politician or office seeker, but he was elected and served as Delegate for Roane in the State Legislature, Twelfth Session, 1875, and again in the Sixteenth Session, 1881. The widow, Elizabeth E., lives at the old homestead yet—1927.

To Marshall and Elizabeth E., his wife, were born and by them brought up there on the farm three sons, but no daughter. The sons' names, Jarrett H., Mark and Orlando.

Jarrett H. Depue, son of Marshall and Elizabeth E., his wife, was born May 27, 1861; married Miss Madora Cuningham on October 1, 1885; she a daughter of Perry G. and Eliza (Allman) Cunningham, his wife, at Walton, Roane County.

Jarrett H. and his wife "Dora," made their home for several of the first years of their married lives at Walton. After his father's death he came to Left Reedy, acquiring the modern residence situate just beyond the creek at the railway station—Billings—together with the stock farm above and below it. He has followed his father's love for cattle and keeps large herds of them. He owns twelve hundred acres of cattle fields in Roane and about the same number of acres in Wirt County.

Jarrett is a sportsman of a single love—fox chasing; always keeps a few of the best breeds of fox hounds; always attends the national meet; enters one or two contestants each time, and captured some prizes but not the first as yet; won first prize for the best looking pair of fox hounds at the National Bench Show in 1924.

Jarrett H. and "Dora" (Cunningham), his wife, have brought up three daughters—no son. Their names, Mabel, Ivy and Elizabeth. Further: Mabel married Dr. Alonzo Beagle on October 7, 1907, her age 21, his age 31; he born in Tyler County, West Virginia. Ivy married William R. Goff, M. D., October 11, 1922, her age 31, his age 31; he is a son of Lewis Summers Goff and wife of Spencer. (See Chapter VII.) Elizabeth married Grover F. Hedges, Esq., of Spencer, June 3, 1913, her age 19, his 28. (See name Hedges.)

Mark Depue, son of Marshall and Elizabeth E. (Jarrett) Depue, followed his father in stock raising. He owns tracts of large acreages not far from Town of Reedy; his home place commencing near Reedy Town and extending up the pike toward Spencer. He married a Miss Clark; they have brought up several children. They have their residence in Spencer while their children attend Spencer High School.

Orlando Repue, youngest of the family, died childless.

De GRUYTER: Correctly "deGruyter."

Otto de Gruyter is the first of this name in Roane County. He was born in Moers Dusseldorf, Rhine Prussia in the year 1852; came to America 1870.

Two brothers of Otto, came to America long before he came. Martin, the father of Julius de Gruyter, of Charleston, was here and served in the Civil War, which ended in 1865. The other brother of Otto and Martin settled in Covington, Kentucky, where he was in the job printing business awhile then ran a drug business.

Otto returned to Germany, stayed a year and came back to Charleston, West Virginia, in 1873. He was an apprenticed watchmaker in his youth and a skilled clock and watch man all his life. Near Osbornes Mills he met with Rhoda J. Hill, daughter of Henry Hill, of a pioneer family of that name—distinguished for their pink blond complexions— and on the 4th day of October 1885, Otto de Gruyter and Rhoda J. were married, his age 33, her age not found. They settled in the Town of Spencer about 1912; here Otto died. To them were born one son and two daughters. Their names, Olin F. de Gruyter and Iona and Eunice de Bruyter; they own and manage a jewelry store in Spencer, carrying also chinaware and books.

Olin F. de Gruyter married Maud M. Hersman on the 7th of September, 1913, his age 26, her age 27. She is the daughter of Hon. Alexander M. Hersman, one time Delegate for Roane in the State Legislature.

DODD:

William E. Dodd, a Virginian, came to Pocatalico country, about Walton shortly before the Civil War—1860-65—having with him his wife, their three sons and two daughters, whose names were Thomas A., Catherine C., William Remly, Annie and Peter M. Dodd. Later they settled on Long Ridge next the Kanawha County line.

We have no information as to Thomas M. Dodd; Catherine C. married Jordan Harper of that place; of William Remley we have no record; Annie Dodd married Ed Welch, and Peter M. Dodd, son of William E., pioneer, married Mildred C. Elmore, and they made their life home on Long Ridge; there to Peter M. and Mildred C. were born five sons and five daughters:

Fannie B., who married Perry Jarvis of Little Sandy; Annie E., wife of James H. Rogers, Huntington; William Everett; fourth child died; George Edward, Charles Irvin, Ida M., wife of Silas P. Robinson; Laura C., wife of William T. Hively; Ollie, who married Lewis Vineyard. No children of a second marriage.

Of the above we write further:

William Everett, third above, married first, Eva E., daughter of Isaac L. Summers, son of James, on the 24th day of February, 1904; to them were born three sons and two daughters. Eva E. (Summers) having died, Wm. E. married Darlie Helmic, of Calhoun County, West Virginia; of this have been born two sons and one daughter.

George Edward, fifth of Peter M.'s children, married Ora, daughter of William F. Ryan of Little Sandy, Kanawha County.

Charles Irvin, sixth of Peter M.'s children, married Allie Daugherty of Long Ridge, November 8, 1908, she the daughter of George Daugherty of Long Ridge. Now (1926) lives at Elk View on the Elk River.

DONOHOE:

Those of Walton District are descendants of an old Virginia family of that name last living in Craig County of that Commonwealth.

Of these, three sons of Major Donohoe of Craig County, Virginia, came to Pocatalico country about the year 1865. Their names: Isaac E., William E., and John Donohoe.

Isaac E. Donohoe died a bachelor.

William E. Donohoe, son of Major Donohoe, married Sarah J. Walker, in Craig County, Virginia, sometime before coming here; to William and Sarah E., his wife, were born sons and daughters as follows:

Isaac A. and Thomas C., both bachelors.

George E. married Emma Mahan.

Eliza J. died, not having married.
William A. died a bachelor at 22.
John D. married Miss Jane Patrick of Roane County.
Robert Walter married Eva Lynch.
Amanda C. died a youth of 13 years, and Mathew Marion Donohoe, last of this family, went "West" about the year 1880, then a young man and not married. Of the above, we state further:

Robert Walter Donohoe, son of Wm. E. and Sarah J. (Walker) Donohoe, was born on July 9, 1860, in Craig County, Virginia, came to Roane, 1865; married Eva A., daughter of John ("Jack") D. and Mary A. (Jones) Lynch, in Roane County, December 15, 1886, his age 26, her age 15; to John W. and Eva A. were born eleven children, their names are as follows:

Marvin L., who married Teressa Vicars.

Flore, not married.

Hubert, married Glada Greathouse, daughter of Marshall Greathouse, of Spencer.

Roy, married Nola Canterbury.

Carrie, married J. C. Pauley.

Ancil, married Georgia Robertson.

Elvie, married Elmer Medley.

Eugene, Mary, Frank and Richard are all youths as yet—1926.

DOUGHERTY: Of Smithfield and Walton. Of Irish extraction, run to blonds in complexion.

It appears that some brothers and sisters of this name, Dougherty, came to those parts of the country while it was yet part of Kanawha County.

There was an Alexander, whose marriage is not on our records. James W. Dougherty married Miss Barbara Hively, August 26, 1856. Phoebe F. married Isaac Cox in 1856, a Phoebe married C. C. Paxton, February 6, 1879; William H. married Emma J. Sergent, June 4, 1885, his age 22, her age 21; William M. married Miss Vina E. Vineyard, August 20, 1889; John W. married Lucinda Moore, June 29, 1878; Elizabeth J. married Samuel Cummings, born in Craig County, Va., the ceremony was on January 9, 1884, his age 22, her age not written; a Henry C. Dougherty married Sarah A. C. Neal, October 23. 1879; the same name to Sadie Naylor, February 3, 1892, his age 50, her's 42; a Chris C. Dougherty married Janie Swank, lives now on McKowns Creek; Virginia A. Dougerty married Allen Lewis White, March 27, 1890, her age 22, his age 23. So much obtained from the county marriage records.

I have been given the following information, except dates, as to George Washington Dougherty and Harvey Dougherty:

Harvey Dougherty married Ann Hively, daughter of Captain John Hively, their chieldren's names: Mary E., who married Henry Helper, September 10, 1883; Janie married George Walker; George W. married Viola Cunningham, August 25, 1882; Mathew H. married Isabell Harper, September 24, 1899; Martin married a Miss Keffer; Charles Dougherty's life we do not know.

George Washington Dougherty married Miss Sarah Ann Hively, September 24, 1859, she a daughter of Captain John Hively. To George W. and Sarah Ann (Hively) were born and by them reared the following sons: Henry A., Howard C. and George Everett.

Henry A. married Miss Dora Looney, November 18, 1886, his age 26, her's 21.

George Everett married Victoria Fisher, June 25, 1890, his age 34, her's 19. G. E. was elected and served one term as assessor of Roane County.

Howard C. Dougherty married Miss Stella Kincaid, May 15, 1905, his age 22, her age 18.

DOUGLASS: Of Spencer and Upper Big Sandy.

Reuben A. Dougles and Emma (Douglass) Woodyard, brother and sister, young school teachers; he came about the year 1876. Emma came about the year 1893.

Ancestry, marriages and posterity:

Andrew Douglass, born on the waters of the River Clyde, Scotland, about the year 1822. With a brother (of the same father and mother) arrived in Virginia, 1844, or thereabouts. The brother's name and in what direction he went has been lost to recollection of Andrew's family. Ruben A. and Emma J. liked to say, "we are of the Clan of 'Douglass the Black,' " though neither was at all of complexion so dark as to partic larly attract attention. My recollections are that Ruben had blue or gray eyes, Emma of a clean white complexion with black wavey hair and black eyes. They claim kin with that branch of Douglasses who have their annual family reunions in Philadelphia.

Andrew Douglass, first mentioned, made his way over into Harrison County, and there, in the year 1845, married Miss Ruhama Dilworth, daughter of a family of pioneers of the Monongahela Valley. They acquired lands on Elk Creek, near "Romines Mills," there made of the lands a good farm and brought up their family of four sons and five daughters. They were devout Presbyterians in their religious connections, and Andrew served as a volunteer in the Union army of the Civil War.

The names of the sons and daughters of Andrew and Ruhama, his wife, are: Ruben A., first mentioned above; Columbia, Andrew, Jr., Marietta, Edward, Jennie, "Sis," Jefferson and Emma J., mentioned above.

Marriages of this family of Andrew and Ruhama:

Ruben A. Douglass was born on the farm near "Romines Mills," year 1847, grew up there and became a teacher in the public schools; came to Roane in the year 1876, here, on October 13, 1877, united in marriage with Miss Mary J. Lewellen, daughter of Jeremiah Lewellen and wife, of Vandal Fork, of Spring Creek; acquired a tract of land near the home of the Lewellens, called the place "Pretty Farm Run" and on this made their life-time home.

From here he went out teaching, was principal of Spencer Independent District Schools in town, one or more terms; affiliated with the lodges, was a Mason, an I. O. O. F. and a Knights of Pythias; elected and served one term as County Superintendent of Schools, years 1893 to 1895.

Ruben A. and Mary J. (Lewellen) Douglass brought up two sons and four daughters; their names: Lewellen Aubra, Rector R., Ethel, Ufa, Vera, Hallie. Of these:

Lewellen A. married Margaret Norris in Parkersburg, year 1914. She was a descendent of the old family Norris of Little Kanawha.

Rector R. married Miss Ruby Mace, July 13, 1923; he 33, she 21 years of age.

Vera, at 20, married Onel McKown, 23, on November 21, 1915.

Hallie, 24, married Harry R. Adams, 34, March 28, 1923. See name "Adams."

We do not have the marriage of Ethel or Ufa.

Columbia Douglass, daughter of Andrew and wife, of Romines Mills, first married Granville Row. To them was born and brought up one son and one daughter, Charles and Jennie. Granville having died, Columbia united in marriage with John Tawney, of upper Big Sandy, on November 27, 1901, he a widower, then 53, and she a widow, age 47.

Andrew Douglass, son of Andrew, Sr., and Ruhama, third child, went to Montana, there taught school, married there, returned here and died. The wife returned to Montana. Of this marriage one daughter was born, she is at this time a teacher in Broaddus College.

Marietta, daughter of Andrew Douglass and wife, married Judson Ward, at Mannington, W. Va.; they resided for a time in Spencer.

Edward Douglass, son of Andrew and Ruhama, married Miss Etta Boyles in Upshur County, W. Va. They brought up three daughters and nine sons; lived many years in Roane and died here. This family scatterd far and near, only one is now in Roane. Cecil, who married Miss Ingaby Post, April 10, 1910, he then 34, she 24 years of age. She is a daughter of Edward Post and wife, of Spencer.

Jennie Douglass, daughter of Andrew and Ruhama, married in Lewis County, Mr. Price Sidebottom.

"Sis," daughter of Andrew and Ruhama, married in Harrison County, a Mr. .... Hall, by profession an architect. He died within a few years. They had one son and one daughter, whose names are, Arthur and Mary Hall.

HISTORY OF ROANE COUNTY   509

Jefferson Douglass, son of Andrew and Ruhama, married in Harrison County, Miss Ann Harrison. He is the member of this family who yet lives on the old home place near Romines Mills. They have brought up three sons and three daughters, we are told.

Emma J. Douglass, daughter of Andrew and Ruhama, while in her teens, married a Mr. Kelley, who died within the year. Later she taught school and came to Roane County as mentioned above, and taught in the Town School, * * * soon married Harry Chapman Woodyard, son of William and Isabelle Woodyard. He was the B. & O. station agent for Spencer at the time of this marriage. Her life from time of marriage is part of that of Harry C., her husband. He was elected and served many terms in the House of Delegates of the United States Congress. She served as his secretary each term, or thereabout. She was diplomatic and was deemed a good "better half." She liked her home in Spencer and the Presbyterian church, in warm loyalty to which she brought up her children. See family name, Woodyard.

DOUGLASS: Elisha, Callahill, Isaac W.

These were three brothers who came here about the time of the Civil War. The first two with their wives and families. All three served as soldiers in the Union army of the Civil War.

We must presume they came here from Boone County, W. Va., for Isaac W. married here, Rachel Runnion, June 24, 1897. "His age 42, her's 22. He was born in Boon County, Virginia," says the record.

DRAKE: Of Big Sandy, Geary District.

The first were three and maybe four brothers. Drakes, descendants of a Colonial family of the James or Roanoke River in Virginia, members of which moved westward, stopping for a generation or two in Russell County, and from there to this Big Sandy in the decade, 1830.

These first were Isaac, Sutton, Admiral and Charles.

Letters of inquiry addressed by the author of this, to two leading descendants of these Drakes, now prominent in Geary District, remain unanswered. We therefore write in part from "hear-say," in part from our own family traditions as helped by conveyance and marriage records, and confine all comments to the family of Isaac and Charles Drake.

Charles Drake, born in Pike County, Kentucky, January 29, 1826, was a son of Charles Drake, born in Giles County, Virginia, Feb. 2, 1780, and Clarissa (Jeans) Drake, born in North Carolina, March 28, 1788.

Charles Drake, II, came to Big Sandy country, 1846 or 7, and here on 11th day of May, 1847, united in marriage with Sarah Ann Bishop, born in Pike County, Kentucky, June 9, 1828, daughter of John Bishop, sr., and wife Margaret Bishop, who was born in Russell County, Virginia, 1810, being, it is observed, a sister of John Bishop, II, pioneer of Pocatalico.

Charles and Sarah Ann, his wife, made their home on Big Sandy of Elk, and there brought up children whose names and births are as follows: William Parrot, Sept. 16, 1850; Marshall G., Oct. 20, 1852; Mahala R., May 11, 1855; Hulda C., Oct. 31, 1858; James Russell, Oct. 16, 1860; America V., Feb. 16, 1863; Newton J., Nov. 24, 1865; and Mary D. M., June 20, 1868. Marriages of this family: William Parrot to Amanda Patton, Dec. 28, 1871; Marshall G., to Elizabeth McQuain, Nov. 19, 1874; Mahala R., to Thomas McQuain, March 21, 1878; America V. to William F. Wilson, April 13, 1881; Hulda to Jacob Cook, 26, Jan. 3, 1884; Newton J. to Cynthia Kiser, Nev. 20, 1888; Newton J. at 25, to Wonder Hall, May 10, 1891; James Russell, 23, to Sarah E. Meadows, 24, April 12, 1884.

It is observed in the roster of enlistments of volunteers from Roane in Chapter I, of this book, that Isaac, Sutton and Charles Drake joined and served in the Union army of the Civil War.

In his biography in Hardesty's History, Rev. Davidson Ross says he married "Nancy Drake, daughter of Isaac and Peggy Bishop Drake."

George C. Drake, son of "Russ' Drake, married Miss Clara H. Spencer, daughter of George Spencer, of Henrys Fork, Smithfield District, on March 19, 1908. His age 22, her age 20. They made their home on main Big Sandy. He has been a popular teacher in the public schools of Geary District from when a mere boy.

Other marriages of Drakes we give from Roane County records as follows: Michael Drake to Lucy Justice, March, 1861. M. G. Drake, to E. McQuain, November, 1874. Isaac Drake to Mary King, August 9, 1875. Almeda Drake to John S. Parker, January 27, 1876. Elizabeth May Drake to John W. Hensley, January 25, 1857. Julia Drake to John King, January 9, 1857. Telitha Drake to James White, 1857. Mary L. Drake to John C. Harold, March 31, 1882. Lydia J. Drake 19 years old, to Camden Iedsome, 22, March 19, 1890. J. W. Drake to Ellen Naylor, April 21, 1877. Ameantha Drake, 17, to James B. Wright, 29, April 1, 1886. Lecta Drake to C. B. Shamblin, January 15, 1888. Priscilla Ann Drake married Christopher P. Tawney. See family name "Tawney."

DRODDY: Pioneer of Walton.

Charles Droddy was the first of this name here. His descendants, though several of them grandsons now past middle age, remember all too little of the family history. It is known, however, that the father of Charles Droddy with a wife and several children were settlers on the Red River in Texas; that Charles served as a soldier in the War of 1812, and with Jackson at the Battle of New Orleans, 1814, however, he must have been a mere boy, yet he drew a United States pension as a veteran of that war, down to time of his death, 1865.

HISTORY OF ROANE COUNTY 511

Charles Droddy was a "trader" of the kind who came up the rivers and bought hides, pelts, furs, venison and bearmeats for the New Orleans market; though we have no definite information as to what errand dropped him into this Pocatalico wilds about the year 1825, the facts are he married here, Miss Sarah Gandee, daughter of Uriah and Mercy "Massie" (Hughes) Gandee, about the year 1826; acquired a large tract of land on which is now the town of Walton. Made a large and attractive pioneer farm and he and Sarah, his wife, spent their long and industrious married life and reared here their family of four sons and three daughters. Their names: Calvin C., George W., Charles Allman, Christopher C., and Floyd E., Malinda, Mary "Polly," and Melissa.

Further of these sons and daughters:

George W. Droddy, son of Charles and Sarah (Gandee), his wife, enlisted as a soldier and served in the Federal armies of the Civil War. He married Martha (Mat), a daughter of John M. Jones, of Cotton Tree Creek. After the war they made their home at Walton, and reared two sons. Their names: Augustus and "Buzz." Augustus, at the age of 24, married Rosie Tanner (Widow Goff), March 31, 1892.

Christopher C. Droddy, son of Charles and Sarah, his wife, was born October 29, 1830, married on Rock Creek, July 3, 1854, Belinda C. Walker, born in Monroe County, W. Va., daughter of Daniel and Catherine (Myers) Walker, natives of Botetourt County, Virginia, who settled on Rock Creek of lower Pocatalico in 1854. Christopher C. enlisted and served as a Union soldier in the "War of the Rebellion." The home farm of Christopher was made opposite the mouth of McKnows Creek, where he and his wife reared their family of five sons and four daughters. Their names, dates of respective births, and marriages—so far as we know—are as follows:

Daniel Miller, 1855, married Margaret Shaver, October 27, 1876. Sarah S., born 1857, married Frank Ferrell. Catherine F., 1859, married George S. Harper, of lower Poca, December 30, 1882. Charles M., 1861, married Mary Ann Harper, December 20, 1884, his age 23, her's 20. George Christopher, born 1864, married Mary C. Jones (then Widow Hensley), daughter of Isaac Jones, of Walton. Leanna J., born July 20, 1866, married Okey H. Boggs, of Wirt County, on June 17, 1886, her age 19, his age 22. Mary E., born 1868, married Charles W. Harper. They, Chas. W. Harper and Mary E., have six children. Ota F., married a Miss Gibson, of Kanawha County. Thomas B., born May 22, 1875, married Martha Hunt, April 17, 1898, his age 22, her's 18. Cornelia E., born March 23, 1877, married Thomas R. Raines, of Flat Fork, May 8, 1898, her age 20, his age 20.

Calvin C. Droddy, son of Charles and Sarah (Gandee) married Miss Mary C. Counts, of Poca, October 19, 1874.

Floyd E. Droddy, son of Charles and Sarah (Gandee) was born October 8, 1850, married July 26, 1875, Miss Mary C. Harless, born in Montgomery County, Virginia, January 13, 1855, daughter of Ballard and Mary (Snyder) Harless. Floyd E. and Mary C., his wife, made their life's home near Walton, where to them were born and by them reared the following children: Eva, July 16, 1876; Sarah J., January 16, 1879; Pruella, October 21, 1881. In his biograph in Hardesty's History—1882—Floyd E. says "he has in his possession a pewter tea pot one hundred years old that was the property of Jesse Hughes, the renowned Indian hunter," his wife's grandfather.

Melinda, daughter of Charles and Sarah (Gandee) Droddy, married Elias Summerfield, son of the pioneer family of Summerfields, of Pocatalico. And "Polly" Droddy, her sister, married Jacob Summerfield, the brother of Elias, above named. We have no information concerning Melissa Droddy, last of the first family of Droddys.

A Walter O. Droddy married a Miss Allie B. Lowe, September 17, 1893, his age 22, her age 18; this from the county marriage records, but we do not have their family connections.

DUKE: Of Reedy.

The first of this family name here was Michael Duke, Sr., and his wife, Sarah, with a family of several children, who came here from west Pennsylvania about 1875.

From recollection of what I have been told by members of the family, the last by John, now (1926) large stock raiser of upper Mill Creek, Jackson County, Michael Duke, the father, was born near Nancy, France, about the year 1825, where Michael's father and mother both died, and the family share of a large manufacturing business of the ancestor Duke and another family was promptly taken away from the orphan Dukes, and Michael turned out alone and pennyless, was at first apprenticed to a blacksmith and ran away from his tyranical master, got himself stowed away on a ship bound for America, landed on the eastern coast at New York or Philadelphia. By reason of his youth and his skill as an iron worker he easily made a good living and made his way by the year 1850 to western Pennsylvania, where he married Sarah ...., we do not have her family name. To Michael and Sarah were born in Pennsylvania several children.

By 1875 he is in Parkersburg, W. Va., bought of McFarland brothers a tract of 669 acres of land, known as the "Camp Place" of Right Reedy, on the Ravenswood and Spencer turnpike, three miles above— west of—Three Forks of Reedy. For this he paid down $500, and promised the residue of the price, $4,000.00, within two years. He met his payments within the time limit and obtained his deed.

As a farmer he was a good one, his observations had been constructive and clear and his methods were those of the Pennsylvania Dutch. He taught the people of his neighborhood their first lessons in reclaiming worn-out, fallow lands, of which the long field on the turnpike was a good example, its fencing long gone, its hillside land of which there was a strip to the run bottom, had been commons since prior to the Civil War—1861—and was washed and cut by gullies made by the drainage from the turnpike. This, within two years, was

HISTORY OF ROANE COUNTY 513

a beautiful, smoothe, green meadow under Michael's management. They all worked, his daughters went to the fields, and were the first to teach the natives what girls could accomplish in the fields, the neighbors all about held to the old Virginia notion that the ladies spin, weave and do house work only. He taught his, that factories would do all such, much better and cheaper, and the daughters' time was more valuable expended in other directions.

To Michael and Sarah Duke were born—all but possibly the last child—in Pennsylvania, the following sons and daughters:

Caroline, who married Jacob Ferguson, lived some years—1892 to 1910—residents of Spencer.

Alfred, maybe, married in Jackson County.

Emily married W. A. Buckanan, of near Jackson and Roane County line, June 23, 1884, his age 23, her's 30.

Elora married Robert W. Seaman, of Reedy, February 20, 1889, his age 26, her age 24.

George Michael married Hallie Goff, daughter of Cyrus Goff, of lower Spring Creek, December 27, 1893, his age 30, her age 24. Michael and Hallie, with their two sons and one daughter, removed to Texas, about the year 1915 or 1916. The names of these sons were Harry and Roy, the daughter's name Bonnie. They settled on a large farm near Abilene, Texas, where Michael, Hallie and Harry. have since died.

Lora married an Otho Gilpin, 1911, his age 24, her age 22.

John, possibly the youngest of the family, married Nettie B. Daniell, of lower Reedy, in Wirt County, daughter of Charles A. and Edith (Wees) Daniell. See name "Daniell."

DULING: Of Spencer, 1891 to the year 1905.

Charles Franklin Duling, subject of this sketch, was born at Malden— On the Kanawha—March 25, 1840, son of Albert and Catherine (Wilson) Duling united in marriage March 6, 1839. Catherine was born on the Great Kanawha near Buffalo, year 1941, or next year or two following, a daughter of Peter Wilson, well known family of pioneers of the Kanawha Valley.

These Dulings were from eastern Virginia, but at what date they settled there we have not searched out. Descendants of the first settler Duling on the "Eastern Shores" are not to say numerous but most all vigorous and active individuals. They have a family reunion each autumn at Fowlerton, in the State of Indiana, where several of the name who venerate their ancestry reside, highly respected as successful farmers.

The ending, i-n-g, tokens the name as Saxon, yet it may once have been "du Ling," or had a Celto-Scotch prefix, Dhu. There has been a Scotch influence in the family, shown in the fact that one branch spells the name "Dulin," and at the same time asserts they are cousins to the family of Albert Duling, of the Great Kanawha.

Charles Franklin Duling, first mentioned, married Miss Sarah Jane Atkinson, born on Elk River near Charleston, a daughter of James

Atkinson and Miriam (Rader) Atkinson, his wife and a sister of their son, George Wesley Atkinson, one term governor of West Virginia, later a judge of the United States Court of Claims.

Charles F. and Sarah J., his wife, made their first home on Elk, near the Atkinson farm, where were born to them three sons and five daughters. In order of respective births: John W., Annie A., James A,. Sallie J., Minette, Nell, Gertrude M., Emma and Howard. And on May 26, 1878, Sarah Jane—wife and mother—died.

Eight years after death of the first wife, Charles F. Duling married Annie Conner, widow with one child, Ethel Conner; he soon sold the Elk River farm and moved to Spencer, 1891, all his family except James A. and the four eldest daughters, with him. Here he engaged in the mercantile business with real estate and general trading mixed. John W., the son, a partner with him for a while.

The block of lots fronting on Market Street and Bowman Street, "Duling Addition," is of their doings. Charles Franklin Duling ended his days here, dying of a sudden illness, December 24, 1905, leaving four sons born of the marriage with Annie Conner, the eldest near twenty-four years of age. Their names, Walter, Everett, Irl, Hugh and Milton. Of these, Walter and Irl are merchants at Huntington. Hugh, a professor in the University at Atlanta, Georgia, and Milton, a physician resident now—1927—at Charleston, W. Va.

Of the family of Charles F. and Sarah J. (Atkinson) Duling, John W. married a Miss Mattie Smith, of Virginia. They now reside at Clifton Forge, he a retired employee of the Standard Oil Company. James A. married Talitha Dorsey, and is a farmer in Nicholas County. Howard married Miss Blanche Levitt, of Parkersburg; they made their home in Charleston, W. Va., where he was a wholesale merchant. He died there, in the year 1925. Left the widow and two daughters.

Sallie J., daughter of Charles E. and Sarah J. (Atkinson) his wife, married Nathaniel Cavender, son of an old family of Cavenders, of Elk River. He was one term County Superintendent of Schools of Kanawha County. He died several years ago leaving one son and several daughters.

Minnette Duling married a Dr. Elliott B. Palmer, of Cincinnati. He died soon, she yet lives in Cincinnati.

Nellie M. is yet a spinster. Emma F. married Charles Garret, of Roane County. She died childless in Pittsburgh, Pa. Gertrude Miriam married, in Spencer, William H. Bishop, author of this book. See name "Bishop."

DYE: Of Poca, part of Smithfield. A different family from that of Reedy.

Robert Dye, Elizabeth, his wife, and their two sons and one daughter, all born in Russell County, Virginia, came from there and settled in

Poca, part of what is now Smithfield District of Roane County, in the year 1853. The sons were John F. and Abram or Abraham; the daughter died in youth.

John Franklin Dye, of above family, married Elizabeth Hall, possibly in Russell County, but they made their home and reared their family here. The names of their children, in order of their birth—a grandson gave me this information—are: Aaron; Mary Ann, married Wilson Jett, December 3, 1880; Margaret, Minnie, William, Jackson, Clark, Franklin and Lee.

Abram Dye, son of Robert and Elizabeth, his wife, first above mentioned, married Louisette Ascue—spelled "Hascue"—in Roane County, W. Va., January 7, 1858. To them were born James M. John M.; Nancy Jane, married Samuel Jackson Hutchinson, March 3, 1887, his age 22, her age 22; Creed F, Lora Emma.

The marriage records of Roane County has it thus: "James M. Dye to M. C. Godby, January 3, 1881"; also "James M. Dye to Melissa Ferrell, April 1, 1886, his age 25, her age ....." John M. Dye married Miss Florinda Smith, daughter of Rev. Jonathan Smith.

DYE: Of Reedy.

The Dye family, of main Reedy in Wirt County, but near the Reedy District boundary, was a prominent family, trading and neighboring at "Three Forks" for twenty-five years—1875-1895—of the sons are remembered Dusossoway, Dennis J. and George, yet here.

Dennis J. married twice, first Julia A. McClung, 1875. After her death he married Mary Duke on February 16, 1890, his age 34, her's 27.

George A. Dye, 23, married Maggie Wyatt, 19, on December 11, 1884.

EDWARDS: Of Walton and Spencer.

Isaac Edwards, first of the name here, was prominent as a miller and business man of Walton for some ten or fifteen years following the close of the Civil War. He served in that war as a Confederate volunteer, under Captain James S. Gandee.

Isaac Edwards was born in Caroll County, Virginia, March 27, 1831, and came with his parents to Kanawha County in his early manhood. In Raleigh County, W. Va., he united in marriage with Emily Jarrell. She was born in Kanawha County, May 22, 1836, the daughter of Madison and Susan (Toney) Jarrell. The children born of this marriage were: Mandeville, September 11, 1853, died within a year; Arminta, May 12, 1855, married George W. Hundley, December 9, 1876; Mathew P. was born September 25, 1857; John L., December 22, 1859; Charles M., March 9, 1863; Giles, March 15, 1865, married Bertha Petty, daughter of William and Melissa (Goff) Petty of Reedyville, this county; William S. was born August 28, 1867.

Giles Edwards, of the foregoing family, settled in the Town of Spencer, about the year 1908; and was one of the three promoters and builders of the Spencer "roller process' flouring mill. His name and achievements are mentioned in the chapter of this book, "History of the Town of Spencer."

Giles Edwards and Bertha Petty were married on Christmas day, 1893, and to them were born one daughter and two sons. Their names: Irma, who married a gentleman in Kanawha County; the sons: Harley D. and Dewitt, young men, yet single.

John L. Edwards married Matilda E. Lowe, December 3, 1879.

Mathew T. married Hannah G. Hunt, July 13, 1880.

ENGLE: Joseph F. Engle, of Big Sandy, first of the name resident in Roane.

Joseph F. Engle was born June 1, 1832, in Pendleton County, W. Va., son of Solomon and Sarah (George) Engle. Some of the Engle family settled in the Monongahela Valley. The George family is prominent in the counties of the Potomac branches.

Joseph F. Engle, first above mention, married Miss Julia A. Hoff, December 14, 1854, in Barbour County, W. Va. She was a daughter of John and Elizabeth (Mannier) Hoff, of Loudon County, Va., and was born in Harrison County, W. Va., on April 2, 1833, one of twelve children of John and Elizabeth Hoff, who shortly before Julia's birth had made their home in Harrison County.

Two years after the marriage of Joseph F. and Julia A. they came to Roane County to make, and made their future home, settling in various places until they at last found Geary District the satisfactory place where they lived the remainder of their lives, useful and respected.

To Joseph F. and Julia A., his wife, were born ten children, five of whom grew up and became citizens of Roane. Their names are: Commodore, born June 12, 1858; John H., August 25, 1861; Elidridge, May 13, 1866 ; Sarah Jane, October 4, 1871, and William H., January 25, 1879. Their respective marriages are as follows:

John H. Engle to Miss Lectra A. Geary, January 23, 1883.

Elidridge Engle to Miss Dora Garrett, December 28, 1897, his age 31, her age 22, " at the residence of T. Garrett."

Sarah Jane Engle to William M. Coon, September 14, 1905. "Her age 34, his age 54. He was born in Wirt County, W. Va."

William H. Engle married Clara E. Tawney, October 18, 1903. "His age 21, her age 18, at the residence of John Tawney." William H. Engle has been sought and used in public office much in his district, and was elected and served one term, four years, as member of the County Court of Roane; was its president for one year, during which roads were improved and several bridges built.

FIELDS: Of Harper, Curtis, Reedy.

Washington Fields, with his wife, Jennie (Ferrell), whom he had married in Russell County, Virginia, came to Lower Flat Fork of Pocattalico country about the year 1850, having with them six sons and two daughters. Their names: Samuel, Thomas, Henry, George W., Elijah, Rachel and Leah. Further about these:

Samuel Fields, first son of Washington and Jennie, married Miss Mary Dearman, August 18, 1866. She was a daughter of Andrew Dearman, lately—then—of Lewis County, to Samuel and Jennie (Dearman) Fields, his wife, were born, all in Roane County, five sons and two daughters, their names as follows:

John Wesley, who married Laura L. McCoy.

Jerome Clinton married Della Naylor, of Kanawha County.

Cyrus Monroe married Esta Rómine, December 2, 1904, his age 28, her age 24.

Thomas married Lorena Jones. Bowers Fields we do not know anything of. The daughters were:

Alice who married John West, April 12, 1885, his age 25, her age 16, and Caroline married a William Westfall.

Thomas Fields, second son of Washington, married Miss Matilda Kiser, in Jackson County.

William Fields, third son of Washington, married Miss Rachel Kiser.

Henry Fields, fourth son of Washington, married Miss Janie Garrett.

George W. Fields, fifth son of Washington, married Miss Phoebe Kiser, in Roane County, September 3, 1868. To them were born two sons and five daughters, named as follows: Abednego, "A. B." B., who married Miss Louisa Lyons, October 4, 1904; Augustus M.; Rosie, wife of Irven Snodgrass; Leah, Rachel, Maud and Alma.

Elijah Fields, sixth son of Washington Fields, married a Miss Ruana Moore, in Roane County, November 16, 1872.

Rachel Fields, first daughter of Washington and Jennie (Ferrell) Fields, married James S. Gandee, November 26, 1872.

Leah, second daughter of Washington, married Joshua Hammond.

FIELDS: Reese B., of West Harper District. His ancestry and other facts so far as we have obtained them are as follows:

James Fields and his wife Sarah (Garrett), both of whom were natives of Tazewell County, Virginia, where they were married and lived for a few years, came from Tazewell County and settled in "New Kentuck," part of Jackson County, about the year 1845. Their six sons, in order of respective birth, were as follows:

Tihlman, Reese B., George, John, Frank P., Lightburn. Further of these:

Tillman (or Tihlman) Fields married a Miss Roush, of Mason County, and made his home there, and there reared five sons and two daughters; Charles C. Fields, now and for several years past, a resident of

Spencer, is one of those sons. He was born in 1866, in Mason County. Married Miss Ella Francis Kirby, also born in Mason County, year 1865, daughter of a family of Kirbys formerly of Tazewell County, Virginia. They have reared two daughters and one son, whose names in order of birth are, Mabel, who married Creed Perdue; Virginia married A. C. Taylor, both residents of Charleston, W. Va. The son's name is Charles, Jr.

Reese B. Fields, son of James and Sarah, first mentioned, married Miss Sarah Ann Rhodes, April 26, 1869. They made their lifetime home in western Harper District, and there reared several children.

George Fields, son of James and Sarah (Garrett) Fields, married— likely in Jackson County—and settled in Roane. We do not have his family names.

John, fourth son of James and Sarah, married and settled in Jackson County.

Frank P. Fields, son of James and Sarah, married Miss Samantha Hatcher, June 19, 1880. They settled in North Harper District near Red Knob.

Lightburn, sixth son of James and Sarah, lives in Jackson County, W. Va.

FETTY:

Henry Middleton Fetty, born year 1840, one of five sons of Isias and Margaret (Carmac) Fetty, residents of Lewis County, western Virginia, in which county both of these families, Fetty and Carmac, had lived many years, farmers about Polk Creek on the Staunton and Parkersburg turnpike. These Carmacs were of a Maryland family of Carmacs. Mrs. Lucy Dodson of Spencer, W. Va., being a sister of Henry M.

In his thirty-seventh year, October, 1881, Henry Middleton Fetty came to Curtis District and married his boyhood acquaintance, Arminta P. Ruhl, daughter of David Ruhl, then residents of Curtis District. Arminta P. being then the widow of Christian H. Steinbeck, having three sons. Of these, see further on in these pages, name "Steinbeck." To these boys he was a good father.

Of this marriage of Henry M. and Arminta P. Fetty two daughters were born at the farm home in Curtis, near Clearence Postoffice, whose names are Maggie D., wife of Paul F. Cottle, now of City of Spencer, married September 14, 1899, and Virginia Myrtle, unmarried daughter yet with her father, their home being in Spencer, and she being a stenographer and deputy of the County Clerk Roy L. McCulty. Henry Middleton Fetty, now in his eighty-sixth year, my nearest neighbor, is yet of clear and considerate mind. In his prime of life was an active attendant and financial supporter of his church, the Methodist Episcopal, and was proud of his part in the building of the meeting house and parsonage at Clearence, near his home. At one time took much interest in the political affairs of the county, was elected and served one term as a member of the County Court, 1904-1908, and was instrumental in getting the first iron and concrete highway bridges in that district.

FISHER:
Romeo H. Fisher, Walton, W. Va. Occupation: Oil Gauger, Eureka Pipe Line Co.

Ancestry and when they came as given by above named:

Wm. Fisher was the youngest of a large family that came to the Kanawha Valley from near Philadelphia, Pa., sometime between 1800 and 1815. His wife was a Miss Samuels, and their children that I know of were: Greenberry Fisher, Leonard Fisher, John Fisher, Mary Fisher and another daughter, I do not remember name.

Greenberry Fisher was born near Sissonsville, Kanawha County, sometime in the year 1822. He married Miss Julia Koonty and they brought up the following sons and daughters: Elben Clark Fisher, Pleasant Summers Fisher, John Wesley Fisher, William Marion Fisher, Ulysses Grant Fisher, Virginia Fisher and Emma Belle Fisher.

Pleasant Summers Fisher was born near Sissonsville Oct. 18, 1852, and married Miss Columbia Ann Casto, daughter of Jacob Casto and Celia (Winter) Casto.

They brought up the following sons and daughters: Romeo H. Fisher, Vaught C. Fisher, Otis Otmer Fisher, Eva L. Fisher, Ava May Fisher, Clairmont Thau Fisher, Fernando Roscoe Fisher, Westa O. Fisher, Bessie Bernice Fisher and Marion Bradford Fisher.

Romeo H. Fisher, oldest son of Pleasant Summers Fisher and Columbia Ann (Casto) Fisher, was born at Fairplain, Jackson County, W. Va., August 30, 1878, and married Miss Icy Howell, daughter of Columbus Howell of Route No. 7, Spencer, Roane County, Oct. 19, 1910. They settled at Walton where he had been employed two years by the Eureka Pipe Line Co., as an oil gauger and has been living there since. They own a home on Cunningham street and are the parents of one child, a daughter, Eloise Fisher, who is now 14 years of age and was a sophomore in Walton High School during the 1926 and 1927 term.

FLESHER:
All the Fleshers of Roane and Jackson Counties, are descendants of the Flesher family, or families, settling prior to the year 1800 in the Monongahela Valley at places included in Harrison and Lewis Counties. From biographs of two sons of the first family of this name in Jackson county, seen in Hardest's History, we gather that Isaac and Elizabeth (Bonnett) Flesher removed from Harrison county and settled on Warth's Bottom in the year 1811, where to them were born William Bonnett Fleshed, in 1822, and Andrew Jackson, born on Mill Creek, January 2, 1827. William Bonnett Flesher married Eliza McKown, born at Mill Creek, 1823, daughter of Gilbert and Lydia (Flesher) McKown, whose parents also came to Spring Creek part of Jackson County in 1811. This is the Wm. B. Flesher who built the large

water grist and flour mill and was himself miller and proprietor for so many years on Sand Creek, three miles out from Ravenswood.

Andrew Jackson Flesher, above mentioned, is the same who settled at Murraysville and there built and maintained for fifteen years the largest boat building and ship yard ever on the banks of the Ohio, in the decades of the War of Secession, "Civil War."

The other Flesher family of Jackson County is that represented by Major Henry Camden Flesher, born at Weston, Lewis County, western Virginia, 1835. He served as a volunteer in the Union armies of the Rebellion, rose to rank of Major, and appears to have come to Ripley as a young lawyer and on September 9, 1869 married Miriam F., daughter of Ephraim S. and Ruami (Wright) Evans, at her father's home on Mill Creek below Ripley. Pauline, wife of Dr. Harlan H. Staata, some time a physician of the City of Spencer, founder of Spencer's first hospital, is the second daughter and third child of Major Flesher and his wife, Miriam F.

H. C. Flesher, Esquire, was many years a prominent practitioner at the Roane County bar, coming from his home below Ripley.

FLESHER: Dempsy P. of next below "Three Forks."

This is the Dempsy P. Flesher whose "Lane" is mentioned in the boundaries of the County of Roane, dividing Roane from Wirt County.

Dempsy P. was born in Lewis County, West Virginia, son of Adam Flesher and wife, and brother of George Flesher, pioneer mentioned in the next following paragraph; he was a prosperous farmer and popular man for twenty years including the period of the Civil War; a supporter of the Methodist Episcopal Church at Reedy. When the Methodist Episcopal people of the "Three Forks" decided to build a "best meeting house" in Roane County about the year 1866, it was located below the village, on the Main Reedy road, midway between the farm residence of Dempsy P., and the village; they gave it the name "Fleshers Chapel." It was a frame building, weather-boarded and ceiled, and painted white. It was sold, to build in the village of Reedy.

We infer from deeds of conveyances signed by Dempsy P. and recitals in them, that his wife's name was Elizabeth Jones, whom he married in Lewis County, West Virginia when both bride and groom were young.

We gather from recollection, confirmed in part by marriage records, that Dempsy P. and Elizabeth (Jones), his wife, brought up one son and three daughters; their names, Robert, Nancy, Elizabeth and Matilda.

Robert married .... They left three sons, whose names were Dempsey, Jr., William and ....

Nancy married William K. Board; Matilda, Thomas Seaman and Elizabeth, James M. Seaman. (See these names.)

FLESHER: George Adam Flesher, 1798-1878, with his wife, first of the name in Reedy.

He was born in the Monongahela Valley on the date above, son of Adam Flesher, of "Indian Warfare" fame. About the year 1820 he married a Miss Sallie Connolly, born 1798, in or near Weston, Lewis County, West Virginia. They made their home at Weston for a few years, then came to this Reedy country in first of the decade, 1830, acquired a large tract of the then unbroken forest lands lying southeast of the "Three Forks' 'of Reedy, up the Left Fork commencing within a quarter of a mile of the "Three Forks" and extending onto the Middle Fork, two thousand acres or more; on this they made their home and there prospered. To them were born there and by them reared the following sons and daughters:

William Kelley, Dempsy, John, Matilda, Alitha, Elizabeth, Sarah and Mary. Further:

William Kelley was killed or died of wounds during the Civil War.

Dempsy, born in 1828, learned the trade of saddlery at Weston, returned and married Eleanor C. Murray, daughter of John Murray and they made their home on that part of the ancestral lands on the Middle Fork of Reedy.

To Dempsy and Eleanor C. (Murray), his wife, were born and by them brought up the following sons and daughters: Virginia L., Ida E., Florence, George Minter, John Columbus, Sarah Elizabeth, Sallie Olive, Martha Eleanor and Thomas Daniel. Their marriages are as follows:

Virginia L. married Albert G. Corbet, April 22, 1881.

Ida C. married Hugh E. McClintoc, of Morgantown, 1896, ages 41 and 39.

Florence married Henry C. Seaman, November 11, 1873.

George M. married Mary Murphy, October 6, 1880.

John C., Miss Roxie Lowe, December 9, 1886, his age 27, her's 18.

Sarah Elizabeth married Mathew T. Lowe, March 17, 1884.

Sallie O., married Robert C. Lowe, September 3, 1887, she 19, he 21.

Martha F. married Hoyt Sheppard.

Thomas Daniel, yet a bachelor, lives at Morgantown.

John Flesher, son of George and Sallie (Conley) Flesher, his wife, born 1831, died 1876.

John Flesher, next above, married on Reedy, Miss Margaret Butcher, the 13th day of March 1859.

They made their home on Left Reedy, on part of the George Flesher lands; this John Flesher farm was for many years the largest and best between "Three Forks' 'and Spencer.

To John and Margaret (Butcher) Flesher, his wife, were born and by them reared on the farm named, three sons and one daughter, whose names were as follows: Andrew L., married Henrietta Sommerville, daughter of Jackson and Sarah (Ott) Sommerville, of Jackson County, Limestone Hill.

Clark and Etta went to the far West when yet young.
Of James, the youngest of this family we have no data.
Matilda, daughter of George A. and Sallie (Conley) Flesher, became the wife of Henry Bushop, of Monongahela Valley. Alitha married Thomas Gough and settled near on the Flesher lands; these are the ancestors of all of the Goughs of Reedy and Spencer.
Elizabeth married Elias Flesher of an unrelated family of Fleshers at Weston.
Sarah became the wife of George W. Callow, of Left Reedy. Mary married Robert E. Lee, of Wirt County, Lees Mills. See "Callow."

FLESHMAN: Of Walton District.

David T. Fleshman and his family were the first of this name here, were prominent for twenty years as introducers and breeders of improved strains of live stock, commencing in the year 1873; theirs is an inspiring example of what industry and good judgment will make out of Roane County lands.

By deed of conveyance dated December 18, 1873, Able P. Sinnett conveyed to D. T. Fleshman his partially improved farm of four hundred acres situate up on McKowns Creek, for the sum of three thousand dollars; how long the Fleshmans had lived here before making this purchase I do not know; the purchase money was in cash down, with a deferred payment which must have been small for no note or vendor's lien is mentioned.

Within ten years, more than two hundred acres of this land were in bluegrass fields stocked with the best breeds of horses, sheep and cattle that the importers of Greenbrier County and the Ohio Valley handled. "The Fleshman stallion and the Fleshman bulls' 'were the talk of the county; how much more satisfactory must be such applaudits than those accorded the successful professional man or public office holder! This farm is an oil field now and of the sons of David T., one has followed him as a stock man. We are informed the others have sold the surface to the brother.

David T. Fleshman was born in Greenbrier County, West Virginia, January 27, 1829, son of John and Catherine (Tuckwiller) Fleshman; John Fleshman having been born in Gallia County, Ohio, March 20, 1803, son of Jesse Fleshman and Catherine, born in Greenbrier County, March 31, 1798, so given in Hardestys. David T. married Miss Sarah S. Dougherty on McKowns Creek, September 28, 1854, she a daughter of James and Phoebe (Gardner) Dougherty; they made their home at first in Greenbrier County, where some, if not all their five children were born. Th names of these and something further is as follows:

Charles W., born June 21 ,1858; Elizabeth J., January 14, 1861; James M., August 3, 1863; Henry Howard, May 15, 1866, and Samuel A., August 27, 1878. Of these sons, Charles W. was one of the school teachers of Roane, when the county system was young and popular. He obtained somewhere a special training as a penman, and organized and taught some classes in penmanship for a few years.

Elizabeth J. Fleshman married O. Mac Chambers, at her home, February 8, 1888, his age 26, her age 26. See name "Chambers" Ch. V.

Henry Howard as "Howard H." married Miss Lulu Jones, of Walton, on October 25, 1891, his age 25, her's 18.

All the above named children of David T. Fleshman and wife were born in Greenbrier County except Samuel Austin, who was born in Roane; he married Miss Maggie Virena Cromwell on September 23, 1900, she a daughter of Robert and Mary E. (Alfred) Cromwell. S. Austin Fleshman acquired the home farm and continues the business of stock raising.

FORE: Early settler of Middle Fork of Reedy.

George W. Fore, born in Prince Edward County Virginia, about the year 1837, came to the Reedy country about the year 1850, with a small 'Show" of the Punch and Judy, and prestidigitor class. On one of these visits he married Irena Chancey, about the above date; she a daughtr of Hiram and Elvira Chancey, large farmers and popular people at the time. George W. and Irena settled in a home on part of the Chancey lands, and lived the full span of their fruitful lives there. He had a lame hand and lame foot from infancy. He taught school and was for many years the county's popular auctioneer.

To George W. and Irena (Chancey) Fore, were born and reared the following children—names from recollection of the author—in order of respective births are as follows: Martha or Tabitha ("Bide"), James D., Elvira, William F., Ida, Thomas Hoyt, George D., Bailey B., Susan and George W., Jr. Further:

Martha married William D. Board, April 15, 1896. her age 30, his 44.

Elvira married E. Adam Fore, born in Southern Virginia.

Ida married Peter Hall, May 2, 1883.

William F. married ....

Thomas Hoyt married Melissa Seabolt, January 26, 1911, his age 30, her's 26.

George D. married Annie L. Wyatt, June 18, 1898.

Bailey B. to Martha Wright, February 4, 1899, his age 23, her age, 21; Thomas H. is a prominent school teacher, and George D. and Bailey B. substantial farmers on small farms once parts of the maternal ancestral lands.

FOX:

Jasper Newton Fox, born in Monongalia County, October 10, 1838, son of Martin and Nancy Fox, natives of Prince William County, Virginia. Jasper Newton Fox married Elmira Anderson in Green County, Pennsylvania, year 1858, lived in Monongalia County until eight children were born of that marriage, and with this family came to Roane County, in 1874, settled on a tract of 230 acres of land lying on Bear Run, which he had purchased just before coming here, all in woods except some small narrow fields along the run. Here in the next ten years following his arrival they made a good farm.

To Jasper Newton and Elmira, his wife, were born twelve children, eight in Monongalia and four after coming here. Of these twelve children only four are yet (1926) living. Their names are, Theodore M., John M., William O. and Joseph A.

Theodore M., born 1861, never married, lives with his brother, John M., at Hartford City, W. Va.

Rev. John M. Fox, of the above family, was born February 17, 1865, has been twice married. His first wife died and his second is yet with him. John M. Fox became a preacher of the Gospel some fifteen years ago, is a Baptist, and is now, 1926, stationed at Hartford City, W. Va.

William O. Fox, a son of Jasper N. and Elmira, was born February 18, 1869, married twice. First wife, Mahala, daughter of Albert Gough, of Reedy, made their home on Bear Run at once. Of this marriage one son and two daughters were born. Mahala died and for a second wife William O. married Glennie, daughter of Alexander Snyder, of Calhoun County, W. Va. One son—died—and two daughters, Chloe, born 1919, and Willa, born 1923, are both with the parents on the old farm.

Joseph A. Fox, son of Jasper N. and Elmira, was born March 27, 1876, married Flora Freeland, of Lower Spring Creek, daughter of Cornelius Freeland. Of this marriage one child, a son, was born. Soon Flora died and Joseph A. next married Corda, daughter of Jackson Walters, of upper Sandy Creek, Jackson County. Of this last marriage four sons and two daughters have been born. Joseph A. Fox has a large part in the old home farm on Bear Run and lives there; one of Reedy's substantial farms.

Jarret N. Fox, son of Martin P. and Anne (Jones) Fox, (Martin P. being a brother of Jasper N. Fox), was born in Monongalia County, Virginia, August 14, 1848; in Green County, Pennsylvania, March 15, 1874, was united in marriage with Mary A., daughter of Philip and Catherine L. (Mauch) McInturff, formerly of Shennandoah County, Virginia, where their daughter, Mary A., was born, 1857. Came to Roane County and settled on his farm on Bear Run, in 1874, coming at same time that his uncle Jasper N. came. To Jarret N. and Mary A. (McInturff) Fox were born, all in Roane County, one son and four daughters, two of which daughters died in infancy. The names of the living are Annie L., born December 22, 1874; Mary A., February 20, 1879, and Ethel A., November 14, 1881. The above Jarret N. Fox was an appreciated Baptist preacher for many years, serving numerous congregations and encouraged building of churches.

Franklin Pierce Fox, brother of Reverend Jarret N. Fox, mentioned above, was born in Monongalia County, western Virginia, June 27,

1854; married in Preston County, 1877, Regina M., daughter of Samuel G. and Martha Sapp. Regina, however, was born in Washington County, Pa., 1861; came to Roane County in 1880, settled on their own farm in that part of Reedy District lying on Spring Creek. To Franklin P. and Regina have been born two daughters in Monongalia County and one daughter and a son in Roane. Their names, Clara M., born February 13, 1878; Bertha Dell, 1879, Ada and Samuel's births we do not have.

Franklin Pierce Fox has been elected by the people and served two terms as a Justice of the Peace of this District.

GAINER: Stock man on Ripley turnpike, father of "Allie" Gainer, business man of Spencer.

Austin Scott Gainer, first of this name here, was born in Barbour County, W. Va., son of Nicholas and Phoebe (Poling) Gainer, natives of the Monongahela Valley, whose later home was in Gilmer County, where Austin Scott, the son, grew to manhood on his father's stock farm.

In the year 1873, in Gilmer County, W. Va., Austin Scott Gainer and Miss Susan Missouri Barnett were united in marriage. She a daughter of the Reverend Allison and Mary (Hickman) Barnett, his wife, of Doddridge County, W. Va.

Austin and Susan M., his wife, made their home in Doddridge County, stock raisers on a farm, where were born all of their children, until the year 1900. In that year they acquired the large farm on Tanners Run, on the Spencer and Ripley turnpike, and established on it the family home. Converted this farm into a good stock farm and has plied the business of raising, buying and shipping live stock ever since.

To Austin Scott and Susan M. (Barnett) Gainer have been born and by them brought up the following named children: Allison Barnett, Nicholas Beeson, Gay, Mary Belle, Dollie, Clarence, Alfred and Granville. Their marriages, further:

Allison B. married in Jackson County, W. Va., Miss Grace Parrish, on April 15, 1903. They have made their home in Spencer ever since, where he has conducted several mercantile businesses in these twenty-four years. Elected and served one term or more as a Justice of the Peace of Spencer District. Mayor of the town of Spencer one or more terms. Their children: Haymond and Clarice.

Mary Belle Gainer married a Mr. Robinson, of Gilmer County.

Dollie married Lewis Bolty in Roane County, January 14, 1903, her age 21, his age 25. Both born in Doddridge County.

Gay Gainer to William E. Donaway, August 18, 1903, his age 24, her's 21. She was born in Roane and he in Wood County, W. Va. He died a few years after marriage and left a daughter, Roxie.

Alfred Gainer, son of Austin Scott and Susan M., married Miss Leeta Crislip, December 20, 1902, his age 24, her's 20. Clarence Gainer married Lona Kelley, December 8, 1915, his age 25, her age 24.

He was born in Doddridge County, she in Roane, daughter of Albert Kelley.

Granville Gainér married Miss Corba Davis, September 6, 1913. He was born in Doddridge and she in Roane County.

GANDEE: Of Gandeeville, first settlers.

Uriah Gandee, first of the name in this country between the Kanawhas, was born in the Monongahela Valley, among its earliest settlers. We have no information at hand as to his ancestors, except those of that family name are found among the Indian fighters and defenders of those settlements.

Uriah married "Massie" (Mercy), daughter of Jesse and Grace (Tanner) Hughes, of the first settlers of the valley. This, the Jesse Hughes of the wonderous fame as a scout, guide and single-handed slayer of Indians; hero of all historians of Border Warfare and Frontier settlements. See "de Hass" Withers Border Warfare, "McKnight," and especially "Border Settlers of North Western Virginia," by L. V. McWhorter, who makes half his title "The Life of Jesse Hughes."

Uriah and Massie (Hughes) Gandee, his wife, came to the upper Pocatalico and made their home near the watershed between the Kanawhas, about the year 1823. They had left the Monongahela Valley some ten years before coming to this safe and satisfactory home. They first settled on the western side of the great Ohio River, on what has been long known as Old Town Flats, at that place their eldest child, William, afterward known as Captain William Gandee, was born in the year 1813. So it is observed that he was a boy of thirteen when they arrived at this place, now Gandeeville. Grace, Massie's mother, came here after the death of Jesse Hughes, which occurred near Ravenswood, in the autumn of 1829,' says McWhorter's, and lived with Uriah and Massie Gandee until her death.

There is much speculation by historians whether Massie or her sister, Martha, was that daughter of Jesse Hughes which was captured by the Indians at her home on Hackers Creek on the Monongahela—1787— and carried away and kept in the Indian camps on Sandusky Plains, where she was surrendered to Jesse Hughes, her father, after the treaty of Fort Harmer, January 9, 1789.

The time of Martha's capture is a notable one in all histories because it was at the time of the massacre of the families of the Wests, Edmund, Sr., and Edmund, Jr., as told by Withers, was on December 5, 1787. McWhorter is positive in his statements, and adds to what Withers tells, the further information that Martha was the eldest child of Jesse Hughes, and "she was then fourteen years old. When captured she was returning home from the house of John Hacker," about four miles up the creek, "where she had gone to get a pup." McWhorter makes the further positive statement that she "was a prisoner two years and nine months." And "Hughes recognizes her as soon as he caught sight of her in the Indian country."

The tradition in the Gandee family here is confirmatory of all McWhorter tells, and that of the other historians as well, except that McWhorter's dates and time are the correct ones. Jacob Gandee, grandson of Massie, now living near Gandeeville, adds that the fireside story in the family, which he had heard so often, was that Martha was captured and carried away as told in Histories, and no word was heard of her for the two and more years ensuing. It was believed she was dead, for the Indians had killed other maidens and children and spared none on that foray. That during Martha's unknown existence another daughter was born to Jesse and Grace, his wife, and they named this child Martha as a return of her that was gone; that when the first Martha was restored to them, there were exclamations, "It is the mercy of God!" So the younger Martha was rechristened "Mercy," which, under the old Virginia manner of speech in which the "r" was suppressed and the "e" sounded as "e" in they, the name "Massie" and hence was always so pronounced. This spelling is that given by McWhorter and others.

Martha married Jacob Bonnett, 1792. See family name, "Bonnett."

Other children of Jesse Hughes, brothers and sisters of Massie Gandee, our pioneer mother, are:

Nancy Agnes, married George W. Hanshaw, long a resident near mouth of Straight Fork, three miles out from Ravenswood.

Rachel, married William Cottrell and lived on Hackers Creek many years and after the death of William, came and settled on upper Spring Creek, about six miles from Spencer.

Sudna, married Elijah Runner and they lived near Sandyville, Jackson County, many years.

Elizabeth, married James Stanley and lived on Mud Run, of Sandy Creek, in Jackson County.

Lourania, married Uriah Sayre, lived in Meiggs County, Ohio, on the west bank of the Ohio.

Thomas lived on the Ohio, not far below Ravenswood, and there died.

William, married a Miss Staats, lived a lengthy life on Mill Creek, below Ripley, in Jackson County.

Jesse, Jr., married Susana Mock, in the year 1800.

To Uriah and Massie (Hughes) Gandee, first settlers of Gandeeville, part of Pocatalico, were born the following named sons and daughters:

Jesse, who married a Miss Mary "Dority," May 3, 1829, Rev. Barnabas Cook officiating clergyman.

Sarah, married Charles Droddy, whose name see.

William, afterward "Captain William and Squire."

Lucinda, married Abram Raines.

Cynthia, wife of Henry Runnion, of Lick Fork.

Harriet, or Hattie, wife of Mac D. Ferrell.

James S. Gandee. He was twice married; first wife being Margaret LeForce, the second wife being Rachel, daughter of Thomas Fields, of

Lower Flat Fork. He afterwards, later in life, moved to Jackson County and died not long ago at Ripley. They reared some children whose names I do not have. Except the daughter, Mahala J., who married Noah F. Pence, January 6, 1881. See Pence.

William Gandee, third son of Uriah and Massie, was born in the year 1813, at Old Town Flats, Meigs County, Ohio. Married a Miss Margaret Casto, of the Jackson County Castos. They succeeded to the ancestral home lands or part of them. William was for twenty-five years a prominent citizen here, taking part in all public affairs; became one of the Justices of the Peace of the county, took part in formation and organization of Roane County, sitting as one member of the first County Court. On outbreak of the Civil War was pro-Union as against secession; became a captain of Home Guards, and led his men in defense of and keeping of legal authority in the county during the five years of that awful turmoil, and so behaved as to hold the friendship and respect of even returned Confederates until the time of his death several years after ending of that conflict. He was elected and served in the sessions of the State Legislature, 1871, as Delegate for Roane County.

To Captain William Gandee and his wife, Margaret (Casto), were born and reared three sons and three daughters. Their names in order of their respective births, are: William, Jr.; Cynthia, who married Henry Patrick; Frederick; George W., who was twice married, first to a Miss Green, next to Sarah Shouldis, of Poca; Martha, who married Thomas Marks, of Walton District; Jemima, wife of Samuel Lee, Jr., and Jacob; and Sarah, wife of George W. Damewood.

Jacob Gandee, son of William, still on the old home lands, and the one who gave me the main facts of the Gandee family, married Josephine Snodgrass in 1872. She was the daughter of Isaac Snodgrass, early settler of Big Lick. To Jacob and Josephine (Snodgrass) Gandee have been born fourteen, of whom nine have grown up and become citizens of this county.

Frederick Gandee, son of William and Margaret (Casto) Gandee, was born here, July 31, 1842; married Carolina Canterbury, daughter of Zadoc and Marcenia (Snow) Canterbury, February 2, 1864, in Walton District. Caroline was born in Monroe County, Virginia, September 25, 1843. Frederick was a "Union sympathiser" during the "War of the Secessions," and he says in his biography, dictated to Hardestrys, 1882, "I was in the seven days' battle at Spencer." He means the series of shootings and surrendered in 1862, by Colonel Rathbone to General Albert G. Jenkins, given in this book in the chapter "History of the City of Spencer."

Frederick served in the regularly enlisted ranks of the Union army, 1861 to 1864, was in the battles of Charleston, Cloyd Mountain, New River Bridge, Lexington, Carter's Farm, Winchester, Hall Town, Martinsville, Berryville, Opequon and Fisher's Hill, as a member of Company B 9th West Virginia Infantry.

After the war he was elected and served two terms as a Justice of the Peace of Walton District; was a Delegate for the County of Roane in the 18th Session—1887—of the West Virginia Legislature.

To Frederick and Caroline (Canterbury) Gandee, his wife, were born the following children: Martha M., 1866; Henry D., 1868, died in youth; Lewis W., 1869; Sarah M., 1871; John D., 1873; Mary J., 1876; Jemima A., 1877; Alice M., 1880, and Zadoc William, May 20, 1882.

GEARY:

Mathew Geary, whose family name was conferred on the magisterial district of that name in recognition of his worth as a citizen of the county, was born in County Down, Ireland, May 10, 1791, died in Roane County, West Virginia, January 24, 1865.

He came to America, having his younger brother, John, with him, and landed on these shores about the years 1823-24; within a year after landing the brothers were found at the salt works—Malden, called "The Licks' 'at that time, learning the ways of the wildwoods of America. John came to his death by drowning in the Kanawha while working there. On Big Sandy of Elk River near what is now the boundary line between Geary District and Kanawha County, lived John Ashley, a pioneer who came from North Carolina and settled there fifteen years previous to the year 1825, among his family was a daughter, Elizabeth Almira, whom Mathew met, woed, won and married at her home there in the year 1825; took her back to the Great Kanawha, where his work was and there they began the long and happy married life of successful pioneers, living on the Great Kanawha the first nine years, during which time money was saved and children born; at the end of this nine years Mathew bought a large tract of land—twelve to fifteen hundred acres—lying about and over that part of Big Sandy where is, what for more than fifty years, has been known as "Osbornes Mills"; Mathew and his family at once moved on this land; Almira was now back among her people, the Ashleys.

Among the things soon done by Mathew was the erection of a water grist mill; for this work he employed Peter Darnell, a millwright. His mill and his home at once became the neighborhood center; there were at that time, 1835, some eight or ten families within a radius of five miles. The history of this neighborhood center is part of the history of Geary District, to which chapter the reader should turn, if more interested in the district than in the Geary family.

To Mathew and E. Almira (Ashley) Geary, his wife were born and grew to manhood and womanhood the following named children:

Isabella, July 25, 1835, married Dr. Patrick McKan, 1851; Caroline married Lewis Ashley, pioneer; Julia married Jacob Young, farmer; Salina M. married Dr. Benjamin M. Helsley, then of Clendenin, later, Walton; Elizabeth married George W. Osborne, of Big Sandy; William A. married Estaline Jarrett; John M. married Phoebe E. Carper; Leona Virginia, born August 15, 1847, married John H. Osborne, December 9,

1868, of her neighborhood; America, born Nov. 24, 1849, married Dr. Lewis A. Rader, April 22, 1868; of further concerning the daughters above named, see the names of their husbands in proper alphabetic place.

John M. Geary, son of Mathew and E. Almira (Ashley) Geary, was born at the ancestral home on Big Sandy, March 25, 1837; on the 28th day of December, 1860, he married Miss Phoebe Elmira Carper, born in Giles County, Virginia, June 10, 1841, daughter of Nicholas and Sarah (Nida) Carper, pioneer residents of Upper Left Hand at the time of this marriage. John M. and his wife appear to have divided the distance between the homes of their families and settled on a large tract of land near and about the mouth of Upper Left Hand, soon a neighborhood center, and afterward for the purpose of a United States post office designation was named "Amma," and at this place they made the well known "John Geary Place," and there spent a long and successful life. To John M. and Phoebe E. (Carper) Geary, his wife, were born and reared the following children:

Lectra A., January 29, 1863, married John Engle, January 23, 1883.

Patrick Vauley, August 16, 1865, married Annie S. Smith, of that country.

Frederick W., born 1868.

Charles Mathew, born 1871, married Elsie B. Riffell.

Amma J., married John H. Parris, merchant of Geary District. See "Parris."

Nora married M. E. Morely, of Geary District, who is a dealer in oil and gas properties.

Myrtle B. married John H. Johnson, skilled workman at drilling oil wells.

William Alexander Geary, son of Mathew and Elizabeth Almira (Ashley), his wife, was born May 5, 1845, at the old homestead, long known as Osbornes Mills; married Miss Esteline Jarrett, born at Clendenin, year 1843, the daughter of Vincent and Caroline (Atkinson) Jarrett. William A. succeeded to the home part of the large acreage of lands left by the father Mathew, and at that home he and his wife spent the long and prosperous life of frugal industry; there they reared their family of eight sons and two daughters, whose names and somewhat further about them we have as follows:

Samuel W. died in childhood.

Annie Silvin, born 1868, married Perry S. Young, March 5, 1893, his age 26; their home is Clendenin; they have three sons and two daughters.

Mathew Byron, born 1871, went West and there married Miss Edna Johnson, of Idaho.

Lewis Melvin, born 1873, yet a bachelor.

Ora Belle, born March 12, 1877, married Thomas E. Vineyard, year 1901; he is of the Vineyard family of Looneyville; also of the City of Spencer; in the chapter of this book: "History of Spencer," see his career. To Thomas Elbert and Ora B. (Geary) Vineyard, his wife, have been born one son and one daughter, their names: Richard, born 1894, and Julia Ann, 1918; their home is in Spencer, West Virginia.

Wehrley B., born 1879, is a merchant of Charleston, West Virginia.

James Morgan, 1881, married Amie Osborne, daughter of Lewis Dranche Osborne.

William Hunter, married Mattie Runnion, of Kentucky; their home is in Ohio.

Okey Jarrett, 1888, married Nellie Belcher, of Clendenin, then; they now live in Oklahoma.

GLAZE:

Henry Glaze, son of a Lewis County family of that name, and his wife, together with several children born to them in Lewis County, came here and settled on upper Spring Creek sometime prior to the Civil War— 1861. The names of those children, we are informed, were Marshall, Stephen S., Isaac M., Henry Granville, and Sarah and Eliza.

Stepren S. served as a Union soldier; died in that service.

Marshall married, was killed by Confederate guerrillas at the home of his father on Spring Creek, sometime during the Civil War; he left a widow and at least one daughter, whose name was Henrietta; she married George Hess, son of a neighbor family, February 19, 1880.

Isaac M. married Miss Sarah Jane Cleavenger, of Reedy, April 14, 1866; made their lifetime home on Left Fork of Reedy on lands adjoining the old Cleavenger farm. To Isaac M. and Sarah J. were born and reared the following children: Melvina ("Nellie"), wife of Dr. A. L. Crislip, mother of Dr. Chester Crislip, of Spencer.

Everette W., who married Cynthia Wright, October 17, 1894, his age 25, her age 20.

Emory, yet a bachelor; Carl and B. Hoy, and Effie. We do not have the marriages of the last three—if married.

Henry Granville Glaze, son of Henry, first mentioned, married Miss Arvilla Rogers, September 10, 1868; she was a daughter of Benjamin Rogers of near Spencer. To them were born and reared two sons named Lonah and Onah.

Lonah Glaze married Bertha McClain of upper Spring Creek, the 28th of April, 1898, his age 23, her age 20.

Clair Glaze, grandson of H. Granville, graduated from the Spencer High School in its class of 1918.

GOAD: Of Geary and Walton Districts.

The prominent Goads, as early settlers were John Goad and James Goad: Squire John of Big Left Hand, now on State Road No. 14, and James Goad of Big Sandy near Osbornes Mills. All we have of the history of this family is as follows:

Aaron Goad and John Goad, two brothers, born in Floyd County, Virginia, about the years, 1820 and 1822, respectively, arrived in the Big Sandy country about the year 1844, young men seeking adventures "in the West."

Aaron soon married ...., a daughter of ....
..............., and made their home on lower Big Sandy; to them were born two sons, named Peter and James, the latter is the Jame Goad mentioned first in this article. We have no further information as to Aaron and his son, Peter, except that Peter married a Miss Mary Long of Ritchie County, West Virginia.

James Goad, son of Aaron, married Martha Carper, a daughter of Nicholas and Sarah (Nida) Carper, of Upper Left Hand, and they began their wedded life and conquest of the forest near Osbornes Mills, and served out all the remainder of their lives at that place. To James and Martha (Carper) Goad were born three sons and no daughters. The names of these sons are A. W. ("Weck") who married a neighbor's daughter, Eva Osborne.

The second son of James and Martha, named C. Ward Goad, as yet has never married, owns most of the home farm, but is an invalid in a Hospital. The third son, Willet Goad, married Ada Runnion, of the Runnion family of Spencer. "Weck" and Willet are business men of Clendennin, (1926).

John Goad, brother of Aaron, both born in Floyd County, Virginia, as first stated, married Mary J. Taylor, daughter of William and Mahala (Cromwell) Taylor, and they began their married lives on Big Left Hand, as stated. Their home and lands soon attracted attention as the best in those parts.

John Goad was a prominent citizen for many years next succeeding the war of 1861-5; was elected by the people and served one term as Justice of the Peace, about the years 1880 to 1884. John and Mary J., his wife, lived a bountiful life and ended their days on the farm on which they commenced. It is now the home of their son, John.

To John, Sr., and Mary J. (Taylor), his wife, were born and grew up the following named children:

Sarah J., who married Joseph L. Jackson.

Ballard Preston, married Lena Foss, Minnesota.

William also married a lady in Minnesota.

Aaron George married Minerva Stewart, of Reedy. See "Stewart."

Edward Jackson married Katie Howell.

Fannie M. married James K. Robinson, of Walton District.

Albert J. married Nellie Knight, of Iowa.

John, Jr., born in 1876, married Mae Lewis, a daughter of Edward and Mary (McChesney) Lewis, of the southern part of Walton District, in the year 1905. Their home is the ancestral Goad place. To John and Mae (Lewis) Goad has been born one son and three daughters, all youths yet at home.

George, the youngest of this family, born in 1878, left in the year 1895, to seek his fortune in the West, settling first in Minnesota.

GOFF: Of Reedy.

Salathiel Goff, of Weston, Lewis County, came to Reedy in 1842, with his wife, Margaret (Flesher) Goff, whom he had married in Lewis County. With them came three sons, John G., Peyton and Alonzo. and three daughters, Elizabeth, born March 17, 1827, married in Reedy, Joseph Stewart, son of the pioneer William Stewart. Rebecca, who became the wife of Josiah Stutler, and Mary, who married Christopher Stutler, brother of Josiah, Sr.

Salathiel Goff owned and made the first of the pioneer farms below the "Three Forks." Dempsey P. Fisher's being a part of this farm. His son, Alonzo, enlisted in the Union cause, 1862, served and was wounded. Peyton enlisted in the Confederate army and served that cause. After that war Salathiel, his wife and two sons, Alonzo and Peyton, removed to Texas, leaving here the three daughters above mentioned and the son, John G. Goff. Salathiel Goff was either grandfather or uncle of William R. Goff, of Spencer.

John G. Goff, of the above family, married Miss Elizabeth Stewart, daughter of William Stewart, pioneer and first settler at "Three Forks of Reedy."

It must be inferred from Roane County marriage records that John G. Goff was born in Lewis County, W. Va., in the year 1825. He made a second marriage, year 1887, to Lavinia Harlow (nee Pursley), his age given as 62, her's 40 years.

John G. and Elizabeth Goff, when first married, lived for a time near Reedyville, later acquired the first farm west of the town of Reedy, where they completed their span of life. They brought up at least three sons; we remember these, their names in order of their ages, Charles, Harvey and Payton Stewart.

GOUGH: Of Reedy.

Thomas Gough, first of the name here, came to Reedy about the year 1835, guessing from the age of his eldest child. He was of French Huguenot descent and from his intrepid disposition must have come from the eastern shores in response to a high spirit of adventure, for he was neither merchant nor soldier at that time. About the year 1836 he married Miss Alitha Catherine Flesher, daughter of George A. and Sallie (Conley) Flesher, of Left Reedy. They obtained a farm out of the Flesher lands and made their lifetime home there.

He was loyal to Virginia in the Civil War, and its armies' trusted scout; chased and fired on so much by Union soldiers of garrisons at Spencer or patrols, and escaped unhit, that it was common remark, "he has a charmed life." For years after the war when anyone picked up a musket ball on Left Reedy his unfailing remark was "There's another bullet that the Yankees fired at Tom Gough."

To Thomas and Alitha Goff, his wife, were born the following named children: Albert, Marshall, Jane, Mary, Pery, Monroe, Jackson, Thomas Jefferson and Florence.

Albert G. Gough, son of Thomas and Alitha C. (Flesher) Gough, married Nancy C. Board, January 5, 1859. She was a daughter of William K. Board, of below Reedy. To them were born the following sons and daughters:
Charles F., Alitha Catherine, Sarah Margaret, Cora Ellen, Anna Letticia, Mahala and Mary Alice. All these married and made homes in and about Reedy at first, later have scattered to other counties and states, except Charles F.

Charles F. Gough, son of Albert and Nancy C. (Board), his wife, married Susan C. Blosser, of Reedy, September 1, 1882; she a daughter of Robert Blosser, killed in the mill explosion in 1866. Charles F. had learned the carpenter trade, moved to Spencer about 1898 and here became a building contractor and followed that for some ten years. To Charles F. and Susan C. (Blosser) were born and by them reared to citizenship in Spencer, the following named children: Peter Frederick; Ella Jane, married John Newlon of Spencer, January 29, 1911, age 24; Samuel R.; Pearl, who married Orel Riley; Skoval K. married Hazel Gilpin, 1919; Ray Albert, married Ruth Runnion (Widow Lamb), June 1, 1926, and is now a young business man of Spencer, W. Va.; Herman Hugh, and Robert Eugene, this last died in first bloom of young manhood.

Further of the children of Thomas Gough, pioneer:
Jane married Jerrard Cline.
Mary Louise was twice married, to the first husband, William Harrison, Hildreth, April 25, 1873; the other husband being Henry Horton.
Pery, married Sevillia Stewart;
Monroe married, 1881, S. E. Cheuveront;
Florence married Louis R. Davis, 1868.

GRAHAM: Of Reedy.

Joseph Graham and Elizabeth Jane, his wife, arrived on Middle Fork of Reedy, purchased five hundred acres of land and commenced a home on it some time prior to the Civil War. He was a real Scotchman of the thin-faced, slender, straight-limbed, erect type. Elizabeth Jane was of a rather rugged broad featured form. They had been married in Baltimore, Maryland, and one or more of their oldest children were born in Baltimore. They were devout Wesleyan Methodists in religious faith and practice. Their sons and daughters were: Melissa, who married T. M. Brunner, in 1866; Mary A., who married Richard "Dick" Dulin; David, William, Sarah Alcinda, and Joseph, Jr.

David and William went "West" about the year 1875; Sarah Alcinda, a young girl of winning charm, married Jacob Tichnell Chancey, son of Roswell R. Chancey, September 8, 1874. See "Chancey."

Joseph R. Graham, youngest of this family, married Miss Margaret (Maggie) E. Davis, of Wirt County. They made their home for some twenty years on the Middle Fork of Reedy, and there reared one son and two daughters; their names: Clarence, who married Alma Fields, in

Wood County; Elizabeth married a Mr. Givens, and Orlie was not married at time we last knew of her. The family moved to and made their home at Rockland in Ohio, just over from Parkersburg, where they have lived for the last fifteen years.

GREENLEAF: Squire John mentioned in Chapter I.

John Greenleaf and his family settled on upper Mill Creek at what is now known as Gay, in Jackson County, "in a very early day,' 'is all we can learn from his descendants. Some entries in the county court order books spell or enter his name as "John Greenleaves." Hardesty's History has it so in its paragraph on the History of Roane County; but conveyances and other papers signed by him has it John Greenleaf. His grandson, Virgil Greenleaf, says he never heard of it as "Greenleaves" or "Greanleaves."

The family tradition is that John Greenleaf was born or spent the first years of his manhood on the upper waters of the Little Kanawha. He was living on his farm on Mill Creek when the County of Roane was formed; his family all grown up then, and had married for second wife, Catherine Cox, widow of Phillip D. Cox—mentioned as pioneer merchant of Village of Reedy. See Ch. V, this work.

To John Greenleaf and ...., his first wife, were born and by them brought up on Mill Creek, the following sons and daughters—written here in order of supposed births:

George Riley, Elliott, Seymore, John, Jr., Benjamin, Thornton, Ruhama "Ruie," Caroline and Mary.

Further about these sons and daughters—Greenleafs:

George Riley Greenleaf married Miss Harriett Raines, June 3, 1856. She is a daughter of John Raines of Flat Fork. The newly-weds made their lifetime home on Flat Fork.

To George R. and Harriett (Raines) his wife, were born and by them reared the following sons and daughters: Filmore, Mary M., John Franklin, Virgil H. These all married and reared families most of them on Pocatalico. Virgil H. married Katie Ryan, September 13, 1891. She was a daughter of Rev. Thomas P. Ryan and wife, of Trace Fork. Virgil H. and Katie have reared three sons and six daughters.

John Franklin Greenleaf, son of George R. Greenleaf and Harriett (Raines), married as "Frank"—Miss Martha M. Hunt, February 10, 1884, his age 23, her's 16. He was chief of police of Spencer one time and lived here.

HALL: Of Middle Geary District.

John Hall is a son of Margaret (Drake) Hall, native of Geary District, was born in 1871; married year 1891, Laura Noe, a daughter of Daniel Noe of the Geary District Noes. He was active and early in life took part in all public affairs; was elected and served his district one term as justice of the peace; many times member of the district board of education; a notary public and scrivener for his part of the county. His farm on Granishe Creek comprises some four hundred acres.

To John and Laura (Noe), his wife, have been born and by them reared five sons and three daughters; their names as follows: Fred, Elbert, Burl and Harry; the daughters: Cloy, Georgia R., and Icy Pearl.

The first three named sons served in the World War; Burl died, after returning, from injuries by poison gas hurled on him at the fighting front.

HALL: Of Geary and Walton Districts.

William and Anna (Fullen) Hall, with their two sons, James and Absalom "Abb", came from Russell County, Virginia, and settled somewhere on the upper waters of Pocatalico in the year 1857; bought some land, cleared and made a small farm home and rearer the children and closed their life-spans here. There may have been a daughter or daughters of this family but we have never heard of them.

James Hall, eldest son of above family, was born in Russell County, Virginia, December 5, 1844; grew to manhood here as above indicated. "In Spencer, February 6, 1867," having just returned from his long service as a soldier of the Union Armies in the "Rebellion" he married Rachel Vineyard, born December 1, 1845, daughter of William and Sarah (Looney) Vineyard. They made their home first on lands near the Vineyards of Smithfield, and later he moved and made his home and farm on head of Left Hand of Big Sandy. To James and Rachel (Vineyard), his wife, were born: Eva, in 1868; Wonder, 1870; Stella, 1872; Susan, 1875; Charity, 1877; James D., 1879, and William V., 1881. The wife, Rachel, having died, James Hall married for a second wife, Nancy C. Justice, a daughter of Captain William Justice, of Left Hand. To them, James and Rachel, were born the following children: Romie Clarence, who married Icy Smith, daughter of the Rev. J. Herby Smith; Annie, who married Robert Burkehart, of Charleston; Brooks, Sallie, Hazel, Cecil, Beatrice; these last five are yet young and none of them married.

Absalom (or "Abb") Hall, son of William and Anna (Fullen) Hall, grew up and yet resides in Walton District; on March 4, 1880, married Rebecca J. Jones, of Walton. After hear death he married Mina Cottle, of Reedy, August 25, 1920, his age 54, her age 42. Mina was a daughter of Charles and Minerva (Stewart) Cottle, and had been formerly married to George Burgess, father of her daughter Beulah. Of the children of Absalom by either wife I do not know.

HAMMACK: Of Smithfield and Walton Districts.

William Hammack and his wife, Sarah, daughter of Wiley Ashley, of Colonial families of Virginia, were married in Kanawha County, year 1822, came to Pocatalico and settled near the mouth of Johnson Creek, about the year 1825. The names of their four sons and four daughters: St. Clair (by the family pronounced "Sinkler"), Sylvester, John, Andrew; Susan, Rebecca, Cynthia and Catherine. All married young and made home farms in Pocatalico Valleys.

St. Clair married Catherine Phillips of lower Poca, November 24, 1840. Their children whom we can name, are Meredith, Martin, and William Wiley Hammack.

William Wiley Hammack was born May 28, 1854; engaged in public school teaching early in life, taught ten terms in all; took active part in all the first teachers institutes commenced in the counyt about the year 1880; married Dicy Paxton, daughter of John and Mary (Vineyard) Paxton. Wm. Wiley and Dicy made their life's home farm on part of the ancestral lands on Poca above the mouth of Johnson Creek; they reared three sons and five daughters whose names are as follows: Henry Lewis, William Clinton, John St. Clair, Laura May, Mary Blandis, wife of Bert E. Summers, near Smithfield line; Lucy Elton, wife of Homer Stump; Eva Susan, wife of Harvey R. Carper, and Mary Octavia, wife of Clary S. Carper.

We have no information on life of Sylvester, John and Andrew, sons of William and Sarah (Ashley) Hammack.

Susan, daughter of William and Sarah Hammack, became the wife of Peter Hammack, the nephew of her father who arrived here a young man from Virginia. Peter and Susan, his wife, made their home on Johnson Creek where they lived a long and useful life. Susan was for thirty years the efficient midwife serving all the surrounding country, the numbers to whom she gave first aid, that arrived to robust manhood or womanhood testifies her efficiency. Of the children of Susan and Peter, we can name, John, Perry and Elizabeth. Perry Hammack was elected and served one term as county assessor, 1904 to 1909. John and Perry owned and operated a sawmill located on Johnson Creek about the year 1900. On an unfortunate day, Perry, working at a log on the carriage while the circular saw was in motion, kicked at a clamp or pointed fastener on top of the log to bend it out of the way of the advancing saw-teeth and his foot struck in such a way that it was seized by the saw-teeth and severed at the ankle joint. This is why he was known as "the lame man" when he was making his campaign.

We have no information as to the careers of Rebecca and Catherine, daughters of William and Sarah Hammack.

Cynthia Hammack, daughter of William and Sarah (Ashley) Hammack, became the wife of Presley Vineyard, senior, and mother of his ten children. See Vineyard.

HARDMAN:

As the name "Hardman" suggests, the Hardmans are of German extraction, from Pennsylvania by way of the Shanandoah, Virginia, and Monongahela country, thence to this upper Reedy; the majority, if not all, members of the family are fair skinned people. We find Thomas Hardman, Sr., mentioned in writings indicating he was among the settlers coming here from Monongalia Valley in the early forties, first clearing up the land at or about where Reedyville now is.

Thomas Hardman and Rebecca (Goff) Hardman reared seven children: William, John, George, Sase S., James E., Drusilla and Tina, all born before the Civil War (1861). These children all married near and reared families. Of descendants of Thomas and Rebecca (Goff) Hardman, we give here the following concerning them:

William Hardman, son of Thomas and Rebecca, married Diana (Burdett), granddaughter of Martin Argabrite of upper Reedy, and made a large farm next above what is now Peniel; the "Bill Hardman place," long spoken of as a best homestead. Their children's names are Thomas, Jr.; John M., married Mollie Fouty; "Sase" I., married Carloine Robey; Rebecca Jane, born 1851, married Thaddeus Kelley of Harper District; Rachel Ellen, married John W. Kelley, a brother of Thaddeus Kel'ey above named.

John Hardman, son of Thomas and Rebecca, married Sarah, daughter of Samuel Romie of Upper Reedy; the names of the twelve children of John and Sarah are, Orlando, who married Margaret, daughter of John Fields; John Middleton, married Electra, daughter of Isaac Scott of Spencer; Lee, George, Ferd, Robert. Josephine, wife of Lemuel Crislip; Mary Carminta, married S. Columbus Thrash of upper Reedy District, who are the parents of A'bertus Lee Thrash, now (1926) cashier of First National Bank of Reedy; Fred Thrash, farmer on the old farm on Middle Fork, and a daughter, Beulah Thrash.

Ninth child of John and Sarah Hardman is Ella, who married Marshall A. C. Board, son of A. Sandy Board of Reedy; Lola and Ada Hardman.

George. son of Thomas and Rebecca (Goff) Hardman; of him we have no information.

"Sase." son of Thomas and Rebecca Hardman, married Tina, a daughter of William Board, on upper Middle Fork of Reedy. James E., fifth son of Thomas and Rebecca Hardman, settled on Colt Run of Left Reedy.

Drusilla, sixth child of Thomas and Rebecca Hardman, married Captain Albert G. Ingraham (we spell it with the "aham" because thus he, himself, wrote it).

Tina, the second daughter and seventh child of Thomas and Rebecca Hardman, became the wife of Kelles Argabrite, son of Martin Argabrite, of upper Reedy.

Four sons of George W. and Rachel (Goff) Hardman, of Lewis County, later Gilmer County, later Calhoun County, West Virginia, made their homes in Roane County; their names: Sylvester, Casset C., George, Columbus and Orlando. The last named two settled in Reedy District (which see); the first named two, about 1867, settled and improved large farms in Curtis District. George went to Calhoun County. There were thirteen children in all.

Sylvester Hardman son of George W. and Rachel, was born in Gilmer County, August 22, 1836; married Martha, daughter of George and Susan (Horton) Crow, in Jackson County, West Virginia, on March 20, 1872. George Crow was born in Green County, Pennsylvania, and

HISTORY OF ROANE COUNTY   539

Susanna Horton was born in County Queen, Ireland; commenced their wedded life together in Monroe County, Ohio, where Martha was born, January 15, 1844. They came to Jackson County, West Virginia, when Martha was three years old, 1847. To Sylvester and Martha (Crow) Hardman, were born in Roane County, three sons and one daughter, names and dates of births as follows: Ira R., December 18, 1872; Susanna, October 3, 1874; Charles C., June 24, 1879, and Owen Ruby, 1885. Of these children of Sylvester and Martha (Crow) Hardman, we further write:

Ira R. married Miss Hattie Clark; they live at Grantsville, West Virginia at this time (1926).

Susanna married William Brown Petty, of Reedyville, 9th day of May, 1894; his age 24, her age 20. Of this marriage of "Susie" and W. Brown, two daughters were born: Edna, who became wife of Guy Sinnett, hardware merchant of Spencer. The other daughter's name is Nina, who is a youth yet with her mother, resident in Spencer; the father, Wm. Brown Petty, having died some years ago.

Charles C. married Gertrude, daughter of James B. and Julia (Hoskins) Thomasson of near Reedyville, June 22, year 1904; his age then 25, her age 22. Of this marriage two sons and one daughter are here; their names in order of their ages are, Floyd, Willis and Martha; the first named now approaching manhood; the second, Willis, a youth about 16 years of age, and the last. Martha, about twelve years. Charles C. Hardman succeeded to the old home place, by purchasing shares, and became a prominent sheep and cattle raiser; was a public lecturer for the department of agriculture at time the State took hold to encourage farming. He died at the very highest of his usefulness and popularity in the State. His widow, Gertrude Thomasson Hardman, and the boys, still have the farm and some remnants of the once high bred stock herd that Charles C. had built up before his death.

Owen Ruby Hardman, son of Sylvester and Martha (Crow) Hardman, was born on the Reedy farm in the year 1885; at early manhood came to Spencer and engaged in the produce business, followed that a few years. On September 24, 1913, he married Martha Grace, daughter of George W. Holswade of Spencer History; his age then 28, her age 25. Of this marriage several children have been born, their names and ages we leave for a biographer. Owen Ruby Hardman a few years ago launched into the road and bridge building business, at which he is reputed to have prospered. He is at this time (1926) president of the Traders Trust & Banking Company, bank of Spencer.

This ancestor, Sylvester Hardman, in addition to making a fine stock farm on Reedy, was some years prominent as a purchaser and transporter of timber of Reedy's big forest; also was elected and served one term as State Senator, 21st and 22nd sessions, 1893-1895.

Cassett Hardman, son of George W. and Rachel (Goff) Hardman, was born when their home was on Hughes River, October 8, 1839, so says his wife; died on Reedy, November 2, 1925. He united in marriage with Miss Isabella R. Burdette, April 9, 1867, in Spencer. She is the daughter of William Burdette (see Burdette). They at once commenced their married life on forest lands on Left Reedy below Reedyville.

He was one of the partnership "Hardman Brothers," who dealt largely in marketing timber from that locality; theirs was soon an attractive and productive farm; later they erected the second of the good frame farm houses of that creek. Isabelle R., now a wiodw, still lives there.

To Cassett and Isabelle R. (Burdette) Hardman were born and by them reared the one son and two daughters: Gay, Leota and Sallie. Further of these:

Leota married Calvin Smith Vandal on September 13, 1887; his age then 24, her's 19. See Spencer District, Chapter VII.

Sallie married, first, Eddie Mount, October 16, 1897; her age then 21, his age 27. Some children were born, and Mount died. Afterward, April 21, 1906, Sallie, widow, married Elzie Cummings, she 26, he 25. He was born in Lewis County, West Virginia. He is noted as having one of Curtis District's finest farms.

Gay Hardman, only son of Cassett and Isabell, his wife, married Miss Tisha Miller, of lower Spring Creek, on the first day of March, 1896, his age 24, her's 19; she was a daughter of Hezekiah and Jemima (Vandal) Miller. One son and one daughter was born of this union.

Columbus Hardman, son of George Washington and Rachel (Goff) Hardman, one of the first of the family to settle on left Reedy, married Miss Jennie Hosey in Calhoun County, about the year 1871; they established their home at once on Left Reedy, one-fourth mile above the place now called Billings railroad station; both here lived out their spans of married life, in a comfortable home. They reared only two children, their names Lora and Harry M.

Lora married Thomas H. Depue, November 18, 1894, her age 21, his age 20. He was born in Jackson County, West Virginia; died here.

Harry M. married Miss Ora L. Hamrick, January 5, 1910, his age 26, her age 21. She was a daughter of G. J. Hamrick, then resident farmer near Seaman. See "Chenowith."

George Hardman, son of George W. and Rachel (Goff) Hardman, married Miss Virginia Burdette, "Dina" the record has it, on October 23, 1867. They made their home in Calhoun County, where they have lived ever since.

Orlando Hardman, son of George W. and Rachel (Goff) Hardman, was born March 8, 1846; married Miss Jennie Thorn in Wirt County, West Virginia, June 20, 1872; she was a daughter of Zadoc Thorn and wife, of Main Reedy below "Three Forks." They made their first home for some years in Calhoun County; then with their family of several children came to Billings on Reedy about the first of 1896, where he erected on his lands next the railroad station the best residence seen there; he died

HISTORY OF ROANE COUNTY   541

there, and there the widow yet lives. His farm when he first acquired it was the tract of more than five hundred acres, called the Hugh Kyger place.

To Orlando and "Jennie" or Virginia (Thorn), his wife, were born and by them reared—as I am informed—two sons and three daughters; their names: Everette, Russell, Lucy V., Rachel E. and Lillie Bell. The girls married at this Kyger and Billings home.

Rached to Edgar S. Harpold, June 7, 1894, her age 19, his age 24; he was born in Jackson County, she in Calhoun.

Lucy V. married John McClung of Reedy, June 26, 1901; their ages not shown on the marriage record.

Lillie Belle married Walter Hugh Ryland, October 16, 1895, her age 20, his age 24; he was born in Richmond, Virginia.

Everette and Dr. Russell T. are at this time young business men stirring mention of themselves sometimes, but whether married or not we can not say.

HAROLD: Of Geary District: Elias Harold first.

Elias Harold and Barbara (Simmons) Harold, his wife, whom he had married in Pendleton County West Virginia, came to Roane County about the year 1850, with all their family then about grown; their names: Jesse, Daniel, Michael, William and John.

Further of this family:

Jesse Harold, son of Elias and Barbara, married Mariah Rogers (widow), daughter of Robert Ogden, on December 20, 1866; they made their home farm on upper Big Sandy; to them were born and by them reared two sons and one daughter whose names and births are:

Jasper Newton, born 1867; George Carrey, 1877, and America Angeline; she married Newton J. Jarvis.

Daniel Harold, son of Elias and Barbara, was twice married: first to Mary Vaughn, August 30, 1866; of this marriage six children were born. Mary having died, Daniel again married, this time with Salina Hart, on July 17, 1886, his age 43, her age 31; of this marriage were born six children.

Michael Harold, son of Elias and Barbara, married twice; first wife, Miss Elizabeth Ogden, daughter of Osborne and Sarah (Petitt) Ogden, of Big Sandy; of this marriage was born one child only, his name Wesley C., in the year 1872. He is now the Reverend W. C. Harold, popular minister of the Baptist Church; served the Baptist congregations of the City of Spencer, in the first years of his preaching.

William Harold, son of Elias and Barbara, married Debora Cottrell; they have three sons and one daughter.

John Christopher Harold, fifth son of Elias and Barbara, was twice married: first wife, Mary Drake, daughter of Sutton Drake, on March 31, 1882; they had one daughter. Mary having died, J. Christopher united in marriage, March 7, 1884, with Caroline Hardway, then seventeen years of age; they have reared four sons and four daughters.

HARPER:

Asa Harper, born in Tazwell County, Virginia (to be distinguished from Asa, born in Russell County, Virginia, son of John and Rachel (Taylor) Harper), settled on the head of Big Left Hand, in what was at that time Kanawha County, now Roane, near its boundary, between the years 1830 and 1840, lived there many years making a good farm and rearing at least three sons; such of his descendants as I have interviewed can not give us the name or family of his wife. This is the Asa Harper—fine engraver, &c.—arrested and carried before a judge sitting at Winfield, about the year 1844, to answer an indictment for counterfeiting the coin and bank notes of the money, &c.; an old citizen of Roane, born in Russell County, Virginia, son of a family well acquainted with the Harpers, says he was a boy some ten to fourteen years old and attending court with his father at Winfield at the time of Asa Harper's arraignment; that Harper made a great furore in court when told by the judge to stand up and answer "Guilty or not guilty to this indictment." Instead of answering direct, "he took from under his coat bags of the coin and stacks of new bills; throwing them on the table in presence of a thronged court room, he calmly said: 'Here's my share, judge, cover it with your larger one on which you have grown so great.' 'Sheriff, do your duty!' shouted the judge; 'take that man to jail; Harper, you're guilty of contempt of court! It is this court's order you be confined in the jail of this county to meditate on the gravity of this offense until such time as you have decided to order your action and conduct yourself with the respect due the majesty of the law and this court; at end of which time you may be again brought before this court to answer, first for this contempt.'" Most of the last of these words of the judge, Harper did not hear, nor anyone else, for the bailiffs were doing their duty and rushing Harper out; he was placed in jail at once, "there to meditate and decide a course of action;" but what his meditations and decision were we do not know.

The next morning after, groups of men could be seen here and there earnestly discussing; Harper was gone from the jail; where, how? who aided?

But Harper's relatives and friends were searching for newly broken ground or recently made heaps and piles for his body, believing Harper had been murdered in the night and his body hidden; for several years in succession at intervals relatives from Russell County and from Pike County, Kentucky, and elsewhere not having word from Asa alive, came to Winfield and searched for his remains. And, our informants and we here, do not assert that the Asa, subject of this sketch, is the same Asa Harper of the Winfield court story.

HISTORY OF ROANE COUNTY 543

However, this Asa who settled in the then faraway forest at the head of Big Legt Hand, is said to have been a very skilled and beautiful engraver.

The names of the four sons of Asa Harper of Big Left Hand, are as follows:

Jordan Harper, who married Catherine, daughter of the Dodd family of Pocatalico, June 17, 1860; these raised four sons and two daughters, names and dates of birth we can give are thus: George Allen, born 1862, lives on Cotton now; Robert, 1866, lives on Cotton near George A.; James Asa, went to Kentucky some years ago; John Peter, whose residence we can not give. The names of four daughters of Jordan Harper are Malinda, Clara, Oma and Ella.

James, son of Jordan Harper, married Erslie Ann Cooper; Hezekiah, son of Jordan, married Margaret McGraw.

HARPER: Armstead and Asa.

Henderson Harper, born in 1822, son of an Armstead Harper, of Russell County, Virginia, who never came to Poca, and Rachel Bishop, who for a second husband married in Russell County, the Armstead Harper brother of Asa and the other Harpers who came here.

Henderson arrived here about the year 1843, a young man it is observed. He was of medium size, rather deep chested, of the middle weight ahletic form, blue eyes and fair skin, and was soon called one of the best hunters and the formidable champion of the rifle at the "shooting matches," which were target shootings at which the rewards to the best at each round consisted of turkey or deer, killed and brought in for the purpose, and first paid for by the contestants by equal contribution. He is the Henderson Harper mentioned in the chapter "The County," as having killed the last of the panthers of Pocatalico country. He was religiously inclined and was a devoted Baptist.

Henderson Harper was married twice, the first wife being Miss .... Gandee, daughter or granddaughter of Uriah Gandee, pioneer of Upper Middle Poca where Gandeeville is now (1926). To Henderson and his first wife were born one son and one daughter, named: The son, Armstead, the daughter, Mary, who married Clark Green of Poca country. The first wife having died, Henderson married for a second wife Debora Westfall, who was a sister of Noah Westfall, and of Barbara Westfall, who became the wife of Andrew "Andy" Stewart, of Reedy, pioneer family.

To Henderson and Debora (Westfall) Harper were born, (all in Harper District at the large farm-home of Henderson, on the Flats west of Cox's Fork), the following children, named in order of their ages: John L.; Rachel, married William Batten; William P., and Malinda, who married Richard Shouldis, of Harper District. Further:

John L. Harper, son of Henderson and Debora, became a Baptist preacher, which work he followed for many years in Roane and near parts of adjoining counties. In later years of his life he was always spoken of as the Reverend John L. Harper. On September 14, 1869, as shown on the Roane county marriage records, which gave no ages at that time, John L. married Miss Melissa Hopkins, of Poca, she the daughter of Robert and Martha (Stalnaker) Hopkins, residents there at time of the marriage. See "Hopkins."

And they made their home and farm on Cox's Fork and there reared their family, the names of whom, in order of births are as follows: Mary, who married Silas Ferrell; Robert, a blacksmith by trade; Jacob M., a lawyer of Spencer, who married Bessie Kester, of Belmont, W. Wa., year 1901, See Chapter City of Spencer; John Marshall, realtor of Parkersburg, married Miss Ida Monroe, see family "Monroe"; Martha married Dr. Noyes, see name "Noyes"; Lelia married a Mr. Walker; Aldie married Elliott Griffith; Eliza married a Mr. Ryerson, and Virgil is the youngest of the family.

HARRIS: Of Curtis District and Upper Spencer District.

Two brothers, Abram Harris and Barton Harris, were respected farmers of the smaller acres for about ten years—1875 to 1885. Each had a family, but the sons have gone elsewhere and daughters have changed their names in marriage.

HARRIS: Of the City of Spencer.

Elias Jefferson Harris was the first of this family to arrive here. He with his wife, Nettie Bernice (Reynolds) Harris, with their five children arrived here in the year 1897. He then a minister of the Gospel was assigned to charge of the Methodist Protestant church of Spencer, by the West Virginia annual conference of the church, of which conference he had been a member for some years previous to his assignment to Spencer charge.

We are not able to state just how many years he was preacher in charge here, but he liked it here, and deeming his family in need of more than the ministry could pay, he resigned as member of the conference and went into business on a small tide of general prosperity, soon acquired ownship in fee of a good home in which he and his wife, Nettie B., have brought up their family.

Ancestry:

Elias J. Harris was born August 14, 1861, in Barbour County, son of John J. and Elizabeth (Marteny) Harris. John L. was a son of George Harris, early settler of the Tigerts Valley, who was a son of Simon Harris, of the Shennandoah Valley, Virginia. Elizabeth Marteny, mother of Elias J., was born near where the City of Elkins now—1927—is, a daughter of George Washington Marteny and wife, pioneers. Nettie Bernice Reynolds was born in Barbour County,

HISTORY OF ROANE COUNTY 545

daughter of .... Reynolds and Susan (Cross) Reynolds; there married Elias J. Harris, April 5, 1882.
The names and somewhat further of the sons and daughters of Elias J. and Nettie B., his wife, are as follows:
Ora was born November 6, 1883, married H. H. Robey. See Robey.
Orville was born July 5, 1884, married Miss Eve Cutlip.
Ottyce, born June 12, 1886, married William C. Hershey, October 27, 1905, he then 37 years of age, born in Fayette County, Ohio, and a resident of McAlister, Oklahoma.
Okey R. was born July 7, 1891, married, and has his residence and business in Spencer, being business manager of The Roane County Reporter, a newspaper and publishing plant.
Orla Virginia Harris, youngest of this family, is a school teacher. She was born June 26, 1896.

HECKERT:
Robert Ervin Heckert, the first of this name resident in Roane County, was born in the year 1856, at Troy, Gilmer County, W. Va., son of Daniel and Mary (Means) Heckert, both born in Gilmer County. Daniel was a son of Adam Heckert, who owned and operated the first mill, at Troy, a water mill later improved by addition of steam power, and was in the family three generations.
Robert Ervin Heckert married Kate, daughter of Mortimer Ireland, of Doddridge County, W. Va., and they came to Roane County in the year 1901, having with them one daughter, Ocie, who grew up here in Roane and married Homer Franklin; since coming to Roane, a daughter, Constance, was born. She is a young school teacher and yet with her parents. Robert and his wife, on first coming to Roane, purchased a farm and lived on it for several years. When he sold it he reserved the oil and gas, and with that and some royalties from wells elsewhere, he enjoys a small income.

HEDGES:
The first of this family name in this county was Charles Thornton Hedges, born in Harrison County, Virginia, May 16, 1813, son of Hiram Benjamin Hedges, born in Berkely County, Virginia, son of Charles Hedges, Jr., born in Frederick County, Maryland, 1749, served as a volunteer in the Continental Army of 1776-1780.
Charles Thornton Hedges, first above mentioned, married, August 28, 1838, Nancy C. Boggess, born November 18, 1818, in Clarksburg, daughter of :.................... Boggess.
To Charles T. and Nancy C. (Boggess) Hedges were born three children, in Harrison County. They came to Roane County about the year 1850, after which five more children were born. Charles T and Nancy C. Hedges, on coming here, purchased a tract of some 800 acres of land situate on Little Spring Creek. On it and of it they made their home for life.

On the outbreak of the War of Secession, Charles T. being loyal to the commonwealth, enlisted in the armies of the Confederacy as a cavalryman. While at home on a furlough seeing after his family and property, he was killed in his own dwelling by Unionists, whether regularly enlisted soldiers or mere zealots, we are not sufficiently informed to say. At the time he was killed his wife was absent on some errand, and the killers left the dead body there in the house where it lay all night, three little children keeping vigil 'til the mother returned in the morning.

To Charles T. and Nancy C. were born eight children, whose names were: Caleb Boggess; John Franklin, died in the Confederate service; Henry Clay, married Miss Alice Robinson, of Harrison County; Charles Edwin; Mary Jane, married John Drainsfield, of Harrison County; Hiram Benjamin, died unmarried; Albert Otho, married Louisa J. Martin, of Harrison County, W. Va.; Fernando R., married Rebecca Foster, daughter of Thomas and Isabel Foster, therefore a sister of Ella Jane, wife of Charles Edwin, his brother.

Charles Edwin Hedges, son of Charles T. and Nancy C. (Boggess) Hedges, was born in Harrison County, W. Va., May 12, 1852, and came with his parents to this Spring Creek country when about two years old, grew up here; in the year 1883 married Ella Jane Foster, daughter of Thomas and Isabel Foster, of Doddridge County, W. Va.; settled and made his home for himself and wife on part of the old patrimonial lands on Little Creek; taught school during winters and between farming months, for some twenty years.

To Charles E. and Ella Jane were born two children, one of whom died in infancy, the other, Grover F. Hedges, grew to manhood, studied law, graduated at the West Virginia University, LL. B., married Mary Elizabeth, daughter of Jarret Depue, June 3, 1913; his age 28, her's 19, lives in Spencer. Charles Edwin Hedges died January 26, 1894.

Ella Jane, widow, married for a second husband, Henry Depue, widower, on June 2, 1895. His age 54, her age 36.

HELMIC: Of Hollywood of Sandy.

Abram White Helmic and Bertha (Skidmore), his wife, were married on Big Laurel in what is now Clay County, came and settled on Hollywood of Sandy, about the year 1856, having with them their six children; five more children were born to them after coming to Hollywood. The names of these children as given by Albert Helmic, from his memory (1926) are:

Lillie Jane, wife of Arthur White, of Geary; Alliene and Oliver, both of whom died in youth; Miranda, died at about thirty-five; Albert, first mentioned; Lorania, who married Thomas Combs of head of Spring Creek; Caroline, died in youth; Asa, who married Nancy, daughter of Granville Lance, of Roane County; Almeda, wife of Shelton West, both died in Clay County; Salathial, married Katherine Brannon, died

HISTORY OF ROANE COUNTY 547

leaving two children; and Nathan, who married Fannie Waugh; of this marriage came a large family, now living about Charleston, West Virginia. Nathan died at or near Columbus, Ohio.

Albert Helmic, of the foregoing family of Abram and Bertha (Skidmore), married Sarah J. a daughter of John Conley of upper Sandy, year 1876; settled on Hollywood and made their home of part of the old family lands; to Albert and Sarah J. were born there, seven daughters and two sons, named as follows:

Rosie, wife of Gus Wilmoth, near Newton.

Ellen, wife of Samuel Tawney, of upper Geary, died.

Louisa, wife of Thos. Brannon.

Parthena was wife of Weck Drake, she being now dead.

Millie, wife of Aimer Elmore; Emma, wife of Ernest Sarver, of Smithfield district.

Bessie, wife of Porter Looney.

HENDERSON: Of Walton District.

Robertus Henderson was the first of this family name who settled in Walton District; he was born in Montgomery County, Virginia, March 16, 1835; shortly after his birth his parents moved to Roanoke, Virginia, where he grew to manhood. We have no information as to ancestry or other members of this Roanoke family. Robertus arrived in Roane County in the year 1860, stopping near.Walton; here on the 14th day of March, 1861, he united in marriage with Nancy M. Looney, daughter of the pioneers, John and Phoebe (Huffman) Looney, near Johnson Creek; Robertus and Nancy M., his wife, acquired a large tract of land nearly all still in forest, situate one mile below Walton, made of it a prosperous home and spent the remainder of their lives in peace and satisfaction.

To Robertus and Nancy M., his wife, were born and by them reared the following named children:

Luella F., February 7, 1862, she married Mandeville B. Snyder; Mary Susan, October 27, 1863, married James H. Dodd, September 18, 1882; Mary Clara A., born December 18, 1866, married David M. Daugherty, December 6, 1888, his age 21, her age 20; Henry M., born January 6, 1870, married Catherine Phillips, February 18, 1892, his age 22, her's 27; Ruth was born May 9, 1872; Giles M. was born June 28, 1874, married Miss Cora Thompson, and they continued the old homestead, or part of it; Lavena D., was born October 1, 1877, married W. P. Humphries; Ross M. was born April 9, 1880, married Miss Edith Garest; Meda M. was born March 20, 1884, married Icy Paxton; Ida M., born August 18, 1886, died 1911.

HENSLEY: Of Walton.

The first of this family name to settle in Walton part of Roane County, was.Doctor Benjamin Morris Hensley, born on the Great Kanawha twelve miles above Charleston, August 4, 1828, son of Samuel Hensley; first practiced medicine from his office at Clendenin. In the year 1856, Doctor B. M. Hensley married Salina M. Geary, daughter of Mathew Geary, of the farms on Big Sandy in what became Geary district; continued to practice out from Clendenin until the year 1872, at which time the doctor and his family purchased property and established their home at Walton, and there remained throughout the remainder of their lives, both having been dead ten years or more at the time of this writing.

To Dr. B. M. and Salina (Geary) Hensley were born the following named children: Wilfred Howard, died in childhood; William Walter, 1863; Wilton Blakey, 1866; Charles Olin, 1874, and Cynthia Mary, 1859, died in youth.

William Walter Hensley of the above family, married Mary C. Jones, daughter of Isaac Jones, builder of the first improved mill at Walton; they have three children.

Wilton Blakely, in the year 1913, married Minnie, daughter of Jacob Helper of the Johnson Creek section of Walton or Smithfield District; Wilton B. and Minnie Hensley have one son, whose name is William Burnard Hensley. Both William W. and Wilton B., are merchants at Walton, also have farms and are general traders.

HESS:

Hiram Hess and his wife, Mary (Fitzwater) Hess, with some sons and daughters, born in Fayette County, or farther east in old Virginia, were the first of this family to settle in Roane County; they came about the year 1852, made their home first on head waters of Poca in what is now Smithfield District. Hiram's son, George, says Hiram Hess was the stone mason contractor who built the stone work of the Gauley bridge destroyed soon afterward in the Civil War. The names of the sons and daughters of the family, so far as we are informed are as follows:

Hannah, who married Solomon Brannon, mentioned in the Chapter: Smithfield District, also in Chapter: Spencer District.

Ephraim, later known as Captain Ephraim Hess, a soldier of the Civil War ,1861 to 1865 (mentioned in the Chapter: History of the County); also served in the war against the Indians known as the Nezperce War. On March 25, 1890, he married Sophronia Murphy, of Spring Creek, his age then 40, her age 20; they have made their home in the far West for many years, where, we are informed, they have reared a family of children.

Evaline, daughter of Hiram and Mary Hess, married Henry Giles, lived many years near and in Spencer.

Frances, daughter of Hiram and Mary Hess, married Andrew Keffer, January 12, 1877.

George Hess, son of Hiram and Mary (Fitzwater) Hess, married, February 19, 1880, Henrietta, daughter of Marshall Glaze of Spring Creek; to George and Henrietta were born and by them brought up the following sons and daughters: Floral, who married Dr. Ross Dodson, December 17, 1919, his age 37, her age 37; they make their home in the City of Charleston, West Virginia.

Beryl, who married George W. Wells, 1915, his age 27, her age 23.

Hobert and Harry, young bachelors; and Kate, who married Howard Marsh.

HILDRETH: First of the name in Roane.

Two brothers, Harrison Hildreth and Robert Hildreth came to Roane County about the year 1866, from one of the counties of the lower Monongahela Valley, where they were born sons of William and Mary Louise (Wadsworth) Hildreth of families of those names, early settlers in New Jersey.

Harrison Hildreth married in what is now Roane County, Miss Sallie Hickman, daughter of Lewis Hickman. To them were born four daughters and two sons; their names in order of births: Ophelia, Martha Ellen, wife of Giles Burdett; Mary Jane, and Sallie; the sons' names: Charles P. and Floyd. The first wife of Harrison Hildreth having died he married Miss Nancy Louise Gough, daughter of Thomas Gough, of Reedy, May 25, 1873, and of this marriage were born two sons and a daughter; their names, Rufus, William H. of Reedy, and Ivy, who became the wife of Harry Clark, about the year 1910.

Charles P. Hildreth, of the above family, married Miss Emma May Tyson, December 10, 1885, his age 20 years, her age 22 years. The bride was the daughter of Calvin Tyson, a then prominent man in the affairs of the county, a land surveyor, had served as a justice of the peace and one term as a member of the county court. Charles P. Hildreth has served a term as member of the county court, and his name as president of the court is seen to many of the proceedings of the court when it was building bridges and pressing for a system of permanent highways. Charles and Emma May have reared some children, one of whom is Roy Hildreth, at this time (1926) prominent in the automobile business of Spencer.

Floyd Hildreth, son of Harrison and Sallie (Hickman) Hildreth, of Little Spring Creek, married, first, Melissa J. Taylor, daughter of a Taylor family of his own neighborhood, on the 22nd day of September, 1888, his age 21, her age 21. There appears a second marriage June 1, 1899. Floyd Hildreth to Virena Walker, his age 31, her age 27.

Robert Hildreth, the other of the two brothers, first coming to Roane, married Virginia Depue, daughter of Jonathan Depue (the name once "dePue") of the Little Kanawha country near the Calhoun-Wirt line.

Robert and Virginia, his wife, later moved to their 250 acres of forest lands on Little Creek in Spencer District, where they made a prosperous home. To them were here born five sons and one daughter, their names: Marshall D., Luther C., Jonathan E. and Curtis Hildreth.

HINZMAN: Of Northwest Walton District.

Abram Green Hinzman, farm and home maker of the above locality, was born in Lewis County, West Virginia, ..., son of Perry Green Hinzman and his wife, Sarah Jane (Swisher) Hinzman, both of whom were natives of the Monongahela Valley. Perry G. was a son of Abram Hinzman, who was of a German family and came into the Monongahela Valley from the Shenandoah or Pennsylvania settlements. Perry Green served as a deputy sheriff of Lewis County for eight years, covering the time of the Civil War—1861 to 1865. To Perry G. and his wife, Sarah J. (Swisher) Hinzman were born and reared in Lewis County, four sons and six daughters, one of which sons was the Abram G. first mentioned.

Abram G. Hinzman and Harriet Jane Morrison were married in Lewis County, August 20, 1879, and arrived in Roane County November 6th, same year with intentions—all things being propitious—of making their lifetime home here. Mrs. Hinzman was a niece of Jacob Morrison, of the neighborhood in which they settled—Big Lick; they were not without encouragement. All went well for them. Abram G. was elected and served three terms as sheriff of Roane County, beginning respectively 1990, 1908 and 1920.

To Abram G. and Harriett J. (Morrison) Hinzman were born and brought up there in Walton District, by them, one son and three daughters:

Reverend Ulysses Ray, who married Cora B. Gandee, October 24, 1901, his age 21, her age 18.

Sarah Zay, who married Henry C. Payne, September 3, 1905, his age 22, her age 22.

Blanche Eva, married Hedgmon D. Belt, March 1, 1905, his age 28, her age 18.

Grace Eva, wedded Virgil E. Rogers, of Spencer, December 1, 1917, his age 29, her age 27.

HIVELY: Captain John; soldier of the War of 1812; member of the committee that laid off the county into magisterial districts, 1863.

John Hively, long known in the county as Captain Hively and as Squire Hively, was born in Monroe County, Virginia, about the year 1796, served in the war with England, 1813 and 1814; married Miss Sarah Lake, in Monroe County. To them were born in Monroe County most of their family of five sons and three daughters, who came with them to head waters of the eastern branches of the Pocatalico, where they settled for their permanent home in the "year 1847," says Mathew Hively, the fourth or fifth son of the family (a twin with Mark) born, he says, in Monroe County, November 23, 1839.

HISTORY OF ROANE COUNTY   551

The names of these sons and daughters of Captain John and Sarah (Lake) Hively, given in order of their respective births, as told me by Hilary Hively, a grandson, are as follows:

Christopher, Madison, James, Mathew, Mark (twins), Ann, who married Harvey Dougherty; Virginia, who married John A. Lowery, in this county, "March 27, 1868, Elder John Hively, officiating"; Barbara, who married William Daugherty.

And further concerning the above family:

Christopher, first son of Captain John Hively, married Miss Emaline Jones, May 1, 1859.

Madison was twice married, first, Miss .... Daugherty; second, Miss Elsie Ferrell; he was father of J. Christopher, Elah and John; Mary, Eliza, and Sarah C., who married George Vineyard, November 9, 1877; they live in Walton.

James, third son of Captain John Hively, married in Craig County, Virginia, a Miss Emelia ....; returned and settled on Rock Creek about the year 1849, where to them were born and reared seven sons and three daughters, whose names in order of respective births are as follows:

Martha Ann, married John D. Canterbury; Sarah, wife of Madison D. Shafer; John L., married Cynthia Summers; Mary C., Frank Newhouse; George M., Jane Noble; Henry F., Lydia E. Lowe; William L., Mattie Woods; Zuinguillius, Victoria Lowe; Hilery married Eva Taylor, April 15, 1897, his age 27, her age 23; she was a daughter of Ira R. and Mahala (Cromwell) Taylor of Walton District, her name as given by her parents is "Loueva." Hilary Hively's farm and residence is on the waters of Cotton Tree; he is the one of this family most widely known. Hansford Hively, youngest son of James, married Miss Belle Lynch, daughter of John Lynch.

Of Mark Hively, son of Captain John, we have no record.

Mathew Hively, fifth son of Captain John, was born in Monroe County, Virginia, November 23, 1839, came to this Pocatalico with his parents in the year 1847; married Nancy C. Cunningham, born in Lewis County, West Virginia, February 26, 1852, daughter of Marshall and Elizabeth (Bonnett) Cunningham; date of this marriage of Mathew and Nancy C., is February 27, 1871; to them were born and reared: Emma K., September 9, 1873, now the wife of "Dot" Whited; George Lonnie, September 23, 1882, married Martha E. Jackson, October 16, 1920, his age 38, her age 33; G. "Lonnie" has succeeded to the home farm and is a prominent stockman of this county. Dr. Howard D. Hively, son of Mathew and Mary C., his wife, is a practicing physician of Charleston, West Virginia.

Ann, daughter of Captain John Hively, married Harvie Daugherty.

Virginia, born November 2, 1883, married John A. Lowery, Sr., on March 27, 1868, in Roane County, "Elder John Hively officiating."

HIVELY:

Reverend John Hively, a Baptist preacher, long of Walton country, whose name appears to so many marriage certificates in the county records, was a nephew of Captain John Hively, who came and settled on main Pocatalico, just below Walton, in the year 1854.

Rev. John Hively was born in Roane County, York, Virginia, married Miss Arminta Dillon. To them were born eight children, of these, three were born in Virginia and five here on Rock Creek, where they settled and made thier home.

John, second son of Rev. John and Arminta (Dillion) Hively, married Martha E. Jackson, June 18, 1866.

William Jackson Hively, son of Rev. John, married Miss Louisa Meadows, daughter of Joshua Meadows—quoting the marriage record— "Father of Louisa present and on consent of father of William J." This informs us that the bride and groom were under twenty-one years of age at the time of their marriage, which was September 15, 1866. Of this marriage we only know of three children born, a son and two daughters. William Jackson Hively died when these were quite small. Their names are, Edward Hively, a substantial citizen of Spencer District; Anna and Sarah J.

Anna married Dennis G. Wolfe, of Spencer District, June 2, 1892, his age 26, her age 17. Children born of this marriage are, Emma, Lillian and Lucile.

Sallie J., daughter of William Jackson Hively and his wife, Louisa (Meadows), married John F. Short, December 19, 1891, his age 27, her age 18. Of this marriage were born some children whose names we do not have. One, however, is Beulah, wife of Walter A. Carpenter, the present sheriff of Roane County. Their marriage was August 30, 1919. Widower, his age 35, widow (Stewart), her age 23.

Some or all of the four daughters of Rev. John Hively married here in Roane County, but we do not have the names of their respective husbands.

HOBBS: Of Spencer. Deputy Sheriff and Jailor about 1872 to 1878; conspicuous as one of the few persisting in the use of the Cavalier pronunciation of the English language.

This was William Epps Hobbs, married in or near Petersburg, Va., about the year 1842, a Miss .... Hobbs, both decendant from a family that settled in early Colonial times in Prince George County, Virginia. Seeking health they came "west," living a while in Greenbrier County, thence came to New California about the year 1855.

To William Epps Hobbs and his wife were born and by them reared and given to the citizenship of this country the following named sons and daughters:

Mary Alphana Magdalene, became the wife of George Deverick, December 23, 1871. Made their home in Roane.

HISTORY OF ROANE COUNTY   553

Margaret Ann Gee, married J. Lee Radabaugh, July 5, 1873, made their home near Spencer and there reared a family.

Elizabeth Eleander, married Thomas Chapman, of Spencer, August 25, 1877.

The two sons were James H. Hobbs and W. M. B. Hobbs. James H. went to Greenbrier County, married there. His home is now in Ocala Florida. William M. B. went from Spencer to Charleston about the year 1877, established a business, married and has ever since maintained his business home there. He is reputed to have grown wealthy.

HOFF: Of border of Curtis and Spencer Districts.

As Andrew Price, president of the West Virginia Historical Society says, whether this name be spelled Hoff or "H-o-u-g-h," it represents the same descendants of Virginians. Hough, as an Anglo-Saxon word, means a joint. Hoff, a Celtic word for hillock. These Hoffs here are big blonde fellows and may be either Saxon-German or Celtic.

John Hoff and his wife, Elizabeth (Mannier) Hoff, were the first of the name here. He was born September 14, 1799, in Loudon County, Virginia, son of Anthony and Lettia Hoff, in the year 1816. John Hoff married, year 1816, Elizabeth Mannier, born in Monongalia County, Virginia, June 22, 1800. They made their first home in Harrison County. Came to the place on the Spencer and Ripley turnpike, State Route No. 5, in the year 1855. There purchased a tract of about one thousand acres, made their home on it and improved it gradually, leaving it to their children. The first school house built for that neighborhood under the free school system after the Civil War, was situate near the turnpike and named "Hofftown" school house, and ever afterward the place has been designated Hofftown, though no town was ever there, and the "temple of learning" was situated on the adjoining Cunningham lands.

The sons and daughters of John and Elizabeth (Mannier) Hoff are as follows: Anthony, Moses, Elizabeth Ann, Julia A., born in Harrison County, April 2, 1833, married Joseph F. Engle in Barbour County, 1854. See Engle; Robert, Cornelius, Trevor, Elam Doudon.

Further about the above family:

Anthony Hoff, first named son of John and Elizabeth, born September 22, 1822, married Miss Indiana Dilworth, in Harrison County. They at once pioneered their home out of the parental lands at the head of Tanners Run of Spring Creek on the Glenville, Ripley and Ohio turnpike. from whence they went out taking part in the affairs of the county, and lived and died there. Their children were Virginia, Napoleon B., Laura, Clay C. and O. Jennings.

Further of these:

Virginia married Hiram W. Goff, September 21, 1868. Napoleon B. Hoff, son of Anthony and Indiana, was one of the first crop of Roane County's young school teachers; was prominent for fifteen years; was elected and served one term in the West Virginia Legislature, sessions

1893. He united in marriage with Miss Mary L. Butcher, March 19, 1878, then neither party being twenty-one years of age. She was eldest daughter of John Butcher, resident on the Ravenswood and Spencer turnpike, three miles north of Spencer. To Napoleon B. and Mary L. (Butcher), his wife, were born and reared several children, of these we name here from memory: Estella, Emmett, Flora (now Mrs. Hugh Burgess, of Texas), Hiram and A. Web Hoff, at present—1927— editor and publisher of the country newspaper, "The Lincoln Republican."

Josephine, daughter of Anthony and Indiana Hoff, married Austin Thomasson, December 1, 1881. See name Thomasson.

Laura, daughter of Anthony and Indiana Hoff, married L. Dow Starkey, of Spencer District, March 1, 1879.

Emma, daughter of Anthony and Indiana Hoff, married L. P. Showen. See Showen.

Clay C. and O. Jennings, two youngest sons of Anthony and Indiana, are farmers, citizens of Roane.

Moses Hoff, second son of John and Elizabeth (Mannier) Hoff, married in Jackson County the Widow Bonnett (nee Corder). They made their home in Jackson County, on the Ravenswood and Spencer turnpike, two or three miles east of Sandyville. They reared some children there, a son, John Hoff, married a Miss .... Mitchell, of Spencer, resided here many years, a daughter, Jane, was the second wife of James W. Seaman, near Reedy.

Cornelius J. Hoff, sixth son of John and Elizabeth (Mannier(Hoff, was born November 21, 1827, married Miss Nancy Smith in Barbour County, near Phillippi; brought her here and they made their lifetime home of the average amplitude on the Spencer and Ripley turnpike, on Tucker's Run, Curtis District, on a part of the ancestral lands, from whence they attended church, labored and reared their family of one son and three daughters: George R., Leig, Ann and Martha. Of these George R., on January 17, 1886, married Miss Mary C. Burgess, of Roane County, his age 28, her age 28. They made their home on the turnpike on the ancestral lands. They have one child only, Mrs. Rufus Kyer.

Elim Douden Hoff, eighth son of John and Elizabeth (Mannier) Hoff, married Miss Louise Donaway, of Roane County, on May 12, 1861. They reared one son and five daughters: Ambrose, Ella, Theo, Florence, Columbia and Minnie Bell. The last being the wife of Harvey Allen Thomasson.

A William A. Hoff married a Miss Serena Ward, in Roane County, W. Va., on May 9, 1883. This name not appearing on the memo from which the foregoing was made up. We presume he is a member of this Hoff family not occurring to the writer of the memoranda.

HOPKINS: Of Harper District.

Robert Hopkins and his wife, Martha A. (Stalnaker) Hopkins, were the first of this name to settle in this territory. Robert was born in

Pendleton County, western Virginia, December 23, 1822, son of Lawrence B. and Mary (Jordan) Hopkins; Lawrence B. Hopkins was born in Rhode Island, year 1760, and was a soldier of the Continental Army of the Revolution; Mary Jordan was a daughter of Captain William Jordan of the Continental Army, who lived in Pendleton County when Mary, the mother of Robert Hopkins, was born, 1794.

Robert and Martha (Stalnaker) Hopkins were married June 19, 1851, and to them were born the following named children ,all on Flat Fork: Melissa J., June 20, 1852; Minerva S., January 23, 1854; Marshall A. C., April 9, 1856; John L., April 15, 1858; Mary S. M., March 14, 1860; A. J. Floyd, July 17, 1862; Martha E. N., August 7, 1864; James O., July 24, 1867. Of these sons and daughters, further:

Melissa J., on September 14, 1869, married John L. Harper, son of Henderson Harper, of Harper District, later spoken of as Reverend John L. Harper; these are the parents of Jacob M. Harper, Esq., of the Roane County bar.

Minerva S. married N. S. Bonnett, September 17, 1879; began their home in Walton District.

Samantha E. married F. P. Fields, January 22, 1880, and they made their home in Jackson County.

Mary S. M. married George W. Mitchell, April 1, 1880; they lived many years at Cicerone, lower Harper District, and there George W. died in 1926.

Martha E. married C. Lowe, of Walton District, April 2, 1871.

John L. married Sarah E. Shouldis, April 15, 1883, and they began life in Harper District.

This wife and mother, Martha A., died in Harper District, at Flat Fork, September 15, 1870.

Robert Hopkins married for his second wife Mary J. Cleek, daughter of George and Bridgett (King) Cleek, in Jackson County, W. Va., on September 24, 1871; to Robert and Mary J. (Cleek) Hopkins were born four children: Bridgett A., October 11, 1872; George Frederick, July 5, 1874; Margaret E., July 21, 1876, and Zuba M., November 14, 1878.

Robert Hopkins was appointed and served as postmaster at Flat Fork, commencing in 1871. Further of his wife, Martha, see name "Stalnaker."

HOWELL: Of Curtis and Reedy Districts. Larkin Howell and Moses Howell were the first to settle in Roane County; so much of their ancestry and descendants as we have gathered is as follows:

Pascal W. and Eliza E. (Marple) Howell, his wife, were early settlers in Barbour County, West Virginia; they were parents of five sons, whose names were as follows:

Larkin D., born 1834, married, lived on Middle Fork of Reedy from near close of the Civil War til his death, 1891; left no child.

William M., born February 19, 1838; married Miss Elzena Tennant in Ritchie County; they settled at Lone Cedar, Jackson County, and reared a family there.

Jacob, married a Miss Mount, and they settled on Muses Bottom in Jackson County.

Monroe, married a Miss Tennant and settled in Ritchie.

Moses Howell married a Miss Mary Jane Peck in Barbour County, West Virginia; she having relatives in upper Reedy, they came and settled there about the year 1857, having with them when they came four children born in Barbour; their names; C. Columbus, America, Victoria, Alvin A.

C. Columbus Howell, son of Moses and Mary Jane (Peck), married Miss Sarah N. Roberts, daughter of Simon Roberts, of Curtis District, December 15, 1877; they made their lifetime home on upper Reedy, where to them were born: Clayton, Annie, Icy, Eva, Minnie; a son, Homer D., who married Miss Hallie E. Thomasson, April 2, 1924, his age 23, her's 22; the youngest of this family is Miss Laura Howell. Icy married Romeo Fisher. See "Fisher," "Robey."

America, daughter of Moses Howell, married J. N. Robey.

Victoria, third child of Moses Howell, married James Cummings, October 24, 1874; settled on Reedy.

Alvin Adams Howell, son of Moses and Mary Jane (Peck) Howell, united in marriage with Miss Emma R. Curry, April 14, 1880; she was born in Pocahontas County, West Virginia, daughter of John Curry and his wife, who at the time of Emma R.'s marriage, lived on upper Reedy. Alvin A. and wife, Emma R., made their home on upper waters of Left Reedy, where to them were born one son, Boyd A., and six daughters, Pearl D., Lulu Z., Willia L., Myrtle M., Goldie N., and Greekia C. Mary Jane (Peck), mother of the foregoing son and daughters of Alvin A., having died, he united in marriage with Miss Gay Carr, 1916; she a daughter of William P. Carr, of Gilmer County West Virginia; no child was born. Since dictating the above Alvin A. Howell has died.

HOWELL: Of Town of Reedy.

Enoch Morgan Howell was born in Nicholas County, West Virginia, February 16, 1849, son of George Warren and Rebecca (O'Balden) Howell, residents of Nicholas at date of Enoch M.'s birth, and both died while this son was a small child. Both George W. and Rebecca, his wife, were of Irish extraction.

Enoch M. enlisted and served as a soldier of the Confederacy; large, strong blond; he returned unscathed as to limbs and physical parts. He appears to have gone to war from Reedy, because he had been here several years before that war; what business or adventure brought him here we are not told.

On the 5th day of May, 1870, Enoch M. Howell and Nancy Conrad were united in marriage at her parents' home in Wirt County, on Main Reedy; she was born February 6, 1851, daughter of Peter and Jane (Blosser) Conrad, his wife; themselves children of pioneers of Main Reedy, she of "Three Forks" Blossers.

Enoch M. was a timber expert and a good manager of timber men; at this he passed several years, then settled with his family in the village of Reedy.

HISTORY OF ROANE COUNTY 557

He was public spirited and took part in all public business; was elected and served as justice of the peace for Reedy District, one or more terms; also has served as mayor of the Town of Reedy since its incorporation.

Enoch M. and Nancy, his wife, have brought up one son and two daughters, Mallie, Guy C. and Ivy.

Mallie married Henry Clyde Law, December 24, 1897; her age them 20 years, his age, 22. (See name Law.)

Guy C. was educated in the Reedy public schools, had his part with the young people of the town; was a member of their brass band; married Miss Ivy Tallman, of Seaman, March 18, 1903, his age 22, her's 21; she a daughter of Samuel and Rosa (Seaman) Tallman. He has become an expert of a branch of the gas business in which he is employed, and lives on Church Street, Spencer, West Virginia.

HOUSE: First of the name in Reedy.

John House was born in Gurnsey (now Noble) County, Ohio, in the year, 1825, son of James House, soldier of the War of 1812, who was a son of a Saxton family of Houses who settled in western Pennsylvania during the times of Indian depredations in those parts. James married a Miss Barnes, daughter of the Maryland family of Barnes, and Days, and with her sometime afterward settled in Ohio, where John—first mentioned—was born.

John House grew to manhood at the place of his birth and in 1850 married Miss Jane Connor, born in Harrison County, West Virginia, in the year 1823, daughter of Reverend Richard Connor, a Baptist preacher and his wife, who was Miss Priscilla Davis, daughter of William and Hannah (Lambert) Davis. The Lamberts and Davises, early settlers in Harrison County, from which county the Reverend and his wife had come to Ohio in the year 1824, when Jane was in her infancy.

After this marriage John taught school, served as township clerk in his native state two terms; was living in Wood County, West Virginia, at the outbreak of the "Rebellion"; was a justice of the peace there under the reorganized Virginia government; went back to Ohio, where he enlisted in the National Guards there and was with it in the chase of Morgan's Raid of historic note; he returned to Wood in 1869.

In the early spring of the year, 1872, John and Jane (Connor) House, his wife, with their family, two sons and one daughter, came to Roane County and purchasing a farm on Left Reedy, some three miles above (south) the village of Reedy, settled there for their lifetime home, from which he went out and took his part in public affairs, especially in educational meetings and religious gatherings, in which he was an appreciated member because of his somewhat better education than the average, but he never sought public office.

The names of the children of John and Jane House are James Finney House, John Albert House and Rachel House.

James Finney House, son of John and Jane, remains a bachelor, and lives at the Town of Reedy; was for some years a prominent school teacher; he is noted as a devotee of all the heavier literature; is in demand at all civic gatherings especially where correct records must be made.

John Albert House, son of John and Jane, in early life married Miss Sarah C. Smith, October 18, 1877, she was a daughter of Brown and Elizabeth (Walker) Smith, of Left Reedy. John Albert taught school for a few years of his first activities; in later years moved to Wood County, West Virginia. To John Albert and Sarah C. (Smith), his wife, have been born some children, but I do not have their names.

Rachel House, the daughter of John and Jane, married Christopher C. Coleman, May 25, 1902, his age 51, her age 42 years; of this marriage no child was born.

HUGHES: Of Spencer and Harper.

Thomas Hughes, the emigrant ancestor of this family was of Welch descent, as the name indicates, and, with his parents, came from Scotland to America sometime prior to the Revolution, and settled at Rahway, New Jersey. He had a son, Thomas, born in New Jersey, in 1768, who married Ann Moore, about the year 1794, and soon thereafter settled in a section of the Monongahela Valley in a part now included in Marion County, West Virginia. They brought up seven children whose names were William, Nellie (Eleanor), John, Josiah, Thomas, James and Mary.

Henry Thomas Hughes, son of William Hughes, and John Wilson Hughes and Elizabeth (Swiger) Hughes, his wife, were the first of the family to settle in Roane County. They arrived in Cassville (now City of Spencer) about the year 1851.

John Wilson Hughes purchased a home in the village and lived here for several years. Henry Thomas was a lawyer and a surveyor, the latter being his principal occupation. His first work observed is a plat of "New California," formerly Cassville, of record bearing date 1852. Of his career see under his name next following this of his cousin, John W. Hughes.

John W. Hughes, the pioneer here, son of Josiah Hughes, Sr., married Margaret P. Jamison, a daughter of William Thompson Jamison, of Butler County, Pennsylvania, a short time before he came to Cassville. Soon after, about 1852, the father, Josiah, with his wife, Elizabeth, and their daughters, Eleanor and Levinia, removed from Marion County to Cassville and Pocatalico, and a little later purchased a tract of several hundred acres of forest lands, having some small improvements on it, lying between the waters of Lower Flat Fork and Big Creek, extending from one to the other, thus covering the head of Trace Fork of Pocatalico. Among the improvements mentioned was that made by John Bishop, grandfather of the author of this book. Josiah

HISTORY OF ROANE COUNTY 559

Hughes, Sr., chose this latter improvement for his permanent home, and it is there that he and his wife, Elizabeth, lie buried. The daughter, Nellie Eleanor married Dr. Edgar A. Barnes. See Barnes. And Lavinia married Silas Counts. See Counts.

Sometime after the year 1855, John W. Hughes and family went onto these lands and near the center on the head of Trace Fork, fixed his house site and there erected commodious farm buildings. His cleared fields soon extended westward to the crossroads long known, as Countsville, a postoffice of that name was later establish there. After the death of Josiah, John W. and family removed to the place on which Josiah, Sr., had resided and there spent the remainder of their industrious and highly appreciated lives. He was prominent in county affairs for twenty-five years. The names of their sons and daughters, brought up and given to citizenship, are: Mary E., Thomas W., Robert A., Henry B., Eliza J., Josiah, Leonidas S., Sophronia E., Luvernia A., Cordelia M., Viola V. and Monroe J.

Of this family we have to say further:

Thomas W. and Robert, twins, were born in New California, in the year 1855. Robert was a soldier boy and was killed in service in the last year of the Civil War.

Thomas William Hughes, son of above named John W. and wife Margaret P., married, 1880, Alice Kelley, daughter of William D. Kelley, of Flat Fork of Poca. They made their home on part of the ancestral lands on Pocatalico, and there reared their children, whose names in order of their respective births are as follows: Ethel, Maggie, Charles D., Lurie, Wilmer Bruce and John C. These made their marriages as follows:

Ethel to James W. Conley, of Poca, October 29, 1899, his age 28, her age 18.

Maggie to Dennis Rhodes, of Spencer, March 1, 1903, his age 24, her age 19.

Charles D. early became a business man in Charleston.

Lurie married Columbus C. Counts, of Flat Fork, March 6, 1904, her age 18, his age 22.

Wilmer Bruce married Elizabeth G. Westfall, January 30, 1910, his age 21, her age 21.

John C. is now—1927—in business at Dayton, Ohio.

Henry B. Hughes, son of John and Margaret (Jamison) Hughes, became a prominent young school teacher; married Roxie Vandal, daughter of A. L. Vandal, of Spencer country; served as Deputy Sheriff for his father-in-law. Next was elected by the people and served one term as Sheriff of the county. Purchased tracts of land and built up a large stock farm adjoining the town of Spencer on the east, introducing the Black Pole Angus cattle in the county. Henry B. and Roxie, his wife's only child, was the son, Romeo, who died in his young manhood.

Alonzo S. "Lonnie S.," son of John W. and Margaret (Jamison) Hughes, his wife, married Miss Maud Taylor, November 15, 1885, his age 23, her age 21. We do not have their careers.

Monroe J. Hughes, son of John W. and Margaret P. (Jamison) Hughes, married Miss Fannie Bates, of Reedy, March 1, 1899, his age 25, her age 22.

Safonia, daughter of John W. and Margaret (Jamison), his wife, married Samuel R. Fields, January 19, 1888, her age 23, his age 24.

Luvernia A. married Henry Clay Taylor, August 20, 1890, her age 22, his age 27.

Cordelia M., we find a "Corda Hughes" united in marriage with Bailey C. Ferrell, September 9, 1891, her age 22, his age 23. Whether or not this is Cordelia M. we do not say.

We have no record of Viola V.

Josiah Hughes, son of John and Margaret (Jamison) Hughes, born on the Harper District farm in Roane County about the year 1860. As soon as grown up was known as an enthusiast on subjects of education; a militant young school teacher in the country schools he taught and at the annual county institutes. Was elected by the people and served as County Superintendent of Schools one term, commencing in 1896. He taught many of the "summer terms" of subscription schools, popular for a long time, commencing with the decade of 1880; is author of some educational books; removed to Charleston, W. Va., where he was some years principal of Eastbank schools. At some time within the foregoing period of time Josiah married Minnie Hamilton, daughter of a Scotch family of that name that came to Virginia, where the marriage took place, by way of Canada, in which part of the "United Kingdom" the Hamiltons lived for a while. This wife is reported as being an enthusiastic school teacher also.

HUGHES: Henry Thomas, of New California and Spencer.

In the decate of the eighteen and fifties, (Thomas Hughes and his cousin), Henry Thomas Hughes, of the Hughes family of the lower Monongahela near Fairmont, western Virginia, and of the New Jersey family of the next preceding pages of this name, arrived with Thomas and commenced his part in the building of this county. Josiah, with his family, at first settled in Cassville (As Tanners Crossroads was then called), and from the youth of the nephew, Henry T., then unmarried, it is inferred that he made his home with the uncle for about one year and until he met Miss Rebecca C. Peebles, a Virginia lady, then visiting the Reverend Joseph Wright, the first Baptist preacher of the village and surrounding country, whose wife, Martha Peebles Wright, was her sister.

Such was Rebecca's charm and Henry T.'s love that he returned to Virginia with her, or followed soon, and they were married at her home in the "Old Dominion." These young people—Henry T. having been born November 28, 1828—at once returned here and purchased an "im-

HISTORY OF ROANE COUNTY   561

provement" located on Left Fork of Reedy Creek about a mile above the then promising village, Reedyville. Just how long they lived there we can not say; Henry T. Hughes had taken a law course as part of his education and had been admitted to the bar; he was also a practical surveyor and his work in either vocation brought him much to the Town of Cassville. We find by a plat of a survey of the town, made by him, dated 1852, that at this date the town was incorporated as the Town of New California, a facetious name, the bestowing of which we are persuaded he did not like, because he was a man of the finer tastes. We are justified from circumstances in saying that he took a leading part in the propaganda and formation of the new county—Roane. He was right there at Reedyville among the strong men of the northern part of the proposed new county and companion in activities with John P. Thomasson, Albert G. Ingraham, Mordecai J. Thomasson and others active in maneuvering for the new county; however, on the 23rd of June, 1856, Henry T. Hughes must have been a resident of New California, for on that date he bought from Alexander West, Jr., all the lands owned by Alexander, Jr., a tract of ninety acres lying to the south of the turnpike, surveyed and platted out a large addition of lots adjoining the first tier of lots fronting on Main Street. On the ninety-acre tract he built a substantial home, locating it on the knoll overlooking the Runnion mill; this was a weather-board and frame house, white with green shutters, easily known as the residence of one of the county's notables, especially for some ten years next after the Civil War. This house has passed through the hands of several notables since: Sheriff P. A. Tallman, Deputy Sheriff A. J. Bowyer, Deputy Sheriff I. I. Riley, and now remodeled is the property of Deputy County Clerk Anderson M. McKown.

Henry Thomas Hughes was elected and served as Roane County's member in the House of Delegates of the State, tenth session, convened at Charleston, year 1872.

The children of Henry T. and Rebecca (Peebles) Hughes, whose names we can give here are: David William Hughes and James Stark Hughes, both at this time (1926) business men residents of San Diego, California; Irena Ann, wife of Charles Bee, a resident business man of Parkersburg, West Virginia; H. Clark Hughes, a prominent resident business man of Pittsburgh, Pennsylvania, and Jennie B., widow of H. Frank Goff, deceased, former sheriff of Roane County, long a resident of the City of Spencer. Her children, two sons and one haughter: Henry T. Goff, now a young lawyer trying it in the City of New York, and Raymond Goff, a business man of the city, not long ago married, and Miss Ruby, living with the mother in Spencer.

HUNDLEY: Of Walton. Later of Spencer.

George W. Hundley, son of Mr. .... and Rebecca Hundley, his wife, was born in Cabell County, West Virginia, year 1855—as figured from age on marriage records; married Miss Mintie Edwards, December 9, 1876, she a daughter of Isaac Edwards, of Walton.

George W. Hundley was elected by the people and served one term as clerk of the County Court of Roane County, ending 1892. He and Mintie, his wife, made their home in Spencer, where he built a good residence; to them was born and brought up one child only; her name, Florence.

The wife, Mintie, having died, George W. united in marriage with Miss Estie Argabrite, October 11, 1896, his age given 41, her's 19; she a daughter of Wiley W. and Mary Argabrite, his wife. Of this marriage were born within the next two or three years one son and one daughter; their names, Raymond B. and Nina Hundley.

There were two daughters of .... Hundley, and Rebecca, his wife, who made their home at Walton; their names, Lucy ("Lucinda"), who married John C. Lowe, of Walton, October 13, 1877; and Miss Emma C. Hundley, who married Christopher C. Lynch, at Walton, March 8, 1885, her age 21, his age 26 (See name Lynch.)

INGRAHAM: First settler of Left Reedy between what is now Billings Railway Station and Reedyville, about the year 1840. Parents of Captain Albert G. Ingraham, of Civil War activities. The name is lately often spelled "Ingram."

Abram Ingraham was the name of the above first settler; he and his wife, both descendants of old Virginia families, came here from Randolph County about the year 1840, having with them several children whose names as given us by Hugh Ingram (as he spells it), a grandson now seventy-nine years old. The names of these five sons and three daughters of Abram Ingraham and wife are as follows: Jesse, Albert G., Jacob, John, Stewart, Jemima, Mariah and Ruhama "Ruie." Their marriages and something of their respective careers are as follows:

Jesse became a sailor on the high seas, and was gone for periods of several years at a time, covering a space of twenty-five years, brought home a wife just before the Civil War and soon thereafter died leaving no child.

Albert G. Ingraham married Drusilla, daughter of Thomas Hardman, then neighbors to the Ingrahams; to them were born two sons whose names were William J. and Franklin. William J. married Miss Martha Burdette, in 1866; this is the Captain Albert G. Ingraham (spelled Ingram) mentioned often in the History of the County and City of Spencer, Chapters I and IX of this book. After close of the Civil War Captain Ingram and his family all went West, first to Missouri, afterward moved to Kansas.

Jacob, third son of Abram Ingram, is grantee in a deed of conveyance of a tract of 350 acres of lands on upper Middle Fork of Reedy, by A. G. Ingraham and his wife, Drusilla; this he improved, sold it soon after and removed to Ohio.

John Ingraham, fourth son of Abram, the pioneer, married Miss Emily Hardman, daughter of a Benjamin Hardman, pioneer and brother of Thomas Hardman, above named; she was born in Ritchie County, West Virginia, says her son, Lycurgus, in his biograph given Hardesty's History in 1882. To John and Emily (Hardman) Ingram, his wife, were born and by them reared the following children, named in order of their respective ages: Hugh, Alice, wife of Jacob Argabrite; Lycurgus and Akbar. Further of this family: Hugh was born in the year 1848, is yet hale and clear of mind, and gave most of the information in this family history; Hugh married Miss Emily Jane Board, daughter of William Board, then a resident of Jackson County, and they made their home in western Curtis District ever since. Their children are five sons and three daughters, whose names in order of their respective ages are, Irven, Florence, Rosie, Alma, Arthur, William T., John and Charles Holly. The last two named are now merchants residing in the City of Spencer.

Stewart Ingraham, fifth son of Abram and wife, pioneers, married a lady in Lewis County and went to the "Far West."

Of the daughters of the pioneer Abram and wife:

Jemima became the wife of Benjamin Riddle and they later became the owners of the pioneer Ingraham large tract of land on Left Reedy, a prominent place for twenty years next before the Civil War; they "went West" about the year 1871. (See name, Riddle in Chapter X of this book.)

Mariah, second daughter of Abram, married first a William Tanner, son of Jesse Tanner near Spencer; she was mother of Josephine (Kyger) Burdette, and Ann (Watson) Roach. (See these latter names in Chapter X, this book.)

Ruhama "Ruie," third daughter of pioneer Abram Ingraham, married Jonathan Vandal, son of James Vandal. (See name Vandal, Chapter VII.) They reared three daughters, their names, Elizabeth "Bett," Catherine and Jemima, the latter married Hezekiah Miller, of Spring Creek, on April 21, 1866.

Lycurgus Inghram (thus spelled by himself), second son of John and Emily (Hardman), was born December 26, 1853, on upper Reedy; on September 22, 1878, married Miss Cynthia A. Harless, daughter of Harrison F. Harless and Elizabeth (Fry) Harless, his wife, both born in Giles County, Virginia, and settled on upper Reedy in the year 1880. Lycurgus and Cynthia A. made their home on part of the patrimonial lands on Reedy, where to them were born and by them reared the following named children: Gusta B., 1879; Jesse W., 1881; Francis B., August 22, 1883, and Virginia, 1885; Virginia married L. Ordway Curtis, August 21, 1905, her age 20, his age 25. See family name "Curtis."

Ackbar Ingraham, son of John and Emily (Hardman), married Miss Louvena Morrison; they lived some years on Reedy; later moved to Wood County, West Virginia; live near Parkersburg now—1927.

JARVIS: Of Lower Harper District.

John Jarvis, born some year of the 1840s in the Little Kanawha or Monongahela Valley, son of a family of early settlers of the Monongahela Valley, is first noticed in Poca Valley, March 11, 1870, on which date he married Sarah Jane Paxton, daughter of Lyle Paxton, Sr.

John and Sarah Jane Jarvis, husband and wife, acquired lands about the head of Rock Creek and there made their home farm and raised their family of three sons and four daughters, whose names are: William, born 1871, married, first Eva Whitney, and after her death he married Ethel Elmore.

John Christopher, 1873, married Mary Paxton.

Benjamin Franklin, born 1884, married Myrtle Beard, of Charleston, W. Va., 1907. Made their home first on the ancestral lands. Being a young school teacher at the time of his marriage, he continued to teach for some years; was elected County Superintendent of Schools and served the term, 1919 to 1923, during which service he purchased a residence and made his home in the City of Spencer, where he and his family reside at this time, he being assistant United States postmaster here—1926.

Benjamin F. and Myrtle Jarvis have one son, Lakin, a lad of about fifteen years, and a daughter, Virgie, who is younger than Lakin.

Margaret Bell Jarvis, of the above family, married William Marshall Jones, son of Manuel Jones, of Poca, in year 1893; his age 23, her age 20.

Laura D. married Silas Phillips, 1894, his age 19, her age 18, "at Green Creek school house."

Virgie married John Wesley Price, of Poca, October 12, 1899, his age 21, her age 21. Virgie died within two or three years. To John Wesley Price (Junior is to be remembered) one son was born whose name is Earl, married Ruth Adams.

Bethel May Jarvis, youngest of this John and Sarah J. (Paxton) Jarvis family, married Fred Jones, June 26, 1907, her age 21, his age 23. He died some time after their marriage and she married Blonda Ray.

JARVIS: Of Upper Geary District.

Thomas Jarvis, of a Calhoun family of that name, married Nancy C. Keen, born 1857, daughter of James and Nancy (King) Keen, of Hollywood, on August 17, 1874. Thomas and Nancy C. Jarvis settled and conquered a farm out of the forest on Upper Middle Sandy, and there raised a family of children whose names we do not have by us.

Nathan Jarvis, of Upper Big Sandy country, came there, and on April 1, 1893, married Melissa Smith, his age 21, her age 20. She was a daughter of William Y. and Julia A. (Cox-Wilson), residents of the spot now (1926) known as Uler. Of the children of Nathan and Melissa we do not know.

He has long been known as an important citizen of those parts.

HISTORY OF ROANE COUNTY 565

JOHNSON: Of Walton District and Spencer.

Enos Johnson, sheriff of Roane County, term 1916 to 1920, came to Roane County from Wirt County in the year 1896, with his wife and three sons. Enos Johnson says he is a grandson of that Henry Johnson who, wih his brother John, two lads thirteen and eleven years of age, respectively, were captured by Indians near their parents' home at mouth of Short Creek, West Virginia, on a day in the month of October, 1788; were carrie daway by two Delaware Indians; killed their captors while they slept in camp, only four miles away, the first night, escaped and returned to their family and neighbors at Carpenter's Fort by early dawn. This is a two-page, 721-722, story in the book, "Our Western Border," by Charles McKnight, and is quoted by McKnight from "De Hass," who recites that it was written for him (De Hass) by Henry Johnson himself in 1851, then residing with his family at Antioch, Ohio, one of which family was a son, Joseph, who married Miss Nancy Hill.

Enos Johnson, first above mentioned, was born in 1857, in Monroe County, Ohio, son of Joseph and Nancy (Hill) Johnson, his wife, the names of Joseph and Nancy's children given in order of respective births are as follows: Harriett, Martha, Enos (of this sketch), William, Joseph and Scott. Joseph and Nancy, with at least the younger members of their family, settled on Right Reedy Creek in Wirt County, West Virginia, in 1868. The son Enos united in marriage with Miss Caroline Gault, born in Monroe County, Ohio, but at time of her marriage with Enos was a resident with her parents in Wirt County. To Enos and Caroline (Gault) Johnson, his wife, were born and by them reared three sons, their names in order of their ages: William David, Robert Everett and Audra Earl. These have all married and made homes and businesses in Roane County.

JONES: Of Curtis District.

Granville Jones, son of Thomas and Betsy Ann (Alexander) Jones. Thomas born in Monroe County and Betsy Ann in Bedford County, Virginia, came to Roane County in 1868, in Curtis District on September 17, 1869. Granville united in marriage with Sarah Jane Settle, daughter of Abner Settle, at the bride's home on Ripley and Spencer turnpike, near the Spencer-Curtis line.

To Granville and Sarah Jane Jones were born at their residence on Left Reedy, the following named children:

James Luther, who married Flora Cummings, of Curtis District. He died leaving two sons and two daughters.

Thomas Abner married a Miss Rebecca Hardman, of a Kentucky family of Hardmans. Thomas A. was first an active young school teacher and served one term as assessor of Roane County.

Annie, became the wife of Asbury Warner, of Curtis.

Emma Alice, married Elmer Sealey, of Pennsylvania.

Maggie Leona, married Charles Ingraham, of Curtis.

Letha Harriett ("Sallie"), married Clem Wolfe, of Upper Spring Creek.

Esta, married Asbury Walker, son of James and Lummie (Bartlett) Walker, of Lower Spring Creek.

———o———

Dr. George Mc. Jones, born in Greenbrier County, Virginia, May 29, 1854, son of A. K. Jones and Delilah (McClung) Jones.

George Mc., married Martha F. Monroe, July 20, 1875, she being a daughter of Robert and Drusilla (McBride) Monroe, who lived in Gilmer County at the time of birth of Martha F., but were residents of Wirt County at time of her marriage.

To Dr. George Mc. and Martha F. Jones were born, Allen, Albert and Genette. This family lived at Reedyville about 1880 to 1885.

JONES: Of Southeast Harper District.

William Jones, born in Lewis County, West Virginia, February 4, 1812; married Anna P. Taylor, a sister of Elijah and William P. Taylor, of Lower Harper. She was born in Russell County, Virginia, February 2, 1822. William and Anna P. Jones settled first in Kanawha County, in the year 1842—so stated in the biography of their son, Norvill. To them were born and grew up, three sons and four daughters, whose names are: Granville, Union soildier, captured at Lynchburg raid, and died in Andersonville prison; Norvill, born in Kanawha County, December 11, 1844; Emanuel; Margaret, who married Henry Taylor, of Harper District; Aretia, married Peter White, of Kanawha County; Sarah, married Archibald Taylor; Harriett, married Elias Moore, of Harper District.

Manuel, third son of William and Anna P. Jones, above, married Elmira Clarkson, of this county, June 18, 1868. To Manuel and Elmira (Clarkson) Jones, were born and reared one daughter and three sons, as follows: Louvinia, who married Thomas Fields, of West Harper District, 1892; his age 24, her age 21.

William M. Jones, married Belle Jarvis, May 25, 1893; his age 23, her age 20.

Moses W. Jones, married Laura Walls, of Kanawha.

Norville, Jr., son of Manuel and Elmira Jones, married Ettie, daughter of Richard E. and Jane Taylor, of Harper District, on January 20, 1895; his age 21, her age 17. To Norville and Ettie, his wife, have been born four sons and four daughters. Norville Jones, of this last paragraph, is a large real estate owner; has served as a member of the County Board of Equilization and Review. Lives yet in lower Harper District.

JONES: Of West Harper District.

Edmund and Malinda (Carr) Jones, one time residents of Harper District not far from the mouth of Cox's Fork, were married in Hardy County, Virginia, and came here about the year 1845. We do not have the names of all the children of Edmund and Melinda Jones,

HISTORY OF ROANE COUNTY 567

however we can give the name and family of one of their sons, named Jacob, who came here with them.

Jacob Jones, son of Edmund and Malinda, was born in Hardy County, Virginia, December 16, 1824, and on February 1, 1853 united in marriage with Rebecca Raines, born in Lewis County, Virginia, January 6, 1836, daughter of John M. and Mary (Hindsman) Raines, land owners, residents of the neighborhood of Poca, at the time of the marriage of Rebecca, one of their several children. To Jacob and Rebecca (Raines) Jones were born and grew up here on Poca, eleven children, their names as follows:

John P., June 9, 1855; Rusina, August 16, 1856; ,William E., November 24, 1857; James C., June 8, 1861; Daniel W., June 8, 1863; Hariett E., August 30, 1865; Lydia D., August 16, 1867; Jacob H., November 18, 1869; Sarah A., February 9, 1872; Joseph M., April 10, 1874; Charles Everett, October 21, 1876.

JONES: Of Walton.

Edmund and Malinda (Carr) Jones, his wife, were residents of Hardy County, Virginia. Henry Jones, father of Edmund, "was a soldier in the Revolutionary War." Edmund and Malinda left Hardy and came to this Pocatalico country in the year 1855. Edmund died July, 1860, and Malinda in 1858.

Edmund and Malinda (Carr) Jones were the parents of sons and daughters, all of whose names we do not know. Isaac, John and Eli are sons mentioned by Isaac in his biography in Hardesty's, and from a granddaughter of William Riley we learn that there was a daughter of Edmund and Malinda (Carr) Jones, whose name was Mary Ann, became first wife of Willam Riley, of Lower Flat Fork.

John and Eli Jones, sons of Edmund and Malinda, both enlisted and served in the Union army, 9th West Virginia Infantry. John was killed in the battle at Winchester, September 19, 1864. Eli was wounded but served until the end of the war.

Isaac Jones, son of Edmund and Malinda (Carr) Jones, was born in Hardy County, Virginia, June 22, 1828; came to Pocatalico country with his parents in 1855; married Melissa J. Stump, June 6, 1860, she being a daughter of Henry and Permelia (Welch) Stump, and born in Gilmer County, West Virginia, June 13, 1842, and was living with her parents at the time of her marriage. whose home was then in Geary District, on Big Sandy.

To Isaac and Permelia (Stump) Jones, his wife, were born, all at Walton, the following children, all of whom grew up at Walton. Henry F., born January 2, 1863; Mary C., April 17, 1865; Waitman P. W., October 12, 1872; Louise F., September 15, 1874.

Of the marriages of these children we find the following on the county marriage records:

"Lulu Jones and Howard H. Fleshman, October 25, 1891; his age 25, her age 18."

"Waitman P. Jones to Dora J. Harmon, September 5, 1895; his age 23, her age17."

Both recollections and even written records are sometimes wrong.

JONES: Of McKowns Creek, East Walton.

John M. Jones, son of John and Jane (Rector) Jones, came to these parts in the year 1858. He was born in Monroe County, Virginia, February 11, 1827. His first wife was Ann E., daughter of John T. and Nancy Ellis. Of this marriage the following named children were born: Augustus C., 1845; Martha A., 1848; Mary J., 1850; Lizzie S., and Eliza F., February 12, 1855; the wife, Anne E. (Ellis), having died August 13, 1861. On February 12, 1864, John M. married Amanda Waldon, born in Washington County, Virginia, 1836. To John M. and Amanda J. (Waldon) Jones were born, prior to 1880, the following named children: John P., February 28, 1866; Isaac S., June 14, 1869, and Bertha V., May 5, 1875. This last Bertie V. became the wife of James A. Gandee, Jr., of Poca country.

We do not have the family record, but are informed that Dr. Edward Clarence Jones, of Spencer (1926) is a son of Mary J., of the above above family, whose husband was another Jones of an unrelated family of Jones's. This pioneer John M. Jones says in his biography that his father, John, was a soldier in the War of 1812, and that his grandfather, James Jones, was a soldier of the Continental forces of the American Revolution.

KELLEY: Of Curtis.

Archibold Kelley, born in Marion County, Virginia, about the year 1818, and his wife, Christina, born in the same county about the same date, daughter of John D. Sharp, arrived and commenced their home on Stover Fork about the year 1848; from other dates we infer five of their seven children came here with Archibold and Christina. The names of their children we can give here, in order of their respective ages, are Reverend William Kelley, long a Methodist Episcopal preacher; John N. Kelley, Harriet, Eliza, Safrona, Blackburn, and Christopher Columbus Kelley. Archibold Kelley soon made a good farm of many acres, and was long an active citizen in the church and secular affairs of the county.

For further concerning this family, as to the daughters, see family names of the men they married, and as to the sons, the following:

Rev. William Kelley went out as a circuit rider of his church; whom he married if he married we do not know.

John N. Kelley married Elizabeth, daughter of Samuel Romine, 1867, then of Romines Mills, Harrison County, and they made their home on the head of Stover. Of this marriage were born: Addison Allen, year 1868, and Ida May, 1871, she is the wife of C. M. McCoy of Left Reedy Creek.

Harriet, daughter of Archibold and Christina Kelley, married in same neighborhood, April 15, 1858, James E., son of Jacob Radabaugh.

Mary Eliza, daughter of Archibold and Christina Kelley, married Lemuel, son of John McCoy, March 14, 1860.

Safrona, daughter of Archibold Kelley, has not married.

Blackburn, son of Archibold and Christina Kelley, was born about the year 1830; was twice married, his first wife being Jane Whetzel, of Harrison County family of Whetzels. Of this marriage, three children were born; their names: William, Orlando and "Ferd." For his second wife Blackburn married .... Hughes, of Jackson County, W. Va. Of this marriage were born one son and one daughter, named Melvin and Cora, respectively.

Blackburn Kelley was a soldier of the Civil War.

Christopher C. Kelley, son of Archibold and Christina (Sharp) Kelley, was born.., grew up on the home farm on upper Stover; married Elizabeth McCoy, born in Barbour County, daughter of John and (Crislip) McCoy. Of this marriage three children were born, named in order of their ages: Annie, wife of Ben T. Board; Calvin Josiah, married..and lives on part of the old home farm; and Dona, who married Irven, son of Hugh Ingraham, of the Ingrahams of Curtis District.

The above named Christopher C. Kelley was many years a prominent personage in his district, active and dependable in civic and church work, especially that of the Methodist Episcopal denomination; served as a justice of the peace, one or more terms; was a member of the county court one term of four years, president of that body in his turn; and was elected by the people and served as Roane County's member in the House of Delegates, 27th session of the State Legislature, 1905.

This family of Kelleys were noted for the number of blonds of the lightest hair and pink skinned blonds.

KELLEY: Of Harper.

William D. Kelley, pioneer of Harper District, was born in Harrison County, Western Virginia, March 28, 1826, son of John L. Kelley and Tracy (Davis) Kelley; John L., born at Front Royal, Va., 1803, son of William Kelley, a soldier of the War of 1812, and Tracy was born in Harrison County, Western Virginia, October 10, 1805, and came to Poca in the year 1855.

William D. Kelley (first mentioned), on the 28th of December, 1848, in Braxton County, Western Virginia, married Margaret Carter, born in Lewis County, Virginia, September 20, 1828, daughter of William L. and Jane (Means) Carter; these four persons arrived and settled in upper Harper on Flat Fork in the year 1849, and within a very few years were reputed to be "well-to-do," and owned a large acreage of improved lands, and kept a crossroads store of general merchandise. William D. Kelley was soon given a commission as a justice of the peace.

In 1862 he enlisted in the Confederate Army, Co. H, 17th Va. Cavalry, and served until Lee surrendered. Soon after returning from the war, he was elected as one of the Commissioners of the County Court of Roane, for a term of two years, then reelected for a term of six, serving in that capacity eight years.

To William D. and Margaret (Carter) Kelley were born, all at the farm-home mentioned, the following children: Tracy J., 1850; Thaddeus C., 1852; John W., 1854; Alice S., 1856; Dexter Lee, 1858; Oscar, 1860; Albert J., 1863.

KELLEY: Of Smithfield and Walton.

Peter C. and Mary (Woodside) Kelley, his wife, moved from Mason County, Western Virginia, to Johnson Creek, upper Pocatalico, near the division line between Smithfield and Walton Districts, in the year 1849, there purchased large acreages and made a farm from the forest and a home known as "the Peter Kelley place," ever since. His son, Claudius P. Kelley, succeeded to this; it was eight hundred acres as entered and taxed about the year 1895.

To Peter C. and Mary (Woodside) Kelley were born the following named children, as given to the writer by their great grandchildren:

John W., who married Miss Eliza Sergent first, Nov. 1, 1856; later Alice S. Looney of Roane County; James, who married a Russell County, Virginia, lady; Franklin, who went to Texas many years ago; Thompson, who married Catherine Cree of Greenbrier County,, West Virginia; Claudius P., who married Charity Vineyard, of Roane; Sallie Stone, who married John B. Stone, long a resident at Roxalana P. O.; and Elizabeth, who became the wife of William Ferrell, senior, of Smithfield District. Of above family, Claudius P. has a biography in Hardesty's History.

"Claudius P. Kelley was born in Mason County (then Virginia) Oct-12, 1845, and in 1849 came to Roane County, then part of Kanawha; Peter C. and Mary (Woodside) Kelley were his parents, and came to this county in 1849. Claudius P. Kelley married Rachel Looney in Roane County, October 14, 1869. [She was the daughter of Peter and Charity (Vineyard) Looney, and was born 1848.] Seven children were born to Mr. and Mrs. Kelley: Peter G., 1871; Charity E., 1872; Lloyd M., 1874; Newton M., 1876; Mary E., 1878; Elizabeth J., 1880, and Susan C., 1883."

KEE: Of Harper, Countsville.

Alfred Newton Kee, the first of the name who settled in Roane County, was born in Lewis County, West Virginia, September 6, 1862, son of James P. and Harriett (Hinzman) Kee.

The Kees are English, and descendants of one of the name who made his home and business in Ireland for one or two generations, and shortly before the American Revolution four brothers whose names were James,

John, Aaron and George came to America, landed "on the Eastern Shore." George, the youngest brother being at the time a mere boy, says the family traditions, and soon after landing all separated from each other. The next we have of certainty is that Aaron Kee has reached Pocahontas County, where he united in marriage with a Miss Heath, and they made their home about one mile from the present site of Marlinton. There to Aaron and his wife were born and by them reared at least two sons whose names were John and James. John Kee came to Upshur County, having learned the trade of tanner; he was employed by Jacob Lorentz in his large tannery there in Upshur and worked in that tannery several years, in the mean time married his employer's daughter, Miss Harriett Lorentz; acquired a tract of three hundred acres of land on Hackers Creek, near where is now Berlin. There John and his wife, Harriett (Lorentz) Kee, spent a long and useful life time. He was elected and served as assessor of Lewis County many terms. To John and Harriett were born and by them reared there on that farm five sons and one daughter, their names: James, Frank, John N., William B. and Alice.

Of those sons, James married Miss Harriett Hinzman, and settled on the old ancestral homestead on Hackers Creek.

To James and Harriett (Hinzman) were born and by them brought up there, three sons and three daughters: Alfred Newton (he first named), Phillip Sheridan, Idress Lee, Kate, Nora and James Frederick (died in Roane County, not married).

Alfred Newton ("Bub") Kee was born September 1, 1862; married in Upshur County, September 16, 1883, Miss Electa C. Robinson. They settled in Roane County ,in the year 1890, for their lifetime home, first in Walton, then acquiring the Adams' farm near Countsville, moved on that fine farm, using it and his other lands in the business of stock raising, at which he has prospered. He has been popular and was his party (Democratic) nominee for sheriff of Roane County once or twice, but the county was from two to three hundred majority Republican at that time.

To Alfred N. and Lectra (Robinson) Kee, his wife, have been born and by them reared the following children, named in order of respective births: Ferris A., Bernice May, Esten B., Idress Lee, Rex, John L., Phillip Pritts, Brell, Kate, Orland D., Muriel, and Rolfe.

John N. Kee, son of Colonel John and Harriett (Lorentz) Kee, married and made his lifetime home at Glenville, West Virginia; these were the parents of State Senator John Kee of Bluefield, who served as State Senator, year 1925.

KEEN:

James Keen, born in Russell County, Virginia, 1828, son of David and Nancy (Bishop) Keen, came to Big Sandy and to Hollywood about the year 1849. On September 20, 1849, he united in marriage with

Nancy King, born in Pike County, Kentucky, daughter of William and Mary (Hamilton) King, pioneers, at time of this marriage living on upper Big Sandy, now of Geary District; the farm made by James and Nancy and which was their home longest, is located on Hollywood.

James Keen was a skilled mechanic as well as an excellent farmer, skilled especially as a blacksmith and worker in iron and steel. He was long an influential man in church and community work; the Baptist church especially, of which he and his family were members; he was secretary of that church for twenty-four years. He served four years as justice of the peace, and six years as president of the district board of education.

Of this marriage of James and Nancy Keen were born eleven children: Elizabeth, February 22, 1851, married John H. Tawney; Nathan S., August 2, 1852, married Elizabeth Upton; William C., August 30, 1854, married Electra A. Smith; Nancy C., June 4, 1857, married Thos. Jarvis; Rebecca A., February 15, 1860, married John B. Vineyard; Phillip J., February 20, 1862, married Elsie Jarvis; James M., October 11, 1867, married Rosie Steorts, 1912; George F., January 23, 1871, married Bertha Reynolds, 1894; Sarah A., 1874, died in infancy; John E., November 27, 1874. The marriage records of Roane County show that a "J. E. Keen, married Lydia Cook, April, 1927, his age 41, her age 26."

KEPLINGER:

Noah Keplinger, 1828-1912, was born in Rockingham County, Virginia, son of a Christian Keplinger and his wife a Miss Lance before marriage. The Keplinger family of Virginia were there before the Revolutionary War, several of Noah's ancestors having served with the Virginians as soldiers of that war. Christian came to Grant County when Noah was seven years old and lived there twenty years. At twenty-seven years of age, Noah, having married in Grant County, left that county and came to Barbour County, Western Virginia, remained there only about six months, coming on westward, arriving in what is now Roane County, in the year 1855. A few yet living remember his flowing red beard, in the years 1890 to 1900.

His first work here was as one of the shingle makers for the roof of the new court house; 1860 he settled on Laurel of left Reedy and became the owner of a farm of sixty acres, increasing this by purchase of another tract adjoining, making a farm there of one hundred and sixteen acres, which he and his family improved to what was known as "a good farm." In the year 1869, he purchased the 163 acre farm on Lick Fork of Spring Creek adjoining the Holswade lands, where he lived nearly all the remainder of his years. Of the family reared by Noah Keplinger we can name here: William Edmond Keplinger, father of Rosa, who is the wife of James Vandevender; Gideon Lee Keplinger, who married Della, daughter of Benjamin Greathouse; Sarah Ann, the wife of Henson Bennett; John Franklin Keplinger, whose wife is Sallie

B., a daughter of .... Scyoc, these have a baby daughter named Catherine Irene; they live in a commodious home on West Main Street, City of Spencer. Bertha Lola, second daughter of Noah Keplinger, was the wife of Benjamin N. Bray; she is now dead, leaving two children: Hoy H. Bray and Zenia Bray.

KINCAID: Of Smithfield and Spencer.

George Washington Kincaid, and his wife, Catherin (Campbell, daughter of Daniel Campbell), who were married in Fayette County, Western Virginia, with their three first born children, came to Roane County in the year 1856; settled near Looneyville. George Washington Kincaid was a son of Thomas and (.................... Davis) Kincaid, who were married in Greenbrier County, West Virginia, both descendants of Scotch-Irish settlers of old Virginia. Fayette County History states that a James Gillispy Kincaid of Greenbrier County, 1807, is the leading name of the family, Kincaid.

The sons and daughters of George W. and Catherine, his wife, were Daniel Thomas, George W., Jr., Seldon, Rufus A., Virginia, wife of Phillip Ellis; Sarah, wife of Elkanah Summerfield; Belle married Hilary Upton; Frances married a Kincaid of another family.

Daniel Thomas Kincaid, son of G. W. Kincaid, Sr., and Catherine (Campbell), was born in 1848, in Fayette County; on April 23, 1873, married Miss Martha E. Brannon, daughter of Solomon Brannon, of Spencer and Smithfield Districts. To Daniel E. and Martha, his wife, were born and by them reared the following five sons and seven daughters: Newman, Melissa, John S., Ott, Lexie, Seldon C., Martha May, Rosco, Ethel, Annice, Emma and Myrtle. These have married and have families and businesses.

George W. Kincaid, son of George W. and Catherine, was born in Roane County; married Miss Lulu Burke, daughter of Peter Burke of Spencer District, February 14, 1877. They reared two sons and two daughters, whose names are Robert, William, Mrs. Darrel Pritchard, and Mrs. Howard Dougherty.

Rufus, son of Geo. W. and Catherine Kincaid, married first Elizabeth Doughert, 1890. She died, then he married Nettie Butcher, of Henrys Fork; they have one child.

John Moton Kincaid was a son of William Kincaid of Dogwood Gap, Fayette County, and was a cousin to the others above mentioned. John M. married Miss Eliza Lowe, October, 1881, and returned to Fayette County.

Seldon Kincaid's career is not given us.

KING: First, William, of Hollywood, Big Sandy; second, John, of Ashley Camp, Left Hand—two brothers, Virginians.

William King was born in Virginia; married a Miss Mary Hamilton, and first lived in Pike County, Kentucky, where their only child, Nancy, was born, November 24, 1834. These three came to upper Bg Sandy about the year 1835; settled on Hollywood, where Mary (Hamilton) King died in the year 1837; William died April 22, 1855.

Nancy, this only daughter, married James Keen, on September 20, 1849. She appears to have been her father's housekeeper for twelve years; she and her husband made their home there on Hollywood where they reared a family and there both died and were buried.—Turn to the family name, "Keen."

John King, second of above Kings, was born in Washington County, Pennsylvania, January 4, 1797, says his youngest son Lewis Frank in a biography he gave Hardesty in the year 1883. Many older persons acquainted with John and his brother William say, "That may be true, but they certainly lived many years in Russell County, Virginia, and in Pike County, Kentucky,". John came to Big Sandy a few years later than his brother William. In Virginia or Pike County, Kentucky, John had united in marriage with Margaret Charles, and to them were born, likely in Pike County, two sons and four daughters, all of whom came with the father here to Sandy, but the mother, Margaret, for some unexplained reason, never came.

The names of those sons and daughters of John and Margaret (Charles) King, in order of their ages, as recollected by Charles B. Ferrell, son of one of those daughters, are as follows: David, Jennie, George, Elizabeth, Margaret and Nancy.

The daughters of this family were mistresses of the household of their father, John King, until about the year 1860, when John brought home a second wife, her name, Juliann, born April 1, 1835. To John and Juliann, his wife, was born a son whom they named Lewis Franklin, and a daughter, Mary A., who married Vincent A. Ledsome, September 17, 1883.

All the children of John King married, and made homes in Geary or Smithfield Districts; all were ambitious to have and to hold largely; there were no tinkers, potters nor professional men in this second generation.

For further of the careers of these daughters, see the family names of their husbands in this Chapter.

As to the sons we can write further, that,

David B. King, son of the above ancestor John, married Sudna West, January 1, 1859. They settled on Dog Creek and there raised a family, the names of individuals of which we do not have, and nothing further, except that there are several "Kings" residents of Big Sandy, most of whom are important citizens. David S., nor any of his descendants, subscribed for a book and made a record of his family as did his brother's son, Wm. R., of whom we write next.

Jennie, daughter of John, Sr., married Aaron Bishop, of Flat Fork, Poca, at that time; Elizabeth married William Noe, Sr., first of the name on Big Sandy; Margaret remained in Pike County and was mother of Captain Wm. Justice of Left Hand; Nancy married John Ferrell of Smithfield District.

George, born in Pike County, Kentucky, married Priscilla Drake, daughter of .... Drake, one of the earliest settlers on Big Sandy; George and Priscilla settled on a large tract of land, on Canoe of Henrys Fork. Their sons and daughters born and reared there were: William Rufus, born December 10, 1853; John M., born 1859.

William Rufus King, son of George and Priscilla (Drake) King, was born on Henrys Fork, December 10, 1853; there married Lovernia Starcher, born there February 15, 1858, the daughter of Josiah P. and Nancy J. (Nichols) Starcher. They began their careers on a large tract of land on Dog Creek, where they made in time a large cattle farm, and reared a family; their names and marriages with ages are as follows:

George W., married Pruda Carper, February 14, 1904; his age, 22; her age, 16.

Joseph P., married Sallie W. Carper, February 8, 1903; his age, 21; her age, 18. Both were daughters of Shelton V. Carper.

Cassie, married French Trout, son of Oscar, on September 17, 1911; "his age, 25; her age, 22."

Mabel M., married Harley Ross, son of Spurgeon, son of Davidson Ross, early settler on Hollywood; this marriage was on April 18, 1914; his age, 22; her age, 19."

William Rufus, Jr., married Mabel, daughter of Nathan Keen, son of James Keen, pioneer, on February 12, 1913; "his age, 21; her age, 21."

Mary D., married Preston Helmic, "July 18, 1908; his age, 22; her age, 18;" and

Pearl, married Clay Reynolds, son of George W. Reynolds, of Virginia.

KISER: Of Western Harper District.

Abednigo Kiser married Rebecca Counts in Russell County, Virginia; came to Jackson County and settled and lived for awhile in that part called "New Kentuck," about the head of Middle Fork of Pocatalico; moving from there to Lower Flat Fork, settling on that stream about two miles below mouth of Coxs Fork, in the year 1866.

To Abednigo and Rebecca (Counts) Kiser were born three sons and six daughters, as follows:

1. Bithinia, married Sam Smith of Jackson County;
2. Elijah, married Martha Slaughter; of him see further;
3. Rachel, married William Fields of Flat Fork, then;
4. Henry, married Margaret Fletcher first, for a second wife he married a Miss Margaret Skeen of Jackson;
5. Elihu, married a Miss Kiser in Virginia of another family;

6. Mary, married Pierce Skeen of Jackson County;
7. Phoebe, married George W. Fields, see name "Fields."
8. Nancy, married John Skeen of Jackson County; and
9. Rebecca married George W. Garrett, settled in Kentuck.

Elijah Kiser, son of Abednigo and Rebecca (Counts) Kiser, married Martha Slaughter of Jackson County, West Virginia, and she died in 1865, at their home on Higly of Poca; to Elijah and Martha were born:

(a) Noah Kiser, who was twice married, the first wife a Miss Brock; the second, Virgie Harper.

(b) Jefferson D. Kiser, born in 1861, married Clementine, daughter of Thomas and Emeline Payne, of Coxs Fork, Harper District. He is a prominent farmer and active in his church, lodges and district affairs. To Jefferson D. and Clementine Kiser were born one son and one daughter, their names: Thomas E., early in life an active school teacher, he married Ollie G. Shafer.

The name of the daughter of Jeff D. and Clementine is Ida J., who married Thomas T. Fields of Flat Fork.

KISER: Of Walton District.

Martin Kiser, the first of this name in this Pocatalico country, came here shortly prior to 1848. He was born in Russell County, Virginia, December 7, 1824, son of Charles and Nancy (le Force) Kiser, of a Colonial family coming to Western Virginia by way of the Shenandoah Valley. Soon after arriving here, Martin Kiser, on July 28, 1848, married Mary Ferrell, daughter of John and Sarah (Alison) Ferrell who arrived from Russell County, Virginia, in 1848, and settled near the mouth of Trace Fork. Sarah Alison was born in North Carolina, 1798.

Martin and Mary (Ferrell), his wife, made their permanent home on the head of Big Creek where they cleared the forest away and made a good home-farm, and there reared their children, whose names—as given by Martin or his family for "Hardesty's History" are as follows:

Nancy, born January 26, 1850;
Sarah J., July 12, 1852;
Martha A., April 20, 1854;
Louisa, February 22, 1856;
Morgan P., June 24, 1858, died at 16;
Robert E., January 10, 1869;
Jefferson D., April 15, 1862, to be distinguished from a Jefferson D., son of Elijah Kiser;

Martin Kiser, above ancestor, was a volunteer in the Mexican War and trained in that army six months.

Simon P. Kiser came to Walton District 1856; he was born in Russell County, Virginia, August 4, 1854, son of Charles and Lucinda (laForce) Kiser, the former born May 9, 1830; the latter May 8, 1835. On February 27, 1879, this Simon P. Kiser and Mary E. Jackson were united in marriage, Rev. Silas P. Whitney, the officiating minister. To these wedded ones, three children were born; their names: Joseph D., 1880; Jamss G., 1882, and Lucinda G., 1882.

KNIGHT:

James K. Knight was born in Harrison County, Western Virginia; in same county married Mary V. Rogers; they came to Left Hand about the year 1844, having then two sons and one daughter; their names: William Payne, Francis, and Emaline. The last named was born January 9, 1834, married William H. Justice, November 1, 1855, and settled next farm to her father. Francis Knight, of this family entered the Confederate Army of 1862, was soon lost to communication with home and never heard from as yet. This left William Payne Knight alone to continue the family name.

William Payne Knight married Sarah Elizabeth Noe, June 11, 1854, his age 23, her's 21, she a daughter of William and Elizabeth (King) Noe, of "Three Forks of Sandy," now Newton; and he and Elizabeth soon made their home on the Knight homestead on Left Hand; continued clearing back and making fields out of the forest.

To William P. and Elizabeth were born four sons: James K., Daniel W., Jackson, and Aaron A., all of whom married wives and founded homes and families in Geary; and one daughter who became the wife of George Carper, son of Calahan C. Carper. Of these, Aaron A. has public notice.

Aaron A. Knight of above family ,in the year 1895, his age 23, her age 22," married Jerusia, daughter of Joseph H. Nutter, of Spencer District, near Richardson, village and post office. They at once made their home on part of the large ancestral lands of Left Hand, where to Aaron A. and Jerusia have been born some five or more children, at home with them now (1926). Aaron A. served as deputy sheriff of this county, years 1905 to 1909, inclusive, and has been elected and served many times as a member of the board of education of Geary District.

KYER: Of Spencer and Spencer District.

The first of the name here was John D. Kyer, born in Botetourt County, Virginia, son of an old family of the name there; he spoke sometimes of two brothers whose names were Charles and Fielding.

John D., while yet young, married in Botetourt County, Virginia, a Miss Martha O'Flaherty, daughter of Hodman O'Flaherty, a miller by trade, who later came to the Spring Creek country while it was under jurisdiction of Wirt County.

John D. Kyer was a first class carpenter, which trade he followed for several years after "coming out of the war," he having served under General Robert E. Lee in Virginia. He was also a good land surveyor, and the real estate records reveal his name often as such surveyor.

To John D. and his wife Martha (O'Flaherty), were born and by them reared to citizenship of the county the following children:

Sarah E., who married Russ Fox, the blacksmith, November 8, 1880.

John W. L., long a resident of Spencer, merchant, carpenter and business man, who married Roxie Arnott, April 2, 1888; his age, 22; her's 16. She was a daughter of Henry M. Arnott, long a resident of Spencer. All now reside at Ravenswood. They have several children.

Lydia A., married Ralph Six of Spring Creek, May 27, 1890; his age, 23; her's 22.

George Forest, married Miss Cynthia Roach, daughter of the Roach family of near Richardson, Henrys Fork, May 8, 1898; his age, 24; her's 18. G. Forest is a first class barber of the City of Spencer. He and Cynthia have reared several sons and daughters.

KYGER: Of Reedy, on the turnpike toward Spencer.

Two brothers: Rollo—"Rolla" the clerks have it—and Hugh Kyger came to this Reedy country possibly as early as the year 1850.

Rolla—Raleigh or Rollo—Kyger was born likely in the valley of the Little Kanawha, maybe in Wood County, year 1819, died at his farm home on Reedy, 1905. These dates are taken from his tombstone.

"Rolla" Kyger and his wife Susan E. (her family name we do not have), settled on a large tract of land, through which ran the turnpike, and made there one of the best and what was the most attractive farms between Reedy and Spencer for the twenty years of 1865 to 1885. There they brought up their family of three sons and one daughter. Their names in order of ages, from recollection of the author, are George W., Annie, Dexter M., and Charles M.

Annie married J. W. Mitchell, December 9, 1882.

Dexter M. and Charles M. each married in another county than Roane; sold their patrimony to the brother, George W. and made their homes elsewhere than here.

George W. Kyger, son of "Rolla' 'and his wife, married Miss Laura Slaven of near Ravenswood. They made their farm home on the pikeside, on part of the old home place; there brought up their several children, all of whose names we do not have. The daughter married Bailey Chambers of Roane.

Some time in the 1890's George W. sold his holdings and with all his family moved to Jackson County.

Hugh Kyger, the other brother above mentioned, was near the age of "Rolla". He was a surveyor and civil engineer and we are told did much of the work of superintending the construction of the Glenville, Ripley and Ohio turnpike, 1848-1850. Acquired many tracts of large acreages of lands in Curtis District and adjoining parts; was a prominent figure especially throughout the period of the Civil War and the years immediately preceding it. He left one daughter, Josephine, who married Wm. C. Burdette.

LANG:

Arthur Wellington Lang, of Tanners Run on the Spencer and Ripley turnpike, was born in Harrison County, in the year 1841, son of Henderson and Mary (Ferris) Lang; enlisted and served as a soldier of the Confederacy, in the 14th Regiment, Virginia Calvary, and was one of the picked three hundred assigned to General Albert G. Jenkins for his famous raid from Virginia into Ohio where horses were commandeered for the Confederate cavalry; and on which raid General Jenkins captured Buckhannon, Weston, Glenville, and Spencer, Ripley and Ravenswood. Mr. Lang "rather liked" Spencer and after that war, returned to Harrison County and there married Margaret Teter. Of this marriage two sons were born: Homer and Arthur W., Jr. With these and the wife, Arthur W. Lang came to Roane County, purchased the farm on Tanners Run, in the year 1901, lives there yet, hale and hearty, though now (1926), in his eighty-sixth year of age. He frequently walks to town since the old turnpike is now concrete-surfaced from town to where it passes his door.

Homer Lang, of the above family, is not married; Arthur, Jr., married. Miss Sallie J. Goff, Feb. 25, 1910; he then 26, she 26.

LAW: Or Reedy.

William A. Law and his family being the first of this name making homes here, came here in year 1899.

The family tradition of ancestry is, that three brothers, Law, came from Ireland and landed in New York, in what year, or even decade is not known; one of these stayed in New York City, one set out for the Northwest, and one has made his way into the Monongahela Valley, his name David W. Law, or he there left a son, David W., within the decade 1840 to 1850.

David W. married in Harrison County Miss Hannah Dennison, about the year 1848, and there they made their home and reared one daughter and two sons whose names were Samantha, "Deed" and William Anderson.

William Anderson Law, the above, was born at or near Cherry Camp, Harrison County, Western Virginia, February 20, 1852, there grew up and married Miss Sarah A. Williams; they began their careers there, and there all their children but one were born. He became a minister of the Gospel; a Methodist first, later a member of the United Brethren Conference of West Virginia; filled many pulpits. They lived a short time in Colorado; returned and made their home with their family in Reedy, 1899, to time of death, 1920.

In Reedy he first began a general produce business and taught his sons general trading; established them and again entered the church ministry. The names and marriages of the sons and daughters of William Anderson Law are as follows: Amos D., Leonidas L., David W., Henry Clyde, Martha Allie, Sarah Elizabeth, "Lizzie", Jemima May, Ray C., Benjamin Stout, Guy Kidd. Marriages:

Amos D., 48, to Claudia Anderson, 25, August 8, 1922;

Leonidas L., 23, to Blanche Seaman, 17, January 1, 1898;
David W., 22, to Stella McGraw, 17, July 1, 1903;
Henry Clyde, 22, to Melvina Howell, 0, December 24, 1897;
Martha Allie, 22, to Lee B. Batten, 24, December 20, 1905;
Sarah Elizabeth, 35, to Walter W. McKinley, 41, October 20, 1912;
Jemima May, 20, to William R. Flesher, 19, December 24, 1898;
Ray Constantine, 32, to Stella Harris, 22, August 8, 1919;
Guy Kidd, of him, yet a young man, we do not know.

LAWSON:

George Patterson Lawson, born in Lewis or Harrison County, about 1841, with his wife, Mary E. (Cutright) and some of their first born children, came to Roane County about the year 1878; purchased a large tract of land lying on head of that branch of Poca on which is Gandeeville, approaching to within one-third of a mile of Gandeeville, now (1926) on State Road No. 14.

The Lawsons here soon made one of the largest farms of that neighborhood. When they settled there all those well grassed fields seen now, were covered with the dense forest that so long sheltered the buffalo, elk and deer that lingered near two large "licks" down near where is now the village.

To George P. Lawson and Mary E. (Cutright), his wife, were born the following children:

Lloyd, who married Mollie Parsons of Jackson County, W. Va.

May, the daughter who died at about twenty-one years;

Arvilla, wife of F. Mint Casto of Gandeeville;

And, Blonda A. and Alonzo, next further mentioned.

Blonda Austen Lawson married Alice Grace Dixon, daughter of Charles Dixon of near Spencer, on the 16th day of April, 1896. To them were born one son, Harley, and one daughter, Opal. Blonda's is one of the large farms of those parts.

Alonzo E. Lawson of above family, was twice married; his first wife, Mary C., daughter of Benj. F. Bailey of Harper District, on the 14th of November, 1896, "his age 18, her age, 20 years. Mary C. died the year 1906. Of this marriage were born two children: Romie and Faye, the latter now the wife of Clyde C. Cleavenger, clerk of the Circuit Court of Roane County. Alonzo E.'s second wife is Stella F. Harper, whom he married August 19, 1908, "his age 30, her age 22." Of this marriage two children have been born.

LAWRENCE: Of upper Spring Creek.

Noah Lawrence and his wife, Elizabeth (Allman), with the first born of their several children, five sons and two daughters, came here from their former home in Lewis or Harrison County about the year 1850.

They were of the third or fourth generation of the Lawrences, early settlers of the Monongahela Valley; and came here and invested inheritances and savings in a large tract of land, virgin forest, on upper Spring Creek.

HISTORY OF ROANE COUNTY 581

The spelling of the name, Lawrence, appears on the county records in different letterings; the first deed of conveyance in this name is one by Alexander; to it he and his wife append their names spelled "L-o-r-e-n-t-z."

Noah and his family were popular people of their part of the county for some twenty-five years.

Of the children of Noah and Elizabeth (Allman), his wife, we are told they were five sons and two daughters. Their names as follows: (1st) Alexander, (2d) Rebecca Ann, (3rd) Peter, (4th) James David, (5th) George W., (6th) Jacob Madison, and (7th) Eliza M. Further about these seven:

Alexander, married Martha A. S. Burgess, September 24, 1860.

Rebecca Ann (2nd) married David Gandee, August 19, 1869.

Peter (3rd), of whom we have no information.

James David (4th) we do not know his career.

George W. (5th) married "Lina" Lowe, December 9, 1871.

Eliza M., seventh child of Noah and wife, married Carr Nichols, October 31, 1877.

Jacob Madison Lawrence, son of Noah and Elizabeth Lawrence, was born in Roane County, in the year 1859; married here, Miss Roana (or Rouena) Bartlett of Little Creek, September 9, 1880. He acquired a good farm on upper Spring Creek, where he made his home, changing in trading, once or twice; last the large farm on what is now State Road No. 14, Spencer to Charleston; died at fifty-five years of age. He was popular for fifteen years; a candidate of his political party once for sheriff of the county; was a dealer and shipper of live stock.

To Jacob Madison and Rouena (Bartlett) his wife, were born and by them brought up three sons and two daughters; their names, Flavius B., J. Rosco and Ira S.; Oma G., and Esta Alice. Of these:

Flavius B., first son of J. Madison and Rouena, his wife, became a popular school teacher of the county and "a learned farmer," meaning, he reads the farm literature and takes part in farmers' and stockmen's meetings. He married at 27 years of age, Miss Margaret M. Camp, 24, on November 6, 1908; she a daughter of John A. Camp.

J. Rosco Lawrence, farmer, son of J. Madison and Rouena, his wife, married Miss Florence Cutright, November 12, 1905; his age, 23; her age then 17; she a daughter of Columbus Cutright of Spring Creek.

Ira S. Lawrence, farmer, son of J. Madison and wife, married Delphia Whited, September 22, 1915; his age then 31, her's 25.

Oma G. Lawrence, daughter of J. Madison and wife, married Bruce I. Hersman, December 6, 1908; his age 21, her's 21.

Esta Alice Lawrence, daughter of J. Madison and wife, married Austin Taylor, she 18, he 24. To them was born one child. Taylor having died, she married John F. Dyer, on September 1, 1907.

LEARY: Pioneer of Middle Fork of Reedy.
Silas Benjamin Leary is the first of this name here. The family is of Irish extraction; and descendants of emigrants who landed on "The Eastern Shore," possibly before the Revolution. I have heard Silas B. say, "The name was once spelled O'-L-e-a-r-y," but as "Leary," they had married and signed their business papers at least one generation before his. He was born June 10, 1823; was a saddler and harness maker, of the entered-apprentice training; worked when a young man in Harrison and Gilmer Counties, then came to Ripley about the year 1856, where he maintained a shop a short time. Visiting Reedy, he there met and married Margaret Roach, in the year 1854; she was born February 1, 1836, daughter of William and Delilah (Carney) Roach, pioneers on Middle Fork of Reedy.

They made their lifetime home on a farm they carved out of the Roach estate. They lie buried in the Roach Cemetery. He farmed in season, and is one of those mentioned as a workman at the James W. Seaman Tan-yard. To Silas Benjamin and his wife, Margaret, were born and by them reared six sons and two daughters, their names in order of respective births: William, Calvin, Sarah Delilah, Conda, Henry, John, Esther, "Hester", and Grigg.

Only one of the name claims a home in Reedy, but further:
William married Miss Susan Victoria Candler, of Right Reedy, January 10, 1883; Sarah D., married Amos B. Mitchell of Jackson County, December 20, 1880; Calvin married Millie Catherine Chancey, May 18, 1883, she a daughter of Calvary Chancey of the Reedy Chanceys; Conda, married Miss Carrie L. Rhodes, of Middle Fork, October 27, 1886; John and Henry each married elsewhere, we have not their record here, both made homes in Clay County, West Virginia, for a time; Esther "Hester" married Thomas A. Chandler, March 22, 1891; his age then 25, her's 20. They have their home in Missouri; he a son of John W. Candler of Right Reedy, one mile above Town of Reedy, at that date.

The children of William and S. Victoria are Charley, and two daughters, Nettie and Maud.

Calvin and M. Kate, his wife, reared several sons; they are at Akron, Ohio, and scattered elsewhere.

Conda Leary is a business man (1927), at Harris, Missouri.

LEASHER:
Jacob M. Leasher or "Lesher" was a farmer and carpenter, long a resident of Left Reedy. His wife was Margaret Bates, whom he married Dec. 6. 1867. See name, "Bates." We recollect two sons: George and Roland.

LEDSOM: Of middle Geary District, Big Sandy, and Daniel Ledsom of Reedy; brothers, and first of this name in Roane County.
Dusoisaway Ledsom (spelt "Dussosaway" in Hardesty's) was born in Wood County, Western Virginia, June 6, 1833, son of Daniel and

Drusilla (Dye) Ledsom. He came to Reedy, thence to Big Sandy country in 1851. He united in marriage with Miss Mary Patton—Big Sandy then part of Kanawha County. "Dissoway" and Mary, his wife, made their home in the forest in middle Big Sandy country on its western side. There they lived their lives, and served their children, whose names are America A., born February 13, 1855; Susan J., November 4, 1857; Vincent A., July 24, 1860; Drusanna, April 4, 1863.

The wife Mary having died, Dusoisaway united in marriage with Miss Eliza J. Drennen, born on Sandy, November 25, 1838. Eliza J. came to the husband's home and mothered the household for the rest of her life. Of this marriage were born the following sons and daughters:

Minerva L., June 5, 1864; Camden L., July 11, 1866; Roena M., May 7, 1868; Daniel C.; February 28, 1870, died a child; Eugenia F., May 18, 1872; Milony F., May 7, 1877; William L., June 13, 1881. Some marriages of both above families:

America Ledsom married Elijah K. Reynolds.

Susan J., married Shelton V. Carper. See "Carper."

Vincent Alexander Ledsom married, September 17, 1883, Miss Mary King, daughter of John King, pioneer of Left Hand.

Camden L. Ledsom married Lydia Drake, daughter of Admiral Drake of Big Sandy.

Eugenia F. Ledsom married Louis M. Payne.

Miltonia "Leonia" married L. M. Cobb, and

William M. Lewsom married Miss Norma Patton, February 20, 1900; he then 19 she then 18 years of age. William L. acquired the paternal homestead and lives there yet.

Daniel Ledsom, of Cains Run, just below the Village of Reedy, married his wife in Wirt County. We have not her name. They were prominent farmer folk there for twenty-five years. Two sons, Nathaniel and George D., were popular grocermen of Town of Reedy for fifteen years, commencing in 1890.

George D. married Miss Clerinda George, January 18, 1891; his age then 22, her's 20. All have gone away seeking their fortunes elsewhere.

LEE: Of Walton and Harper Districts.

First settlers of this name here were three brothers: Samuel and Thomas of Big Creek and Robert of lower Flat Fork.

Samuel Lee with his wife, Elizabeth (Potts) Lee and two sons, Nathaniel Potts Lee and William D. Lee, came here from Harrison County, Western Virginia, in the year 1857, purchased a farm on head of Silkets Fork and soon were prominent people of those parts.

Samuel Lee, the father of above named Samuel, Thomas and Robert, was born in Ireland; on coming to America he met Elizabeth M. McCabe and in Wilmington, Delaware, they were married and at once or soon came to Harrison County, Western Virginia, where were born the above named three sons; the son, Samuel, on December 22, 1819, who there grew to manhood and married Elizabeth Potts, born in Harrison County, January 13, 1817. She was a daughter of Nathaniel Potts, born in Walton Parish, Cumberland County, England. To them were born: Nathaniel P., Samuel, Jr., Virginia, and William D. Lee.

Nathaniel P. Lee, son of Samuel first above named, and his wife, Elizabeth, early settlers here, was born in Harrison County, July 11, 1844, came with his parents to Pocatalico country as first stated; married Messelva Paxton, October 5, 1877, born in the Pocatalico neighborhood, July 12, 1849, daughter of John and Mary (Vineyard) Paxton. Near on a part of the Lee lands they made their life-time home-farm. Nathaniel P. Lee was an active and popular citizen of the county for twenty years or more; served as a Union soldier in the Home Guards of Captain William Gandee, in which service he had a leg broken by a musket ball from an enemy gun, March 5, 1865, from which wound he never recovered full use of the limb. We are told that this happened in a skirmish on the Roach farm on Reedy. He served as constable, deputy sheriff, and in several district offices. To Nathaniel P. and Messelva (Paxton) Lee, were born and by them brought up the following named children:

Webster, born October 14, 1878;

Lloyd, April 24, 1880;

Cora, March 5, 1882.

Samuel Lee, Jr., married Jemima, daughter of Capt. William Gandee.

Virginia, daughter of Samuel Lee, pioneer here, married Chester D. C. Jones in Walton District, March 11, 1875; to them were born several children.

William D. Lee, son of Samuel and Elizabeth (Potts) Lee, married Hester Ann Snodgrass, April 22, 1880; she the daughter of Jacob and Julia (Curtis) Snodgrass, settlers on Big Lick, who came there from Boone County, Western Virginia. To William D. and Hester Ann, his wife, were born and grew up some sons and daughters: Stella, Julia, Ernest, Antoinette, Helen and Dainey.

Thomas Lee, son of Samuel, Sr., and his wife, Elizabeth (McCabe) Lee, born on the Monongahela, came to Roane at the time his other two brothers, Samuel and Robert, came; purchased lands on Big Creek, in Walton District, and made his home there. He was noticeable at the county seat, at court and other times of public gatherings, because of his tall figure, prominent nose and heavy shock of hair, which in 1894, and a few years before and afterward, was iron gray. He and his wife reared several children of whom we can name here as follows: William, Hannah Jane, Thomas, Jr., Charles, John L., Samuel, Jr., and R. B., who died and left a son named Roseevlt to whom Thomas on dying left most of his estate.

Robert Lee, son of Samuel, Sr., and Elizabeth (McCabe) Lee has not left us any record of himself.

LESTER: Of Reedy.

The first of this family name in this part of the State, was John C. Lester, born in Pike County, Kentucky, in the year 1834, married Miss Rebecca Brown about the year 1854, at her home on Middle Reedy, then in Jackson County, now called "Peniel." She was a daughter of James and Dorcas (Carney) Brown, who moved to Mill Creek shortly after Rebecca's marriage.

What we know of the ancestry of John C. Lester is from fireside remarks, in the home of the parents of the author of this book. Recollections of such family remarks are in effect about as follows:

John Lester, the elder, was of a Virginia family and appears among the Kings, Drakes and Bishops, in Russel County, Virginia; later in Pike County, Kentucky. He was a dealer in horses. He was father of at least three children, two sons and one daughter, whose names in order of their respective ages were: James, Eliza and John C. James' mother was a Bishop,—this is the horseman "Jim Lester," prominent in Jackson County several years next following the Civil War. Eliza, the daughter, united in marriage with Moses Bishop in Jackson County, Western Virginia, about the year 1853. They had four sons whose names are Harvey, Isaiah, Jeremiah and Wilk Bishop. The youngest child of John Lester, Sr., was the John C., first mentioned.

The mother of Eliza and John C. was a Miss .... King; John Lester, Sr., was killed by "horse raiders" 'either in Missouri where he had collected a drove for the Eastern markets, or in Kentucky. He was on the road with his drove, when he was shot in the back, the bullet cutting through the rim of his saddle; soon after John's death his wife also died, and the three children: James, Eliza and John C., were brought to this country by the grandmother who became the owner of a farm on left Reedy. She was always referred to as "Granny King." She always expected that John C. Lester, her grandson, would "grow up and avenge his father's death." But as observed John C. married as soon as grown; then came the Civil War. In this he was loyal to Virginia; and the cause needed cavalrymen who were able to furnish their own mounts. John C. enlisted in the cavalry and rode away to Virginia's battle fields. Though married, and only twenty-eight years old, he was "a dashing colonel of cavarly," I have heard remarked. On return from the war, he took to business in his dashing way; became a cattle dealer, built up a farm of some two hundred and fifty acres, "the Wright and Granny King" places included; and died at the age of forty-six. To John C. and Rebecca (Brown) Lester were born and by them brought up there on Reedy, two daughters and five sons, their names in order of respective ages are, Sarah Jane, Pery, Wellington H., John M., James Brown, Etta May, and Charles D. Lester. Their several marriages are as follows:

Sarah Jane married William Knopp;

Perry married Miss Mary Roberts, daughter of Col. T. A. Roberts of Reedy;

Wellington H. married first Mattie Riddle who died not having any child; later he married Miss Lizzie Lee of Wirt County; served one term as County Superintendent of Schools of Wirt, also one term as County Superintendent of Schools, Calhoun County. They have a large stock farm in Calhoun now; brought up one son, Kenna Lester, delegate in State Legislature two terms.

John M. Lester married Miss Nannie Stalnaker, daughter of Marshall Stalnaker of Right Reedy and Sandy divide; 2nd day of April, 1885, "his age 20, her's 21. He soon showed industry and a cavalier desire for leadership and to share in the large things to be had. He was elected and served two terms as a justice of Reedy District; studied law, was admitted to the bar and practiced some; helped promote establishment of two banks at Reedy where he made his home, acquired a good income and died while yet young. John M. and Nannie (Stalnaker) his wife, were parents of the following sons and daughters: Ethel Anice, Elva, Roy, Emmett E., and Elpha Mabel. Of these, Ethel A. married Cadmus G. Cottle, October 18, 1911; Emmett E., married Miss Odra Elizabeth Depue, December 16, 1921, his age 28, her's 18.

James Bee Lester, son of John C. and Rebecca, married Miss Mary Curfman, July 8, 1893, his age 21, her's 22; she a daughter of Samuel Curfman.

Charles D. Lester, son of John C. and Rebecca, married Miss Mary A. Smith, September 1, 1889; his age 20, her age 19. She was a daughter of Elijah Smith of Left Reedy.

Etta May Lester, daughter of John C. and Rebecca, married John Joseph Bryant, August 17, 1899; the age of each then 23. He was born in Wirt County, West Virginia.

LEWIS:

Asbury Lewis, long of Smithfield District, later of Spencer, popular for some twenty years as a cattle dealer and good citizen, was born in Harrison County, year 1840; he married in that county Miss Olive Post, 1866. To them were born, grew up and married, George L., Judson R., Orville and Laco. All came to Roane County about the year 1882 to 1884.

George Loman married Miss Ella, daughter of Jacob Chambers, November 12, 1890, "his age 23, her age 26."

Judson Romie married Fannie Clarkson, April 7, 1901; "his age 23, her age 23."

Laco married Miss Lena Hurt, in Virginia. They live in Livingston, Alabama. His wife, Olive, having died, Asbury Lewis married Miss Frances Catherine Looney, February 28, 1884. She is a daughter of Daniel Looney, Sr. To them were born and grew up two daughters, whose names are Eliza and Jennie. Eliza married Rector B. Rowe.

HISTORY OF ROANE COUNTY 587

LEWIS: Edward Lewis, son of James A. and Prudentia (Wilson) Lewis, was born in Charleston, Western Virginia, August 24, 1838, died in Roane County, 1902.

James A. Lewis, the father of Edward of Roane County, was born in Bath County, Virginia, 1794, served as a soldier of the War of 1812, died in Kanawha County, 1860. Prudentia Wilson, wife of James A. and mother of Edward, was born in Ireland in the year 1801, died in Kanawha County, 1867.

Edward was married twice, the first to Anna L. McChesney, October 21, 1858, she born in Rockbridge County, Virginia, December 7, 1838, died June 4, 1865, leaving one child, named Prudentia, born October 23, 1861, grew to womanhood and became the wife of Dr. William Campbell. See the family, Campbell. In the great "Rebellion" Edward Lewis enlisted in Stonewall Jackson's Brigade, Co. I, 4th Va. Infantry, at Richmond, October, 1864, with one of his brothers, John F. Lewis. John Lewis, another brother, soldier of that same army, had been killed in battle at Winchester, September 19, 1864.

Edward visited Rockbridge County again, and there on October 9, 1867, Mary M. McChesney, sister of the first wife, became his wife. She was born February 22, 1841, daughter of James and Frances A. (McNut) McChesney. Edward Lewis in his biography in Hardesty's, says he "Settled in this county ,then Kanawha, in the year 1854." From this date he was a settler in what is now Roane County, two years before his first marriage. Here at the place of his first settlement, near Southern line next Kanawha County, he owned seven hundred and fifty acres of land, made a large farm, and cattle and horse buyers visited his place, though for many years deep in the forest, six or seven miles from Walton, where they were sure to find some stock to drive away.

Here were born all the children of the married life of Edward and Mary M. (McChesney) Lewis, their names as follows: Fannie M., (Simpson by marriage) was born September 19, 1868; William A., January 31, 1871; James McChesney, September 3, 1873; John Edward, May 22, 1876; May (Goad by marriage), September 15, 1878; Lucy J. (Mrs. James Lynch), August 24, 1881. Mary M., the mother of these and widow of Edward Lewis, died about the year 1915.

This large tract of land owned by Edward Lewis descended to his children above named at time of his death, intestate, Prudentia Campbell had preceded him in death by a few years. At time of his death an oil company held a lease giving its exclusive right to explore for and produce oil and gas of all this large tract, holding it at the price stipulated in the leases of twenty-five cents per acre.

The widow and heirs decided to have this 750 acres partitioned among them, by proceedings of court; the writer, author of this history, was attorney for the plaintiff and made and presented to court all papers and orders of the partition proceedings, and as the circuit court's commissioner made deeds to the several heirs, to each his allotment; here hangs a more instructive story: When in consultation as to instituting the suit for partition, the heirs moving the matter, were informed that as the law then was, the oil company might object to such division and complain that it had not bargained to deal with so many persons, and the court sustain its objection, thus preventing partition. This was met by the plaintiff's deciding that twenty-five cents per acre per annum, was not worth bothering with, and decided to bring the suit without making the oil company then owning the leasehold a party to the proceedings, which was done, and the cause completed and a deed made to each heir for his moyety in acres, by metes and bounds, except the share of the deceased, Prudentia Campbell, which had descended to her children and that share was conveyed to them as joint owners. The widow it was argued by the heirs was of right getting that twenty-five cents lease money paid by the holder of the leases, and it did not hurt the share of any one. But:

After a few years oil was struck on the western side of the original 750 acres, and slowly extended on the nearest three shares; the money for production being paid to the holder of the share on which such producing wells were located, and nothing to the others.

This continued until some three hundred thousand dollars had been obtained by the holders of these shares having produced oil and gas wells on them.

Then a suit in chancery was instituted by Dr. Campbell for himself and children, alleging and contending that such a division of lands as shown in that partition suit did not partition nor divide the minerals or mineral rights, and praying for an accounting; the court of last resort sustained the contentions and ordered an accounting and a refunding by those of the heirs who had received it, the full and proportionate shares of all money received for oil and gas to those heirs from whose "surface shares" no oil or gas had been produced or marketed. The accounting and reimbursements were made as ordered. We have not heard whether or not this engendered a family feud; let us hope it did not.

LONG: Of Reedy.

John C. Long was born at Holly Meadows, Randolph County, Western Virginia, June 1, 1831, son of James and Barbary A. (Johnson) Long, both born in Randolph County; he, 1781; she, 1800.

John C. Long was twice married. His first wife was Samantha, daughter of Houston and Ingaby (Thompson) Booth, whom he married in Harrison County, where she died only one year later. His second wife was Margaret V., daughter of John and Hannah (Corder) Pickens, whom he married in Barbour County, West Virginia, February 21, 1867; John C. Long came to a large tract of land which he had purchased from Harrison County owners situate on and about the head of Longs Run, on the line between Curtis and Reedy Districts, extending to the coves of Buffalo of Mill Creek, about the time he married first, 1857. He enlisted on the Confederate side, and served with General Albert G. Jenkins as a member of his staff. After the war was over and he had married Margaret V., they came to the lands above mentioned and began the making of a farm, at which they worked, as all such pioneers had to work, right there for the next twenty-five years; he sold to Melville W. Morrison, his brother-in-law, his farm and to the Bonds and others the farms they made in that locality.

To John C. and Hanna (Pickens) Long five children were born; their names in order of their ages, are: James Lee, several years an attorney-at-law in the City of Charleston, West Virginia, was born 1868; Icy Boothe, 1872; Rose Altha, 1875; William W., 1879, died 1880.

John C. Long was a large, fair-skinned man with blue eyes, and of a counterance suggesting playful humor and good sense.

LOONEY: Of Walton and Pocatalico.

John and Phoebe (Huffman) Looney, his wife, came and commenced their home in this county in the year of its birth, 1856. John was a brother of Robert of Smithfield.

He was born in Botetourt County, Virginia (Craig County now), January 14, 1814, son of Joseph Looney. She was born in same county, February 16, 1816, daughter of Jacob Huffman. They appear to have lived in Tazwell County for a time, from which county they came to Roane County with their family of sons and daughters, whose names are as follows:

David Giles, Lewis, Nancy M., Mary A., Permelia D., and John Madison.

David Giles Looney, son of John and Phoebe (Huffman) Looney, his wife, was twice married; first wife Clara S. Peters, born 1838, married November 17, 1863. Of this marriage were born five children: James Lewis, September 19, 1864; Phoebe E., April 23, 1866; Jacob H., August 16, 1867; Christain P., March 18, 1869 and Rebecca A., January 13, 1871. The wife, Clara S., having died, David Giles Looney married Mary E. Hammack, March 8, 1874. Of this marriage two sons and two daughters were born; their names and births: Barbara J., January 25, 1876; Charles R., February 10, 1878; Henry P., August 15, 1880, and Fannie E., January 15, 1883.

James Lewis Looney, son of David Giles and wife, Clara, united in marriage with Mary Lucretia Barr, February 7, 1889; his age 20, her age 21. She was born in Gallia County, Ohio, daughter of Jacob Barr, who settled with his family on Long Ridge, some time in the 1880's. James L. and Lucretia have reared three daughters and one son: Grace, Sylvia, Pearl and Jacob Christopher.

Grace married Dr. Waitman T. Smith, November 11, 1914; his age 26, her age 23; Pearl married Hubert S. Adams, November 25, 1918; his age 27, her's 26; Sylvia married Lyle H. Tracy, January 19, 1924; his age 32, her age 26.

Jacob Christopher married Aubra E. Casto, June 3, 1919; his age 23, her's 21. James L. Looney and all his family, except Grace, live in Spencer now, 1927.

Lewis W. Looney, son of John and Phoebe (Huffman) Looney, was born in Tazewell County, Virginia, February 20, 1856. On February 13, 1864, he married Rebecca F. Gibson, born in Greenbrier County, West Virginia, January 8, 1842, daughter of Robert H. and Mary (Spotts) Gibson, at time of this marriage living near Charleston, W. Va. Rebecca F. Gibson received the first teacher's certificate issued in Roane County under the free school system. Lewis W. and his wife, Rebecca F., made their lifetime home on Round Knob Creek of Upper Poca. They felled the forest and made many fine fields there. Their's was known for many years as the best farm of that part of Walton District. The names and dates of birth of their children are as follows:

Mary Esta, July 6, 1864, wife of James Madison Butcher; Mattie J., October 1, 1866, married James J. Taylor, 23, April 7, 1887; John Houston, January 26, 1869, married Miss Laura Ethel Ferrell, August 22, 1900, his age 31, her age 18;' Lloyd G., August 17, 1873; Phoebe Susan, July 12, 1876, married Madison (Mat) L. Ferrell.

Of the above family John Houston Looney is most widely known; was a successful school teacher for many years, commencing quite young. He succeeded to and owns the home farm on Round Knob; keeps the farm; is a student yet and keeps well posted in current affairs.

Of the three daughters of John and Phoebe (Huffman) Looney, we are told Nancy M. became the wife of Robert Henderson; Mary A., the wife of John W. Lynch, year 1866, and Permelia D. wife of Presley Sergent. See names, Henderson, Lynch, Sergent.

John Madison Looney, son of John and Phoebe Huffman Looney, was born in Monroe County, Virginia, 1856, came here with the family in the year 1856. He married Cynthia Vineyard, daughter of Delana Vineyard, January 30, 1883. Soon acquired a large farm at mouth of Johnson's Creek of Poca; dealt also in stock and was popular as a first farmer for twenty years. Was elected and served one or more terms as a Commissioner of the County Court. His name is on several highway bridge plates as such member, or as president of the Court of year, 1900 and onward. To John Madison and Cynthia (Vineyard), his wife, have been born on dates in order of name given, the following children:

Gillie Myrtle, Sydney Delana, now an M. D.; Melissa, Delana V., Velma R., became the wife of Coy C. Conley, April 26, 1916;her age

20, his age 26; George H., Theodore Roosevelt, Catherine Delores and Quentin A. The last four, being children at home yet.

LOWE: Of Harper District.

James Lowe, son of a John and Sarah Lowe, natives of Monroe County, Virginia, John having been a soldier in the Revolutionary War, came to the Lower Flat Fork country about the year 1845. In the year 1847 he married Catherine Harper, but we do not know of which of the Harper families she is a daughter, it has been observed that the first wife of the pioneer Asa Harper was a Mary J. Lowe, whom he married in the year 1840, according to Asa's biography in Hardesty's History, he settled here in 1835. There were four brothers of Asa Harper here at that time, some of whom had grown daughters.

To James and Catherine (Harper) Lowe were born: William H., 1850; Lisha A. H., 1852; John M., 1854, and Sarah C., 1856. The wife and mother, Catherine Lowe, died in December, 1856, soon after the birth of Sarah C. On August 11, 1857, James Lowe married Hannah, daughter of Peter and Martha (Bell) Dearman, of Upper Harper, then widow of William H. Raines, deceased, having a daughter two years old at the time of marriage, named Mary A. Raines. To James and Hannah were born, Martha J., 1858; Matilda E., 1861; Adaline F., 1866; James G., 1868; Cora B., Dec. 10, 1871, and Samuel E., February 1, 1875.

LOWE: Of Upper Spring Creek and Spencer.

As to ancestry of this family, our definite information commences with Levi Lowe, an early settler in the country between the Greenbrier and New rivers, later included in Monroe County, and that his family came over there from the valley of the James River some time prior to the year 1793. From biographies and other literature it is observed that the Lowes were English and that some arrived in New England, others Pennsylvania and the Carolinas. Different spellings of the name is indulged in; it is observed that those of the North spell it "Low," in Virginia it is spelt "Lowe," and in the South both spellings appear.

Levi Lowe, above mentioned, was married or married, and he and his wife, about the year 1790, made their home there between Greenbrier and New rivers, and reared a family. Of these we have the following name: Bradley, Mathew, Joseph, Samuel; and daughters, Lethia, who married a Dinsmore, and Sallie, who married a Mr. Warren, or Waren.

Bradley Lowe, above mentioned, came to the upper Pocatalico and settled among the Vineyards and Looneys in the first of the decade, 1845 to 1855.

Mathew Lowe, of above mention, was born in 1793, and died in Roane County, 1884. He had married in Virginia, Miss Elizabeth Clark, born 1801, died 1856. Their first home for many years was in Monroe County, West Virginia, where all their children were born. The names of these: Charles B., Samuel H., Levi C., Morris J., Granville, John,

Columbus. All these came to Roane County about the year 1855, likely having had a good report of the country from the Unkle Bradley, who had preceded them here by some years.

The wife, Elizabeth (Clark) Lowe, having died, Mathew married again. The children of this second marriage were: Adaline, who married William Arnott; Elizabeth Ramsey, Clementine Mann, Rebecca, Sinnett and Agnes Wyatt.

Further of above families:

Samuel Henry Lowe, son of Mathew and Elizabeth (Clark) Lowe, was born in Monroe County, Virginia, November 29, 1828; married Catherine Meadows, born March 28, 1832. This couple made their home on Rush Creek near Pocatalico, near Charles and Emeline, the brother and sister.

To Samuel Henry and Catherine, his wife, were born and brought up the following named sons and daughters:

Martha A., born March 25, 1852, married James W. Nida on December 15, 1878.

Henry A., January 9, 1854, married Julia A. Pursley, November 25, 1875.

Mathew Thomas, October 16, 1855, married Miss A. A. Ferrell, October 27, 1878. Of this union a scon named Howard was born; and this first wife having died, Mathew T. married Miss Sarah Elizabeth Flesher, daughter of Dempsey Flesher, of Reedy, on March 17, 1884.

Charles G. was born December 10, 1857, married Sarah E. Wade, November 11, 1876.

Floyd F., born February 18, 1860, married Malinda Santee, September 11, 1880.

Ward S., February 25, 1862, married Emma S. Callow, of Reedy, November 26, 1886.

Louverna B., born April 8, 1864, married Peter C. Looney, 1882.

Robert C., March 10, 1866, married Sallie O. Flesher, of Reedy, September 8, 1887.

Roxalana E., born January 8, 1868, married John Columbus Flesher, brother of above Fleshers, on December 9, 1886.

James Patrick, born April 26, 1870, married Miss Florence Workman, of Spencer, June 3, 1899.

Elizabeth C., born March 2, 1872, married William E. Burke on January 6, 1893.

George H. Lowe, born September 19, 1874, married Minnie Hersman, October 1, 1898.

All the foregoing sons and daughters of Samuel H. Lowe and Catherine, his wife, have made businesses, homes and readed families. James P. is a general merchant in Spencer. He and his wife, Florence D., have one son, Paul Lowe, now a young man of Spencer. Mathew T. died some years ago leaving the wife, Sarah Elizabeth (Flesher), and one son, Homer D. They are—1926—proprietors and managers of the "Lowe Hotel," of the City of Spencer.

Charles B. Lowe, son of Mathew and Elizabeth (Clark) Lowe, his wife, united in marriage with Miss Emaline Meadows prior to formation of Roane County, all Pocatalico then being under the jurisdiction of Kanawha County.

Charles B. and Emaline acquired a tract of several hundred acres of land, all in dense forests, on Round Knob Branch of Pocatalico and made a hundred or more acres of it into clear and fertile fields. There spent the remainder of their lives, coveting nothing, envying no one. The names of the five sons and three daughters and marriage of each:

Henry J. to Julia Pursley, November 22, 1875.

Harvey Houston to Sarah Jane Hammack, October 2, 1873.

H. H. Lowe, widow, 40 years old, to N. J. Ryan, 39, February 16, 1890.

John C. Lowe to "Lucy" Lucinda Hundley, October 13, 1877.

James Anderson Lowe, 26, to Sarah J. Mitchell, 16, December 26, 1886.

Lewis Washington Lowe, 20, to Barbara Ellen Carpenter, 20, April 26, 1888.

Elizabeth S. Lowe to William Snyder, March 2, 1868.

Pauline "Lina" Lowe to George Lawrence, December 9, 1871.

Mary Ann Lowe, 21, to George W. "Dock" Pursley, 26, March 5, 1885. He was born in Botetourt County, Virginia.

Morris J. Lowe, son of Mathew and Elizabeth (Clark) Lowe, was born in Monroe County, West Virginia, June 3, 1836. On September 29, 1859, married Miss Mary Camp, daughter of William Camp and his wife, of Spring Creek country; acquired a large tract of land in Walton District lying between Round Knob and Rush Creek of Poca. On this, in the forest they commenced, worked and achieved a home of satisfaction, a competence of old age and gave the country seven sons and three daughters, as follows:

Samuel L., born July 25, 1860, no marriage record here.

John J., born December 2, 1861, married Fannie J. Ferrell, 19, on March 1, 1888; William T., April 26, 1863, married Sallie Roberts, of Reedy, March 14, 1893; Elizabeth A., January 6, 1865, married Festus Sinnett, March 12, 1885, his age then 24; Henry J., born December 8, 1866, married Miss Ella G. Gibson, November 6, 1892, her age then 20; Mandevilla J., born January 6, 1868, married Miss Louise Hayes, daughter of G. Warren Hayes. Mandeville became a graduate physician, located in Parkersburg where he has practiced some fifteen years, known as Doctor Lowe. Everette C., seventh child of Morris J. and Mary, his wife, was born October 7, 1890, died; Charles C., born September 5, 1873, married Emma S. Sinnett, October 8, 1897, his age 23, her's 20, a second marriage was to Lectra Canterbury; Martha S., and Addie E. (twins), born June 15, 1877; Martha S. married J. Kellum Snodgrass, October 16, 1898, ages, she 21, he 22; Addie E., married

Melvin Snodgrass; Otmer Overton, born August 15, 1879, married Miss Theo Law, daughter of L. F. Law, of Spencer, died soon after marriage. Of the above family, Henry J., excellent farmer near Spencer, is most widely known hereabout. He and his wife are the parents of Wilbur T. Lowe, the popular grocer on Main Street; his wife, Erline (Goff), whom he married August 15, 1919, his age 26, her's then 20 years.

William T., son of Morris, above mentioned, has resided at Gandeeville for long, possibly ever since his marriage. He is a prominent farmer there, having all the comforts of a farm with village conveniences of gas for light and heat, and the paved State highway past his door.

Levi Clark Lowe, son of Mathew and Elizabeth (Clark), was born in Monroe County, West Virginia, August 8, 1823; on June 23, 1859, married Miss Sarah E. Camp, daughter of William Camp, who was at the time a recent arrival from Monroe County with his family. L. Clark was a school teacher, but soon acquired a farm on Charles Fork of Spring Creek, ánd there he and Sarah, his wife, made a comfortable home and brought up a family. The names of these children in order of respective births are as follows:

Sarah Jane, who married A. B. Jordan, died shortly afterward; Henry Clay, C. Edward, Morris Pembroke, Robert, Elton A. and Susie. Their marriages:

Henry Clay, at twenty years of age, to L. C. Gandee, 21, March 8, 1888; C. Edward, 29, to Dora B. Nichols, 19, on April 23, 1899; Morris Pembroke, 19, to Lillie B. Valentine, 18, October 29, 1880; Robert G., 23, to Eliza D. Stalnaker, 22, December 27, 1893; Elton A., 27, to L. E. Davis, 30, January 30, 1902; Susie, 21, to Howard Snyder, 21, November 17, 1921.

Of this family of Levi Clark Lowe, Henry Clay resides in Spencer, and has for some years been rental payer for the United Fuel Gas Company.

Rev. Morris Pembroke Lowe resides on his farm, but is a Baptist preacher and in charge of various congregations in the county.

LUKENS:

The first of this name who came here was Thomas D. and Amelia (Brunner) Lukens, his wife, and their nine children, who purchased land lying on the divide between Spring Creek and West Fork, at head of Beaver Dam Run.

Thomas D. Lukens was born in Noble County, Ohio, about the year 1826. Amelia Bruner was born in Ohio County, West Virginia, about the year 1832.

This Lukens family arrived here November 17, 1876.

The names of the nine children of Thomas D. and Amelia Lukens are as follows:

Theodore M., who married Jennie Hughes, of Jackson County, West Virginia. Her family we do not know.

Mary Ann, married James Carbel in Athens County, Ohio.

Fred H., married Mary E. Bennett, daughter of James T. Bennett, of Barnes Run, Spencer District.

John Bruner married Elizabeth Jane Connolly, daughter of Charles and Matilda (Greathouse) Connolly, of Henrys Fork, on April 18, 1885. To John and Elizabeth J. were born, at their home on the ancestral place, three sons and three daughters.

William J. married Addie Miller of Illinois.

Eli B., married Miss Ilo Rader of Missouri.

Christina married John W. Wells, and they later made their home on Upper Flat Fork of Poca for some years. They reared several children, among them is Frederick Wells, yet of Upper Flat Fork, in Smithfield District.

Sarah E., married Samuel Bennett, son of James T. Bennett, above mentioned.

Lydia E. married John Frederick Beeker, of Athens County, Ohio.

LYON:

In the year 1872, Peter Lyon and Alfred and William ("Billy") Moore arrived from Green County, Pennsylvania, and settled. Lyon on the Mill Creek Reedy divide near the Spencer and Ripley pike, and the Moores settled on the creek at Peniel.

Peter and Elizabeth (Kern) Lyon, his wife; he was born in Jefferson County, Ohio, February 22, 1819; she in Fayette County, Pennsylvania, April 11, 1838, and they were married November 25, 1858, in Green County, Pennsylvania. Of this marriage eight daughters and one son were born. Alice J., 1859; Della, 1861; James D., 1862; Nora, 1864; Annie B., 1866; Lizzie M., 1868; Effie, 1870; Virginia M., 1873, and Jessie L., 1876. The last two children were born in Curtis District. The family was noted as promoters of vocal music in their neighborhood.

ALFRED MOORE, born in Green County, Pennsylvania, 1841, son of Thomas and Rachel (Maple) Moore, natives of Pennsylvania. Thomas being a son of John A., soldier of the War of 1812. Alfred married in Green County, Elizabeth S., daughter of Samuel and Nancy (Patterson) Guthrie, year 1864. Of this marriage four children were born. Zora M., 1865; Nancy W., 1867; Margaret L., 1868; Virgia, 1877. Alfred Moore will long be remembered as a faithful attendant at Masonic Lodge at Reedy. Margaret L. is yet a resident of Roane County.

"Billy" Moore, brother of Alfred, lived some fifteen years, a good farmer residing on north side of the pike in the first "plank and weather-boarded" farm residene of that immediate neighborhood. The farm was of some two hundred acres comprising the creek bottoms down the creek. He was noted as the best violinist of the Reedy county. He went back to Pennsylvania, leaving the memory.

LYNCH:

John D. ("Jack") Lynch and his wife, Mary J. (Jones) Lynch, both born in Monroe County, Virginia, lived a while in Creenbrier County, came from the latter county to Walton, part of Pocatalico, in the year 1854, with their sons. Here Mary J. died and "Jack" Lynch married a second wife, Rebecca Hundley, a widow, at that time having one son and three daughters, "the Hundley children." Further of all these:

John William Lynch, son of John D. and Mary J. (Jones) Lynch, was born in Greenbrier County, July 9, 1841. Here on Pocatalico John William Lynch married Mary E. Looney, daughter of John and Phoebe (Huffman) Looney, March 1, 1866. To them were born five sons and four daughters, named as follows: Harvey Madison, William Silas, Woody L., Sylvan Otis, "Otto," James A., Emerson Permelia B., married H. C. Hively. Phoebe J., became the wife of James A. Robertson, December 26, 1887, his age 20, her age 17. Eva A., married Robert W. Donohoe, December 15, 1886, he 26, born in Craig County, Virginia. Sarah ("Sallie") F., married Peter H. Camp, August 18, 1894, his age 21, her age 17. For more about the daughters, see names of their husbands.

Wesley L. Lynch, son of "Jack" D., married Talitha Allen, February 3, 1871; made their home on Trace Fork. We do not have names of their several children, except I recollect the following: John, William, Edison, Dora, Myrtle, Lloyd, Carrie and Walter.

Lewis C. Lynch, son of "Jack" D., born June 27, 1853, in Greenbrier County the year before they made their home in (then Kanawha) Roane County, August 20, 1876. Lewis C. married Elizabeth Allen, born in Fayette County, West Virginia, June 14, 1860, daughter of Archibold and Elizabeth (Sparr) Allen, who became residents of Roane County, year 1867. To Lewis C. and Elizabeth (Allen) Lynch were born— prior to 1884—one son and two daughters: Dora E., born July 17, 1880; Howard E., March 27, 1882, and Effie May, July 3, 1883. Lewis C. was blacksmith at Looneyville for some years, and was proprietor of a general store there in 1883.

Christopher C. Lynch, son of "Jack" D. and Mary J. (Jones) Lynch, on March 8, 1885, married Emma C. Hundley, at Walton, daughter of Rebecca Hundley and deceased husband, Mr. Staple Hundley, Rebecca for second husband become the second wife of "Jack" D. Lynch—a fimily wedding indeed. Chris C. Lynch, of this paragraph, was a good carpenter and builder and lived for some years in Spencer. We do not have the names of any children of Christopher C. and Emma C. Lynch.

Two other sons of John D. "Jack" Lynch and Rebecca (Hundley) Lynch, were Frank, who died in childhood, and Gorge W., who married Nannie Berry, November 10, 1886, his age 25, her age 17; of whose careers we have no information.

Charles C. Lynch, son of John ("Jack") and Rebecca (Hundley) Lynch, was born in Roane County, 1864. January 1, 1893 he married

Effie H. Walker, his age 29, her age 25, at the residence of Newton K. Walker, near Walton, on Pocatalico. To Charles C. and Effie K. were born one son.

The above Charles A. Lynch has been an active and prominent citizen of the county for twenty-five years; served as member of the County Board of Equilization and Review of values of realty and property for taxation. Now—1927—is a member of the County Court of Roane.

All the above Lynches are noted for their blonde complexion, pink skin, light hair and blue eyes.

For something of the Hundleys, see the name in its alphabetical place.

LONGFELLOW:

Michael Longfellow, of near Spencer, 1866 until about the year 1890, was a stalwart man about six feet two in height, heavy brown beard of the John Ruskin shape, pink cheeks and blue eyes. His son, Winfred or Wilfield, "Win" also bearded, was usually taken for Michael's brother.

Persons who knew them often were questioned about them, would reply, "New Englanders, offspring of the poet, Henry W."

Michael's younger son, Otto, gives me the following bit of the family history from his recollection, though it is said there is a biography made by Michael and left with some of the family. Michael Longfellow was born in the State of Maine about the year 1850, a son of a large family there of the name Longfellow. For an unexplained reason Michael ran away from his Maine home when about thirteen years of age. Soon his wanderings brought him to Morgan County, Ohio, near Pennsville, where he liked it and grew up the neighborhood's boy. There near Pennsville he married a Martha Harris, a daughter of John Harris, of Pennsville. To Michael and Martha were born there, "Win," the son above mentioned.

Martha having died at Pennsville, Michael married her sister, Permelia, and to them were born at that place all their children— soon mentioned—except one, the youngest. About the close of the Civil War the whole family came here and settled on a tract of wood land lying on Coal Run, about one mile east of Spencer, purchased by John Harris for the daughter, Parmelia. Of this tract the Longfellow farm was cleared out and made.

The children of Michael and Permelia Longfellow were six. The son, Stace; daughter, Lee; Annie, who married Fred Perrine, son of Miles, deceased; George Faris ("Dock"), and Otto, "Ott." The last three are all of this family left here.

MACE: Of Spencer District.

These are all descendants of a Henry Mace, son of a Mace who arrived from England "on the Eastern Shore," whether of Maryland or Virginia we can not say. The expression "Eastern Shore" was used very often as designating Maryland among the pioneers here. This ancestor arrived on the "Eastern Shore" just prior to the Colonial Revolution; loyal to King George IV, and was soon killed by zealots of the Revolution.

Among, or his only child was Henry Mace, who came "West" by way of the Monongahela Valley, where he tarried awhile and married. Shortly after his marriage he is left a widower with one child, Jeremiah Mace. Henry is next found an appreciated settler on West Fork near Arnoldsburg, about the year 1825. With him a wife, who was a Miss Cogar before her marriage, and some children, among whom is Jeremiah, of the first marriage. There near Arnoldsburg they found confidence, peace and prosperity. There they made their lifetime home, died there and were there buried.

The names of the sons and daughters of Henry and wife (Cogar), as given us by a grandson written in order of their respective births, are Jacob, Peter, Archibold, Henry Harrison, Nancy and Margaret ("Polly") Cottrel.

These others all married in due time and settled at various places on the waters of the West Fork or Henry's Fork. Some reared large families and some had no children. We concern ourselves with the two who settled in what is now Roane County. The elder of these was Jeremiah Mace. He acquired some five or six hundred acres of land on the west side of Henry's Fork, at the mouth of Laurel Creek. Soon—1849—the Glenville, Ripley and Ohio turnpike was made through this land, right past his door. We do not know the name of his wife. They reared no son or daughter of themselves, but adopted one, Joseph Corder. Jeremiah Mace's was known for twenty years as the best place on the turnpike between Spencer and Glenville.

Henry Harrison Mace, usually mentioned as "Harrison," son of Henry and .... (Coger) Mace, his wife, married Miss Salina Starcher, in the year 1860. She was a daughter of William ("Blue Head") Starcher, a pioneer of the lower Henry's Fork country about what is now Rocks Dale. He had patented some large tracts of land there on both sides of the Henry's Fork, and conveyed to Henry Harrison a tract of three hundred acres lying on the west side of the river, which is the boundary line between the counties of Roane and Calhoun. This tract extended from the Henry's Fork clear across to the coves of Triplett Creek.

Here on this tract, in the unscathed forest covering the tops of many rolling hills, Harrison and Salina, his wife, made their home and pursued with health and vigor the making of their part of Roane County, and here spent a long and prosperous life, and likely a happy life. They at once took part in business and past-time affairs at the Town of Spencer. He was a charter member of the Masonic Lodge, "Moriah Lodge No. 38, A. F. & A. M.," of Spencer; often was one of its officers and seldom missed a communication throughout, from date of its charter, A. D. 1869, to the time of his death, year 1923.

He was Protestant 'in religion and lead in the erection and maintenance of the neighborhood church, named "Blue Head Chapel." The names of the children of Harrison and Salina (Starcher) Mace, given in order of birth, are: William H., married Eliza Jane Short, 1892, his age 27, her's 25; Allen, who married Miss Priscilla Carr, Sardis, Ohio, in the year 1905. He is a railroad conductor and they live in Spencer and have two daughters; Van, third son of H. H. and Salina Mace, married Miss Sarah Roach, of Calhoun County, they have resided in Spencer for some years; Webster, fourth son, married Miss Maud Stalnaker, March 6, 1913, his age 36, her age 21, she a daughter of Whitman Stalnaker; Minerva, first daughter of H. H. and Salina Mace, married George W. Starcher, December 5, 1878; Nancy Jane, married Robert M. Short, May 30, 1880.

Melissa, second daughter of H. H. and Salina Mace, married Charles Joseph Glover, November 15, 1889, his age 32, her age 22. He was born in Ritchie County of an old family of the name. Charles J. and Melissa have made their home in Spencer ever since. He was a good carpenter and was long a contractor and builder here, and at other places away from here. To them were born and by them reared here in Spencer, one son and one daughter, being Ray and Faye.

Margaret (Maggie) Mace, married Archibold H. Bartlett, September 19, 1891, her age 19, his age 21.

Lillian M., married Robert J. Knotts, of Calhoun County, September 26, 1900, his age 24, her's 21.

Virginia, married Marcellus Boggs, a contractor of Spencer, who has since died; she now a widow residing in the City of Spencer.

In Hardesty's History we read as follows: "The first white child born on Henry's Fork was Solomon, son of Henry and Rachel (Townsend) Mace." This was about the year 1814.

MARKS: Of Walton District.

Morgan Marks was born in the Monongahela Valley, about the year 1800; married Sarah Cain, in upper Little Kanawha Valley, while both were young. They began married life about Glenville and lived there possibly twenty years, then came to the upper Poca country at Gandeeville about the first of the decade of the eighteen hundred and fifties.

To Morgan and Sarah (Cain) Marks were born several children, of whom we can name here as follows: Thomas. C., Cornelius, John, Phillip, Pery and William C.

There were some daughters of Morgan and Sarah Marks, but we do not have their names.

Of those six sons above named, only three came with or followed their parents and became citizens of Roane. Those were Thomas C., Cornelius and John.

Thomas C. Marks, son of Morgan and Sarah (Cain) Marks, on January 2, 1866, married Martha Gandee, daughter of William and Margaret (Casto) Gandee, of the cross-roads, later called Gandeeville. To them were born eight children, at their home in Walton District. Their names, Cornelius, Jr., Lewis, Alfred, Ezra, William Wesley, Sarah and Amanda.

Cornelius Marks, second son of Morgan and Sarah (Cain) Marks, was born near Glenville, West Virginia, 1845, married Louisa, daughter of Perigrine Hayes, on April 16, 1870, and they commenced their married life on a beautiful tract of land adjoining Gandeeville, where they spent the remainder of their lives.

To Cornelius Marks and his wife, Louisa, were born two sons and three daughters, as follows: Howard, now—1926—a resident of Jackson County, West Virginia; Rouena, married Frank M. Conley, son of Elias Conley; Chessie, who married Dr. Calvin Camp, September 24, 1899, ages not given on marriage record. Dr. and Mrs. Chessie Camp have been residents of the City of Spencer for some years, where the doctor maintains an office; Peregrine French, took the medical course and graduated at the Medical Department of the Louisville University, married a Miss Josephine Byrd, and they have made their home in the Town of Walton for some years, where the doctor maintains his office.

John Marks, third son of Morgan and Sarah (Cain) Marks, married Rachel A. Harper, daughter of the Harpers of lower Pocatalico, July 3, 1867. They settled below and near Walton Village, where they maintained for many years a good home farm.

Of the five daughters of Morgan Marks and his wife, Sarah Cain Marks, one or more may be among the following:

Amanda B., married Spencer C. Stalnaker, October 1, 1893, his age 22, her age 19.

Isabelle, married S. E. Conley, August 13, 1899, his age 19, her age 22.

Jemima F., daughter of John Marks, married Samuel Greenleaf, August 6, 1890, his age 22, her age 20.

Margaret A. Marks, daughter of Thomas Marks, married Sylvester A. Wilson, March 17, 1887, his age 21, her age 18; and a Sarah Marks married Solomon Runner, November 17, 1856.

Phillip C. Marks, of the above family, we are not positive of which branch, married Angelina Gandee, August 23 1870. They settled in Calhoun County, we are told.

MATTICS: Of Spring Creek and Reedy.

Thomas Scofield Mattics and his wife, with two sons and two daughters, came to Roane County about the first of the decade, 1860. a grandson says they came here from Greenbrier County.

It is seen in deed books of the County Court records that one Elwood Mattics, of Philadelphia, on February 28, 1865, is grantee of Lemuel

HISTORY OF ROANE COUNTY 601

Crislip, a tract of 315 acres of land "adjoining lands of H. T. Hughes and others" on Left Reedy; also that in same year, C. H. Progler and wife, of Jackson County, West Virginia, at the price of fourteen thousand dollars paid, conveyed to "Elwood Mattics of the City of Philadelphia," two tracts of land on Spring Creek, the first containing 380 acres and the second 580 acres; also, P. H. Thomasson conveyed to Scofield Mattics, year 1865, a tract of land on Left Reedy in consideration of a conveyance by Scofield Mattics to him—P. H. Burdette—a tract of "269 acres situate in Greenbrier County, West Virginia, adjoining the lands of John Mattics."

Scofield Mattics, first above mentioned, appears to be the sole Mattics who settled in this county at that early date, 1865, the others never having made a home here.

The sons and daughters of Scofield Mattics, Sr., and his wife are as follows: Eleanor, wife of M. D. W. Boggs, married 1869; Elizabeth, married John E. Boggs, April 10, 1876; Mathew, married Malinda Hardman, September 26, 1881, and George married Miss Margaret Ann Boggs, August 12, 1870, she a daughter of M. D. W. Boggs and Charity (Vandal) Boggs, his wife.

To George and Margaret Ann (Boggs) Mattics, his wife, were born five sons and two daughters: Scofield M., who married Annie Cheuvront, October 26, 1901; Elidridge ("Dick"), married Ive Hylbert, 1903, his age 23, her's 16; George, Jr., married Alma Deaton, 1909, his age 25, her's 22; Charles E., married Mary Smith, April 11, 1921, his age 35, her's 22; Sadie B. and Gertrude, the daughters of George and Margaret Ann, may be single, I see no marriage recorded.

McCAN: Of Geary.

Patrick McCan, M. D., son of Richard and Monica E. (Goff) McCan, was born Christmas Day, 1822, in Lewis County, Western Virginia. His father, Richard, having been born in Ohio, July 4, 1799, and was living still in Meigs County, of that state, about the year 1882, when Dr. McCan gave his memoir to the writer of Hardesty's History. We can not tell why, in that memoir, something further of the ancestry of Richard McCan was not given, and why he—Richard—came back from Ohio, married and lived for some time in Lewis County, where Patrick was born.

This relationship to the Goffs furnishes some, though meager clue to the reason for young Doctor Patrick McCan's coming to Roane County, a graduate of Sterling Medical College, about 1851. On May 22, 1851, Patrick McCan and Isabella A., daughter of Mathew and Elizabeth A. (Ashley) Geary, were united in marriage at the Geary home on lower part of Big Sandy, where these newlyweds began life's work we do not know. In his memoirs he says, "At the beginning of the Civil War Dr. McCan relinquished a good practice and enlisted, September 9, 1862, in Company K, 7th Ohio Cavalry. He was detailed regimental surgeon, and was brigade hospital steward at Bean Station,

East Tennessee; received honorable discharge July 9, 1865, and is soon seen at his home in Geary District, near Osbornes Mills, the revered reliance of many miles of country for medical service. He must have enjoyed the sublime solitudes of a surrounding forest, for we called at his home on Pigeon Creek while on an electioneering trip in the year 1904. It was a commodious frame building, having well kept door-yards, garden, out buildings and fields all pinched in between towering tree-covered hills. He owned some hundreds of acres in this district.

Of the married lives of Dr. McCan and Elizabeth A. (Geary) McCan, were born five daughters and nine sons, however, of all these only one of the name McCan—Carrico F.—is now in Geary District.

The names of these fourteen children as given by Dr. McCan in his memoir, are Mary A., born 1852, married William A. (Foster) Smith; Esther E., 1857, wife of Isaac P. (Foster) Smith; Martha E., 1858; Eva C., 1859, died in youth; Addie B., 1875. The sons: Richard B., 1854; Jesse D., 1861; Ambrose B., 1863; Sherman G., 1866; Bertie H., 1867; Patrick H., died; Carrico Franklin, 1871; Shelby Ryan, 1873; Charles W., 1876; Benjamin W., 1880.

McCARTY: Of Middle Reedy.

"Mr. McCarty" came to this part of Reedy shortly before the formation of Roane County—1856—purchased a large tract of land for a farm. He and his wife were of the "Slave Holding Class" of old Virginia, but of what county we do not know; none of his family is left in Roane County. We have seen him, but never knew his first name, as he was always spoken of as "Mr. McCarty." One of his slaves, known as Joe Lee, was brought here. He was faithful to the family until the last member was gone about his own business; attended the master, "Mr. McCarty", to his grave, though Joe was the elder by a year or more. Out of respect for such fidelity as Joe's, the people of Reedy buried Joe in the white man's cemetery, of Middle Reedy.

We believe that of the family of three daughters and two sons of Mr. McCarty and his wife, three of the older ones were born in Virginia, the two younger boys in Roane.

The names of these children that I can give are: Almeda, wife of Newton B. Armstrong; Sarah E., wife of John W. Cain, Jr., which two family names see in their places; and Mason McCarty and Spurgeon McCarty, the two sons mentioned.

McCAULY: Of Curtis District.

Came here about the year 1859, two brothers, John S. McCauly and Solomon McCauly, sons of Henry and Mary (Burkham) McCauly, of Lewis County, Western Virginia. Henry McCauly owned a tract of eight hundred acres of land lying just below Reedyville, and extending across the dividing ridge between the two Reedy Creeks, this tract Henry sold and conveyed to his sons, John S. and Solomon McCauly, the larger part next, the Left Hand Fork, to John S. and the ridge part to Solomon, five or six years after they came here.

John S. McCauly, son of Henry and Mary, was born in Lewis County, Western Virginia, about the year 1822. In Lewis County he married Mary Alkier; of this marriage eight children were born, three sons and four daughters in Lewis, and one son here on Reedy; of all these only one yet lives, Joseph W. McCalla (they have changed the spelling in late years), who married Jane, daughter of Hezekiah Boggs, who came from Gilmer County and settled on Colt Run, of Curtis District. Jacob Boggs many years a fruit raiser of near head of Colt Run, now farmer at Murraysville, Jackson County, is a son of this same Heziakiah Boggs.

Solomon McCauly, son of above named Henry and Mary (Burkham) McCauly, after coming to Roane County married Jane Blackburn, of Jackson County. They brought up on the farm in Curtis, two sons and one daughter. The daughter's name, Rebecca; one son, Perry, went to Kentucky many years ago. The other son's name was Joseph Henry McCalla.

McCROSKY: Of Geary, Walton, Spencer District.

Mary Jane McCorsky, widow of John H. McCorsky, who died in Glies County, Virginia, in the first of the decade, 1850, with their six sons and three daughters came to Roane County about the year it was founded (1856), and established a pioneer home for herself on Big Sandy. The names of these sons and daughters are as follows: James Henley, William C., John Robert, Paris L., Harvey Chapman and Giles Franklin, Amanda, Talitha and Virginia.

Further of this family:

James Henley married Miss Sarah Ann Keiffer, went west; John Robert married Miss Lydia Ellis, he was many years the first-class blacksmith at Spencer, West Virginia; Paris L. married a Miss Susan A. Snodgrass, year 1871; Harvey Chapman, went "west"; Giles Franklin, married Roberta Barnhouse, January 17, 1883.

William C. Mc Crosky, above mentioned, son of John H. and Mary Jane McCrosky, was born in Giles County, November 1, 1842; helped with making of the family home on Big Sandy; enlisted and served in the Union armies, 1862-1864. On return furlough, on Sandy, January 15, 1864, he united in marriage with Louisa Drake, born on Big Sandy, then part of Kanawha County, May 1, 1848, daughter of Solomon and Elizabeth J. Drake, pioneers there. William C. McCrosky became owner of the old home place and was a prominent figure in Geary District religious and secular affairs for twenty years; such as member of the Board of Education and Justice of the Peace one or more terms. To William C. and Louisa (Drake), his wife, were born and reared the following named sons and daughters: Sutton M., 1869; Elizabeth J.,

1866; Charles W., 1871; John Henry, 1873; Harvey W., 1876; Mary E., 1878; George W., 1880; Virginia B., 1882, and Martha, 1884.

Of these, three daughters of Mary Jane, the widow: Amanda, while yet a Miss, went to the far "west." Talitha married Martin Aldrich and went to Kanawha County. Virginia died, not yet having married.

McCLUNG: Of Reedy. First one, year 1853.

Mortimer Allen McClung, with his wife, Mary (O'Dell) McClung, and one child, were first here.

Mortimer Allen McClung was born in Greenbrier County, Western Virginia, November 12, 1831, one of several sons of Alexander and Jane (Withrow) McClung. Alexander born September 7, 1803, Jane December 1, 1806, both in Greenbrier County, and Alexander was a grandson of that William McClung, "the first Anglo-Saxon resident in Greenbrier." The foregoing, though in quotation marks, is what Mortimer A. McClung says of his ancestry in his biography dictated himself in Haresty's History, but not in his own words.

Mary O'Dell was born in Nicholas County, Western Virginia, October 17, 1834, daughter of John W. and Mary (Bails) O'Dell—spelt by themselves: Odell.

Mary and Mortimer A. McClung were united in marriage in Nicholas County, April 9, 1852, and came to Reedy the following year, where their first home was—I have not inquired—but as early as 1870, their's was a large farm lying on Folly Run reaching over onto Cains Run, about a mile and a half from the "Three Forks."

He was an industrious man, his education a little better than that of other such farmers of the county; studied law, either before or soon after his marriage; was a familiar friend of Joseph Smith, at that time Judge of the Circuit Court; a circuit which inclded then Nicholas, Kanawha, Jackson and maybe Wirt. Mortimer A. practiced in Roane County Courts, was a devout Baptist and took active pride in his church's business. He was a large, florid blonde man, a smiler. He and his wife spent their long and productive lives there on that farm and left it a heritage to their children, whose names are as follows:

Mary J. A., Bowen C., Fluvana M., Amanda F., D. Judson, John A., Signora P., "Nora," Matilda H., Roxalana V., Samuel T. and Parker. Of them and their marriages we can say somewhat further:

Mary J. A. McClung, born January 16, 1853, married Dusaisaway T. Dye, September 27, 1875.

Bowen C., born 1854, died 1880, not married.

Fluvana M., July 3, 1856, married John H. Bates, of Reedy, March 2, 1871.

Amanda F., born January 19, 1859, married Newton C. Smith, of Roane County, November 16, 1878.

D. Judson, born November 27, 1860, married Lenora "Nora" M. Seaman, September 19, 1882.

John Allen, born March 16, 1863, married Lucile V. Hardman, June 26, 1901. Marriage record shows no ages.

Lenore "Nora," born November 27, 1867, married George M. Chenowith, December 13, 1891; her age 24, his age 24. He was a son of Ira S. Chenowith, of Reedy.

Park W., born September 12, 1870, married in Wirt County, West Virginia, became a physician and practiced at Elizabeth, Wirt County. Served overseas in the World War, died at Elizabeth, 1925. Left a widow and some children there.

Matilda H. McClung, born November 11 1872, married J. C. Youcy, March 17, 1895, her age 22, his age 27. He was born in Minnesota, U. S. A. They made their home on Reedy. Farmers.

Roxalana V. McClung, born April 5, 1876, married Nevil Lakin Chancey, May 29, 1897; her age 21, his age 20.

Samuel T. McClung, son of Mortimer Allen and wife, was born April 24, 1878, married—in Spencer—Miss Georgia Stansbury, each then 27 years old. She was born in Jackson County, West Virginia, daughter of Jonathan and Henrietta (Pennybacker), his wife, descendants of pioneers of Jackson County. Both the Stansburys and Pennybackers being descendants of early settlers of the Shennandoah Valley.

Samuel T. and Georgia have been residents of Spencer ever since their marriage. At present are lesees and managers of the Arlington Hotel. They have a son and a daughter.

McCOY: Upper Left Reedy, Curtis District.

John McCoy and Nancy (Crislip) McCoy, his wife, natives of Lewis County, or somewhere in the Monongahela Valley, with some or all of their first born children were the first of the name here. They settled on the Upper Reedy some time before the Civil War—1861.

The sons and daughters of John and Nancy McCoy are as follows: Abraham, Asbury, J. Ezra, Elizabeth, Alminia and Savena. Further, some marriages and descendants:

Abraham McCoy, son of John and Nancy (Crislip), his wife, married Miss Rebecca Burdette, likely before erection of Roane County. She was a daughter of Ellison Burdette and wife of Left Reedy. Of the names of the children of Abraham and Rebecca McCoy we have as follows: Clamont M., John, Ira and Everette.

Clamont M. McCoy married Miss Ida Kelley, August 28, 1889; his age 22, her's 19. They have their farm home on Left Reedy and have brought up some children.

Elizabeth McCoy, daughter of John and Nancy (Crislip) McCoy, married Christopher C. Kelley. See name Kelley.

Savena, daughter of John and Nancy (Crislip) McCoy, married Rev. William W. Kelley, March 9, 1867.

Lemuel McCoy, son of John and Nancy (Crislip) McCoy, was twice married; first, to M. Louisa Kelley, March 14, 1860, she a sister of C. C. Kelley, above mentioned. Of this union two children were born,

Melciah and Eugenia. Melciah married and made a home farm on head waters of Left Reedy. Eugenia married Scott Miller. M. Louisa having died, Lemuel McCoy married Miss Ruth E. Haynes, October 6, 1869, she a daughter of John Haynes, then of Upper Reedy.

To Lemuel and Ruth E. McCoy were born and by them brought up the following children: Erlando, Artennis "Tennis," Ellet, Alice, Laura, Gertrude and Orla. Their marriages are: Artennis, first to Carrie Davis, second to Myrtle Shafer in Kanawha Conuty; Alice, at 14, to Henry Law, 22, on October 25, 1891; Laura E., 18, to John Wesley Fields, 24, on March 28, 1901; Gertrude, 22, to Henry Reger, 25, July 16, 1907, he born in Ohio; Orla, 18, to Otto D. Norman, 21, August 31, 1909.

McINTOSH: Of Spencer.

The first of this family name here was John McIntosh, Sr., a skilled tailor of the kind who had served his apprenticeship; a veteran of the Mexican War, had married Miss .... Keeney, a daughter of a pioneer family, then of Reedy, made their home and opened shop in "Cassville"—now City of Spencer—about the year 1846. He carried on his business here for some years.

He was one of several of the clan, McIntosh, from the Clyde, Scotland, who settled in Canada at a place called Galt, near Toronto, thence came to the Ohio River. He enlisted in the United States Army, possibly at Ripley, Jackson County, and on return came here—"Cassville."

In Chapter II, Curtis District, we mention a first preacher, given in Hardesty's History as " Rev. John Keener," and say we have no information as to whence he came. This wife of John McIntosh must have been his daughter, and his name Keeney, because no one ever heard of any "Keener" on Reedy.

To John and .... (Keeney), his wife, were born one son and one daughter only. Their names were John Angus, and Salina. The latter married Charles Harpold, of Jackson County, West Virginia. and they made their lifetime home in Ravenswood, and brought up three sons, William, Edward S. and Charles P.

John Angus McIntosh, son of John and wife (Keeney), enlisted in the Confederate armies, a mere boy, from Jackson County, served through the Virginia campaigns and came home at its end unscathed.

On August 12, 1867, in Spencer, John A. McIntosh and Ella D. Smith were united in marriage, "on consent of C. C. Smith, her guardian," quoting from the county marriage records. This means that her parents, George Smith and wife, of Ripley, were dead before this marriage.

John A. and Ella D., his wife, made their lifetime home in Ravenswood, but kept up much business in real estate situate here in Roane; owned by himsef and wife. His principal business was his general store at Ravenswood, later specializing in the hardware business.

He was noted as a devout member of the M. E. church, South, and his wife and him, both as pioneer militant workers against the sale and use of intoxicant liquors, even in the days when imbibing them by great and small was popular.

To John Angus and Ella D. (Smith), his wife, were born and by them brought up one daughter and two sons. Their names: Mary Alice, Frederick Frelinghuysen and Charles Leon. Of these:

Mary Alice married, in Ravenswood, Mr. J. Smith Green, and they made their home in Pennsylvania or New York.

Charles Leon married and made his home in Ravenswood.

Frederick Frelinghuysen, in the year 1895, married Miss Hariet Chapman, born in Cincinnati, Ohio, 1872, only daughter of Ezra and Margaret (Callahan) Chapman.

Frederick F. and Harriet lived the first ten years of their married life in Ravenswood, where Frederick F. was with his father, John A., in the hardware business. In the years 1902, 1903 or 1904 he established a hardware store in Spencer in partnership with N. O. Rudman, "McIntosh & Rudman," and moved his family here for permanent residence in the year 1906. He built the first brick structure hardware store in Spencer, on Market street.

To Frederick Frelinghuysen and Harriet, his wife, were born and by them brought up one son and two daughters, whose names are: Frederick F., Jr., and Dorothea Ellen and Mary Alice.

Frederick F. Jr., son of Frederick F. and Harriet McIntosh, went into the hardware store with his father here in Spencer. He married Miss May O'Brien, of Spencer. She a daughter of .... O'Brien and Mary (McMahan), his wife, and a granddaughter of Judge William H. O'Brien, of Ripley.

McKINLEY:

Thomas M. McKinley, for some years addressed "Squire McKinley," settled on the head of Bear Run, on what was made, later, the road from Spring Creek to Kyger—now Billings—in the year .... He was born in Harrison County, Western Virginia, July 18, 1824, son of Jonathan and Elizabeth (Rector) McKinley, as said in his biography in Hardesty's, written in the year 1882.

The name McKinley shows him of Scotch extraction, but whether of the colonists of Pennsylvania, Maryland or Virginia, in each of which were so many Scotch, we are not told. Jonathan McKinley was born in Monongalia County, western Virginia in the year 1798, Elizabeth Rector, January 14, 1801. The Rectors were long a prominent family of the Monongahela country, some of this name in Jackson County, West Virginia, say they are of a Faquier County, Virginia, family.

Thomas M. McKinley was twice married, the first wife, Catherine M. Neel (Neil, rightly), born in Wood County, Western Virginia, February 27, 1834, married Thomas M., November 23, 1852, died March 14, 1858. Of this marriage three daughters were born: Mary E., November 30,

1853, married Moses, son of Bailey Cleavenger, March 11, 1875; Flora J., October 28, 1855, married John C. Cleavenger, brother of Moses, 1877, and Catherine W., born February 3, 1858.
For a second wife Thomas M. McKinley married Elizabeth Hall, in Ritchie County, November 22, 1859, she being the daughter of William and Mary (Lowther) Hall, a Loudon County, Virginia family that settled in Harrison County, Western Virginia, where this daughter, Elizabeth, was born, in the year 1831. Of this marriage of Thomas M. McKinley and Elizabeth, the following children were born, all in Ritchie County, West Virginia, except the last named: Robert Lee, May 23, 1861; Emma, May 15, 1865; Rector, February 22, 1867; Virginia, March 23, 1869; W. Walter, February 14, 1871, and Sarah C., November 19, 1872.

McWILLIAMS:
John McWilliams, a veteran of the Union army of the War of the Secessions, 1861 to 1865, his wife, Helen M., daughter of Samuel Pue, was a sister of Rebecca, the wife of M. V. B. Monroe. John and Helen weer married in Monroe County, Ohio; came to Roane County about the year 1878, made a home farm of a tract of seventy-five acres of land on the head of the Elk Fork of Mill Creek. This appears by the records to have been conveyed to Helen in the year 1882; left the farm and became a resident of the Town of Spencer about the year 1886; srving as a Deputy Sheriff and Jailor of the county under Benton Mathews, Sheriff.

The children of John and Helen (Pue) McWilliams, whose names we can give, are: Zilphia, the wife of Charles Morgan, formerly of Jackson County, later for some years a resident of Spencer. Charles and Zilphia Morgan have raised two sons and one daughter: Clement, John and Eunice. All this family now live in Akron, Ohio, and Zillia, the wife of Floyd Rhodes, formerly a Jackson countian, several years in the livery-stable business in Spencer, now a resident of Belpre, Ohio, opposite Parkersburg; Zilla (McWilliams) and Floyd Rhodes have reared several children, whose names we can not give here.

MILLER:
Samuel Miller, a soldier of the War of 1812, born in Green County, Virginia, April 25, 1796, and Rebecca (Carpenter) Miller, his wife, after living a short time on Spring Creek near the Boggs' and Depues', moved upon a tract of one thousand acres of forest he purchased, lying about the mouth of Stover Fork about the year 1830. He soon made a large and valuable farm of some hundreds of acres on which he lived for many years. He there raised a family of several, among whom were Anderson Miller, who married Mary McKown, a daughter of Gilbert McKown, mentioned in the history of the City of Spencer; Anderson (waggishly called himself, sometimes, "Purty Anderson"), with Mary, his wife, settled on lower Spring Creek, becoming the

parents of James Albert, yet living on the old Spring Creek farm. Arthur G. Miller, long a banker in Grantsville, and Jefferson Miller, a resident of Spencer, dealing in oil leases and royalties. Another son of Samuel Miller, older than Anderson, named Thomas, lived a long and industrious life on a part of the one thousand acres on Stover Fork, completing the work of conquering the forest and making a good farm. Thomas was twice married, the first wife being Drusille Kirby, mother of William Anderson Miller, now a resident of Spencer; his second wife being Emily Phillips, mother of John Wesley Miller, yet living on a farm on the head of the same creek in Curtis District.

William Anderson Miller, above mentioned, married Sarah Jane Roberts, daughter of Daniel and Margaret (Board) Roberts. Wm. Anderson Miller and wife have lived many years in Town of Spencer, and here brought a family of several children; of these we can name from memory as follows: Esta, Holly, Pruda, Glenn, Camden, and Orville.

MITCHELL:
The first of this name settling in these parts was Thomas Mitchell and his wife Margaret ("Peggy" Snyder) Mitchell, natives of Floyd County, Virginia, who came direct here from there where the New River is not larger than Spring Creek, bringing with them their thirteen children: nine sons and four daughters, about the year 1845.

They at once, or had, purchased a tract of one thousand acres situate on the divide between the Kanawhas, adjoining the lands of Uriah Gandee, lapping over on the Spring Creek side to where the crossroads, village, Speed, now is, on State concrete Road No. 14.

Here the Mitchell pioneer home was made within a few hundred yards of the Kanawha's watershed; and these lands kept as an inheritance for those same children, born in Floyd County, and their descendants.

The names of these children are:
1, Henry; 2, James; 3, Samuel, 4, Granville; 5, William V.; 6, George; 7, Charles; 8, Thomas Pride; 9, Susan; 10, Mary; 11, Nancy and 12, Margaret Elizabeth.

The marriages and families of the foregoing as given us by Charles Mitchell, grandson of the pioneers, Thomas and "Peggy", he being a son of Thos. P. Mitchell, are as follows:

Henry, first son married Mary Harmon; bought the Doty Tanyard in Spencer.

To Henry and Mary (Harmon) Mitchell were born and reared near the Tanyard mentioned, three daughters and one son; their names: Mary, who married John "Pat" Murphy, who for many years was Spencer's best blacksmith, was a merchant a few years and died here.

James M. Mitchell, son of Henry S., married Mary E. Crouse, of a good family of the name Crouse in Fayette County. James M. Mitchell became the owner and manager of the Tannery in Spencer. (Of this see the Chapter: City of Spencer.) To James M. and Mary E. (Crouse)

Mitchell were born three sons and two daughters: Martin, now (1926) in the motion picture business in Detroit; Wallis; Minnie, a school teacher; Joseph and Ruth.

Nancy (Nannie) Jane, daughter of Henry S. and Mary (Harmon) Mitchell, his first wife, married Charles C. Cleavenger, November 29, 1876. He was son of Bailey Clevenger. (See that name, also the Chapter City of Spencer.) To Nancy Jane (Mitchell) and husband C. C. Cleavenger were born two sons and three daughtrs, as follows: Robert W., May, Bertha, Carrie (known as "Dock"), Nell and Mason.

James, second son of Thomas Mitchell and Margaret (Snyder), married and remained in Virginia.

Samuel, third son of Thomas and Margaret Mitchell, remained in Floyd County, Virginia, became a teacher of vocal music; during war, 1861-5, went South and was never heard of afterward by the family here.

Granville, fourth son of Thomas, remained in Virginia.

William V., fifth son of Thomas Mitchell and Margaret, married Ellen Underwood in Floyd County, Virginia, came to Roane County about 1856, to his father's wide homestead. The names of children of William V. and Ellen (Underwood) his wife, are, first, Lizzie, who married John Huff, son of Mose (or Anthony) Huff of Jackson County. John and Lizzie, his wife, lived many years in Spencer, died here and left several children, among whom was a son, Albert.

Robert, first son and second child of Wm. V. never married.

Charles Thomas Mitchell, second son and third child of William V. Mitchell, above mentioned, married Sophia Butcher, daughter of John Butcher of Spencer District on Ravenswood turnpike.

To Charles Thomas and Sophia (Butcher) Mitchell were born and brought up three daughters and one son, whose names are, Wilda V., wife of Dr. James Justice, married February 25, 1907, his age 29, her age 26; Blanche, now (1926) widow of Ira S. Bartlett, deceased, is a clerk in a Charleston bank; Verna, who married Samuel A. Simmons of Spencer, "18th December, 1904, his age 23 years, her age 18 years;" and Clyde T. Mitchell, linotype man, married Daniese, daughter of Dr. Samuel S. Holroyd in Mercer County, West Virginia.

George Mitchell, sixth son of Thomas, pioneer. No record.

Charles, seventh son of Thomas and "Peggy" Mitchell, pioneers first mentioned, died in the Union service of the War of 1861 to 1865.

Thomas Pride Mitchell, eighth son of Thomas and "Peggy" Mitchell, pioneers first mentioned, was thrice married; first wife was Miss Harmon, sister of George Harmon. To Thomas P. and (Harmon) Mitchell were born two sons: first, George Washington Mitchell, long of lower Harper District, married Mary S. M. Hopkins, March 29, 1880. They reared several children, the oldest of whom were Hoyt and Homer. Second son of Thomas Pride and first wife, Harmon, was John W. Mitchell, who went to Oregon and is believed to have died in Portland of that State.

The second wife of Thomas Pride Mitchell was a Miss Combs; to them no child was born; she died.

The third wife of Thomas Pride Mitchell was Nancy Edwards, sister of the pioneer, Isaac Edwards, miller and business man of Walton. To Thomas Pride and Nancy (Edwards) Mitchell was born one son and one daughter, their names: Charles and Sarah Jane.

Charles Mitchell last mentioned, married Elizabeth Margaret Santee, daughter of .... Santee.

To Charles and Elizabeth (Santee) Mitchell were born and grew up, in this county, four sons and two daughters. Their names we do not have.

Susan Mitchell, ninth child of Thomas Mitchell and "Peggy, died a spinster at seventy-two years of age.

Mary Mitchell, tenth child of Thomas and "Peggy", the pioneers, was first wife of Elijah Wagoner of Charles Fork. She died childless.

Nancy Mitchell, eleventh child of Thomas, the pioneer, married Gordon Farley, of Rush Creek.

Margaret Elizabeth, twelfth child of Thomas and "Peggy", pioneers, became the second wife of Elijah Wagoner, above mentioned.

Lewis M. Mitchell, fourth child of William V. Mitchell, on 13th September, 1877, married Miss Nannie R. Conrad, of Reedy, Wirt County, West Virginia, daughter of Jacob and Abigael Conrad. Of the children of Lewis M. and Nannie Mitchell, two sons: Oakland Kenna, May 7, 1880, who lives at Reedy, in Roane County ,and Rufus lives at Parkersburg, West Virginia; and one daughter, whose name is Esther B., born August 4, 1878.

MONROE: Or Curtis District, 1887.

Martin Vanburen Monroe was of a New England family of Monroes; born in Belmont County, Ohio, son of Curtis Monroe and wife who both died when Martin Vanburen, their son, was only two days old. He grew to manhood in Belmont County, Ohio, and married, 1858, Rebecca Jane, a daughter of Samuel Pue, a Virginian, then a farmer of near Bellsville, Ohio. For some reason Martin Vanburen Monroe's name appears written "M. V. B. Monroe." By deed of conveyance dated May 16, 1887, Samuel Silcomb, attorney in fact for the heirs of Lot M. Morill of Kenebec County, State of Maine, grantee of the North American Land Company, conveyed to M. V. B. Monroe a tract of six hundred and fifty-four acres, situate on the head waters of Elk Fork of Mill Creek in Curtis District, reciting as the purchase price, six hundred dollars in hand paid.

This is the last land in Roane County sold and purchased at such low price.

Mr. Monroe at once moved from Ohio onto this large tract of land, then all in the original forest, and within a few years had conquered from the woods large fields and made a substantial homestead on which was a united and happy family of six children, besides the two that died very young. He was an enthusiast on the subject of the higher education; was a practical surveyor and had taken a course in law in a school of law or in an office in Ohio. The names of the children of Martin Vanburen Monroe and Rebecca Jane Pue, his wife, that we can give here, are:

Chalmers Lee Monroe, 1859-1925; married Alice Belle Neff, an Ohio girl. They at once made their home in Curtis District on or near the family lands. They raised six children whose names and business we cannot give in this connection. Chalmers was for some years a school teacher of Roane County; he and his family moved to Parkersburg a few years ago where he died in the year 1925, just when the income from his lands was making life's opportunities broad in that he most liked.

Samuel Clark Monroe, born 1864, third son of M. V. B. Monroe and Rebecca Jane, like his brother Chalmers L., went to Ohio for a wife and there married Martha Neff, of Monroe County, Ohio. They now live at Belprey in Ohio. Samuel and Martha have reared three daughters whose names are, Nannie Harriet, wife of Herman Carpenter of Jackson County; Alice, yet with them, not married, and Emma, wife of Wellington Payne of Roane County.

Sylvania, fourth child of M. V. B. and Rebecca J. Monroe, was born about 1869, married Albert Kelley, son of the Squire William (Bill) Kelley of Flat Fork, Roane County. They now (1926) maintain a home in East Spencer.

Harriett Ellen, fifth child of M. V. B. and Rebecca J. Monroe was born, about the year 1871, married Webster Riley, son of Squire William Riley, of Roane County history, Webster and Harriett Ellen live in Charleston, West Virginia. They are conducting a large mercantile business.

Ida, sixth child of M. V. B. and Rebecca J. Monroe, born about the year 1874 or 1875, is the wife of John Marshall Harper, son of John L. and Jane (Hopkins) Harper of Harper District, this county; John M. and Ida Monroe Harper made their home in Parkersburg a few years ago where they yet live. John M. Harper is a "realtor" there. They have raised to manhood two sons: Raymond, "Ray" and Bruce.

Jefferson Pue Monroe, the seventh child of M. V. B. and Rebecca J. Monroe, born about the year 1876, now resides in Kentucky, where he went a few years ago.

Agatha, eighth child of M. V. B. Monroe and Rebecca J. Monroe was born about the year 1878, married Arthur Lee of Wirt County, West Virginia, their place of residence and business at time of this writing we do not know.

MORRISON: Of middle Harper District.

Jacob Breck Morrison was for twenty-five years a prominent and influential citizen of his part of the county.

He was born in Lewis County, West Virginia, in the year 1827; married in Lewis County, Mary A. Achard, who was born in Rockbridge County, Virginia; to them was born in Lewis County one child, who died, a youth of 17 years. They came to this part of Roane County about the year 1865; purchased a large tract of land having on it some small improvements.

To Jacob B. and Mary A. (Achard) Morrison were born in Roane County, the following named children: Margaret, wife of Thomas J. Shouldis; Sarah Columbia, wife of George W. Roberts, settler of upper Reedy in Curtis District; Catherine, who married Floyd Raines of Harper District.

Sylvanus ("Van") Morrison, born in the year 1862, married Miss Sarah Ann Johns of Jackson County, W. Va., 1890; succeeded to the home farm by purchase of the shares of the other heirs of Jacob B., deceased; also owns the Thomas Raines farm. To Sylvanus and his wife Sarah Ann, have been born two sons and three daughters. Continuing about the family of John B. Morrison: Lucy married John Garrett; John married Miss Ida Raines of Flat Fork, and Harriett, the youngest daughter, married James Stanley.

MORFORD:

The first of this name who settled in Roane was John Morford, born in Green County, Pennsylvania, year 1834, son of Isaac and Elizabeth (Brown) Morford, natives of Pennsylvania, and of Scotch descent.

John Morford married Margaret Taylor, in Green County, Pennsylvania, where she was born in the year 1832. To them were born, all in Green County, Pennsylvania, the following named children: Elizabeth, Angeline, John P., Isaac Newton, and Ona.

Margaret having died, John Morford married for a second wife, Hannah Taylor, who was a sister of the first wife, Elizabeth. To John and Hannah (Taylor) Morford were born: Priscilla V., Mary J., Patrick and Hagan. In November, 1878, John Morford with all the above family, except Elizabeth, Angeline and Thomas, arrived in Roane County and purchased and settled upon a large farm on Triplett Run in Spencer District, where they were soon deemed one of the important families of the county. John was a farmer and stock dealer; and these are the ancestors and families of the several Murfords mentioned in the chapter of this book, "History of the City of Spencer." Of this family:

Isaac Newton Morford married Sophia Springston, daughter of the Springstons of Spencer District, at her home on the 25th February, 1881. I. N. was elected by the people and served one term, four years, as a justice of the peace of Spencer. He owned a good farm; later, was for long an employee of the Carter Oil Company. He and his family reside in the City of Spencer. Their names in order of ages: Ocie, Ruby, Lois, Harold, Charles N., and Ivan N.

John P. Morford married Theodocia Bartlett, January 15, 1881; she the daughter of .... Bartlett, of Triplett; John P. (Dr. "Jack") was a dentist for some years before his death, though his main business was as a farm owner. The three dentists Morford of Ch. IX are his sons.

Patrick Hagan Morford, also first a farmer, married Lizzie Newlon 10th January, 1897; she the daughter of Salathiel J. Newlon of Triplett; these live in City of Spencer and are parents of Byron and John Morford.

MOSS: Of Middle Reedy.

Robert J. Moss was first of this name to become a resident of Reedy. He was born in Louisa County, Virginia, year 1840; his parents coming to Harrison County where Robert J. grew up. He came to the Little Kanawha about Burning Springs when a young man, engaged in lumber and flatboating; came to Reedy, there on June 10th, 1868, united in marriage with Miss Eliza V. Rhodes, daughter of Samuel and Parthena Rhodes, his wife; they made their life time's home on the Middle Fork of Reedy three miles above "Three Forks;" where he built up a farm of some two hundred acres, more or less. To Robert J. and Eliza V. were born and by them brought up—except the two or three younger ones—the following named children: Richard H., Minnie C., James M., Holly O., Fannie L., Robert V., and William H. Moss.

The wife Eliza V. having died Robert J., united in marriage with M. Elizabeth Rader, August 6, 1899, she a widow Wyatt at the time and a daughter of Harvey H. Rader and wife. See name "Rader."

To Robert J. and wife M. Elizabeth were born the following children: John H., Glen W., George C. and Buel Moss.

Robert J. Moss died in September, 1908, from injuries when thrown to the ground by an unruly steer he was driving on the highway. He left an estate of some eight to ten thousand dollars of personalty, and real estate of a similar value, mostly bequeathed and devised for maintenance and education of his younger children, by will written and witnessed in year, 1895.

NAYLOR: Of Geary District.

The older people pronounced this name so as to rhyme with Tyler. They were of the earliest families in lower Big Sandy.

Adam Naylor appears to have been the first of this name here, as shown by marriage records and deeds of conveyances; also an Absalom Naylor appears about the same time.

Tarleton V. Naylor next appears on the records; he was a prominent character for twenty years in this Big Sandy country; married Miss Catherine Hensley, February, 1880. Both were young. He owned at ont time large tracts of land on Eastern side of the Big Sandy.

HISTORY OF ROANE COUNTY 615

Tarleton V. Naylor and his wife Catherine left several children, so have many other Naylors of this family. We give some marriages from the records of this county:
Naylor, Andrew, to Mary Drake, June 21, 1858.
Naylor, Abraham, to Belinda Deal, February 19, 1867.
Naylor, William, to Sarah Taylor, 1867.
Naylor, Jacob to Margaret Drennin, October 31, 1873.
Naylor, Michael, to Eleanore V. Smith, April 5, 1875.
Naylor, John, to Nancy Ann Arthur, August 29, 1882.
Naylor, McClellan, to Nancy C. Justice, April 30, 1883.
Women:
Naylor, Farciba, to Wiley Horner, May 7, 1856.
Naylor, Margaret, to George E. Brown, January 22, 1867.
Naylor, Eliza J., to John W. Ross, February 26, 1867.
Naylor, Mary C., to Michael Deal, January 2, 1869.
Naylor, Sabina, to James E. Deal, March 23, 1867.
Naylor, Frances E., to Benjamin F. Armstead, November 29, 1872.
Naylor, Susan, to John Short, September 22, 1873.
Naylor, Anna Barbara, to Solomon C. Schoolcraft, December 23, 1874.
Naylor, Rebecca J., to St. Clair Thompson, March 23, 1876.
Naylor, Ellen, to J. W. Drake, April 2, 1877.
Naylor, Emily, to Albert White, March 8, 1877.
Naylor, Ellen, to Aaron Hensley, April 2, 1877.
Naylor, Labanna, to Isaac P. Smith, April 30, 1877.
Naylor, Lucretia, to Jefferson Thompson, October 27, 1881.

Ages and place of birth of the parties do not appear on our records before the year 1882.

NEELY: Of Curtis District.

James Mason Neely was born in Monongalia County; there married Minerva M. Lemley, also born in Monongalia, daughter of Jacob Lemly or l-e-y; they came to Curtis District, about the year 1879, purchased a tract of 130 acres of forest lands lying on the divide between Middle Fork of Reedy and head of Frozen Camp of Mill Creek; made that lands into an average farm of those parts; brought up three children whose names are:
Ettie, who married Isaac Hinzman;
Everettie, married Samuel M. Silcot; and
Seth, born in Monongalia County, West Virginia, 1876, and married Ollie Walters, 6th October, 1900; his age 24, her's 18. Ollie was a daughter of Silas Walters and wife, neighbors of the Neeleys. To Seth and Ollie (Walters) Neely were born the following named children:
Charles Clifford, 1891, a school teacher now;
Hazel Victor, Blondis C., and Denver Paul. Seth and his family live at this time in the City of Spencer; he is a carpenter by trade.

NOE: Of Geary District.

William Noe, the first of the name here, was born in Patrick County, Virginia, February 13, 1809, of an old colonial family arriving from England with "the Cavaliers," bearing for centuries—as said by a descendant of a family, neighbors to the family Noe, in Virginia—the names "Lowe;" the change was opined to have been made from mere caprice, there being known no other reason for abandoning the honorable, historic name of Lowe.

We must infer he came, like many an other Virginian (he was neither poor nor needy), braving adventure for the thrill of it, and further like them, to settle down after adventure no longer thrills, to found an ancestral estate, deep in the midst of nature's overflowing bounty, where came together three branches of the clear, clean waters of Big Sands of Elk, awakening to dominance in him some atavistic spirit which felt itself again on the banks of the Shannon or the Clyde among the Druids.

At the home of William King, on Big Sandy, an older adventurer in these forests, already well surrounded with fields and provided with buildings, William Noe found, woed and wedded Elizabeth King, born in Pike County, Kentucky. The time of this wedding must have been in the year 1835 or before; for Samuel Noe, a son says, in Hardesty's History, that he was born on Big Sandy, May 21, 1936.

William Noe was a notable pioneer for thirty-five years; was a justice of the peace and long a leader and supporter of regilious organizations.

Other children besides Samuel mentioned were, Aaron Noe, who married Sarah Ann Griffith, July 31, 1856; she a daughter of Hugh Griffith; he 23, and she 19.

Mary Noe to George W. Tawney, February 11, 1858.

Daniel W. Noe to Elizabeth Anderson, November 26, 1872.

William A. Noe to Eliza Spencer, September 14, 1884.

Beverly L. Noe to Lecta B. Ross, November 20, 1904; she then 19 years old, he 32; she a daughter of Isaac Newton Ross and wife of Big Sandy. Beverly L. Noe is and has been for some years the village and country of Newton's popular physician and surgeon; to Dr. Beverly L. Noe and Lecta B., his wife, were born and by them brought up two daughters: Dorma E., wife of William L. Chambers, and Miss Evaly, a teacher.

NOYES:

William W. Noyes, first of this name resident of this county, was born in Charleston, West Virginia, son of Isaac Noyes, a resident of Charleston.

William W. Noyes married Elizabeth Frances Smith, who was born at Guyandott, Western Virginia; they came to Roane County about the year 1860. In an old record of bonds in the county clerk's office, one of the few books saved from the conflagration of the court house in 1887, is an official bond of W. W. Noyes, H. D. Chapman, surety ,in penalty $3,000, it is recited that "W. W. Noyes was duly elected Recorder of the county' 'at the election, 1864, for the term of two years. Again he appears to have been elected recorder of the county, as recited in another bond, "whereas at an election duly held on the 22nd day of October, 1868, W. W. Noyes was duly elected Recorder for the term of two years from the 1st day of January, 1869."

To William W. and wife, Frances, were born five children: Adelbert, John S., one which died in infancy, Isaac Wright, also died in youth, and Charles Bradford.

Adelbert, son of William W. Noyes, married Lucy Rogers of Marietta, Ohio. To Adelbert and Lucy Noyes were born two sons whose names were Chester Smith, and William Wallace Noyes.

Chester S. Noyes married Arminta Dye.

William Wallace Noyes II became a graduate of a National Medical School, married Martha E., daughter of Rev. John L. Harper of Harper District, "at the home of the bride's father, August 18, 1901; his age, 29; her age, 21." Doctor W. W. Noyes made his home for a while at Red Knob in that district, and from there practiced his profession; removed from Red Knob to City of Dunbar on the Kanawha, 1912 or 1915, from which place he continues his medical practice; the wife and companion of his earlier efforts still with him.

OGDEN:

William and Elizabeth (McIntire) Ogden were early residents of Marion County, Western Virginia. We are informed that William and Elizabeth Ogden had three sons: Presley Benjamin, Robert and Osborne. Of these, Presley was long a prominent physician and surgeon of his native county; he is also the father of Hershel C. Ogden of Wheeling, at this time (1926) owner and published of the newspaper, *Wheeling Intelligencer*, and owner and director of several smaller newspapers of the State of West Virginia.

The brothers, Robert and Osborne Ogden, both came and made their homes in Roane County, acquiring farms lying just above the Village of Newton, about the year 1855, which farms, by frugality and good judgment, they soon made prominent among the better farms on Sandy, and there both lived until their deaths several years ago.

Robert Ogden before coming here had married in Marion County, western Virginia, Mariah Smith, a daughter of a Pennsylvania family of Smiths. To Robert and Mariah were born two sons and one daughter, named respectively, William Wesley, born, 1857; Harrison B., who died in youth; and Mary A., who married Millard, son of Reverend Davidson Ross of near Newton, which couple made their home henseforward in Geary District, and have left of their marriage several children whose names we do not have.

William Wesley Ogden, son of Robert and Mariah above mentioned, in the year 1885, married Maggie, daughter of Kelles Chewning, near

Linden, of upper Henrys Fork country. For history of the Chewnings see Chapter, Smithfield District.

To William Wesley and Maggie (Chewing) Ogden were born two daughters and one son, both of the daughters died in early youth; the son, Robert Kellis, is a business man, partner or comrade with his father at their home in Charleston, West Virginia, at this time, 1926.

William Wesley Ogden's first public work was that of school teacher, next surveyor of lands, then for some years one of the larger timber dealers in marketing the last of that country's big oak, poplar and walnut trees; on his marriage, and death of his father, he succeeded to ownership of the old home farm, which he attended and improved while also attending to the other businesses mentioned. On arising of the oil and gas business he plunged into buying and selling of rights and interests in the oil and gas of the country which he plied with such judgment for a few years that, a competence being acquired, he took a home in the city, Charleston, as above mentioned, there to enjoy the comforts and conveniencies of modern city life, for which he is generally said to be well prepared financially. Roane County of right claims him as her citizen. In addition to what is given above of his services, we must here add: he served the county one term as deputy sheriff under the Sheriff, P. A. Tallman; was elected and served one term in the State Legislature, session 1910, as delegate for Roane County. See Chapter III.

Osborne Ogden, son of William and Elizabeth (McIntire) Ogden, mentioned as coming to Geary District with his brother Robert in the year 1858, appears, from the biography of John P. Rogers in Hardesty's History, to have united in marriage with Miss Sarah Petitt, and that they made their home on Big Sandy. Of their children we are told of one, Rocina E., born November 17, 1861, married John P. Rogers, April 17. 1879. Not 18 years of age, it is observed.

See family name, "Rogers".

O'HARA: Pioneer school teacher of Reedy.

James O'Hara was born December 15, 1815, in the Town of Altrest; Parish of Donaghady, County Tyrone, Ireland; married Miss Elizabeth Jane Flesher in the Town of Weston, West Virginia, September 8, 1840; she was born there September 5, 1823. They came, a few years later, to Reedy, where James devoted his time to teaching school, and may be rightly accredited with being the first resident professional school teacher of Reedy.

At the time of the arrival of James O'Hara and Elizabeth, his wife, at Reedy, there lived two families of Fleshers near Three Forks, but of which family she was nearest related, we are not informed. He was long an influential citizen of Reedy on account of his intelligence and marriage relations; in his old age he acquired a farm on upper Middle Fork of Reedy near Peniel, closed his days there and there lies buried.

HISTORY OF ROANE COUNTY 619

To James and Elizabeth (Flesher) O'Hara, his wife, were born and by them reared the following sons and daughters: Anna A., August 12, 1841; Charles, August 30, 1844; Florence L., June 6, 1849; Albert W., October 18, 1850; Elijah F., July 4, 1855; and Mary Elizabeth, July 27, 1860.

Florence L. O'Hara of above family married Samuel Price Cotttle, February 5, 1871. They made their home near ePniel many years and reared some sons and daughters. See name, Cottle.

Charles O'Hara of the above family was for several years clerk of the first State Hospital for Insane located at Weston, West Virginia, was possibly the first clerk of that institution. Elijah F. married and has lived at Weston, W. Va. many years.

OSBORNE: Of Geary District, Osbornes Mills.

George Osborne, born in England March 17, 1792; died on Big Sandy, of Elk of the Kanawha, U. S. A., 1868.

George Osborne crossed the ocean in company of two of his brothers, all three of whom landed on the "Eastern Shores". Of two of these we have no information; but George Osborne is found in Greenbrier County, where on the 16th day of July, 1815, he united in marriage with Miss Susanna Fleshman, born 1794, died January 21, 1867.

George Osborne and his wife are next found making a home for themselves in the forest on Big Sandy of Elk of the Great Kanawha, year 1822 or 1823, which home for about twenty years was up on Big Sandy only about one mile from its mouth. Here they brought up their family of twelve children; first five of the older children were born in Greenbrier County; the other seven on Big Sandy.

The names and dates of birth of these twelve are as follows: Archibold P., August 25, 1816; Elizabeth, March 18, 1818; Charles, April 29, 1819; Jane D., July 14, 1820; Isaac E., January 18, 1822. These were all born in Greenbrier; John, March 4, 1824; David, December 27, 1825; Mahala, March 10, 1829; Harvey, April 5, 1831; Caroline, June 8, 1832; George W., February 23, 1834, and William H., May 25, 1836.

Again, their marriages, either in Roane or Kanawha:
Archibold P. to. Elizabeth Snyder (the widow Atkins).
Charles to Nancy Jarrett.
Jane D. to Mr. Lockhart of Wirt County.
Isaac F. Saliena Hart.
John to Jane Carpenter.
David to Elizabeth Rucker.
Mahala to Richard Cart.
Harvey to Ozilla Darnell.
Caroline to William Johnson.
George W. to Elizabeth Geary, likely of record in Kanawha County.
William H. to Mary Darnell.
Of the foregoing Osbornes we mention further as follows:

George W. and the three sons of Isaac and his wife, made homes on Big Sandy near Osbornes Mills and were prominent in their business.

George W. Osborne, son of George and Susanna (Fleshman) Osborne, as above shown, was brought up on the Big Sandy; united in marriage with Elizabeth Geary, daughter of Mathew Geary and wife, pioneers of Big Sandy. They made their farm home on a large tract of land near Osbornes Mills, reducing many acres of the forest to fertile fields that brought them prosperity; and there brought up their family of three sons and two daughters, whose names are Edgar Ward, Isaac G., Alfonse B., Cynthia G. and Hattie C. And of these:

Hattie Carrie married John William Looney, September 28, 1892; her age then 25; his age 28. See family name "Looney."

John H. Osborne, son of Isaac F. and Saleina (Hart) Osborne, was born February 1, 1848; married Leonia Virginia Geary, December 8, 1868; she a daughter of Mathew Geary and wife, pioneers. See name, Geary.

We are not giving the names of their children except Stella, who married J. T. Parris, April 1, 1897, each 24 years old.

Lewis D. Osborne, son of Isaac E. and Salina (Hart) Osborne was born December 31, 1851; on October 13, 1875, married Miss Louisa Stump, daughter of Major Henry Stump and his wife. See name, "Stump." They made their home at Osborne Mills, where he was a popular timber dealer until about the year 1890. We are told of only two children, whose names were, Charles D., born 1879, and Ocie D., born December 22, 1881. Ocie, when 22, married Nelson J. Carper, 27, on March 30, 1904.

Millard F. Osborne, son of Archibold P. and Elizabeth, his wife, married Miss Flora Stump, April 5, 1880.

C. "Ham" Osborne, son of Charles and Nancy (Jarrett) Osborne, married, at 27, Julia Corder, 24, on March 23, 1884. These last had their home at Osbornes Mill for some years.

PARRIS: Of Big Sandy, Geary District.

James T. Parris arrived here from England shortly before the year 1897. Our informant does not know his ancestry nor county or parish in which he was born; nor when he came or at what port he landed; or why he came here; all of which would be interesting, but must be left to a biographer.

By the marriage records we are informed that he united in marriage at Amma, in Geary District, on the 1st day of April, 1897, with Miss Stella A. Osborne; his age 24, born in England; her age, 25, born in Roane County. Stella A. Osborne is a daughter of John H. Osborne and L. V. (Geary) Osborne, his wife, which family names, see.

James T. Parris and stella made their home at Amma, where he conducted a mercantile business many years. To him and his wife Stella A.

were born and brought up, we are told, "one son and one daughter; their names, Ruth Parris and Paul Parris."

PERKINS: Of upper Reedy, Curtis District.

Eli Perkins and his wife whose name or family we do not have, were married in Fayette or Greenbrier County and just prior to time of the formation of Roane County, 1856, with their two sons and four or five daughters; the eldest of whom were already of marriagable age, settled on upper Left Fork of Left Reedy Creek; made a farm there and were well spoken of by neighbors for some twenty years. Of the sons and daughters of Eli Perkins and wife we are told of the following: Morgan, who married a Mary Griffith; Lafayette, who married Miss Alma McCoy of Reedy, June 24, 1858; and Susie, who married a Mr. Safereid.

Morgan and Mary (Griffith) Perkins, his wife, made their farm home on upper Reedy many years; there brought up four sons and two daughters. Of these:

William Perkins, son of Morgan and Mary, married Miss America Miller, daughter of Scott Miller, of Left Reedy, Curtis District. Of this union only one child was born; his name, Byron Dewey Perkins. Byron Dewey was a popular pupil of the Spencer High School and its foot ball team, years 1920 to 1925. In the year 1926, B. Dewey married Miss Estel Heck, daughter of Albert S. and Estella (Crislip) Heck, of City of Spencer History.

PAXTON:

A distinction is to be observed between two early settlers in Walton District of this family name, Paxton; they have not the same mother, place nor time of birth.

Lyle Paxton, pioneer farmer, of Straight Creek and Rock Creek country of Walton District, was born in Kanawha County, year 1822, son of Thomas and Dicena (Cartright) Paxton, settled in Walton District in the year 1858; was twice married; for first wife, he married Barbara Hammack about the year 1843. She died in the year 1861. To Lyle and Barbara were born the following children: America, 1844; John V., 1848; and Sarah J., 1850. For a second wife Lyle Paxton married, in Roane County, December 7, 1862, Artenia Summers, daughter of St. Clair Summers. To Lyle and Artenia were born six children whose names were Julia L., born 1864; Lyle, Jr., 1866; Minnie C., 1868; Fannie, 1873; Leona I., 1875, and Ernest T., 1878.

Lyle Paxton first above named served as a Captain of "Home Guards" auxiliaries of the Union armies, 1863 to 1865; he died from being crushed by a falling tree on his farm, February 24, 1879. The men of this family were of auburn hair and beard, clean complexion and large athletic build.

Thomas B. Paxton, blacksmith, of Walton Village, for several years commencing in 1866, was born in Botetourt County, Virginia, May 22,

1814, son of Thomas and Mary (Plott) Paxton. In Craig County, Virginia, January 10, 1839, he married Mary, daughter of Henry and Catherine Britts. Mary was born in Botetourt County, Virginia, August 8, 1814. To Thomas B. and Mary Paxton were born Samuel B., 1839; Alcy C., 1841; Sarah, 1844; Mary, 1847; Victoria, 1854, and Amanda, 1858. In his biography in Hardesty's, it is stated that Thomas B. Paxton settled in Roane County, in the year 1866. How many of his older children came here with him we can not say.

NOAH FRANKLIN PENCE: Of Walton District.

Four of this family, two brothers and two sisters, came to Roane County to make their homes about the year 1872; all were born in Augusta County, Virginia, children of Ruben D. and Mary (Wise) Pence, his wife, ruined financially in war's devastations in Virginia, 1861 to 1865. These four came "West," about 1866, tarrying in Lewis County, West Virginia ,five or six years. The names of the other three are George W., Maggie and Martha.

Noah Franklin Pence married Mahala J. Gandee, January 6, 1881. She was a daughter of James S. Gandee of Gandeeville. They soon acquired a farm and made their permanent home on Silkets Fork. They were parents of the following sons and daughters, named in order of their respective ages: Florence, wife of BenJamin F. Fields; Roy R., who married Dulcie McKown of Spencer District; Myrtle, married William Edward Raines of Poca country; Addie J. married David Holley Boggs of Geary District, "June 30, 1910; his age 23, her age 22;" Orvie Cecil, born 1889, married Miss Dona Phillips, daughter of George W. Phillips of Big Sandy, "November 24, 1910; his age 21, her age 18." They live at Walton where he is cashier of the Poca Valley Bank; he has been with that bank since the year 1916, near eleven years now.

PERRINE: Of Spring Creek and Spencer:

Miles Perrine, first of the name here, married Miss Angeline Wees, (or Wiese) some time before the Civil War. They made their home half mile below Spencer. He was an enlisted Union soldier in Ninth West Virginia, injured at Cloyds Mountain, died soon afterward at his home. To Miles and Angeline, his wife, were born and grew up, Emma, who married Zadoc Goodwin; E. Lewis married Miranda Harris, December 24, 1878; Frederick married Anna M. Longfellow, 1887; Junius M.; Rebecca Harris of Spring Creek; J. Catherine married J. D. Grady, September 21, 1886, her age 18, his 24. They live in Spencer District, near line of Reedy. Joseph married Rebecca Ward, daughter of Job Ward. Grant Perrine was a son of Miles and Angeline. We do not have anything of his career.

PETTY:

William Petty, born in what is now Wirt County, West Virginia, June 5, 1843, son of Rowland and Catherine (Ott) Petty, came to Roane County in company of his brother Rowland, in the year 1865. They were sons of Rowland and Catherine (Ott) Petty, his wife, both born in Wirt County while it was a part of Wood County; Rowland on 23rd day of May, 1810; Catherine on 16th August, 1816. She was a daughter of Phidellis and Mary Ott, his wife.

In the sketch of the history of Wirt County, in Hardesty's History; a "William Petty' 'is named among the first settlers of Wirt County, 1796, with William Beauchamp, John Petty and others; the Pettys were among those who came there from the Monongahela Valley, we fear there may be some confusion of Williams and Rolands.

William Petty, II, above named, married Miss Melissa Jane Goff, April 2, 1867. She was born January 9, 1845, daughter of Major William R. Goff and wife Sarah (Bush), at the Goff homestead at eastern side of the Town of Spencer. William Petty acquired, or had acquired at time of marriage, a tract of several hundred acres of lands at Reedyville, Curtis District; on this he and the wife Melissa J. (Goff) made their further life-time home.

The names of the sons and daughters of William and Melissa J., his wife, are, Cora A., born October 16, 1868; Rowland R., February 24, 1870; Bertha M., May 27, 1872; Margaret C., August 26, 1874, and Sarah E., December 13, 1876. Their marriages:

Cora A. to Harley D. Wells.

Rowland R. has been twice married. He has succeeded to the home farm at Reedyville. We do not have his children's names.

Bertha M. married Giles Edwards. See Edwards.

Sarah E. "Sallie," married R. H. Copenhaver, August 2, 1902; his age, 25; born in Kanawha County. They reside there.

Rowland Petty, II, before mentioned son of Rowland or William Petty, and his wife, Catherine (Ott), pioneers of Wirt County, was born there, as indicated by marriage records, in the year 1846; came to Reedyville vicinity, 1865; there married Miss Elizabeth C. Thomasson, year 1867; made a tract of land, possibly three hundred acres, into a large stock farm; has lived there ever since; never has sought political office or public notice, but contributes to churches and neighborhood affairs. Rowland and Elizabeth (Thomasson), his wife, reared two sons and two daughters; their names, William Brown, Joseph A., Carrie and Agnes, whose marriages are as follows:

William Brown Petty to Susie Hardman, May 9, 1894; his age 24, her age 19. She is a daughter of Sylvester Hardman. Susie, now a widow, resides in Spencer, the eldest daughter of W. B. and Susie is wife of Guy Sinnett. See name, Sinnett.

Joseph A. Petty, 21, to Madge Smith, 21, on July 21, 1895.

Carrie Petty, 21, to A. I. Mount, September 29, 1890; he born in Harrison County; she in Roane.

Agnes Petty and John R. Showen, 27th April, 1904; his age 38, her's 28; both born in Roane County. See "Showen."

PRICE: Of Pocatalico.

John W. Price, born in Russell County, Virginia, October 7, 1836, and James H. Price, his brother, was born in the same county, July 6, 1842. These two brothers came with their mother, Lavina, and settled in western part of Harper District in the year 1855, both brothers served on the Confederate side through the War of the Secessions. There was another brother of these two, named William Price, who was killed during the war, in Harper District, though not an enlisted soldier.

John W. Price married Margaret, the daughter of Joseph and Rebecca (Neely) Presley, January 3, 1867, in Jackson County, West Virginia, she also, having been born in Russell County, Virginia, October 25, 1845; the Presleys having come to Roane County when Rebecca was one year old.

These Prices cleared and made into good farms a fair share of their part of the district.

To John W. and Margaret (Presley) Price were born and by them brought up, four sons and three daughters, whose names and dates of births are: Joseph Presley, November 7, 1867; Rebecca J., April 4, 1869; Mary L., April 28, 1871; William E., October 20, 1873; Celia S., November 13, 1875; John W., January 7, 1878; and George N., November 6, 1880. Of these we note here, Joseph Presley Price. He attended the public schools of the district, was an apt pupil developing a business brain out above the ordinary; became a shrewd trader; a crossroads merchant and later was elected sheriff of the county, in which office he served the four year term, 1912 to 1916 with efficiency and commendable credit; during this service he made his home in the City of Spencer, where he yet resides, his wife, the sweetheart of his young manhood, with him. She is Kate, the daughter of Elbert Smith, and was born in Harrison County, West Virginia. Joseph P. Price and Kate his wife have had only the one child, her name is Ruth. She is the wife of Brady Reed, a resident of Spencer.

Joseph P. and Kate Price became the foster parents, of Earl Price, a son of John Wesley Price, the brother of Joseph Presley Price, when the wife of John Wesley died and left Earl, an infant of only .... years of age. Earl Price married Ruth Adams, the daughter of Phillip C. Adams, mentioned in the chapter of this work, "City of Spencer." Earl and Ruth have their home here.

PRICE: Of Spencer District and Henrys Fork.
First here:

HISTORY OF ROANE COUNTY 625

John Price and Rose Anna (Wayts) Price, with several of their first born children, were the first of this family name in the above mentioned locality.

John Price was born in Monroe County, Virginia, year 1818; is later in Wetzel County, Western Virginia. There he married Miss Rose Anna Wayts in the year 1837. She was born in Wetzel County. They made their home there in Wetzel for a few years, then removed over into Ohio. From Ohio they all came to Calhoun County, West Virginia, about the year 1882; from Calhoun into Roane in the year 1900.

In Roane they acquired lands, and became good farmers. John and Rose Anna, brought up and gave to the citizenship of the county five sons and four daughters, whose marriages and samewhat further about each, is as follows:

Margaret Elizabeth; we have no information of her.

Mary Bell married Ira G. Reip, 29th April, 1888; his age, 23; her age, 22.

Sarah Adelaid, married Andrew Mace, 23rd January, 1899; her age, 22; his age, 23. Of Artie, we do not know.

Winston Price, at 21, married Ida May Mace, 19, on the 8th of January, 1891. They reside in Spencer now—1927—and have a family.

Archibold, at 44, married Naoma A. Parsons, 37, on February 16, 1916.

Artie H. Price, 22, to Icy May Mace, 19, October 1, 1902.

John Price, 22, to Flora Mace, 18, December 23, 1897.

Howard Price and Herbert Price are the youngest of the children of John and "Rosanna" (Wayts) Price.

PURSLEY: Of Spencer District.

Hudson Pursley and Elizabeth (Short) Pursley, his wife, whom he had married in Botetourt County, Virginia, about the year 1840, with some of their first-born children, came to Roane County about the year next following the Civil War. Elizabeth "Betty" was a sister of William, Hiram, George and Hatchet Short, all of whom came from Botetourt about the time the Pursleys came.

Hudson and his family acquired land and settled on Charles Fork of upper Spring Creek, and there completed their span of life. Their children's names were Sarah J., William E., Louvinia, Andrew J., Thomas Reedy, Jesse Hudson, Julia Ann, Andrew Jackson, George W., C. Austin and Martha M.

The list given us by a member of the family has on it the names of at least three children who died before marriage. First marriages of members of above family:

Of Sarah Jane we have no information.

Caroline married a John Johnson in Botetourt.

William E. married Miss Nellie Wright of Spring Creek, on January 2, 1869; they brought up a large family.

Louvinia married John G. Goff of Reedy, August 24, 1887; she then as "Widow Harlow," age 41, his age 62.
Thomas Reedy married Elizabeth Snyder, 1891; he 39, she 26.
Jesse Hudson married Louisa Snyder, September 13, 1877.
Julia·Ann to Henry Alex Lowe, November 22, 1875.
George W., "Dock", married Mary A. Lowe, March 5, 1885.
Martha M. "Mattie" to T. Albert Thompson, October 10, 1882.
C. Austin Pursley, possibly youngest of this family, married a Miss Silcot, in another county.

Some of the above Pursleys have brought up large families, many of them yet in the county.

William E. and his wife, Nellie (Wright) Pursley, are parents of several active business men. Reedy Pursley of Roane Grocery Company, is one of this family.

RADABAUGH: Pioneers of upper Left Reedy.

Jacob Radabaugh, veteran of the War of 1812, with his wife, Ruth (Winnings), whom he had married likely in Upshur County, for they came here from that county with some children, prior to the Mexican War, 1845, some of which children as shown by marriages must have been nearly grown up when they arrived. From conveyances it appears he held title to some thousand or more acres of land extending from near Reedyville up the left fork of Reedy, on which he made his ample and for many years known as a best farm in those parts. He died in 1876, but the wife, Ruth, lived some years longer.

We are able to name the following one son and two daughters of this family: James E., Cinderella and Elizabeth.

Cinderella married Lorenzo D. Holbert and Elizabeth wedded a Thomas Lanham.

James E. Radabaugh, son of James and Ruth, his wife, succeeded to the home farm. He volunteered and served as a Union soldier in the War of the Rebellion, erroneously reported as killed in the battle of Cloyds Mountain. He had married Miss Harriett N. Kelley, April 15, 1858. To them were born the following children: Peter T., Columbia, Ulysses, Alma, Augie, Ira, Isaac Newton, and America. Their marriages:

Peter T. to Sarah E. Tawney, 15th May, 1888; Columbia to Wm. Frank Wilson, October 15, 1877; America to George M. Carrickhoff, November 18, 1885, he born in Upshur County; Ira to Martha A. Davis, September 17, 1893, his age 24; Isaac Newton to Orlie L. Conley, November 10, 1895; Alma to Alvin N. Conley, May 4, 1893, her age 23, his 24; Augie married Theodocia Winter, and we do not have the marriage of Ulysses.

RADER:

Dr. Lewis A. Rader was born in Kanawha County, western Virginia, March 9, 1847, his parents being Bennett and Ann E. (Cobb) Rader, the former born in Jackson County, the latter in Kanawha County, closed their lives in Mason County.

Dr. Lewis A. Rader enlisted in the Union army in the month of March, 1863, and served in Co. I, 13th Regt., West Virginia Vol. Infantry. Later came to Roane County, and on April 22, 1868, united in marriage with America A. Geary, daughter of Mathew and Elizabeth M. (Ashley) Geary, of Geary District. The Doctor and wife made their home at Gandeeville for so many years, from which point he practiced medicine until old age compelled him to retire; often for several years in succession he was the only physician within a radius of ten miles; the reliable country doctor, riding many a long lonesome road on many a stormy night to relieve distress and suffering. The doctor and his wife both died in the City of Spencer, in the year 1925.

Of the marriage of Lewis A. and America A. Rader, his wife, were born, prior to 1883, the following children: Alton C., born June 2, 1872; Emory, April 11, 1875; Lillie Lee, March 27, 1878; Flora W., June 25, 1879, and Icy G., February 26, 1882. Emory is a resident of the city of Spencer, now, 1927.

RADER: Of Reedy.

The Raders are descendants of Colonial families of Eastern Virginia—maybe the Shenandoah Valley. A James Rader came into Jackson County immediately after the War of 1812, others by way of Greenbrier, Nicholas, Kanawha and Mason Counties, in each of which counties they appear to have tarried at least one generation, some of whom remained while others came on westward.

The most prominent of the name in Jackson County was E. Hart Rader, of upper Mill Creek parts, born year 1816, son of James and C. (Allen) Rader; his was the finest of the farms; he was in the height of popularity just prior to the Civil War and for fifteen years afterwards.

John Rader, of the same parts of Mill Creek, who must have settled there about the year 1845, came there from Nicholas County, in which county he had married his first wife, Miss McClung. His second wife was Nancy Duddington. He reared a family in Jackson County, their names: Joseph, George, Adison, William, Charles, Franklin, Harvey, H. (the resident of Reedy), Margaret, Sarah, Mary, and Susan. Of these, Franklin married Miss Dorcas Riddle, of Reedy, on 14th of July, 1858.

Harvey H. Rader, son of above family of John Rader, was for a period of twenty-five years a prominent resident of and about "Three Forks" of Reedy; served as a soldier in the Confederate armies of Virginia; returned unscathed from all those battles, and on August 5, 1867, united in marriage with Miss Sarah Burr Watts, daughter of William and Elizabeth (Burr) Watts, of Reedy. They first were farmers in Wirt County, where some of their children were born; afterward, Harvey H. was some years a merchant in the Town of Reedy. They brought up four children; two sons and two daughters, whose names, in order of respective births, are Lulu, Eddie—died at 16—Elizabeth and Lorenzo D. Rader. Further of these:

Lulu married William H. Gibbs, son of W. Brown and Mattie (Greer) Gibbs, of Reedy.

Elizabeth H. was twice married; first, to Louis H. Wyatt, of Reedy, on June 26, 1892, his age 23, her's 21. Of this marriage two children were born, named Nettie and Azel. The husband, Louis H., having died, Elizabeth H. married Robert J. Moss, born in Louisa, Virginia; at time of marriage a widower-farmer of Middle Fork of Reedy. This marriage was on August 6, 1899, her age then 29, his 58. Of this marriage five children were born and brought up.

Lorenzo D. ("Lennie"), son of Harvey H. and Sarah B. (Watts) Rader, was born in Wirt County, 1875, died at Reedy, February 27, 1926. He was for some years clerk in his father's store; after death of his father became sole owner and passed his life in his general store at Reedy. On July 15, 1894 he united in marriage with Miss Allie Roberts, his age 19, her age 17 years. They reared two children, their names Vivian and Horace. Miss Vivian became administratrix of her father's estate, and continues the store business at Reedy.

Laura, daughter of Harvey H. and his wife, married Barney Wyatt, of Reedy, December 3, 1902, her age 22, his age 25. They have eight children.

There were Rader pioneers of Reedy other than the family above named, but my information is indefinite as to their relations to each other. Some names of Rader men of Reedy appear in the lists of soldiers in the Civil War as printed in Chapter I, of this book. Also:

A Susan Rader became the wife of Mordecai J. Thomasson prior to formation of Roane County.

A Mariah Rader, born in Jackson County, year 1815, was the wife of Levi Pickerel, pioneers of Reedy.

An Isaac M. Rader, born in Jackson County, Western Virginia, year 1845, son of James and Catherine (Cunningham) Rader. Isaac M. married in Roane County, Amanda J. Alfred—widow Ferrell then— October 29, 1882, He was a blacksmith, miller and farmer of Flat Fork of Poca, in Harper District, for several years. They reared a family.

RAY:

In the year 1856, three brothers of this name, Ray, all born in Albermarl County, Virginia, arrived at Walton, Western Virginia. Their names: Zedekiah, Ira and William.

Zedekiah Ray had married in Albermarl County, Lou Ella Clatterbaugh, and she came with him. They made their home in Lower Harper District and reared a family of which we can name here: Edward H., Mary E., who married John W. Long, of Harper District,

HISTORY OF ROANE COUNTY   629

1890; his age 19, her age 18. Nancy Jane, who married Moses Coon, of Higby, 1889; his age 24, her age 17. Edward H. Ray, for some time principal of Spencer Independent School, died about the year 1918. The youngest of this family, Okey Ray, resided for some years on Higly.

Ira Ray, second of above brothers, married Fannie Cummings. We do not have the names of their family, if any.

William Ray, brother of "Zed" and Ira, was born in Albemarle County, Virginia, May 15, 1838; came to Roane the year the county was formed—1856—to get away from having to drive Negroes, so his son told me; married Artentia Summers, daughter of St. Clair and Susan (Hammack) Summers, in Roane County, 1863. Settled, first near Walton, afterward made their home for life on a farm near head of Green Creek. To William and Artentia (Summers) Ray were born and by them brought up. William H., who married Catherine Shafer, of Kanawha County; Byrd St. Clair, born in 1874, married Lillie, daughter of Lewis Jones, of Kanawha County, West Virginia, year 1901. To Byrd St. Clair and Lillie were born five sons and three daughters. Byrd St. Clair taught school a number of years, was elected and served one term as assessor of Roane County, and is now (1924-6) Mailing Clerk in the State Road Department at Charleston.

Esta, daughter of William and Artentia Ray, married John Larch, of Lower Pocatalico; Nancy, her sister, married Jacob deYoung, of Lafayette, Indiana.

REED: Of Geary District.

Nathan I. Reed, was born in Barbour County, Virginia, in the year 1836 a son of Alexander and .... (Reader), his wife. In that same county Nathan I. married a Miss Annice Catherine Engle, daughter of Solomon Engle and his wife. To Nathan I. and AnniceC. (Engle), his wife, were born, all in Tigarts Valley, near Phillipi, three sons and four daughters, all of whom came with their father and mother to Roane County, in the year 1876, and first settled on Flat Fork of Poca, on a tract of forest lands purchased with intention of making a home farm of it; built the usual house in the woods, cleared some fields then sold out and moved to Geary District, in the year 188 . having purchased a tract of unimproved lands lying on Big Sandy one-half mile below Amma. They improved this, made an average farm of it, and here Nathan I. Reed and his wife spent the remainder of a likeable and blameless life. He was prominent in the local affairs there for a space of some forty years.

The names and something further of the children of Nathan I. and Annice C. Reed, his wife, as given me, are: Elmanzie E., married Homer Dan Hoff, year 1879; Jasper Newton, see further in this paragraph; Leburey Jackson, married Fannie S. Parker, 1884; his age 21, her age 18; Theressa married George Marion, of Kanawha County; Isopher Z., married a Miss Flemming, and Lulu Bell, married Seymore

C. Petitt, year 1889, his age 21, her age 17. They reared two sons, Lonnie and Wehrle. Jasper Newton, the above son of Nathan I., married Miss Cora Belle Bradley, 1879, his age 26, her age 20; they made their home in Roane County. He is now—1927—one of the managerial force of the O. J. Morrison & Company store of Spencer. To Jasper N. and Cora B., his wife, were born and reared, three sons and one daughter, whose names are Luther L., William Brady and Oris Hayes, and Goldie B. Their marriages are as follows:

Luther Loral, married Miss Cora Dearman; William Brady, married Ruth Price, December 30, 1919, his age 22, her age 21; she is a daughter of Joseph P. Price and his wife, formerly of lower Pocatalico; Oris Hayes, married Ruby Kiser, daughter of Noah Kiser of Pocatalico.

Goldie Bly, the only daughter of Jasper N. and wife, married Captain Harry Holswade, year 1920, his age 35, her age 25. They reside on part of the Holswade ancestral lands.

W. Brady and Oris Hayes both are members of the O. J. Morrison Store Company force in their Spencer store, and each owns his home in Spencer.

RHODES: Of Reedy.

Samuel Rhodes, first of the name settling in Reedy, was born in Rockbridge County, Virginia, about the year 1800; there married Parthena Vandine, lived there in Rockbridge County several years, during which their first three or four children were born. They came to Jackson County, Western Virginia about 1845, settled near Ripley and lived there some ten or fifteen years, then came to the Middle Fork of Reedy, purchasing a farm near mouth of Staats Run, where they completed their lives. This Samuel Rhodes, though born in Rockbridge County, is to be distinguished from the Samuel of the family of Rhodes of the same county who left Rockbridge and settled on Upper Mill Creek.

To Samuel and Parthena (Vandine) Rhodes were born four sons and three daughters, all of whom came with them to Reedy. Their names, John Woodard, Sarah Ann, Eliza, Martha, Louise, Isom, Virgil and Catherine.

John Woodard Rhodes married Lucinda Parsons, of Jackson County, West Virginia. They lived and died on the old ancestral place on Middle Fork of Reedy. Their bodies lie interred in the Roach cemetery nearby. On the ample stone marking the grave is this inscription: "John W. Rhodes, 1831-1902—wife Lucinda, 1832-1904."

To theme were born and grew up the following sons and daughters: Louisa, died, not having married; Dorcus, wife of Henderson Williams; Albert and Allen, twins. Albert M. went to Texas many years ago. Allen W. ("Bunn") married Sarah E. Watson, daughter of Simon Watson, then of Right Reedy. To "Bunn" and Sarah were born two daughters, Gertrude and Nellie. Gertrude married Robert McCutchen, of Reedy; Nellie married William Stephens, now residing at Rockport,

Wood County, West Virginia; Carrie married Conda Leary, of Middle Reedy, October 27, 1886; they went to Harris, Missouri, shortly after marriage. Maggie married Charles Goff, of near Town Reedy.

Sarah Ann, daughter of Samuel and Parthena Rhodes, was twice married. Her first husband was Alexander Chancey, son of Hiram, of Reedy; Alex and Sarah Ann reared three daughters, Leilia, Jane and Martha. Leilia married Leroy M. Eagle, of Buffalo, of Mill Creek; marriage records showing her name as "Cora Chancey," February 26, 1877. They later made their home many years in Parkersburg, West Virginia. Of the marriages or otherwise of Jane and Martha I do not know. Alexander Chancey having died, Sarah Ann married for a second husband, John Corder, January 16, 1874. To them were born one child, a daughted, her name I do not know. Corder died December 5, 1876, aged 54 years and ten months.

Of Isom, Virgil and Catherine, children of Samuel Rhodes and Parthena, his wife, we have no information.

Eliza married Robert J. Moss, born in Harrison or Lewis County. See Moss.

RHODES: See paragraph "Community Centers" in Chapter Harper District.

Peter Rhodes, the Lower Flat Fork miller, is the pioneer of this family. Peter and his brother, Samuel Rhodes, were born in Rockbridge County, Virginia, about 1807 and 1809, respectively, and came to Jackson County and settled on Upper Mill Creek, near what is now —1926—United States Postoffice "Gay."

This arrival may have been as early as the year 1840. Rev. John H. Smith, of Harper (1883), says he married "Letta Rhodes in the year 1860," but does not say whose daughter she was, nor where the marriage took place. However, soon after the War of "65,," Peter is found at the mill, built by Parrot Ferrell, a mile or so above the mouth of Trace Fork; had improved the mill and henceforth it was known as "Peter Rhodes" Mill. Of Peter's children whom we can name, is his son Marion Rhodes, who succeeded to the mill and other property of Peter when he died, 1924, at the unusual age of one hundred and sixteen years. More remarkable is the fact that at one hundred and twelve, thirteen and fourteen, he was stilll attending the little mill, and would carry in all grists except such as were in the large bags.

Samuel Rhodes, the other brother mentioned, had married in Rockbridge County, Virginia, where part or all of his six children were born, who later became residents of Jackson County. Their names in order of their respective births, are: Matthias, Archibold A., Andrew, John Wesley, George W. and Eliza.

Of the foregoing children of Samuel Rhodes, we concern ourselves here with John Wesley and George W. only, because these became citizens of Roane.

John Wesley Rhodes, son of Samuel, above mentioned, married Mary Allen in Roane County, West Virginia, December 30, 1875. A poor scribe causing her first name to be written "May!" She was a daughter of Henry and Elizabeth Allen, and his wife, whose home for long previous to the marriage of Mary, was on upper Left Fork of Elk of Mill Creek, and near Gay United States Postoffice Mary died and was buried.

To John Wesley and Mary (Allen) Rhodes were born—all near United States Postoffice "Gay"—one daughter and four sons. Eva L., who married William E. Greathouse, son of W. M. D. and wife, on May 9, 1917, his age 44, her age 40.

Dennis married Maggie Hughes, of Flat Fork, March 1, 1903, his age 24, her age 19. He was a field man in the employ of the United Fuel Gas Company at time of the marriage. He was one of the first natives to learn that business. Dennis and Maggie made their home in Spencer, about 1915, where he is in the mercantile business. They have a family of several children.

Dayton married Maud, daughter of Charles C. and Martha (Stewart) Casto, formerly of Jackson County, "at the Grand Hotel," Spencer, West Virginia, April 13, 1902, his age 32, her age 22. They have three daughters and one son, Phillis, Martha, Virginia and Charles. Theirs is one of the several good brick residences of the city. Dayton commenced as first garage owner of the Town of Spencer, and dealer in the Ford automobiles, and is reputed to have grown wealthy in the fifteen years of the growing automobile business that ensued.

Ferdie Ephraim, commenced some years ago in a dry goods business in the city, Dennis later joining him. They are reputed to be great financial successes. On September 19, 1917, Ferdie E., married Olla Thompson, his age 33, her age 32. She is a daughter of Thomas Albert and Mattie (Pursley) Thompson.

Emmet, the youngest, not married, "was killed in action," on a battlefield of France, in the World War.

George W. Rhodes, fifth son of Samuel, ancestor first mentioned, married Miss Jane Reynolds, of near Ripley, and to them were born the following named children:

John Wesley, who married Ettie Craddock, and began as a farmer near Spencer. We do not have dates or ages. They had two sons in the World War, one of whom, Romie, on the monument "Okey," "was killed in action."

Charles Holt married Miss Irene A. McKown, daughter of Ephraim McKown, Sr., of upper Spring Creek, on January 21, 1894, his age 30, her age 24. To Charles H. and Irene A. have been born and grown up, several children. Their home is in Spencer, where for fifteen years C. Holt has been in business, first as a stone and brick work contractor, and later as a partner of the Rhodes, Meredith, Thomasson Plaining Mill Company, or "Spencer Brick Company."

William Downtain, traveling salesman, married Florence Stalnaker, daughter of William A. Stalnaker, of Calhoun County, West Virginia, his age 27, her age 21. They have their home residence in Spencer.

Oliver Dow, trader, farmer, married Oma, daughter of J. Lee Radabaugh, of near Spencer, on November 30, 1905, his age 25, her age 20.

Theodore, married Ocie Crislip, of Spencer, May 16, 1909, his age 23, her age 20. They went to California some years ago, where they yet live.

Cora B. Rhodes, youngest of this family, is a trained nurse, and joined her brother, Theodore, in California a few years ago, and is there now—1926.

An Alexander Rhodes, born in Rockbridge County, Virginia, married Miss Mahala Edens, in that county, came to Jackson County, about the year 1850, for their son, Llewlelyn Rhodes, long a resident of Gay, marr'ed there in Jackson County in the year 1854. He served as a Union soldier of the war—1862 to 1865—Alexander made his home on Flat Fork prior to 1880, and has left there several descendants whose names and careers we do not have.

Isaiah Rhodes married Amanda Jolly, settled on Flat Fork. They left four sons and three daughters.

RIDDLE:

Benjamin Riddle and Jemima, daughter of Abram Ingraham, his wife, of Left Reedy. These settled there on some five or six hundred acres of land. The Abram Ingaham lands as to part including the Mordecai Thomasson farm improvement, about the decade of 1840 to 1850. They reared several children. The whole family sold out and "went west," leaving here about the year 1871.

Of this family are remembered Albert G., who, at 21, married Clerissa Sheppard, 25, of Lower Reedy, April 17. 1854. John, who marr'ed Miss Belle Collins. Thomas, who married Miss Jennie Collins. Bo'h 'hese misses being school teachers, daughters of Edmond and Elizabeth Collins, of Long Bottom, Ohio; these marriages were about the year 1871-?. There was a youngest son named Benjamin, Jr.

A'bert. son of Benjamin and Jemima, who married Clarissa Sheppard, made his home for self and family on a tract of land overlooking the Middle Fork of Reedy, three miles from the "Three Forks." He was a soldier in the Confederate service; went west and was lost to his family, being two sons and three daughters. Their names, Samuel, who married Miss Lillie Straley, May 6, 1879; Benjiman Franklin, married Miss Delilah Elizabeth Candler, August 7, 1892, his age 33, her age 24. He holds the old home farm. I can not recall the name of the eldest daughter, the other two were Leora, who was, for awhile, a popular teacher, then made her home in the "West." Mattie, married Wellington Lester, died childless soon after marriage.

RIDDLE: Of Curtis District.

James Riddle, with his wife and family came from Lewis or Harrison, on Upper Reedy, prior to the Civil War. Was at once priminent in neighborhood and county affairs. He is the James Riddle who served as one of the committee which apportioned the county into "Townships" in 1863. His wife died and he married Mrs. Rebecca (Wetzel) Curtis, widow of Captain William Curtis, on February 7, 1867. Of the first marriage we can name two sons: Elijah M., one time Delegate for Roane in the State Legislature, and Tobias, long a resident of Curtis District. Of the second marriage we know of one son, Phillip H. Sheridan Riddle, who married Miss Lavina Hoge, March 3, 1887, his age 19. He is a farmer of Middle Reedy. They have some children, at least one son of engaging mein.

Fletcher S. Riddle, of which family we do not know, married Nancy E. Burdette in the year 1856.

RIDDLE: Alfred and Symiramis, of Left Reedy.

Alfred Riddle was a son of Salathial Riddle and wife, residents of Calhoun County. He had one sister, Delphia Stalnaker, of Gilmer County; a half sister, Louisa "Lou", who married W. "June" Deem. The marriage record has it thus: "J. Deem to Lou Riddle," August 28, 1883. "June" was a son of Thomas Deem, of a Wood County family of Deems. W. June and wife left Reedy and went to Oregon about the year 1887, where they have resided ever since.

Alfred Riddle married Miss Symiramus Goff, of Gilmer County, about the year 1862, and they lived for the first year or two with Salathiel in Calhoun County, where the first child was born. He enlisted and served in the Conferedate armies in Virginia, and on returning came to Left Reedy, where he purchased a tract of two or three hundred acres of land, most all in forest; engaged in timbering and clearing this; built the second good frame house erected on that creek, situate a quarter of a mile up the creek from the Ravenswood and Spencer turnpike. He was prominent for twenty years in District and County affairs. To Alfred and Symiramis, his wife, were born and by them reared, three daughters, their names in order of births: Julia, Lyle and Nancy. Julia was born in Calhoun, was twice married, first when 16, to Louis Hamilton Burke, February 5, 1880, second to Charles E. Hall, June 24, 1894, her age 24, his age 39. He was born in Ritchie County, West Virginia. One son was born of her first marriage, named Holly H. Burke. Several children were born of her and Hall's marriage.

Lyle M. married Benjamin Forest Gilmore, November 7, 1898, his age 29, her's 27. Born in the State of George; they make their home in Charleston.

Nancy married Emory L. Shafer, June 12, 1895, her age 21, his 23. He was born in Monongalia County, West Virginia.

HISTORY OF ROANE COUNTY   635

RIFFE: Of Smithfield District.
William David Riffe and his wife, Harriett (Boggess) Riffe, born in Monroe County, Western Virginia, with their several children came to Roane County about the year 1875, purchased lands on the head of Laurel Fork of Pocatalico and there attacked the dense forest which had already vanquished the first settler who commenced a home there and left a cabin, which was the first home of these Riffes in Roane County. The Riffes proved invincable, cleared back the stubborn forest and made a good home, which twenty years later sheltered a happy and prosperous family, the names of members of this family which I can give here are: Rev. Henry Kiser Riffe, and Rev. Andrew Clay Riffe, both regular preachers of the Methodist Episcopal church of West Virginia; each, for many years, has served on divers charges throughout the State. Rev. H. K. has had the City of Spencer churches one or more years. He is now stationed at Parkersburg, West Virginia. M. Carl Riffe, a third brother of this family, keeps the old home farm yet. A daughter of this family, whose name is Nannie, married Rev. G. N. Day, also a preacher of the M. E. conference for some years before retiring, making a suburban home at Spencer, where he died about the year 1924, leaving surviving him Nannie, the wife, and some children, grown.

RILEY:
The Rileys, of Harper District, pioneers of Middle Harper and mentioned in the chapter of this work, Harper District, and the chapter, History of the County, besides their careers in Roane County have left something of their family progenitors in a biography by George W. Riley, in Hardestys.

Jesse Riley, a soldier of the United States Army of the War with Great Britain, appears to have commenced a family life in Stafford County, Virginia, about 1812 or 1814, after that war was over, where Elijah Riley was born. He married Sarah Carter, a daughter of a Carter family of Stafford County, Virginia, and they soon came "west", settling for a while in Harrison County, near Clarksburg. We next find Elijah and Sarah (Carter) Riley, as settlers on Elk River in Kanawha County, possibly as early as the year 1820. Their settlement on a large tract of land of some thousand acres, mostly lying on a single branch of Elk River, was known for twenty years and spoken of as "Riley's," and that branch flowing through the large tract of Riley lands, to this day bears the name "Riley's Branch."

With the family of Elijah and Sarah there on Elk River were the two sons, George W. and William, later to come to Flat Fork of Pocatalico. George W., the elder of the two. We give here further about them:

George W. Riley was born in Harrison County, Western Virginia, June 23, 1814; came to Elk River with his parents, Elijah and Sarah, as above stated. He married April 14, 1850, in Doddridge County,

Western Virginia Louisa, born in Lewis County, June 14, 1812, daughter of James Arnold, of the Arnolds of the Monongahela Valley.

George and Louisa lived at or near Glenville during her life—she died there. To George and Louisa (Arnold), were born one son—John Elliott, and three daughters: Theresa, who married Amos Kelley, of Roane County; Salina, who married Benjamin Romine; Sa`lie, who married John W. Ball, and lived a short time in Harper District.

John Elliott Riley, son of George and Louisa (Arnold) Riley, married Mary E. Somerville, of Roane County. They made their home in Harper District. To John Elliott and Mary (Summerfield or Somerville) were born: Jonathan Kendal, Louis Monroe, who about 1876, made his home on the ancestral lands many years. Served on term as a Justice of the Peace of Harper District; never married and now lives in City of Spencer. George W. Jr., next in age to Lewis M.; Albert Lee, Alfred Irven and Elizabeth Catherine, wife of Amos W. Phillips, of Roane County. Louisa died and after her death George W. Riley, pioneer last above dealt with, married for a second wife Elizabeth, daughter of Roradam and Ruth (Woofter) Nutt, an old Virginia family of that name. Elizabeth was born in Lewis County, Western Virginia, June 14, 1812—two years older than her husband, George W. Riley. He says in his biography (which omitted that first marriage and family) "the same year of our marriage, 1850, we came to Roane County" and settled on Lower Flat Fork of Poca, at the mouth of Cox's Fork; there made the farm and built the mill.

To George W. and Elizabeth were born the following children, (in Harper District, of course): Frances Irven, William Perry, Albert Marsden, Amanda, the school teacher, who married Jacob Tichnell Chancey of Reedy, and Louisa, who married Richard Parrot Ferrell.

William Riley, son of Elijah and Sarah (Carter) Riley, was long a resident of the head waters of lower Flat Fork. William "Squire Bill" Riley served many years as a Justice of the Peace of that locality while a part of Kanawha as claimed by some and by others a part of Jackson County. At least we find him a Justice of the Peace for Jackson, took acknowledgements of deeds, administered the oaths of office to the other members of the first County Court of Roane County.

William Riley was twice married. His first wife being Mary Ann Jones, sister of Isaac Jones, of Walton District, therefore a daughter of Edmund and Malinda (Carr) Jones, who came from Hardy County, West Virginia, in the yera 1855, says Isaac Jones in his biography, and from marriage record of Isaac I. Riley to Mary Lulu Goodwin, September 28, 1884, his age 26, her age 18. Edmund and Malinda Jones must have been living near Walton as early as the year 1855.

William "Squire Bill" Riley married a second wife, Elizabeth Jane Taylor. Of this marriage were born one son and one daughter, Webster and Malinda.

Of this family of Squire William Riley we can say further:

HISTORY OF ROANE COUNTY 637

Isaac I. Riley married for wife Mary Lulu Goodwin, dates above given. Isaac was long active and prominent in Roane County affairs. Served one term as deputy sheriff of the county. For further see Chapter City of Spencer and Chapter VIII, Walton. Of this marriage of Isaac and Mary Lulu (Goodwin) were born—as we can name from recollection—two sons and five daughters, their names as follows: Oral, Charles, Oma, Grace, wife of Richard Hayes, of Spencer; Belva, Ruth and Anna.

Webster Riley, son of William Riley ("Squire Bill"), married Harriett Ellen Monroe, daughter of M. V. B. Monroe, of Curtis District; she was born in Ohio. The marriage records have the date of this marriage May 1, 1890, his age 22, her age 19.

Webster Riley began active as a young man, later moved to Charleston, West Virginia, and there established a large business, dry goods store, and he and his wife, Harriett Ellen, have their home in Charleston at time of this writing, but we are unable to give names of their children.

ROACH:

William and Delilah (Carney) Roach, of the earliest settlers on Middle Fork of Reedy, came there about the year 1823, onto a tract of four hundred acres of land purchased by William for the purpose of adding to its acreage and making of it an ancestral home, all according to the Scotch and Irish fireside philosophies in which these two had grown up.Delilah was born in the Monongahela Valley, year 1800, daughter of William Carney, sister of Jesse Carney and Charles Carney, the latter one time sheriff of Jackson County, about the year 1850. Delilah Roach was also a sister of Hannah, wife of Levi Casto, of Jackson County, who died about 1856.

William Roach was born in the year 1800, somewhere in Maryland, where his father died at about the time of William's birth, and his mother at once married a Mr. .... Collins and within a year a brother was born, named Edmund Collins. These four left Maryland within two or three years " for the West," arrived and settled on a large farm in the lower middle of Long Botton, Meigs County, Ohio, extending from the river back into the hills. They had funds to start with and soon a fine farm was made, and there these first settlers lived the remainder of their lives, no other children being born to them.

News of the War of 1812, with Great Britain, brought alarm to the old settlers and the spirit of adventure to the boys, William and Edmund. They ran away from home and joined some Virginia troops on hurrying march to Detroit over a trail not many miles north and back from the Ohio River. The boys were received and petted by the soldiers, and allowed to go with them to Detroit. The boys were camp help, and William, the elder of the two, was placed on the rolls as an enlisted soldier. Too young it appears from above dates.

But whatever error there may be it must be in the dates of births of the boys, yet on the grave-stone of William, at Reedy, it is "Born 1800."

And grandmother Delilah Roach (maternal grandmother of the author of this history) drew a United States pension as a widow of William Roach, an enlisted soldier of the War of 1812, for several years within my own recollection.

William and Edmund were surrendered at Detroit to the British as soldiers of General Hull's army.

On relinquishment of prisoners of war by the British at the end of that war, William and Edmund started eastward with a company of Virginia troops. Edmund stopped at Cincinnati, and William remained with the travelers until "Kanawha Licks" was reached. There he tarried and began work at the Ruffner Salt Works, and continued with them until he was twenty-three or twenty-four years old. Keeping up his knowledge of the whereabouts of Edmund, who by that time had become a steamboat pilot, they decided they would visit their old home at Long Bottom, which they did, Edmund by the river and William horseback overland, down Mill Creek, and there near what is now Ripley, stopping at William Carney's for the night, he met a heart-to-heart response in the daughter, Delilah Carney, and they were soon married. William at once resigned his work at the Salt Furnaces on the Kanawha, which had risen to that of superintendent, and came to Reedy and commenced the home first mentioned.

Their home soon became the community center, rivaling that of the Stewarts at Three Forks. He built a horse mill for grinding of breadstuffs, which brought the settlers there. He made the largest and most commodious farm house and out buildings, that have never been exceeded in commodiousness as yet, though many good frame residences have been erected in Reedy within this one hundred years.

Being a good judge of stock, his stallions and his bulls brought him neighborhood renown. His home was deemed always open to the preacher and school teacher, though he was not a reader nor a public worshiper at religious meetings, his home was the assembling place for preaching and religious worship for many years. Private tutors for his children were occasionally kept for short intervals, but their main education, the little they received, was obtained at subscription schools at Three Forks where the Stewarts and Seamans joined in the educational enterprises of the times. The boys walked to school, the girls rode horseback in months of good weather, and boarded with some resident near the old log building in which "school was kept." William established the cemetery for the neighborhood on his lands, which bears his name and holds his remains. William Roach died about the time of the first news of secession reached the neighborhood, leaving his widow and family, among whom were three large young men, loyal to Virginia against all the world.

HISTORY OF ROANE COUNTY 639

To William and Delilah (Carney) Roach were born and grew up there on Reedy, the following named children: Charles, who married Ellen Skidmore, of Jackson County, West Virginia; John never married; Mary married John Corder; Sarah, born December 16, 1833, married John Bishop, 1854, then of Racine, Ohio; Margaret, married Silas B. Leary, of Ripley, West Virginia, she born in 1835; Nancy, married Edward B. Combs, and they settled on Mill Creek in Jackson County, and there reared a large family; the youngest son of William and Delilah Roach; Jesse married Ann Watson, of Reedy, August 29, 1870.

Jesse Roach was long a prominent personage of the county, first after returning from "the war" he was Township clerk, then elected and served a term as Justice of the Peace, then was elected and served a term as Delegate from Roane County in the 17th, and again in the 19th session of the State Legislature, years 1885 and 1889, respectively. He lived some four or five years in Sullivan County, Missouri, or near the town of Harris, Missouri; returned to Reedy where he spent the last ten years of his life establishing a hardware business, there died leaving an estate of some fifteen thousand dollars, net, to his children.

To Jesse Roach and Ann (Watson), his wife, were born the following named children, in order of their ages: Arthur Cyrus, now a merchant of Harris, Missouri, married there, Miss Cecillia R. Watson, daughter of William H. Watson, born in Missouri, and has a family; Ella Florence was born 1879, married Dr. .... Jett, of Fayette County, West Virginia, where they have their home; Hallie C., married, at Reedy, Miss Jennie Smith, April 2, 1904, his age 27, her age 24; Mollie, the youngest of the famly, married in Spencer, P. Ward Riley, September 24, 1902, his age 24, her age 23. She was born in Roane, he born in Kanawha County.

At the time of the death of William Roach, 1861, the five hundred acre farm had about two hundred acres of cleared fields, well stocked. As we before remarked, those three stalwart sons were loyal to the old commonwealth, they were pro-"Secesh," and no more garrulous and fault finding man ever lived than Uncle Charles. Uncle John, the bachelor, was a cavalier in courtesy and courage, and when Colonel Roberts, late member of the first Wheeling convention, was arrested in the public road where it passed through the Roach farm, by Captain Albert G. Ingraham, bearing orders from General Henry A. Wise, Uncle Charles and Uncle John, being familiar friends of Captain Ingraham, were by the pro-Unionists, deemed either aiders and abettors of the Roberts arrest and his sufferings, or as a reprisal measure, Charles and John were forthwith arrested and hurried off to Camp Chase, Ohio. There Uncle Charles was a nuisance because of his sarcasms and was soon liberated, but Uncle John was kept until Roberts was released from Libby, where he had been taken.

For further of the Roaches in the Civil War, read under the family names, "Bishop," "Baker," "Ingraham," "Roberts."

ROCK:
Harvey O. Rock, the first of this family name resident of the county, was born in Botetourt County, Virginia, about the year 1845, and came to Walton at the close of the Civil War, 1865, a young carpenter and house-builder by trade. He was a welcome addition to the busy people desiring to change their residences from the old log houses to the frame weatherboarded and painted ones.

On September 16, 1869, Harvey O. Rock and Ann Eliza Hundley were married at the home of her mother, the bride being a daughter of Rebecca Hundley, widow, and her deceased husband, having two other daughters and one son, George W. Hundley, who afterward became clerk of the County Court, and was prominent in county business and politics for some ten years, 1900 to 1910. Jackson D. Lynch, of Walton District, married the widow, Rebecca, and here these Hundley children, George W.; Lucinda, who married John C. Lowe; "Liza," wife of Harvey O. Rock, and Ennina, wife of Charles Christopher Lynch, were spoken of as the family of Jack Lynch.

To Harvey O. Rock and Ann Eliza, his wife, were born, in Roane County, the following children, named in order of their births: Jennie, wife of "Bud" G. Lynch, son of Jackson D. by a former marriage. To them was born a child named Cecil G. Lynch; Hattie Rock, who married W. A. McCrosky; George William, died not having married; Rebecca, wife of Perry Webster Caldwell, of Poca; Fred Waitman Rock, married Martha Fields, daughter of William Fields ,of Jackson County, West Virginia; now with his family lives in Spencer, a houses painter by trade; Lucy Belle Rock married Charles Wyley, who later died leaving two children whose names are Wayne Wyley and Virginia Wyley.

ROBERTS:
Colonel Thomas Asbury Roberts, school teacher, land agent, soldier, early settler in Reedy, was born in the suburbs of the City of Baltimore, in the year 1808. William A. and Amanda Frances (Hanson) Roberts were his parents, devout Methodists, and the babe was christened in accordance with the rites of the Methodist Episcopal church of Baltimore, Thomas Asbury Roberts.

William A. Roberts, father of Thomas A., was one of the three sons of a Roberts born in Ireland, who landed in Baltimore before the Colonial Revolution and did his bit in that mighty struggle culminating in the independent United States of America.

Of the three just mentioned, one went to Virginia, another to the farther Northwest Territory, the third, William A., remained in Baltimore for some years, uniting in marriage there with Amanda F. (Hanson), and there became the parents of Thomas Asbury. While he was yet a small boy his parents emigrated to Ohio with him, purchasing and settling on a large tract of land west of Zanesville, at a place later named "Fultonham." There Thomas Asbury grew up. From private and public schools he obtained what was deemed by those pioneers, a good education. He is first spoken of publicly as a good school teacher.

In the year 1837 he married Mary Porter Fultonham, of the nighborhood of that same name. Of this marriage three children were born, named respectively, Irenus, Benedict and Samuel W. The last a citizen of the village of Three Forks Reedy for many years.

The first important public notice of Thomas Asbury Roberts was when Thomas Corwin, governor of Ohio, under the Great Seal of that State, commissioned him a Colonel of Militia. Let us quote from the Commission itself, which we have only a few hours ago had under our own eyes:

"TO THOMAS ROBERTS, GREETINGS:"
"It appearing to me that on the twentieth day of May, 1842, you were duly elected Colonel of the First Regiment of Cavalry, Second Brigade, and fifteenth Division in the Militia of this State, and we having confidence, etc."

On the back of the Commission is written the acceptance of the Commission and oath of office, taken and subscribed: "Thomas A. Roberts."

In the year 1844, Thomas A. and his wife, Mary Porter Fultenham Roberts, with their two first-born children, came to Reedy, his business being that of a "Land Agent," such being the designation of the salesmen appointed by companies and other large land owners to stay on the grounds and sell lands for them. He also owned "wild" lands himself, on Pocatalico, head of Reedy and elsewhere, which he made sale of from time to time; he also taught schools at Reedy several terms, scattered through some five or six years. At this time the Colonel and his wife, Mary, were both in weakened health. Mary P. returned to Fultonham, where she soon died.

The Colonel's business at Reedy required his personal attention, he returned there within a year or so after the death of his wife, Mary P., and there, on November 11, 1852, he, the widower, married Susan, daughter of William and Mary (Board) Stewart, then one of the prosperous of the first settlers of Reedy. His farm covering all the lands on which is now the Town of Reedy and adjoining farms.

Of this marriage came four sons and six daughters, whose names and further mention we give after relating here some episodes of public interest in the further useful though injured life of Colonel Roberts.

For nine prosperous years next after his marriage with Mary Stewart Roberts, graciously mothering his motherless sons, their lives and all others of the people of Reedy ran as serenely smooth as the streams by which they lived, sensitively trantranquil as the age-old forest surrounding them, ominous calm of impending storm, war, internecine war, most cruel and all-pervading of wars.

Virginia threatened to secede from the Union; a convention of leading men of these western counties assembled at Wheeling, May 13, 1861, printed and sent broadcast fourteen resolutions condemning the action of Virginia, the number "eight" of these was: "RESOLVED, that in event of the Ordinance of Secession being ratified by a vote, we recommend to the counties here represented, and all others disposed to co-operate with us, to appoint on June 4, 1861, delegates to the general convention to meet on the 11th of that month at such place as may be designated by the committee hereinafter, to devise such measures and take such action as the safety and welfare of the people they may represent may demand—each County to appoint a number of representatives to said Convention equal to double the number to which it will be entitled in the next House of Delegates." * * * *

Virginia ratified the Ordinance of Secession on May 23, just ten days after the resolution "No. 8," which direct what the people should do in that event.

Roane County appointed Colonel Roberts its representative to that second Wheeling Convention. Would he accept this dangerous mission? Should he?

In all the Reedy country one family only—this the Chanceys—and they only peaceful farmer folk, were in sympathy with the measures of the Union; from everywhere came reports of enthusiastic gatherings of those loyal to the "Old Dominion" and against the measures of the Union; but Colonel Roberts accepted the necessary duty to his county, and went to and gave his vote for the Union and the formation of this new state out of the counties represented.

General Henry A. Wise, ex-governor of Virginia, at once proclaimed this action of that Wheeling convention and of the people of the counties aiding and abetting it, as bold treason to be put down by condign punishment of all taking part. His prompt action in the premises and marshalling of troops supported by all the Southern Confederacy, and personally accompanying his armies into the Kanawha Valley with orders to coerce the counties, and of his deluge of Captains Commissions to his sympathisers everywhere, are matters of familiar history.

Colonel Roberts returned to his home from that Convention and boldly advised, "The Union is great, its powers mighty and its cause just; wisdom beckons to support of the Union." He soon received Federal orders to assist in recruiting and training of Union soldiers. But?

Within a few days after his return from the Wheeling Convention, while quietly resting in his home, he was informed that his eldest son was under arrest and held at a place up on the Middle Fork some two miles distant. He went at once to see about the son, his wife accompanying him, and when they reached the place of the Roach farm he was there met by Captain Albert G. Ingraham, commanding twenty soldiers, who at once informed the Colonel that he was under arrest on a charge of treason to the Commonwealth of Virginia and the Southern Confederacy. Captain Ingraham then proceeded, displayed to the Colonel his commission as Captain, and read to Colonel Roberts his orders from Governor and General Henry A. Wise, among the several parts of which were the words: "Arrest, forthwith, all and every person who took part or supported that Wheeling Convention; take then dead or alive, and send them to Richmond, where we will bury the dead and hang the living."

In the Colonel's memoirs of this, he says he was then and there handcuffed with metal shackles, thrown on his horse, his feet tied beneath the beast, which was then whipped out in front of the detail, whose orders were already known to them, and started for Richmond; one awful night of pain and hunger; next night at Gauley Bridge the same and worse; so on, relates the Colonel's memoirs until Richmond and Libby Prison; June, July, August, September, October and when November arrived he was exchanged; set at liberty in consideration of release by the Federal authorities of a Confederate held by them on a similar charge.

Once back home he forthwith began assisting in recruiting soldiers for the Union; the first year of this he was compelled to assist his recruits to Ravenswood or Parkersburg, where they would be within protection of Union soldiers. This accounts for so many Roane County men's names appearing enlisted in Wood, Jackson or Kanawha County. Two companies, the 11th and part of the 13th regiment owe most of their enlistments to his activities.

Colonel Robert's whole course during that awful war was such that, when it was over, little or no malice was shown against him. About 1869 when the Roach farm, where took place that arrest by Captain Ingraham, was partitioned among the heirs of William Roach, every one of whom was a contentious Confederate and aider and abettor of Rebel soldiers, except Sarah Bishop, Colonel Roberts was one of the chosen commissioners to set over to each heir his due part of the estate, "according to quantity and qaulity." All were satisfied with the division.

The names of the children of Thomas A. and Susan Roberts, we promised, are, in order of their ages: Leroy Windfield (("Scott"); Alonzo Dempsey; Theodore Thomas, and daughters, Mary Frances, Amanda Eliza, Iva Nettie, Hattie Lillie ("Bird"), Sallie Eulalia and Estil Allie.

ROBERTS: Of Curtis.

William and Elizabeth (Engle) Roberts, husband and wife, came from Barbour County and settled on Stover, above Kelley's, about the year 1843. Their six children, here mentioned in order of dates of their birth, are Daniel, James, Malinda, Simon, John and Emmett, of these we note further, as follows:

Daniel married Margaret, daughter of Alexander Sandy Board, of near Three Forks Reedy. Of this marriage of Daniel and Margaret we can give names of four children, as follows: Sarah Jane, wife of Wm. Anderson Miller, Lloyd, Emmet, Jr. and Nevil G., all born and raised on the old home farm.

James, son of William and Elizabeth Roberts, married Rebecca Ann Board, daughter of a Jackson County family of Boards. James, Rebecca Ann and their children went to Montana, about the year 1878, thence a few years later to Oregon.

Malinds, daughter of William and Elizabeth Roberts, married John Reed, in Barbour County, they later coming to Roane County. He served as a Union soldier in the Civil War. These are parents of Herbert Reed, of Reedy.

Simon, son of William and Elizabeth Roberts, married Elizabeth, daughter of Augustine Hickle, on Left Reedy in Curtis District. Of this marriage were born three sons and two daughters, named William Sanford, Armeda Belle, Lillie, Arthur and Samuel. Samuel and Armeda Belle each has for home, part of the old paternal estate. Above named William Sanford Roberts married Nora, daughter of William Board, of Middle Fork. They (W. S. and Nora) have ten children, five sons and five daughters.

John, son of William and Elizabeth Roberts, was twice married, first a Miss Parsons, for a second a Miss Argabrite.

Emmett Roberts, Sr., son of William and Elizabeth, the pioneers, married Rebecca Jane, daughter of Thomas Miller, son of Samuel, the first settler here.

ROBEY:

Randolph Robey and his wife, Louisa (Hardy) Robey, whom he had married in Marion County, Western Virginia, with several children born of that marriage, arrived and purchased a large tract of land on upper Left Fork of Left Reedy. There, in the forest, commenecd their home, about the year 1851.

An oral family history, as given me by Hamond H., a grandson of Randolph Robey, says that the Robeys are of English descent; that four brothers coming from England landed in Baltimore, there separated, one going to Philadelphia, one remaining in Baltimore, and the other, Randolph, first mentioned above, came "West," stopping in the Monongahela Valley where he married as stated. He was a soldier of the Mexican War and his widowed wife, Louisa, after his death, drew a United States pension.

To Randolph and Louisa (Hardy) Robey were born, all in Marion County, the following named sons and daughters: Hezekiah; Caroline, who married Salathiel S. Hardman, of Reedy, March 19, 1857; William H., who married Sarah Thomasson, of Reedy, November 24, 1859, and died about the year 1865, leaving two children, Shirley and Emma, the latter became the wife of Dr. David Stewart, of Three Forks of Reedy, who later practiced many years at Creston; Elizabeth married Samuel Miller; Mary I. married Menzie Jenkins, year 1871, and John Nelson, the youngest son, succeeded to the home farm on Reedy, by purchasing the shares of his brothers and sisters in the ancestral lands, as appears by deeds of conveyance. Randolph Robey never conveyed any lands after this county was formed, 1856.

John Nelson Robey, son of Randolph and Louisa, was born in Marion County, Western Virginia, June 21, 1841; a Confederate soldier, 1861-65, married America Howell, July 26, 1872, she being a daughter of Moses Howell, of Upper Reedy country. She was a sister of Columbus and Alvin Howell, of Upper Reedy. They cleared and made into cultivated fields many acres of forests.

To John Nelson and America (Howell) Robey were born the following children:

Lillian, who married J. Frank Keplinger, died 1891, not having had a child.

Howard Lee, long a cashier of the first bank in the City of Spencer, called "The Bank of Spencer." Howard L. later served in a bank at Point Pleasant, West Virginia, and while there married a Miss Catherine Long, of Mason County.

Fleet Monroe died a prosperous young man, never having married.

Hamond Harry married Ora, daughter of Elijah J. Harris, of the City of Spencer, October 27, 1905, his age 24, her age 22. This is the H. H. Robey mentioned in the chapter of this work, "City of Spencer," first to have a movie in town, and first to put in an electric lighting plant; at present (1926) owner and manager of the Theatre "Auditorium."

John E. Kenna, the son, died, never having married.

Ollie J. Robey, married Joseph Mel Schwinder, of Spencer, December 9, 1908, his age 25, her age 24.

ROGERS: Of Geary and Smithfield Districts.

In a memoir of John P. Rogers, in Hardesty's History, he says he was born in Gilmer County, Western Virginia, June 4, 1850, son of Seth and Mary (Drake) Rogers.

John P. "Jack" Rogers was the Village of Newton's tanner and popular man there for ten years, about the 1880s. There, on April 17, 1879, he united in marriage with Miss Racina E. Ogden, she a daughter of Osborne and Sarah (Petitt) Ogden, born November 17, 1850. "Jack" Rogers was a deputy sheriff of Roane County for one or more terms, under Andrew Vandal, then "High Sheriff."

The other Roger's we mentioned were Edgar S., who married Mahala Ann Rollinson, March 29, 1880.

Phillip, who, we are told, also married a Miss Rollinson.

Mahala, who, we are told, married Solomon Myers.

Benjamin M. Rogers, the one who leaves a later impress of the family name, married Miss Ellen Virginia Upton, on December 22, 1872. They made their farm-home near Newton, on Big Sandy, for many years, and there brought up two sons and five daughters, whose names are Charles Nelson, John Spencer, Vernia, Lysta, Locia, Willa. Of these:

Charles Nelson Rogers, son of Benjiman M. and Ellen V. (Upton) Rogers, married Miss Melissa Sarver, November 25, 1903, he then 23, she 22 years old; she a daughter of Hon. John A. Sarver, of Smithfield District. See name "Sarver."

Charles N. is a superintendent for the United Fuel Gas Company, of the field of Clover Run.

Charles W. and Melissa, his wife, have some children, two of whom are Miss Opal and Miss Justine, both students at the Spencer High School.

ROMINE: Of Curtis and Harper Districts.

Samuel Romine and his wife, Nancy (Dearman) Romine, natives of Harrison County, where they had been married, left there and came to upper Left Fork of Reedy in the year 1854. To them were born and by them reared five sons and two daughters, all except one of which children were born in Harrison County. Their names given for this writing by the grandson, Earl Romine, are as follows:

Elizabeth, Sarah, Benjiman, John Middleton, James K. P., George and Christopher. Respective marriages and further:

Benjamine Romine, son of Samuel and Nancy, his wife, married Miss Etalina Riley, of Lower Flat Fork, October 9, 1865. They made their life-time home on Flat Fork and reared a family whose names we do not know with full certainty.

John M. Romine, son of Samuel and Nancy, married Miss Sarah Riley, of Flat Fork, September 15, 1866. They made their home on Flat Fork and there reared a family.

James K. Polk Romine, son of Samuel and Nancy, married a Miss Julia Runnion. They made their life-time home on upper Left Reedy. Names of their several children we do not have.

George Romine, son of Samuel and Nancy, married twice, first to Miss Emma Walker, next to Elvira Casto, daughter of John Casto, of Harper District, November, 1895, his age 47, her age 24. They reared two sons and one daughter.

Christopher C. Romine, born in Roane County, son of Samuel and Nancy, married Miss Ida B. Winninner, on October 9, 1889. She was born in Morgan County, Ohio. They made their home on the parental farm or near it on upper Reedy. To them were born and by them reared to citizenship three sons and four daughters. Their names, Nelson, Everett, Earl, Carl, Ottie, Bertha, Lora and Edith, the latter are two young girls yet at home.

Marriages of the others:

Everett Earl married Miss Laura Howell, January 4, 1916, his age 24, her age 22. She was a daughter of C. C. Howell, of Reedy.

Bertha married a Mr. Cottrell and Ottie married a Mr. Miller.

Marriages of Romines whose parentage I do not know:

George Romine to Carrie Hardman, April 19, 1896.
Samuel L. Romine, 23, to Mazilla Rhodes, 20, July 9, 1899.
Holly R. Romine, 22, to Velma C. Lester, 20, December 14, 1913.

ROSE: Of Spencer, year 1873.

John Rose was born in Green County, Pennsylvania, 1824, son of Jacob and Rebecca Ross, his wife, both born in that commonwealth, desecendants of Colonial settlers there.

John grew up where born, and was three times married, each time in Green County, Pennsylvania. First to a Miss .... Ammons; second to Ernestine Odenbaugh; third to a Miss .... Kinney. He moved with his family—children of the first and second marriage—settling in Roane County in the year 1873, having purchased, or purchased on arrival, the tract of 163 acres which included what is now that part of the City of Spencer, designated as "Holswade Addition," at south end of Market Street. There made a home for himself and family for several years. Later sold this and made his home further up the creek for the remainder of his and his wife's lifetime.

To John Rose and wife (Ammons) several children were born in Pennsylvania, but we do not have their names.

Of the wife, Emeline Odenbaugh, were born Lucretia, John Pinkney, William, Thomas and Mary. All in Pennsylvania.

Of the wife, Sarah Kinney were born Ingraham, Jane, Lane and Harry S. ("Budd"). Some of the marriages of this family:

Lucretia married Joshua T. Reynolds, of near Spencer, on March 15, 1884.

Ingraham married Martha Garrett, September 20, 1897, his age 24, her age 22. He died after a few years, leaving children.

W. Lane married Louise Miller, December, 1902, ages not entered. She was a daughter of Neal Miller, of Curtis District.

Harry S. "Budd" married Miss Grace Greathouse, March 15, 1913, in city of Akron, Ohio, his age then about 25, her's 18; she a daughter of Webster and Eva (Nichols) Greathouse, his wife, of Spencer, West Virginia.

Jane, daughter of John and Sarah (Kinney) Rose, married in Spencer, A. Lee Kelley, on November 1, 1893, her age then 18, his 25. They made their home in Spencer several years after marriage. He erected a three story brick building on Market Street, opposite northwest corner of Court Square; had his clothing store in it first. A. Lee and Jane (Rose) Kelley have brought up some children, but I am not told their names.

ROSS:

Rev. Davidson W. Ross is the first of this family name in Geary District. So far as we find he came alone, a young man scarcely twenty-one years of age, and at once purchased a large tract of land, about or above "Three Forks of Sandy." He says in his dictated biography in Hardesty's History, that he "was born in Pike County, Kentucky, January 6, 1831, son of Rease A. and his wife, Isabelle (Anderson) Ross," both these of Colonial families of old Virginia. Here, near "Three Forks of Sandy," Davidson W. Ross, on July 14, 1850, married Nancy Drake, born in Pike County, Kentucky, June 8, 1833, daughter of Isaac and Margaret "Peggy" (Bishop) Drake, of Virginian Colonial families, who settled here on Sandy about the year 1844. It is regrettable that Davidson W. Ross did not leave more information of the family he left behind when he came here, so young, yet so well provided with money, and a better education than any other of the settlers at that date. A lone young man determined to found a home and family in the depths of an immense forest. He soon became a leader; added a mercantile business to his other many pursuits. Promoted getting the first United States postoffice established at Newton, 1857, the name of which he bestowed, in compliment to his baby son, Isaac Newton. He became a regular preacher of the Baptist faith, which he followed for fifteen years, becoming generally spoken of as the "Reverend Davidson Ross"; was seven years postmaster, six years the Justice of the Peace. A useful man.

Of the marriage of Rev. D. W. and Nancy (Drake) Ross, we can here name the following children: George W., born 1851; William E., died in ifancy; Isaac Newton, February 9, 1855; Lewis Phillip, June 27, 1857; Millard F., June 11, 1859; Rease H., January 12, 1862, died infant; Margaret I., December 25, 1865; Ulysses S., February 27, 1867; Spurgeon C., January 24, 1872; Talitha, died in infancy, and Forest R., was born April 26, 1878.

Of this Ross family we note further: That Isaac Newton Ross married Elizabeth Tawney, daughter of the pioneer family of Tawney's of Upper Sandy, and made a good farm and raised a family of children on it. His first public service was that of school teacher, which he followed the first years of his young manhood; was a member of the county board of teachers' examiners several times, about the years 1881-82-83; was elected and served one term, four years, as Commissioner of the County Court, its president for the year 1907 or 1908, during which time the court began the erection of iron bridges and a general improvement of the county roads. And further:

The son, Louis Phillip Ross, also began as a public school teacher, young, and when lacking just one month of twenty-one years of age, May 18, 1878, says the marriage record, united in marriage with Clara Wolfe, one of the first of the female teachers of the county, and the daughter of Joseph B. and Elizabeth (Alkire) Wolfe, of near Spencer. Some time shortly after marriage L. Phillip took a medical course at one of the Ohio Valley medical colleges, and went West, about 1898, his wife and daughter, Willa, soon following, and established himself in practice of his profession in Oklahoma, and has ever since resided there and been spoken of as Dr. Ross.

RYAN:
Rev. Thomas P. See Ch. IV, Harper District.
James R. of Walton District.
James R. Ryan and Diana (Neal) Ryan, his wife, came from Fayette County, West Virginia, and settled first on the Ridge North of Walton, later made their home on McKowns Creek.

To James and Diana, his wife, were born in Fayette County, the following named children: Nancy J., William F., Sarah M., and James R.; and after coming to Pocatalico, about 1855, to James R. and Diana were born: Conry M.

Hannibal D. Ryan, youngest of the children of James R. and Diana Ryan. was born, June 6, 1864; married first, Nancy E. Whited, after her death he married Miss Martila Riley, daughter of Albert Riley of the Pocatalico country. Hannibal D. Ryan has been taking a prominent part in affairs of the county since his early youth; he was elected as justice of the peace of his district, Walton, and served the term 1912 to 1916.

Ryan, Thomas P., Esq.
Ryan, William St. Clair, Esq.

SARVER: Of Walton District:
Barnabas Sarver was born in Craig County, Virginia, son of................
.......................; married Miss Jemima A. Caldwell in the same county, ...day of.............................; she was a daughter of.............................

Barnabas and Jemima (Caldwell) his wife, came to Roane County in the year 1875, lived awhile at Walton and afterward made their home on Johnson Creek, near Smithfield boundary.

To Barnabas and Jemima Sarver were born three sons and one daughter whose marriages and ages are as follows:

John Madison Sarver married Emma S., daughter of Edgar E. Smith of Shamb ins Mills, "March 18 1897, his age 24, her age 20." They live at Parkersburg, West Virginia.

Edward Jackson Sarver, son of Barnabas and Jemima, married Ruby Parril daughter of Dewitt and Lydia (Miller) Parrill, of lower Spring Creek, "September 30, 1914, his age 33, her age 25;" both the parties were school teachers at time of marriage; E. "Jack" Sarver and family, wife and one son, have resided in the City Spencer for the last five to seven years. He is abstractor of land titles for the United Fuel Gas Company, a subsidiary of the Standard Oil Company of U. S. A.

Mary E., daughter of Barnabas and Jemima Sarver, married Robert Wesley Kerns, October 18, 1908; his age, 22; her age, 23.

Okey C., youngest son of Barnabas and Jemima Sarver, died at age of 22, not having married.

Sarver, Hon. John A.

SEAMAN:
David and Thomas Seaman are mentioned in Hardesty's as among the first settlers of Reedy country, then a part of Wood County. David and his posterity appear to be the Seamans of Reedy District.

David Seaman, with his wife and family, came to Reedy from Monroe County; the names of the children of this early settler, David Seamen, are: Silas B.; John, who went to the Burning Springs locality; George married a Miss Boggs and made his home at Conrad's Run country; and Willet Seaman, who went to and began as a citizen in Mason County, western Virginia; and the names of the two daughters of David Seaman were Susan, who became the wife of Moses Doolittle, then of Jackson County; and Elizabeth, who was wife of a Mr. Candler, a trader on the Ohio, who soon met his end by drowning, leaving his wife, Elizabeth, with one child, John Candler. For further about John Candler and the Doolittles see their names in alphabetic places in this chapter.

SEAMAN:
Silas B. Seaman, son of David Seaman, first of this name here, was born in Monongalia County, Western Virginia, April 7, 1804, and Margaret Burdette, born in Monroe County, western Virginia, December 19, 1809, daughter of Willis Burdette, were married at the home of her parents on Middle Fork of Reedy, January 11, 1829; she just past nineteen years of age and he twenty-five.

What, if any relation, Silas B. was to the Thomas Seaman, mentioned in Hardesty's as pioneer with William Stewart, we cannot say.

Silas B. and Margaret Seaman, within a few years, had the best and most commodious farm home in the country of the Right Fork of Reedy, about one mile and a half from the "Three Forks,' 'embracing all the country about what is now "Duke" of the railroad station; a thousand acres, mostly lying to the southward extending over on waters of the Middle Fork.

Silas B. soon became a prominent man of that locality including the "Three Forks;" as usual in such cases, he was appointed by the Governor of Virginia, a justice of the peace, and served many years, and for many years was addressed as "Squire Seamen;" he was noted for his good humor and facetious wit, and at periods to indulge too freely in plentiful brandies distilled in Reedy in his day, but "always genteel drunk or sober." He was a charter member of the Reedy Masonic lodge, A. F. & A. M. No. 72 of the State, and regular attendant at seventy-five years of age; he was a good judge of a horse and always rode a beautiful mount.

Of this marriage of Silas B. and Margaret (Burdette) Seaman, were born James W., Moses A., David, Thomas P., Henry C., and the following daughters: Susan, who married Christopher C. Board of Reedy; Sarah E., who married Kenner Hutchinson, of near Sandyville, December 23,

HISTORY OF ROANE COUNTY 651

1872; Caroline, who married .... Woodyard, last near Reedy; Julia, married Payton, son of Joseph, son of the pioneer William Stewart of Reedy; and Rosie, who married Samuel Tallman, was last of the name Seaman to have a home at the old Silas B. Seaman place, on the Ravensgood turnpike, at what is now Dukes Station.

Moses A. Seaman, son of Silas B. and Margaret (Burdette) Seaman, was born on Reedy, April 2, 1832; married Miss Edith I. Stalnaker, July 14, 1853. She was born August 14, 1836, daughter of John and Susan (Chenowith) Stalnaker, then recent settlers of his neighborhood. Moses and Edith made their life-time home on Seaman Fork of Right Reedy Creek, which was long deemed a large and prosperous farm. There to them were born and by them reared the following sons and daughtrs: Sarah E., October 19, 1854; Virginia A., June 12, 1856; Silas B., April 14, 1858; Lenora M., June 29, 1860; John Milton, July 31, 1862; Emma B., September 15, 1864; General Lee, September 21, 1866; Loverna V., February 4, 1869; Matilda J., January 16, 1871; Edgar L., June 6, 1873; Cordelia M., December 6, 1879; William H., April 14, 1881, died in youth. Their respective marriages are as follows:

Sarah E. to Kenner Hutchinson of Jackson County, West Virginia, December 23, 1872; Virginia A. to Dr. J. T. Hartley of Jackson County, West Virginia, November 27, 1878; Silas B. to Marietta Board of Reedy; Lenora M. to Judson D. McClung of Reedy, September 19, 1882; John Milton to Annie Smith of Left Reedy, November 8, 1885; Emma B., to Joseph H. Nuzum of Jackson County, West Virginia, July 12, 1885; General Lee to Miss .... Ruble of Wirt County, West Virginia; Louverna V., as "Verna" to Millard F. Lewellen of Spencer, March 8, 1891, he then 34 years old; Cordelia M. to William Stalnaker of a Calhoun family.

James W. Eeaman, son of Silas B., Sr., and Margaret (Burdette) Seaman, is the Seaman who built and operated the tanyard on the Ravenswood turnpike in Reedy. He married Miss Elizabeth Flesher, January 12, 1859; she a daughter of Dempsey P. Flesher of Main Reedy. Their children's names so far as we recall are, James Dempsey, Robert W., and "Agatha." There may be others, as James W. was married a second time to a Miss Jane Hoff, daughter of Moses Hoff of Jackson County. Robert, of the above family, married Miss Flora Duke, February 20, 1889; his age 26, her's 24. See Duke. James Dempsey as J. D. Seaman, Jr., married Miss Eva Hardman of upper Middle Fork of Reedy, November 6, 1906; his age 36, her age 23. J. D., Jr., is a general trader, resident of Spencer, at this time (1927), also owns most of the paternal lands on Reedy and devotes it to stock raising. Robert W. also runs a stock farm near or part of the Seamen lands.

David Seaman, son of Silas B. and Margaret (Burdette) married about the time of close of the Civil War. He and his wife made their home on Seaman Fork, for several years known as a good farm, 1870 to

1885. The names of the children of David Seaman and his wife, whom we recall, are Martha, who married Dempsey P. Flesher, Jr., August 18, 1881; he son of Robert Flesher of Main Reedy; Flora married W. Scott Cottle, November 9, 1884, her age 21, his 31; and John R. married Mary M. Smith of Left Reedy, May 5, 1887, his age 28, her's 21.

Thomas P. Seaman, son of Silas B., and Martha (Burdette) Seaman, married Matilda Flesher, January 4, 1861. She was a daughter of the Dempsey P. Flesher of Main Reedy.

Henry C. Seaman, son of Silas B. and Martha (Burdette) Seaman, married Miss Florence Flesher, November 11, 1873; she a daughter of Dempsey Flesher of Middle Fork of Reedy. Henry C. and his wife went to the "Far West" some time after marriage.

SERGENT: Of Spencer and Pocatalico in Smithfield.

James Madison Sergent, first leader of the family name and his family, are mentioned in Chapter VII, Spencer District; and in Chapter IX, City of Spencer. However, James Madison was a justice of the peace of Reedy District for one or more terms of office, next after the Civil War.

James Madison Sergent and his brother, Henry D., and possibly another brother, came here from Russell County, Virginia, some time in the 1580's; a sister, Sallie Combs, widow of Cullen Combs, with their large family, came here about the year 1870.

Henry D. Sergent, above brother, married Miss Phoebe Drake, November 4, 1858, in Roane County. She was a daughter of that Drake family that settled on Pocatalico and Henrys Fork.

These Sergents were large men of fair skin, light hair and brown beards. Henry D. Sergent and wife brought up several children, but we do not have their names. All are active and prosperous citizens.

SHAFER: Of Rock Creek, Harper District.

Jacob Shafer and his wife, Jane, daughter of John and Rachel (Taylor) Harper, were the first of this family name to settle in this southeast part of Harper District, possibly as early as the year 1849.

The names of the children of Jacob and Jane Shafer that we are able to give, are:

John, Sarah Ann, Susan, David, Henry, George, Isaac, and Asa.

"Old Jacob" and Jane (Harper) Shafer, father and mother of the above family, cleared and made a farm and were respected people there for some twenty-five years. Both died there some years ago.

I do not venture to give the marriages of the several above named Shafers, because the marriage records show several "David Shafers," "G. W. Shafers" and "John Shafers," but no information as to what family any one of them belongs.

SHOWEN: Of Curtis District.

The first of this family name to make his home in these parts was John Showen, born in Germany about the year 1800. We have nothing further of his career, until we find him in Monroe County, Virginia, where in the year 1823, he united in marriage with Sophia Swopes. There in Monroe County they made their home for some twenty years or more, and to them while in that county were born four sons and two daughters, all of whom came to the Reedyville country about the year, 1850. The names and years of respective births of these children of John and Sophia (Swopes) Showen are as follows:

James Allen, born October 24, 1824.

Nancy Jane, November 7, 1827, married John I. Haynes, of Reedy;

William Preston, born October 27, 1831, married Nancy Artemesia Parsons, daughter of William Parsons (known as Hare Lip), then resident of Reedy;

(4) Jacob Harrison married Mary Parsons, he was killed in the War of Secessions, and Mary the widow married Wiley W. Argabrite;

(5) Elizabeth Katherine, 1835, never married;

(6) John Morris S. Shown, June 3, 1839, married Margaret Thomasson, daughter of Mordecai Thomasson of Reedy;

(7) Lewis Irvin, July 26, 1851, married Susan Falen, or Phalen, of the Great Kanawha. Further and again:

William Preston Showen, third son of John and Sophia (Swopes) Showen, above mentioned, married Nancy Artemesia Parsons, and made their home near Reedyville for remainder of their lives. To them were born; Jacob Jenkins, 1864; John Roland, 1865, married and made his home on Reedy; Lewis Preston, 1867, married Emma Kate Hoff of Curtis District, 1895. She was a daughter of Anthony and Indiana (Dilworth) Hoff, of Curtis District. To Lewis P. and Emma Kate have been born five sons and two daughters. Their first rate farm is near Reedyville, the place of their nativity.

Mary Jane Showen, fourth child and first daughter of John and Sophia (Swopes) Showen, married William Lyda Davis of Left Reedy of Curtis, Mary Jane and W. Lyda reared four sons and four daughters.

Victoria Shown, seventh child and last daughter of John and Sophia Showen married George H. Bennett. They have reared two sons, Ortie and Lewis Roland Bennett.

SIMONS:

Stephen H. Simons with his wife, Rhoda (Calla) Simons, with several children, came to Roane County from Barbour County, West Virginia, and commenced their home here on upper Cox's Fork in Harper District, in the year 1876. Stephen and Rhoda were both born in Barbour County and were married there, both of old prominent families long resident of Barbour; both lived here in Roane for the remainder of their lives.

Stephen Simons was a good farmer and dealer in live stock and was prominent in affairs of the county for twenty years; was elected and served one term as county assessor in the days when that office valued all the property and real estate of the county for tax purposes; later sold his farm and became a resident of Spencer, and carried on various businesses, chief of which was that of a butcher shop and meat market.

To Stephen and Rhoda (Calla) Simons were born and by them brought up the following four sons and two daughters:

Walter, who married Elsie Jarrett and settled in Spencer, where they have brought up a family. Other children of Stephen and Rhoda, were:

Alva Hampton; Stella, who married Ehud Roberts of Curtis District; Robert; Lora, who married Holly Miller; and Donald and Iven Simons.

SIMMS: Of Reedy, now scattered:

Martin W. Simms was the first of this name here. He was born in Harrison County, Western Virginia, June 12, 1815; died in Roane County, February 15, 1882. Married in Lewis County, Miss Susanna Wagoner (a grandson spells it "Wagner"), about the year 1835; she was born, 1814, in Lewis County, the daughter of William Wagoner, a frontier settler and Indian fighter of the Monongahela Valley in time of the Revolution. Martin and Susanna began their married life in Lewis County, where they lived the first seven years, and came to Reedy country in the year 1845, acquired lands and there made their farm and home near the Wirt County boundary line.

Martin and Susanna were parents of the following Simms's: (1) Granville, (2) John Wesley, (3) Ned, (4) Henry M., (5) Pery, (6) Luther M., (7) Olive, (8) Lizzie, and (9) Elizabeth.

(1) Granville married Sarah Sheppard; their children were Charles, Benjamin, Henry H., Samantha, and Louella. Charles Simms, son of Granville, married Miss Lizzie Price; their children's names were, Granville, Susan, Tessie and Everett.

Benjamin Simms, son of Granville, married Emma Smith; their children's names were, Edgar, Lee, Charles, Camden and Herbert. Of the other children of Granville and Sarah Simms we do not have any information.

(2) John Wesley Simms, son of Martin and Susanna (Waggoner) Simms, was born in Lewis County, October 20, 1839; married Miss Anne E. Pickerell, in Roane County, December 18, 1867. She was born in Roane County, March 11, 1849, daughter of Levi and Mariah (Rader) Pickerell, who came to Jackson County from Faquier County, Virginia, in 1815. John Wesley and Mariah, his wife, made their home in the Simms neighborhood, and were parents of several children. Of these our informant can give us the following: Okey Johnson, born in 1868; Ida M., 1877; Louella and Mabel, mentioned by John Wesley in Hardesty's History, we know nothing.

(3) Ned, third son of Martin, was a soldier in the Civil War and was drowned in the James River in Virginia while in military service.

(4) Henry Maddison Simms, fourth son of Martin and Susanna (Waggoner) Simms, married Miss Roselynn Walker, acquired a farm in the Simms' neighborhood and there they made their lifetime home and reared their family of five sons and one daughter; their names: Martin B., Archibold Thomas, Francis Llewellyn, Dora, Macklin Everett, and William Elvin. Further of these:

Martin B. married Lena Price.

Archibold Thomas, son of Henry M. Simms and Roselynn, became a salesman of organs and pianos; spent some years at this, then settled in Charleston, West Virginia, where he married Miss Bessie N. Saunders; opened a large musical instrument store in Charleston from which he continued the business of piano and instrument sales, and has prospered. To A. Thomas and his wife Bessie N. have been born Clarence W., Julius A., and Margaret L.

Frank Llewellyn, son of Henry M. and Roselynn Simms, is yet a bachelor. Macklin Everett married Dixie Boggess. Their children are, Bernard, Thelma, Howard and Harold. Dora and Willied E. died not married.

(5) Perry Simms, fifth child of Martin and Susanna, married Miss Nannie Full; their children are Thornton and Samuel.

(6) Luther M., sixth child of Martin and Susanna, married Catherine Sleath. Their children are named Lewis, Grover, Roy and Rosa.

(7) Olive Simms, daughter of Martin and Susanna, married Lewis Full. Their children are, Nora, Kate, Rosco and Homer.

(8) Mary Eliza, daughter of Martin and Susanna, on 19th December, 1872, married W. P. Price, her age 19, his age 19; their children, Ora, Martin, Nancy, Estella, Holly, and

(9) Susan Elizabeth, daughter of Martin and Susanna Simms, married, March 8, 1872, A. J. Pickerell. Their children are, Samuel, Ella, George, Clyde, Clay, Lulu and Minnie.

SINNETT:

The first of this name in the country was John Sinnett and Elizabeth (Propst) Sinnett, his wife, both born in Pendleton County, Virginia, he November 12 and she August 18, 1787. Patrick Sinnett, the father of John, was "born in Ireland and served three and one-half years in the Revolutionary War."

The family relation of John Sinnett above mentioned to Able P. Sinnett, of Kanawha County, the Able P. Sinnett, county surveyor of Kanawha County, who surveyed the boundary lines of the southern part of Roane County on its formation, we do not know.

Samuel Sinnett, born in Ritchie County, Western Virginia, July 15, 1825, son of John and Elizabeth (Propst) Sinnett, says in his biography after giving the day of his birth, "Came to Roane County, then Kanawha County, with his parents, in 1837."

The handiwork of this family first claiming the attention of early settlers was that of the home and "Sinnett Farm" on McKowns Creek of Walton District.

Samuel married for a wife, Leah, daughter of .... Sergent; Leah was born April 15, 1832, in ...., and died September 23, 1864. Of this marriage of Samuel and Leah (Sergent) Sinnett, were born the following children: Eliza J., October 7, 1852; Sarah C., February 11, 1857; Thomas H., October 12, 1858; Festus T., December 4, 1860, and W. David, July 11, 1863, died in youth. Leah having died, Samuel married Sarah B. Peters on Augus 9, 1866.

Of the marriage of Samuel and Sarah B. (Peters) Sinnett, were born the following children: Albert B., June 7, 1867; Henry N., November 19, 1868; Able P., February 9, 1870; Lewis E., June 25, 1871; Mary A., May 2, 1874; Laura M., 1876; Emma S., August 28, 1877, and Samuel C., May 4, 1881.

Festus Sinnett, son of Samuel and Leah (Sergent) Sinnett, pioneers last mentioned, married, March 12, 1885, Eliza A. Lowe, daughter of Dr. Morse Lowe of Rush Creek of Poca; "his age 24, her age 20;" to Festus and Eliza A., his wife, were born the following sons and daughters:

Mary A., who married A. Clyde Rader;
Ona married Harry L. Dyer;
Mabel, who married Ronald Thompson;
Elsie married Lieut. Frederick Wright;
Addie married Okey Harris.
See family name of above husbands.

Guy Sinnett married Edna Elaine Petty, 7th February, 1917, his age 27, her age 21; he is in the hardware business, City of Spencer.

H. Brooks Sinnett married Lulu Simmons of Spencer, West Virginia, 2d May, 1917, his age 24, her age 19. He, the other member of the frm Sinnett & Wright carrying on a drug and soft-drink business in City of Spencer.

Everett M. Sinnett, bank clerk, mayor of City of Spencer, 1927, married Marie Parrish, 26th September, 1919, his age 28, her age 27. She was born in Jackson County, West Virginia, daughter of Calvin Parrish, a prominent farmer of upper Mill Creek.

Henry N. Sinnett, son of Samuel and Sarah B. (Peters) Sinnett, was born November 19, 1868, married Viola Hickman, "March 19, 1893, his age 24, her age 22;" she was a daughter of Wilson Hickman of upper Spring Creek. Henry N. and Viola have a farm of large acreage and a nice farm home situate half mile below and east of Gandeeville, on State Road No. 14. They have some daughters now, 1926, in their teens, maybe a son or sons.

SMITH: Of Geary District.

John and Frances (Cochran) Smith, both of pioneer families of old Virginia, were united in marriage in Pocanhontas County, Western Virginia, about the year 1835, and came to upper Sandy about the year

1843. Of this marriage were born five sons and six daughters; their names: James J., born in Pocahontas, 1836; William Y., in Pocahontas, 1840; Newton, about 1838; Franklin died when a youth and Joseph N. The names of the six daughters are, Margaret, who married Lindsy Drake; Mary, wife of Alkanah Carper; Martha, wife of Charles Shackleford of Tennessee; Lydia, married John Boggs, of Sandy; Eliza married Isaac, son of Reverend Davidson Ross of Geary; Lectra, who was wife of William Keen of Hollywood. Eliza Ross is the youngest of this family. For further of these daughters, see their husband's family name. This John Smith of Pocahontas, was an energetic man, a preacher by authority of the M. E. Church; a Union soldier, corporal of Co. B, 9th W. Va. Regiment Vol. Infantry, died in service at Sulphur Springs, August, 1862. Of his sons above mentioned we say further:

James J. Smith, son of John and Frances, wedded Emma Rodgers, in Clay County, December 6, 1860. She was born in Kanawha County, daughter of Levi and Naoma (Skidmore) Rodgers, April 29, 1842. They made their home on upper Sandy; there, to them were born twelve children, whose names are: George B., born in the year 1862; Newton J., Hannah V., 1866; Frederick, 1868; Julia, 1869; Susan, 1871; James C., 1873, died 1875; Charles L., 1876; Flora G., 1878; Ida, 1879, lived only one month; Clay, 1880; Hunter, July 14, 1882, and Emma.

William Y. Smith, son of John and Frances (Cochran), was born in Pocahontas County, 1840; was twice married. First wife, Melissa Jarrett, of her were born Alice D., 1866; and Buena A., died at three months age, 1868; soon also died this mother. September 1, 1870, William Y. married Julia A. (Cox) Wilson, widow of Walter Wilson, a federal soldier, who died a prisoner of war, June 4, 1865. She was born in Gilmer County, March 16, 1839, daughter of Isaac and Mary (Nicely) Cox. At time of death of her husband Walter Wilson they had two sons: William F. Wilson, born December 15, 1860, and Robert F., April 10, 1863. To these two sons of his deceased comrade in war, he was pleased to be and proved a good father, taking and joining these to his motherless Alice at their home on Sandy. Of this marriage of William Y. and Julia A. were born six children. Their names and births are: John, born 1871; Melissa, 1873; Mary F., 1875; William C., 1877; Floyd, 1879, and Thomas F., December 7, 1881. William Y. Smith served ten years school trustee; three years in the Union army, quarter master, re-enlisted in Co. B, 4th W. Va. Regt. Cavalry; was elected and served one term as Roane County's delegate in the thirtieth or thirty-first session of the State Legislature, 1911 or 1913.

Newton Smith, born about 1838, son of John and Frances Smith, brother to William Y. last mentioned, served as a soldier in the Union army; went to Kansas, in the year 1869; married a wife in Kansas and yet has his home in that State, at Chanute. He is here in Roane now (1926) visiting the scenes of his boyhood days; yet a strong though aged man.

Joseph N. Smith, son of John and Frances, was born in the family home on upper Sandy, July 1, 1854; married Ann Eliza, daughter of Andrew and Amanda J. (Riffle) Cruikshank, born in Nicholas County, Western Virginia, 1863. Of this marriage the following children were born: Everett A., April 26, 1881; and French W., born May 7, 1883.

The Cemetery on the public road at Uler is 100 square rods of the ancestral lands of this family. By a Deed of Conveyance dated June 4, 1910 (Deed Book No. 50:315), William Y. Smith and his wife, Julia, conveyed this "place of the dead" by aptly ingenous words to Trustees, as "A place of Interment of the Smith family of which John and Frances Smith, his wife, were the fore parents;" naming "as Trustees: John Smith, W. C. Smith, Floyd Smith, T. F. Smith, G. B. Smith and John A. Ross," "To be kept in perpetuity, that in case of death, removal or otherwise incapacitated to serve as Trustee, his eldest living son shall be created Trustee in his stead."

It is observed by referring back to names of his children all these Trustees are sons of William Y., except John A. Ross.

SMITH:

The part of Harper District, between Wolfe Creek and Higly, and not far from the farm of the Prices just mentioned, is the last home of the Reverend John H. Smith, and where he and his, through many years commencing on his return from service as a Union soldier of the Civil War, conquered the wild forest and made the farm-home on which grew up some sons and daughters, destined to continue community and public service.

Rev. John H. Smith was born in Russell County, Virginia, October 22, 1837, married Letta J. Rhodes, daughter of.................................... on Christmas day, 1860. The children of Rev. John H. and Letta J. Smith whose names and dates of births we can give here, are Benjamin A., June 15, 1867 ,now physician and surgeon of City of Spencer, mentioned in the chapter on "History of Spencer," was a delegate for this county in the twenty-eighth session of the State Legislature, year 1909. Dr. Benjamin A. Smith married Mrs. Foglesong of Sissonsville or lower Poca, who is yet with him. Rev. John H. Smith, on death of Letta, March 3, 1875, united in marriage with Victoria J. Hackney, daughter of Archibold Hackney, born in Scott County, Virginia, at time of Letta's marriage, an old settler of the country about the head of Higly, is also the father of the Reverend James Hackney, a graduate of a Baptist theological school of Louisville, Kentucky, and of the Reverend Joshua Hackney of the same church and same theological school. The only child of Rev. John H. Smith and Victoria J., his second wife, whom we can name here, is Dr. Arthur Archibold Smith, a graduate of a Chicago medical school. He, while quite young, married Carrie, the daughter of Wesley Lynch, an old settler of Trace Fork. Dr. Archibold A. Smith is now practicing his profession in Boone County; and is the popular general medical man for one of the big coal companies of that part of the State.

SMITH: Of Smithfield. Rev. Jonathan, Elkana.

Nicholas P. Smith and Barbara (Bennett) Smith, his wife, came here from Barbour County, West Virginia, about the year 1854, and settled on a large tract of forest lands on Poca between the mouth of Rush and Laurel Creeks. With Nicholas and Barbara were their two sons, Edgar E. and William Randolph T. Smith, and a daughter named Christ:ne, who married Robert Ferguson, long the blacksmith of the Town of Spencer.

William Randolph T. Smith married Catherine Jarvis of Calhoun County, long worked on the old home place. This adjoined the large farm of Rev. Jonathan Smith, of Smithfield District. William R. T. accumulated and cleared up lands until about the year 1913. Oil was struck on his 200-acre tract there, October, 1911; well after well has been drilled in on this tract until at the present time, he tells me, there are "only sixteen good producers." Some five years ago he voluntarily complained that his check from the Eureka Pipe Line Company for sales of oil from his wells for the month was just twenty cents less than two thousand dollars; that it had been so near two thousand dollars for so long, he "just hoped it would be two thousand this time." I do not venture here how much he may be worth in cash at this time. Of the children of William R. T. and Catherine I can name here: John Wesley, born 1872, graduate now of a medical school "University of the South," and is a practicing physician of Gassaway, West Virginia; Waitman Taylor, born April 20, 1889, graduated from Louisville Medical College, May 30, 1913, later married Grace, daughter of James L. Loomey, of City of Spencer; Dr. Waitman T. Smith is now practicing his profession at Glenville, West Virginia.

The other children of W. R. T. Smith are Dora E., who married Christopher Ferrell of the pioneer family of Ferrells, and Lizette, who married Samuel E. Steel.

SMITH: Pioneers of Left Reedy.

Jacob C. Smith and Sarah, his wife, who was a daughter of a family of Smiths not related in blood to Jacob, the husband, came from Kanawha County and settled on Left Fork of Reedy on lands adjoining those of the pioneer George Flesher. Elijah Callow, a son-in-law, in his biography in Hardesty's History, states it thus:

"Jacob C. Smith, her father, was born November 26, 1813, and her mother, Sarah Smith (Smith) was born April 19, 1814, in Ritchie County then Virginia." Jacob C. died in the year 1870. Jacob and his wife with some children must have settled on Reedy about the year 1848.

To Jacob C. and Sarah, his wife, were born and reared there on Left Reedy the following named children:

Jacob Brown, John D., Elijah, William R., Catherine, Rebecca, Hannah, Rowena, Fisher and Orpha.

The marriages and children of the above family, so far as marriage record and recollections of acquaintances serve us, are as follows:

Jacob Brown, son of Jacob C. and Sarah, married Miss Elizabeth Walker, sister of Rev. Park Walker, later of Huntington, West Virginia. Their sons and daughters are as follows: Sarah C., married John A. House, October 18, 1877; Emma, married but left no children; Mary, married John R. Seaman, of Reedy, 5th May, 1887, his age 28, her's 21; Arizona, married Jonah Sheppard, of Wirt County, 3d March, 1884, his age 23, her's 19; Anna C., married John Milton Seaman, 8th November, 1885, her age 19, his 22.

William Park Smith (son of J. Brown Smith and Elizabeth Smith), married Louisa Cottle, daughter of David S. Cottle, May 21, 1905, his age 25, her's 21. He is a merchant and general trader of the Town of Reedy. They have one son, David Brown.

Continuing the family of Jacob Brown Smith:

Addison G., seventh child, married Maud Golden, 10th April, 1898; his age 22, her age 21.

James K., not married, and Otis Smith, the youngest of this family, married and lives in Ritchie County, West Virginia.

John D. Smith, son of Jacob C. and Sarah, his wife, pioneers first mentioned, married Miss Emma Delia Ashley, October 28, 1856. They made their home in the virgin forest on part of his father's tract of land lying near the divide between Left and Middle Forks of Reedy; made a farm there and there John D. died in the first of the decade, 1870. At present I can think of only one child born to John D. and Emma Delia (Ashley) Smith. This was a son named James Lee Smith, a resident attorney at law of Elizabeth, Wirt County, West Virginia, for many years.

Elijah Smith, son of Jacob C., and Sarah (Smith) Smith, married a Miss Charity Mays. They made their residence on part of the old home lands, on the creek. They reared some children, but we have the name of only one child; she, Mary A., who became the wife of Charles D. Lester, son of the neighbor, September 1, 1889; his age, 20; her age, 18.

William R. Smith, son of Jacob C. and Sarah, his wife, married Miss Melissa Callow, October 24, 1868. She was a daughter of George and Sarah M. (Flesher) Callow, and born, says her father's biography, "February 26, 1848."

William R. Smith and Melissa, his wife, made their home on Left Reedy, on the turnpike six miles north of Spencer, where they cleared up and made a large farm; he dealt in buying and selling stock for many years. To William R. and Melissa, his wife, were born and reared on the farm only three children. Their names:

George, who married Miss Lonie A. Ward, 19th November, 1891; his age, 21; her age, 19. Charles married a Miss Allie Jarrett of Long Ridge about the line of Roane and Kanawha Counties. She is a daughter of Columbus Jarrett, farmer on the Long Ridge. The daughter, Eva B., married James P. Vineyard, December 14, 1891; her age, 21; his age, 21.

The daughters of Jacob C. and Sarah (Smith) Smith: Mary Catherine married Elijah Callow, July 15, 1852; Rebecca married Andrew Mays; Hannah married George Mays, 1871; Rowena married Alexander Chancey, July 12, 1875; Fisher married Mr. Jerome Hickle, and Orpha A. married Clement Tallman, 7th November, 1884; his age, 58; her age, 42; he was born in Marion County, Western Virginia.

SNODGRASS: Of Smithfield.

Anderson Snodgrass, born in Craig County, Virginia, son of Caleb and (............ Nida) Snodgrass, came to Roane County about the year 1868, and soon married M. Josephine, daughter of Daniel Looney, senior. They made their home, becoming a large farm later, on the head waters of Henrys Fork, near what was afterward named as United States post Josephine, his wife, whom we can name here, are, the sons: Doctor Okey Snodgrass and Doctor Frank Snodgrass. One of these is located in Maryland and the other in the Far West; and the daughters: Lucy, who became the wife of Albert Hopkins; Fannie, the wife of Edward Tuning of the Tuning family of that neighborhood, now residing at Parkersburg, W. Va., and the youngest, Sallie, married Howard Weaver and yet lives near Tariff. Some few years ago Anderson and M. Josephine left this county and became farmers, resident of the State of Maryland, thence they removed to a place known as Delta, Pennsylvania, and now reside at that place.

SNODGRASS: Of Walton.

The first persons of this family name to settle in Roane County were two brothers: Robert and Isaac Snodgrass, both born in Giles or Montgomery County, Virginia. Both married wives in Giles County or in Boon County, Western Virginia, in which last named county they lived for some years, then came to Roane County, about the year 1857; had purchased a tract of about four hundred acres, all except a small patch, still in the virgin forests. This lay on the creek about one mile below Gandeeville. There they made their homes, and finished rearing their families, many of whom yet reside on parts of the patrimonial lands. Of these two we further say:

Robert Snodgrass's wife was Elizabeth Ferrell. To them were born in Boone County and came with them here: Jacob and George Washington.

Jacob married Julia Curtis of Lincoln County, and to them were born one daughter and five sons: Hester Ann, who married William D. Lee, and they settled and reared a family near Gandeeville. The sons are, Jos. Shelton, died a young man; John Leftridge died at about twenty-one; Albert Maywood, now a teacher, and James Kellum Snodgrass, at this time, 1926, county superintendent of schools of Roane County.

Isaac Snodgrass first above mentioned, before coming here, had married Emily Curtis in Boone County; to them were born three children in Boone County; their names, Hyatt, who married America Vineyard; Josephine, who became the wife of Jacob B. Gandee, and Robert, who went "West;" Isaac Wesley ("Wes"), born in Roane County in 1859, married here twice; first wife, Mary C. Vineyard, daughter of Delana Vineyard. To them were born seven children. Mary C. having died "Wesley" married Harriet Greenlee, stepdaughter of Henry Summers. To them have been born four children. Isaac Wesley Snodgrass is the siniging master of the neighborhood.

SNYDER: Of Charles Fork, Spencer District.

John Wesley Snyder, born in Pendleton County, Virginia, 1813, with his wife whose name before marriage with John W. Snyder, was Elizabeth Grogg, born in Cold Bottom, Highland County, Virginia, year 1818.

John W. and Elizabeth Snyder lived only a short time in Highland County, then removed to Doddridge County, Western Virginia, where all or most of their eight children were born, all except the oldest of these children. The father, mother and the seven, together came to Roane County in the year 1866,—one of the hundreds of migrations following the close of the "Civil War," War of the Secessions.

This family bought a tract of land on the Charles Fork of upper Spring Creek, and there plunged into the then unbroken forest of that particular spot. Other settlements had been made on this creek previously, and they had neighbors within one mile either up or down the creek.

The names of the children of John W. and Elizabeth (Grogg) Snyder and somewhat further concerning them are as follows:

1. Mary Ann, the first child, married Samuel Cox of Middle Island Creek, Doddridge County, and never came to Roane to reside.

2. William, son of John W. and Elizabeth Snyder, married and settled on Big Creek, Walton District. He was twice married. On April 12, 1868, he married Elizabeth Lowe, daughter of Charles Lowe. The name of his second wife was Nancy J. Ryan, daughter of James R. Ryan. William was father of several children whose names are, Frances, Charles J., Henry A., Lloyd Nathaniel, John Everett, Esther J., Daniel W., Clendenin, Louisa D., Edward T.

3. Alfred married a Miss Hulda McCluster of and in Lewis County, West Virginia, and settled on Big Lick, in Walton District. State Route No. 14 passes the residence in which Alfred and Hulda Snyder lived

for so many years. We do not know the names of their six, seven or eight children.

4. Israel Snyder, son of John W., pioneer of Charles Fork, married Emily Smith in and of Roane County, November 9, 1869; made his home on head of Spring Creek, a nice place yet, at foot of the hill on the Spencer side of the watershed between the Kanawhas; some time after marriage he lost a hand in some kind of a mill accident.

To Israel and Emily were born and reared at the home just described, the following named four sons: William Snyder, oculist, of Clarksburg, West Virginia; Herbert, Ora V., and Romie.

5. Eliza Snyder married Reedy Pursley, son of Hudson Pursley of Charles Fork.

6. Louise married Andrew Jackson Pursley, and son of the above named Hudson Pursley.

7. Edward Tunstall Snyder, youngest of the above family of John W., was born in Doddridge County, Western Virginia, September 24, 1857, and was one of the family when they arrived on Charles Fork. On June 28, 1881, E. Tunstall married May L., a foster daughter of Eli Radabaugh, on the Spencer and Glenville turnpike, Roane County. Edward Tunstall and Mary L. Snyder, after marriage, made their resirence on the ancestral home on Charles Fork, to which they succeeded by maintenance of the father John, who lived to a very old age, or by payments to the other heirs of the deceased fatherr, John Snyder.

There on that farm were born to E. Tunstall and Mary L., his wife, four sons and seven daughters. Some of these are young folks at home now.

STALNAKER: John and Susan, his wife, of Reedy.

John Stalnaker, born November 6, 1804, died March 30, 1862; Susan (Chenowith) Stalnaker, his wife, was born year 1812, died in Reedy, April 7, 1862. Both were descendants of Virginian colonists or of those early settlers of the Shenandoah Valley.

John and Susan possibly began their married life in Randolph County, Western Virginia, as it was some times said they came from Randolph County some time in the 1830's; acquired a large tract of forest lands lying acros sthe divide between a small right hand fork of Sand Creek which empties into the Ohio River at Ravenswood and the Seaman Fork of Right Reedy Creek.

Here they made their home-farm, ample in all that constituted the pioneer home of all sufficiency of those days; noted for its hospitality of the back-woods kind. To John and Susan Stalnaker his wife were born and by them reared and educated—in the R R R—three sons and three daughters; their names: Marshall, Milton, Edith Lndiana, Martha A., Jennie and David.

Marshall Stalnaker, son of John and Susan, married Miss Jennie Paxton, when and of what family we do not know. He became a land surveyor; was influential in all parts of what is now Roane County, for some twenty years, 1840 to 1860; succeeded to ownership of the parental home and continued its popularity where John and Susan entertained Marshall's friends until time of their deaths, first mentioned. The names of the children of Marshall and Jennie Stalnaker, his wife, were, Viola T., Nannie, Iona I., and Clementine B., "Todd;" their marriages as follows:

Viola T. to James B. Shreve, August 23, 1879;

Nannie to John M. Lester, March 31, 1885; ages, she 20, he 21. See "LESTER."

Iona I. to Elmore E. Cain, September 29, 1890; her age 23; his age 25.

Clementine B. to Charles W. Craig, May 20, 1894; her age 24; his age 24. He was then resident of Reedy, born in Washington County, Ohio.

Milton Stalnaker, son of John and Susan, pioneers, leaves us no record, having left when a young man.

Indiana Edith Stalnaker, daughter of John and Susan, married Moses Seaman, of Reedy, July 14, 1853; died, 1881. See family name, "Seaman."

Martha A. Stalnaker, daughter of John and Susan, was born, February 1, 1834; married Robert Hopkins, June 19, 1851; died September 15, 1870. See "Hopkins, Robert."

Jennie Stalnaker, daughter of above family, married James Wiblin.

David Stalnaker, youngest of above family, had his home in Clay County, along about the year 1894.

STALNAKER: Of Upper Spring Creek.

The first persons of this name settling in Spencer District arrived in the year 1875, being three sons and two daughters of the family of a Samuel Stalnaker, a pioneer who settled near Clarksburg about 1810, and whose wife was an Elizabeth McWhorter, a young woman whom he married at her father's home in the middle Monongahela Valley about 1825.

To Samuel and Elizabeth (McWhorter) Stalnaker, were born (all in Harrison County), four sons and three daughters whose names were as follows:

Andrew, John, Charles, Marion, Levi, Sobieska, Walter, and Whitman; Julia and Elizabeth.

Of those seven children, Walter (familiarly mentioned as "Wat" Stalnaker) came here in the spring of 1875; and John, Whitman and the girls, Julia and Elizabeth, all came in the fall of the year 1875. Of these last two, Julia was the wife of J. Marcellus McWhorter, first clerk of both circuit and county courts of Roane County, and Elizabeth who came with Walter ("Watt", on August 30, 1875, married Charles Dixon, who settled on upper Spring Creek, near where Speed now is, and at which place they yet live.

John Stalnaker, son of Samuel and Elizabeth Stalnaker, first named, had married in Barbour County, a Julia Ann Stalnaker, daughter of a family of that name of no known relation to John's family. To John and Julia Ann were born in Barbour County ,three sons and four daughters, all of whom—then of ages 2 to 12 years—constituted the family of John and Julian Stalnaker when they arrived on upper Spring Creek in the year 1875. The names of these children and marriages when grown up are as follows:

Samuel Jr. married Manda Jane Watson, March 18, 1882. Ages were not recorded at that time.

Henry Sobieska, son of John Stalnaker, married January 6, 1901, Mary Melissa Davis, daughter of Ellis and Mary E. (Hersman) Davis, and settled on a part of the John Stalnaker farm on upper Spring Creek. Henry S. and Melissa have one daughter and four sons.

Martin Wayne, son of John Stalnaker, married Lillian Ferrell of Harper District, January 9, 1896, his age 26, her age 21, at the residence of J. B. Casto in Spencer, West Virginia.

Hannah Etta, daughter of John Stalnaker, married Joseph L. Santee, April 22, 1878, in Roane County.

Elizabeth Dessie, daughter of John Stalnaker, married Robert Lowe, son of Clark, December 27, 1893; "his age 23; her age 22."

Alverta, daughter of John Stalnaker, married Charles N. Cottrell, February 3, 1901; his age 30; her age 21.

Mary Jane, daughter of John Stalnaker, likely the eldest, married Frank Marion Watson, April 9, 1879. Their good farm and commodious home is on State Road No. 14, about four miles south of Spencer.

Walter ("Wat") Stalnaker, son of Samuel and Elizabeth Stalnaker, married Rubenia Wagoner of Harrison County; they, with several of first born children, came to Roane County, in the spring of 1875; choose a farm on upper Spring Creek, there cleared and plowed; also engaged in the sawmill business.

Their children born and married, ten in all, are named as follows:

Elizabeth Ann, born in Harrison, married Alexander M. Hersman.

George Whitman Stalnaker, son of "Wat," married Priscilla V. Morford, February 23, 1887; "his age 20; her age 19." She was the daughter of John Morford.

Unice, daughter of "Wat," born in Harrison County, married William Crihfield, in Roane, near Gandeeville, November 2, 1883; "his age 20; her age 20."

Elwood A., son of "Wat," married Sarah Nichols, "December 23, 1891; his age 22; her age 19."

Mary Olive, daughter of "Wat," married Marcellus Davis of upper Spring Creek, September 13, 1885; "his age 23; her age 17."

Spencer C., son of "Wat," married Amanda B. Marks of Gandeeville,

October 1, 1893; "his age 22; her age 19." She was daughter of Thomas Marks.

Ida M., daughter of "Wat," Stalnaker, married Thomas P. Skeen of Jackson County, February 13, 1896; "his age 26; her age 17."

Dessie, a daughter, and Everette and Robert H. Stalnaker, children of "Wat," have all lived and married here in Roane but we have not their rcords.

Whitman Stalnaker, son of Samuel and Elizabeth (McWhorter) Stalnaker, married Virginia Waggoner, in Harrison County, West Virginia; came to Roane County in the fall of 1875.

Whitman, sometimes mentioned as "Whit" Stalnaker, engaged in farming and making his farm by clearing away the forest, also engaged in the portable sawmill business.

To Whitman and Virginia Stalnaker were born one son and one daughter, both in Harrison County. The son died in infancy or youth; the daughter, Emma Louisette, grew up and married in Roane, John Lindsy Santee, August 1, 1886; "his age 22, her age 18."

To Emma L. and John L. Santee were born two sons and one daughter. They make their home in Roane.

STARCHER: Of upper parts Lower Flat Fork.

The first of the family name Starcher settling here were Stephen and Charity (Hinzman) Starcher, both born in Lewis County, Stephen, 1813, Charity, 1819, and came to this Flat Fork country some time in the 1840's, and purchased a large tract of native forest lands near the Riley settlement, and of it made a fine farm, long known as the "Starcher place." Stephen and Charity (Hinzman) must have been married in Lewis County and came here soon, because two of their sons, Isaac and Marion were enlisted Confederate soldiers of the War of "Rebellion," 1862-5.

Stephen Starcher and his wife Charity soon made one of the best of the farms on the upper part of Lower Flat Fork. He was an influential citizen for some twenty years. A peacemaker in the turbulent time of the "Civil War."

They reared seven sons. Of these Marcellus and William H., the latter died some three or more years ago, I have known for many years. Marcellus lives now (1927) in the City of Spencer.

An M. Starcher married Miss Lelia D. Barnes (see Barnes) on the 11th day of June, 1883, in Roane County. We take this as being the Marcellus named above.

STARCHER: Of Henrys Fork, Smithfield District.

Josiah Starcher, of what family we do not know, married Miss Nancy Jane Nichols, possibly of a Little Kanawha family of Nichols's, near the year 1855, and they made their home at once on the Henrys Fork and there reared the following children: Lovernia, Amanda, Belle S., John C., Lucy and Annie.

Lovernia married Wm. R. King (see King); Amanda married Nathan Ellison, 1874; Belle S. married Leroy Bissell, February 15, 1891; her age 23; his age 25; Annie married William D. Dillon, May 31, 1891; her age 23, his age 24; John C. and Lucy are yet single.

DANIEL STARCHER, son of William "Bluehead" Starcher and .... Tanner, of near junction of Henrys Fork with West Fork of the Little Kanawha, about the year 1858 to 1860, married Miss Emily Moore. They settled on upper Henrys Fork and soon made the good average home of the times in those parts, and there reared four daughters and four sons, whose names are, Salina, Mary, Samuel, John, Charles, Ira, Ora and Nancy.

Salina married, first, William Holland, January 24, 1881. They had one son and one daughter. Her second marriage was with George Gillenwater, May, 1886, she then 26, he 24 years of age. They brought up two sons and one daughter. Mary married Daniel Webb. Samuel married first Edith Holland. To them were born two sons and five daughters. Edith having died, Samuel married Miss Belle Holland. They have two sons and five daughters.

John Starcher, son of Daniel, married, first, Jennie Norman, on January, 1889, he then 19, she 21. They have several children. Jennie having died, John married Miss Maud Love, August 14, 1909, he 39, she 27 years of age.

Charley Starcher, son of Daniel, married Bertha Young, March 1, 1893; he 19, she 19 years old. They have several children. Bertha having died, Charles married Sarah Holland, August 24, 1908; he 34, she 31.

Ira Starcher, son of Daniel, married Cora Webb, August 25, 1897; he 19, she 18 years of age.

Ora married Alexander Moore.

Nancy Starcher married Alonzo Nutter, December 13, 1891; she 17, he 20 years old.

STEEL:

Nelson Steel and his wife, Helen M. (Hutchinson) Steel came from Craig County, Virginia, and settled on Cotton Tree, in Walton District near the Geary District boundary, in the year 1856. To them were born sons and daughters. Of these we are able to name here, Frank, William Downtain, Samuel Eredman, Laura and Clora.

Frank Steel of the above family married Martha, daughter of Captain William H. Justice of Geary District. Frank and Martha were about the same age, we observe in the bioraphy of her father that she was born July 14, 1868.

Samuel Eredman married Lizette, daughter of William R. T. Smith and his wife Catherine (Jarvis) Smith, who at the time of this marriage resided at Hammack in Smithfield District, now of the City of Spencer, West Virginia.

Laura Steel, daughter of Nelson and Helen M. married John Sherman Gandee, of Cotton Tree.

And Clora became the wife of Lee Reed of Cotton Tree.

We have no information of the life of William Downtain Steel.

STEINBECK:

Christian Henry Steinbeck and his wife, Araminta P. (Ruhl) Steinbeck, former residents of Lewis County, West Virginia, arrived in Curtis District on upper Middle Fork of Reedy, and commenced their home there about the year 1872. Of their marriage four sons were born, two in Lewis County and two after coming to Roane. Their names are: Grant, whose career we do not have.

"Perry G., born in Lewis County, married in Curtis District, Ella A. McCoy, August 20, 1891; his age 22; her age 21."

Louis Otmer, born in Roane County; on May 5, 1895, married Elsie, daughter of Benjamin F. Conley of Harper District; his age then 22, her age 21. L. O. Steinbeck is at this time owner of a stock farm in Curtis District of about three hundred acres, being the old Charles Sharp farm, the Fetty farm and part of the paternal homestead, is a resident of the City of Charleston, however, where he deals in timber and lumber on a large scale.

George F. Steinbeck, born in Roane County, son of Christian H. and Arminta Steinbeck, married Maud, a daughter of Asby Crislip of Left Reedy in Curtis District, "February 18, 1895, his age 38, her age 36." They live on and own the Asby Crislip farm at mouth of Stover.

Christian H., the father of above named Grant, Perry G., Louis O. and George F. Steinbeck, died at his home on Middle Reedy about the year 1879. His widow, Arminta, two years later married H. Middleton Fetty, who thus became a father to these sons who yet hold him in due filial esteem.

STEORTS: Of Geary District.

Isaac Lee Steorts, the more widely known member of this family at time of this writing, 1927.

The family Steorts:

The first we have of definite facts is that George Washington Steorts was born at or near the mouth of Hackers Creek on the Monongahela, son of a Steorts who was born in Germany of the blond German stock, married and made his farm home there about Hackers Creek. George Washington grew up there where born and married Miss Amanda Jackson, daughter of the renowned Jackson family of that locality, a sister of Minter Jackson mentioned in Chapter IX, History of the City of Spencer; also a cousin of Federal Judge John J. Jackson.

George W. and Amanda, his wife, made their home for the first several years of their wedded life, near where married, leaving there with their family and making their home on head of Right Hand Fork of Big Sandy about the year 1864, having acquired a large tract of lands there.

The names of the sons and daughters of George W. and Amanda (Jackson) Steorts, his wife, are Horace, William W., Alvincy, Eunice, Theodocia, and John Steorts.

All these married and went in diverse directions.

John Steorts married Miss Mintie Hire of Big Otter. He succeeded to the old home place, where he yet lives.

William W. Steorts, son of George W. and Amanda, his wife, was born in Lewis County, Western Virginia; married Miss Rosie Boggs, December 25, 1888; his age 27, her's 17; she a daughter of Isaac and Mary E. (Garee) Boggs of Big Sandy.

They made their first home over on a branch of Big Otter Creek. He died at about forty-two years of age, leaving the widow, Rosie, and four sons: Earl, Isaac Lee, Charles Marshall and George Ernest.

Of these, Isaac Lee Steorts, born March 19, 1891; married Miss Maud Keen age, 20, on September 18, 1916 (of Hollywood and Sandy). Of this marriage two daughters were born. The wife Maud, having died, Isaac Lee married Miss Lethia Wright, May 28, 1920; "her age 27;" she a daughter of Samuel K. Wright.

Isaac Lee and family live near Newton, Roane County. He is an active dealer in oil and gas properties and has large interests in that abounding locality.

STEWART: William Stewart, pioneer of Reedy.

William Stewart, pioneer, was born in Green County, Pennsylvania, June 23, 1790, joined Pennsylvania State militia and came to the Ohio, and served about Wheeling with him his brother Charles Stewart, Patrick Board and Henry Blosser, all natives of Peensylvania, and there first heard of Reedy Creek and decided to make their homes at its "Three Forks." See names: Blosser and Board.

William Stewart married Mary Board, a sister of Patrick Board, about the time they set out for Reedy, which must have been about the year 1817 or 1818. His oldest son Joseph's birth is given in Hardesty's as occurring at Reedy in the month of May, 1820. William was a blue eyed, pink blond, short, and in his old age a pompous rollypoly man.

He selected a large tract of land covering all the wide basin between the hills on the west side of the juncture of the three forks of Reedy; and built his home out on the promontory where the first rays of the rising sun kissed away the fog and the dew. That was their life-time's home. There they made what was for many years the best farm in Reedy, and there they reared their large family. Their names in order of births: Joseph, John, Bee, Andrew, Alfred, Mary, Susan, Sarah, Jane, Mary, Elizabeth and Minerva, eleven in all.

These sons and daughters all married, some with sons or daughters of Reedy, others elsewhere, but most all married before formation of the county of Roane and their marriage records are in Jackson, Wirt or Wood County.

Joseph married Elizabeth Goff, May 12, 1845, she born in Lewis County, March 17, 1827, daughter of Salathiel and Margaret (Flesher) Goff, at time of the daughter's marriage, but recently arrived on Reedy. They made their home on head of Right Fork of Reedy near Sandy Summit; reared a large family.

Andrew married Barbara Westfall, of the Pocatalico Waterfalls. Susan to Col. Thos. A. Roberts; Mary to Andrew B. Chancey; Elizabeth married John G. Goff; Minerva to Charles Cottle; Sarah J. to Charles M. Boggs. See all these names in this Chapter X.

The Andrew above named is the "Andy Stewart," the Reedy miller for so many years.

The children reared by Andrew and Barbara, his wife, so many as we can recall, are:

Dr. David, many years a resident physician of Creston, Wirt County, his wife Emma Robey. See Robey.

Elizabeth, who married Andrew J. Ott, of Wirt County, December 22, 1873; and others I have forgotten, and Emma the youngest daughter married William H. Armstrong.

STEWART: Of Reedy, formerly of Jackson County.

William P. Stewart, born in Jackson County, 1834, died at Reedy, 1911, was a son of John and Lucinda (Knopp) Stewart, the former born in Monongalia County, Virginia, the latter in Rockbridge County, Virginia, settled in Jackson County at an early date, some years prior to 1834.

William P. Stewart, above, married in Roane County, Anna, daughter of Alexander and Hannah (Staats) Ables, on November 12, 1857; Alexander Ables was born in Pennsylvania. Anna was born in Jackson County, western Virginia, January 5, 1831; married first, Christian Starley, born in Lewis County, Western Virginia, and he died 1852. Of this marriage twin daughters were born, Margaret A. and Hanna E., December 10, 1852, and William P. was their respected stepfather.

He and Anna made their home in Reedy the year next after their marriage, where both spent their long and fruitful lives. He taught school, was a good trader and took part in all public affairs; served one or more terms as a justice of the peace of Reedy District.

To William P. and Anna (Ables Straley) his wife, were born and by them reared, in addition to those two girls of first marriage, the following children:

Flora A., February 27, 1862, wife of J. N. Board; Minerva L., October 11, 1863, wife of Aaron G. Goad; Myrtle V., 1865, married Clauson Dix, 25, November 17, 1887; Dorcus P., April 12, 1867, married Harvey Lee Starkey, M. D., June 19, 1892; Magnus Fleet, April 11, 1871; he became a graudate physician and commenced in Lewis or Harrison County, West Virginia.

HISTORY OF ROANE COUNTY 671

STRALEY: Pioneers of Middle Reedy.
Jacob M. Straley should be considered as the pioneer Straley. There was an Abraham or Abram Straley lived for a few years on upper Middle Fork in the decade following the Mexican War, maybe before that decade lived about where the Ripley turnpike crosses. A Stephen Straley lived on upper Mill Creek, not far from Ripley, a brother to Jacob M. of Reedy, who was a prominent farmer for some years following the Civil War.

Jacob M. Straley married Miss Hannah Staats, 1857. His sister, Cinderella, married William T. Staats, brother of Hannah, year 1858. These were children of John and Margaret ("Peggy" Carney) Staats, of pioneer families of Mill Creek country in Jackson County. See name, Staats.

Jacom M. Straley and Hannah, his wife, made their lifetime's home on Staats Run of Reedy, in the dense forest they pitched their cabin and made a good farm and there brought up their family of three sons and two daughters, whose names were as follows:

Elias, George W., Leslie, Lillie and Mary.

Elias and Leslie went to the State of Missouri when young and not married; married there and made their homes.

George W. married Miss Henrietta Dix, of Reedy, March 20, 1884; his age 24, her's 24. She was a daughter of Jacob Dix and wife; born in Barbour County.

Lillie Straley married Samuel Riddle, of Middle Fork of Reedy, May 6, 1879.

Mary Straley married James Leonard McMillion, December 30, 1876; her age then 22, his age 27. He was born in Wirt County, West Virginia, son of Robert McMillon and wife.

Mary's husband, James L. McMillion, having died, she unitel in marriage with A. W. Rhodes, of Reedy.

STUTLER:
The first of this name in this county was John Stutler II, long a resident on Kinchelo Creek, Harrison County, Western Virginia. He was born in Harrison County, 1787, grandson of John Stutler I, and Mary (Newberger) his wife; this John I, served as a soldier of the Revolution in the ranks of Virginians, after which he and his family came to the Monongahela country, of which family we are informed were three sons: Robert, Elias and John II. Robert and Elias each married a daughter of Jonathan Hughes, a brother of Jesse, hero of border warfare. Robert was father of several daughters and one son. Elias Stutler was father of eleven sons and three daughters; the Stutlers of Calhoun County on the Little Kanawha are descendants of Elias, through Benjamin Franklin Stutler; the most generally known of this branch of the Stutler family at this time is Boyd B. Stutler, employee of the State printing department at Charleston, West Virginia, and he made investigations and gives us the foregoing information as to the Stutler family tree.

Boyd Blynn Stutler is a son of Daniel E. Stutler, attorney at law and Emily B. (Heckert) his wife.

John II married in Lewis County, Miss Mary Carder. To John Stutler II and wife were born four sons and one daughter, their names in sequence of their ages: Rebecca, born March 15, 1822, became the wife of Alexander Sandy Board, which see; Josiah, John III, Christopher and Manly, the last named died in the War of Secession, 1863, or thereabout.

After the death of his wife in Harrison County, John Stutler II, widower, stone mason by trade, came with his above daughter and sons to Jackson County, settling for a time on Sand Creek about five miles eastward and up the creek from Sandyville. About the year 1848, he removed to Reedy near "Three Forks," established his home there, from which home his above named children went forth and married and made each a home for himself. Further of this family.

Josiah Stutler, son of John and Mary Carder, was born in Harrison County, Western Virginia, August 16, 1824; February 5, 1852, married Rebecca, daughter of Salathial Goff, resident and large land owner one to three miles below "Three Forks." Josiah and Rebecca soon made their home in the depths of the dense forest of the first branch creek emptying into Main Reedy on the eastern side about one mile below Three Forks. They soon had title to about two hundred and fifty acres there, and as the years passed made a good homestead surrounded by many fields cleared and brought to excellent production by Josiah, Rebecca and their several children whom we will presently write about. Josiah was a man industrious and frugal; moderate and just in all his opinions; his conduct through the stormy vicissitudes of the "Rebellion," though an outspoken southern sympathizer, was such that he was Reedy's first justice of the peace elected next after that war, succeeding Squire Roswell R. Chancey, neighbor to the Bishop family (my father's).

Squire Chancey had long been the petted loyalist of the Union authorities; any man of less breadth of intellect would have been spoiled and filled with prejudice, therefore with resentment at the election of one of "the enemy;" my father who had served all through as a Union soldier seemed to regret that authority should thus so soon pass out of the hands of known and tried Unionists; but, I remember Squire Chancey's remarks on the occasion: "Tomorrow I will meet Josiah Stutler, the newly elected justice and hand over to him the docket and other books of the office." "No, Josiah Stutler is a sensible man and will be fair with all; I will administer the oath of office to him." This was done on the next day just as Squire Chancey said he would do. Squire Stutler must have served more than one term as justice, or else those years of my impatient youth dragged out longer than actual time marked. I mean, I was impatient to reach manhood.

To Josiah and Rebecca (Goff) Stutler were born the following named children that grew up:

Amanda, born 1852, married F. Lewis Smith, Nicholas County, West Virginia.

HISTORY OF ROANE COUNTY 673

Melissa, 1856, married Caleb D. Kimes, of Wirt.
William, 1858, married Mary E., daughter of Jackson Sommerville, of Jackson County. He, William, was for a few years prominent in Roane County, first as a prosperous young man, next as a successful school teacher, then served one term as County Surveyor of Lands. Went to Missouri about 1886; his wife died in Missouri, married again, 1904, this wife being Miss Minnie Gray, of Boynton, Missouri. We are told William owns large and valuable properties at his home in Missouri. Further of the family of Josiah:

Sixth child, Susan, married George W. Mitchell, of upper Spring Creek.

Mary married George A. Hylbert, of Wirt County.

Nancy married James W. Conrad, of Wirt.

Margaret married John K. Daniel, of Wirt.

Lemuel H. married Louisa Fox, of Spring Creek.

Josiah, Jr., born July 8, 1878, married Kate W., daughter of Robert M. and (McIntire) Wells, of Buffaloe, West Virginia, May 7, 1902. Josiah, Jr. taught school six years for his first public activities; engaged the meanwhile in farming and stock raising, having acquired the family homestead on Stutler Run; was elected member of the County Court and served the county one or more terms as such member; succeeded in the oil business; moved to City of Spencer about the year 1924, having bought the Bowman property on Main Street, where he now (1926) lives. To Josiah, Jr. and Kate W. (Wells), his wife, were born five children: Virginia Rebecca, 1903; Roland Alonzo, 1906; Ruth Carolie; Ralph Emerson, 1915, and Reta Joanna, 1921.

Christopher Stutler, son of John II, pioneer, married Mary Goff, daughter of Salathiel Goff, they reared a large family

John Stutler III, son of John II, married and brought up a family in Reedy.

STUMP:

Henry Stump, long known as "Major or Captain" Henry Stump, was born in Lewis County, Western Virginia, January 25, 1819, son of Michael and Elizabeth (Bush) Stump, of Colonial families of those names. Henry married Permelia Welch, daughter of one of the Welch family, the name of which is perpetuated in the city Welch, McDowell County, West Virginia. Permelia was born in Harrison County, July 15, 1821, daughter of John and Elizabeth (Arnold) Welch, who later settled on Elk Fork of Mill Creek. His mill on Elk Fork being one of the objects named in Roane County boundary lines. In his biography found in Hardesty's History, Major Stump does not give the date of his settlement in these parts; incidents of the history of Roane indicate he was there some years prior to the Civil War. He was one of those who surveyed the county and was Major of a Militia company which he assembled and trained on fields at Walton and on the bottom at mouth of Johnson Creek. Isaac Jones, who settled at

Walton was his son-in-law, married his daughter, Melissa J. June 1860. Major Stump, here at Walton on outbreak of the War of Secession, enlisted a company of soldiers for the Union cause, and was rewarded by a captaincy in the mighty Union army, captain of Company K, 13th West Virginia Infantry. "Among the battles in which he took part were Berryville, Winchester, Kernstown, Martinsburg, Fisher's Hill and Cedar Creek. He was twelve years County Surveyor of Roane, and served as Delegate for Roane in the second State Legislature, 1864. In the year 1904 being a candidate for "state's attorney" as the office of prosecuting attorney was then called. I visited Captain Stump at his home and saw him for the first and last time. He saw us approaching the house and came out and greeted us at the gate, and took us to his rooms. Us? I was with Elijah Riddle, a veteran who soldiered with him, and at this time a candidate for election to the House of Delegates. Captain Stump was delighted, yet of the grave and sincere manner, with this call by his old comrade in arms and dangers.

They talked animatedly of the war, of achievements and hopeful prospects, hardships endured and perils escaped. Incidentally he addressed me with this: "I have never been paid for my services in surveying the boundaries of the county necessary on its formation; you will find our report somewhere in the court house if it did not go up in flames when the court house burnt." I said why were you never paid? He said: "For the first four years the county funds were so needed for erection of the court house that I felt I should not press for my pay; then the war came; that over, sentimentalists enfranchised the rebels; they took the reins of county government and have persistently delayed my pay, twenty some years now. You are a son of a veteran, we hope you will be elected." Captain Stump was of medium height, broad of shoulders and of a very fair, clear skin. It was a warm day and he had his coat off, otherwise he dressed as if expecting company.

The names and birth dates of the children of Henry and Permelia (Welch) Stump, as given by him in the memoir before mentioned, are Irwin C., September 25, 1840. This is the Irwin C. Stump delegate to the first Wheeling convention, one of those General Henry A. Wise ordered arrested and sent "to Richmond where we will decently bury the dead and hang the living." Irwin C. was not buried nor hanged. His residence, year 1882, was given as San Francisco, Calif. Melissa J., born June 13, 1842, married Isaac C. Jones, of Walton; Laverna C., married and had her home in Charleston; Charles E., July 29, 1847, became a physician, married Elizabeth, daughter of Elijah Hughes, of Ohio. Dr. Stump practiced from Newton several years. Names of the children of Dr. Charles and Elizabeth (Hughes) Stump are Irwin C., a physician of Clendenin, West Virginia; Lulu May, wife of Theodore R. Simmons, mentioned in the chapters, Smithfield District and History of the City of Spencer. Harry Rudolph

HISTORY OF ROANE COUNTY 675

Stump, business man of Clendenin, West Virginia. Cora E. (Widow Davies), of Charleston. Kittie, wife of Otto Engle, of Amma, Roane County. Dennis E., lives in Charleston, West Virginia. Henry Clay and Harry C., both of Clendenin, West Virginia.

Names of other children of Major Henry and Permelia (Welch), his wife, are Mary E., born 1850; Louise M., 1854, wife of Lewis D. Osborne, of Osborne's Mills; Flora E., 1862, married Millard F. Osborne, of Osborne's Mills, April 8, 1880. For further see family names of husbands.

SUMMERS:

The Summers's of Roane County are descendants of a pioneer family of that name among the first settlers of Kanawha County. The following is gotten in part from a biography of Christopher C. Summers in Hardesty's, and in part from Amos W. Summers, grandson of St. Clair Summers and his wife, Susan (Hammack) Summers, settling soon after the War of 1812, on Elk River in Kanawha County, near Jarrett's Ford. St. Clair was a United States pensioner on account of services rendered as a soldier of the War of 1812. To St. Clair and Susan (Hammack) Summers were born there at Jarrett's Ford, five sons and two daughters. Their names in order of their births are as follows: John, born in 1817; Martin; James; Henry; Andrew; Artentia, who became the wife of Lyle Paxton of Poca, and Arminta, who married William Ray, later settling on Rock Creek, and Elizabeth, who was the first wife of Squier Young. Of John, son of St. Clair Summers, we do not know. Martin, son of St. Clair Summers, married Lucinda Hively, daughter of John Hively, of Poca, January 6, 1860. To them were born five sons and four daughters, their names as follows: James Madison, who settled on Poca Fork, Kanawha County; George Martin; John H., married Barbara Hammack, December 25, 1860; Giles Lewis, married Maggie Farley; Elliott; Virginia, who married John Dodd, of South Walton District; Sarah Susan, wife of David J. Cummings; Lucinda, who became second wife of David J. Cummings.

James Summers, son of St. Clair and Susan (Hammack) Summers, was born near Jarrett's Ford, Kanawha County, December 26, 1826, married Sophia Phillips, born May 22, 1827. They came to Roane County in the year 1853, settling and making their last home near head of Rock Creek. To James and Sophia Summers were born five sons and two daughters, their names:

Christopher C. Summers, son of James and Sophia (Phillips) Summers, was born in Kanawha County, Western Virginia, January 26, 1850, married Rebecca Ward in Roane County, August 23, 1874; she born in Barbour County, Western Virginia, April 8, 1852, daughter of Aquilla Ward, mentioned in the History of Spencer. To Christopher and Rebecca (Ward) Summers was born James Otis Summers, April 30, 1880. This is the J. Otis Summers of City of Charleston, City

Clerk, etc., (1924-5-6). Christopher C. Summers kept a general store at Walton for several years, about 1885 to 1895.

Sarah Jane, second child of James and Sophia Summers, married John H. Cummings, of southern Walton District, December 23, 1873.

Cynthia, third child of James and Sophia Summers, married John Hively, son of James Hively, of Walton District.

Isaac L., fourth child of James and Sophia Summers.

Mary A., fifth child of James and Sophia Summers.

Amos W., sixth child of James and Sophia P. Summers, married for first wife, Bird Smith, sister of William Smith, of Forks of Green Creek. After her death he married Miss Nannie Ison, of Carter County, Kentucky, who is with him in their home at Circleville, Ohio. They have one child. Of the marriage of Amos and Bird (Smith) was born a daughter named Maisie, who became the wife of Dr. L. C. Young, born in Wirt County, West Virginia, now resident of Lexington, Kentucky.

Amos W. Summers was active early in life; taught school in Roane County; was elected and served one term as clerk of the County Court of Roane County, West Virginia, years 1902 to 1908.

Henry Summers, fourth son of St. Clair and Susa (Hammack) Summers, married Jane V, Hammack, daughter of Delana Hammack. Theirs was the first farm east of Walton bridge, was a prominent place from the year 1870 to 1885.

The names of the children of Henry and Susan "Gussie," as remembered by their neighbors were: George, Lewis, Fry, Delana, Peter, William, and one daughter named Dicie, who married William Harmon, their home, first farm on Poca above the mouth of Johnson Creek.

Andrew "Andy" Summers, son of St. Clair and Susa (Hammack) his wife, we are told, was thrice married. First wife, Miss Mary Tilford, whom he married in the State of Kansas, afterwards returned here and made their home on Rock Creek, Roane County, West Virginia. Of this marriage were born Robert Summers and Henry Summers.

This first wife having died, Andrew united in marriage with Bertha Groves, of Roane County, July 23, 1874. Of this marriage, we are told, were born two daughters, their names, Mary, who married Leander Fields, and Linnie, who married Edward Cummings.

TALLMAN: Of Smithfield District.

Samuel M. Tallman and his wife, Lucinda (Cox) Tallman, with some of their first born children were the first of this family name to settle in Roane County.

Samuel M. Tallman was born in Pocahontas County, Western Virginia, December 26, 1820, son of James and Jemima (Gilispie) Tallman, and James was a son of Benjiman and Rachel (Lincoln) Tallman, both born in Pennsylvania about forty miles from Philadelphia. "Rachel Lincoln was an aunt of Abraham Lincoln," says Samuel M., in his biography in Hardesty's History, "and Benjiman held a captain's commission in the Continental Army during the War of Independence."

Lucinda (Cox) the wife of Samuel M., was born in Lewis County, Western Virginia, April 17, 1828, daughter of Isaac P. and Mary (Nicely) Cox, pioneers settling on upper Pocatalico in the year 1844.

When a young man Samuel M. had learned the carpenter trade and sometimes worked at that trade during his early married life. He was a tall, strong man, of quiet yet positive demeanor and much respected.

To Samuel M. and Lucinda (Cox) Tallman were born and by them brought up the following named children:

James B., 1852; Julia A., 1854; Peter A., 1856; John W., 1858; Samuel, Jr., 1862; and William Crawford, 1865.

Efficient and industrious in their personal affairs none of the above family sought public office, however, William Crawford Tallman, while a young man, served his home district (Geary) as a Justice of the Peace, and Peter A. served the County of Roane one term as its sheriff. He became a large land holder and stock raiser of Smithfield District.

Peter A. Tallman, above mentioned, united in marriage with Miss Martha J. Ferrell, November 20, 1879; made their home in Smithfield District many years, where to them were born two or three sons and one daughter, the latter named Olive.

William Crawford Tallman married Miss Lizzie Springsto, of the family near Spencer, December 27, 1886; his age 21, her age 25.

TAWNEY: Of Upper Geary District.

The first of this family name who came here was Daniel Tawney, born in Virginia, June 30, 1804, and arrived here in the year 1854, with him his wife Lavisa (Harless) Tawney and their four sons and three daughters, all born in Giles County, Virginia, having first stopped a while on Hurricane Creek of Big Sandy, and later coming to Granishe ("Grannys") Creek in Upper Geary.

Daniel, the father, afterward returned to Virginia on a business trip and there died in 1863.

The names of these four sons were George W., Christopher, William H., David and John H. Tawney.

These four became joint purchasers and owners of a tract of about one thousand acres of land that lay on "Grannys" Creek, shortly after arriving here.

Being "strapping"—a term in those days meaning being both strong and large—they went to work making "howling wilderness" into fertile fields, and the Tawney place was soon heard of. These lands are owned by descendants yet. Further information as to this family is:

George W. Tawney was born in Giles County, Virginia, April 9, 1827, came here, as above stated, in 1854 and on February 14, 1857, married Mary Noe, born August 19, 1840, near "Three Forks" of Sandy, the daughter of William and Elizabeth (King) Noe, who at time of her birth had been there some five or more years.

To George W. and Mary (Noe) Tawney, his wife, were born Daniel W., March 27, 1861; Sarah E., February 25, 1863; David J., May 6, 1865; Hiram J., August 16, 1867; George, April 14, 1872; Samuel R., June 7, 1874, and Ruami F., September 16, 1881. Miranda, their first child, and Lovisa, their sixth, each died in youth.

Of the respective children of George W. and Mary Tawney we can relate further: That Daniel W.—nicknamed "Link"—married Mary H. Haley; his age 26, her age 18, and settled on Dog Creek.

Sarah Elizabeth, on March 15, 1888, married Peter T. Radabaugh, of Curtis District; his age 29, her age 25. They made their home in Curtis District for several year, then removed to Missouri.

David J. Tawney, on September 13, 1889, married Cynthia Carper, on Left Hand, her age 18, his age 23.

George F. Tawney married Emma Schoolcraft.

Samuel R. Tawney was thrice married, first Ellen Helmic, May 2, 1897, his age 22, her's 19; second, Jennie Rowe; third, Mabel Keen, who, at time of her marriage with Samuel R. Tawney, was the widow of William Rufus King, Jr., deceased.

Ruamia Florence Tawney married William O. Sergent, September 17, 1902, her age 21, his age 27. She died about the year 1920, leaving surviving her two sons and three daughters.

Aaron Tawney married Flora Alma Graham, August 22, 1903, his age 25, her age 19. She was a daughter of W. I. Graham. Aaron was successful, carried on a large farm in Geary District. To Aaron and Flora were born six sons and four daughters.

Christopher P. Tawney, son of Daniel and Levisa (Harless) tawney, married Priscilla Drake, July 19, 1866, and they made their farm out of the joint lands above mentioned. To them were born and by them brought up four daughters, the names of three of whom we do not have, the one, Rebecca, married G. W. Scott, and they live in Kanawha County.

William H. Tawney, son of Daniel and Lavisa (Harless) Tawney, married Louisa Griffith, daughter of Hugh and Miriam (Boggs) Griffith, and to them was born one child, a son, named Hugh H. Tawney, who married twice, but of neither marriage were children born. He has always lived on the old Tawney lands.

David Tawney, son of Daniel and Lavisa (Harless) Tawney, married Elvira Young.

They went to Kentucky where we hear they have reared a large family.

John H. Tawney, son of Daniel and Lavisa (Harless) Tawney, the last named of the family first arriving here, was also born in Giles County, Virginia, before the family came here, on March 22, 1848, died at his home in upper Geary District, October 1, 1916.

John H. Tawney married Elizabeth Keen, April 19, 1867; she was a daughter of James Keen, of Hollywood.

HISTORY OF ROANE COUNTY 679

They made their home, a large stock farm, on the head waters of Big Sandy, lived there many years, became a successful large farmer, a man of force and usefulness to all about him; a supporter of the church and schools. At the age of eighteen years he became a devout member of the Baptist church, and enjoyed its fellowship throughout the remainder of his life.

To John H. Tawney and Elizabeth (Keen), his wife, were born twelve children. Something further and their names we are given as follows:

Dora E. married Robert F. Wilson.
James W. married Nancy A. Ross, of his neighborhood.
Emma married Ulyssis S. Ross, son of Davidson Ross.
Daniel C. married Lulu Drake, of the Geary District family.
Lucy married S. C. Ross.
May Belle married C. W. Drake.
Clara E. married William H. Engle, of Lower Geary.
Mary E. married O. E. White.
Rosa F. married U. S. Ross, becoming his second wife.
Roxie F. married J. W. Milster.
Robert L. died in infancy.
John S. married Leona Ross.

After the death of Elizabeth, the mother of all the foregoing children of John H. Tawney, he married Columbia Roe, widow, November 28, 1901. No child was born of this union.

TAYLOR: John and Anna P. (Hunt) Taylor. See Chapter IV, Harper District.

William and Mahala (Cromwell) Taylor, his wife, of a Virginia or Tennessee family of the name, came from Russell County, Virginia, and settled on lands on the divide between head waters of Pocatalico and Big Sandy about the year 1851. William was born April 11, 1811, and Mahala was born in April 1809—dates in biography of Beverly J. Taylor in Hardesty's. William and Mahala (Cromwell) Taylor, when they arrived here had four sons and one daughter, named as follows: Beverly J., born in Russell County, Virginia, September 22, 1831; Samuel L., born in Meigs County, Tennessee, August 9, 1838; Ira R., born in Russell County, Virginia, July 10, 1847, and Andrew F., born in Russell County, Virginia, December 20, 1850. These four sons of William and Mahala all grew to manhood, married and made prosperous homes and reared families in Roane County. Beverly J. and Andrew in Geary, and Samuel and Ira R. in Walton, all not far from the division line of Geary and Walton. The daughter, Mary J., became the wife of John Goad, of Walton District, about the year 1858. See Goad.

Beverly J. Taylor, of above family, was twice married, his first wife being Artemesia Darnell, and with her he settled in lower Geary District. Of this marriage five children were born, three of whom died in infancy. A son, David C., born April 14, 1859, was long an influential citizen, and continued the large farm his father had acquired and made. A daughter of Beverly J. and Artemesia, named Annie B., born 1861, reached twenty-one or more, but we have no further information about her. Artemesia (Darnell) died some time prior to the year 1872, and on February 26, 1873, Beverly J. married for a second wife, Lucy J. Woody, of Mason County, West Virginia, she being the daughter of William G. and Mary A. (Keys) Woody. Of this marriage were born three children, the first died in infancy, the others were Florence G., May 11, 1876, and of the other, born March 12, 1883, we have no information.

Samuel L. Taylor, son of William and Mahala (Cromwell) Taylor, pioneers, married Mary E. Hindman, daughter of Josiah Hindman. To them were born two sons and five daughters, whose names are as follows:

Henry Clay, long an excellent school teacher of the county, between years 1890 and 1900.

Daniel Webster.

Maud, who married Lonnie S. Hughes, of Roane County.

May, who became wife of Homer Cottle, of Spencer, June 2, 1895; his age 26, her age 25.

Ava, who married W. J. Patterson.

Kate, who married R. E. Cart, and Virgie, wife of Peter C. Kelley.

Andrew F. Taylor, born in Russell County, Virginia, on December 20, 1850, son of William and Mahala (Cromwell) Taylor, married Mary F. Osborne, May 20, 1870. She was born in Kanawha County, January 8, 1850, daughter of A. P. and Elizabeth (Snyder) Osborne, and they made their home-farm in Geary District, where to them were born four daughters and one son:

Amy E., September 2, 1874; Louise M., December 16, 1876; William B., July 1, 1878; Mary E., November 9, 1879, and Iva H. September 3, 1882.

Ira R. Taylor, son of William and Mahala (Cromwell) Taylor, was born in Russell County, Virginia, July 18, 1847, married Sarah F. Dougherty in Roane County, West Virginia, March 31, 1870. She was a daughter of Alexander and Nancy (Robinson) Dougherty, and was born in Greenbrier County, West Virginia, December 12, 1851. To them were born, here in Roane: Lueva, 1871; Emma N., 1873; Louverna, 1876; Silas E., 1879, and Cora S., 1882.

Henry D. Taylor, and a Charles Taylor, sons of William and Mahala (Cromwell) Taylor, have left us no record of themselves.

THOMAS:

John Enoch Thomas, Justice of the Peace of Spencer District, resident in the city at time of this writing. Of this family we are told the following:

Enoch Thomas, a Connecticut Yankee, while a young unmarried man, left his parents in New England, came seeking his fortune and settled in the south end of Jackson County about the year 1818, 1819 or 1820; married Annie or Anna Carney, daughter of William Carney and sister of Charles Carney, a pre-war sheriff of Jackson County. She was also a sister of Delilah Roach, of Reedy, of Hannah, wife of Levi Caston, of Mill Creek, and of Dorcus, wife of James Brown.

At the time of her marriage to Enoch Thomas, Anna was a widow, having been twice married previously. First, to Cornelius Straley, of which marriage she had two children, and second, to .... Randolph, by whom she had one child. The son, Riley Randolph, there grew up, married and founded a family in Jackson County.

Enoch and Anna, with their family, became owners of large acreages of lands in Jackson county which he improved. He was a prominent citizen of Jackson County for more than thirty years.

To Enoch and Annie (Carney), his wife, were born and by them reared the following children:

Elizabeth ("Bettie"), George, Jesse, Malinda, Hiram, Elias A., and Nehemiah M. S., who was elected by the people and served three terms as Justice of the Peace of Washington District, of Jackson County.

Elias A. Thomas, of above family, married Miss Harriett Shiverdecker, of a family of that name near Raymond City, on Kanawha. They reared five sons and one daughter, their names: Jerry M., John Enoch (first mentioned), George Custer, Samuel Robert, Yuluia Ann and Elsworth D.

THOMASSON:

John Poindexter Thomasson, first of the name here, large land holder, active in formation of the county.

John Poindexter Thomasson, subject of this sketch, was born in Louisa County, Virginia, near Louisa Court House, year 1782, and there united in marriage with Miss Nancy Hancock, born 1783, the date of which marriage we have not searched out, however, the date of birth of one of the older children is given as of the year 1809. John P. appears to have come to the Reedy and Spring Creek country as early as 1828. In what year he moved his family here we do not know. Records show him at Clarksburg in 1840, at which time he purchased at a Federal court judicial sale, several hundred thousand acres of land of the "Clayborne Surveys" cornering near the mouth of Hughes River of the Little Kanawha and extending southward to the Kanawha County boundary line, which he claimed was an east-and-west line some two miles south—up creek—from where Spencer and Reedyville now are. Further of this purchase and his career we write in the History of Curtis District, the County and of the City of Spencer, in chapters above referred to.

The names of the sons and daughters of John P. Thomasson and Nancy (Hancock), his wife, are as follows: Austin H., Elizabeth, Anna H., Mary Louisa, Mordecai James, James E., Pleasants Hites, Edmond James and Martha Ellen.

Of the above family we are given, by R. Millard and Arthur C., great grandsons of John P. and Louisa, his wife, further information as follows:

Austin H., born June 19, 1809, went to North Carolina and there, in Stark County, married Nancy Creioz, December 1, 1835.

Elizabeth, born February 22, 1811, married John Chopel.

Anna H., born November 19, 1812, married Ellison Burdette, on Reedy, then deemed in Jackson County, January 4, 1838. See "Burdette."

Pleasants Hites Thomasson, sixth child of John P. and Nancy (Hancock) Thomasson, was born March 19, 1819, married Miss Emily Rader, December 23, 1842. They soon left this country, seeking their fotune elsewhere.

Edmond James, son of John P. and Nancy Thomasson, their seventh as named, leaves to the present no record; neither do we have anything as to Martha Ellen, born June 8, 1830, eighth child of this family. Except, we find on the copy of the family record that "James E. Thomasson married Mary J. Burdette, October 6, 1842."

Mary Louisa, born July 4, 1814. Of her we have no further information.

Mordecal James Thomasson, fourth child of John P. and Nancy (Handcock) Thomasson, was born June 8, 1817, married on Reedy, January 21, 1841, Miss Susan Rader. See "Rader." Made out of the depths of the forest on left fork of Reedy midway between what is now—1927—Billings and Reedyville, the first good farm of those parts; it was prominent for thirty-five years as the "Thomasson and Riddle" places; reared there eleven children, their names as follows:

Will, Robert, George W., Lewis A., Austin, Nancy Ann, Elizabeth C., Eliza J., Margaret Mazilla, Minnie B., James B. and Mattie. Of these we write further:

William, when a young man, went to Kansas. Parsons, Kansas, was his last address.

Robert was with William in Kansas when last heard of.

George W. was also with the two above brothers for several years. He returned and married Mrs. Mollie E., widow of John Burdette, daughter of .... Hoff, November 18, 1897; his age 49, her age 45. No child born.

Lewis Allen, son of M. J., married Emaline Parsons, November 6, 1872, made their home-farm on Left Reedy, where to them were born the following children: Ida A., Lonnie, Harvey Allen, Ruben Millard.

HISTORY OF ROANE COUNTY 683

Ida A. married Forest W. Heaton, January 23, 1908, her age 23, his age 25. He was born in Wood County, West Virginia.

Lonnie married Miss May Lewis, of Urbana, Ohio. Harvey Allen married Annie B. Hoff, December 2, 1899, ages, 22 and 21 years, respectively.

Ruben Millard taught school for a few years while yet young; located in Town of Spencer where he embarked in a general insurance business; married in Spencer, Miss Bessie Harold, January 23, 1908, his age 28, her's 23. She was born in Charleston, West Virginia. He was elected and served on term as mayor of the City of Spencer, year 1913. He is public spirited and used often on business or church committees.

Clyde Clayton married Clara Bowers, lives in Akron, Ohio.

Hoyt, youngest of this Lewis Allen Thomasson family, married Pearl Phillips, October 9, 1912, his age 22, her's 20. They live in Akron, Ohio.

Austin Thomasson, son of Mordecai James and Susan (Rader) Thomasson, was born on Reedy, year 1852, married Miss Josephine Hoff, of his own neighborhood, on December 31, 1881. They made their farm-home on upper Reedy and there reared and gave to the country the following named three sons and four daughters:

Arthur C., business man of City of Spencer, architect and member of the firm "Spencer Brick Company." See Chapter IX of this book. He married Miss Ida Harold, November 29, 1911, his age then 26, her age 28. She was born in Charleston, West Virginia. They maintain a neat home on North Beauty Street, and have a daughter named Elinor.

Maud married Jeremy G. Reedy, April 23, 1921, her age 31, his age 30.

Cordia married John Meadows.

Pearl married Arthur Fisher, October 20, 1921, her age 24, his 24 years.

Virgil is a youth at this time in high school.

Harry B. and Blanche died in youth.

Nancy Ann, daughter of Mordecai J. Thomasson, married Washington Huddleston, December 28, 1859.

Elizabeth C., daughter of Mordecai J. Thomasson, married Roland Petty, 1869.

Eliza J., daughter of Mordecai J. Thomasson, married William Nathaniel Patmon, April 10, 1876.

Minnie B., daughter of Mordecai J. Thomasson, married James M. Simmons, of Smithfield District history, December 23, 1888. Mattie, the youngest of this family, remained a spinster.

James B. Thomasson, son of Mordecai James, was born December 4, 1859, married Miss Ettie Juliett Hoskins, born in Calhoun County, but in Ravenswood at time of marriage. Of this marriage were: Gertrude, wife of C. C. Hardman; Hallie, wife of Homer D. Howell (see Hardman-Howell), and a son, Holly B. Thomasson.

THOMPSON: Of Spencer, Upper Spring Creek.

William W. Thompson, with his second wife and some children of both a first and second marriage, were the first of this family name to settle here, 1857. He was prominent here for fifteen years; was a Justice of the Peace. Long known as "Squire William Thompson." Graduated his three oldest children in college. S. Blackamore and John Brown as physicians.

William W. Thompson was born in Harrison County, Western Virginia, July 12, 1812, son of John and Pattie (Jackson) Thompson, both born in the Monongahela Valley, of Fauquier County parents, who died in Barbour County.

William W. Thompson was twice married. His first wife being Susan K. Tomlin, born in Fauquier County, Virginia, daughter of Stephen and Sarah (Norris) Tomlin; Willim W. and Susan K.'s marriage taking place in Harrison County, August 4, 1833. She dieu there, August 26, 1846. They made their home near Clarksburg or at Clarksburg, where to them were born and by them reared the following named children: Stephen Blackmore, November 24, 1834; John Brown, May 16, 1839; Martha N., November 11, 1840; Francis Marion, January 1, 1844.

The wife, Susan K., having died, William W., in Clarksburg, May, 1848, married Miss Susan Marrow, born near Oldtown, Maryland, February 15, 1823, daughter of Robert and Susan (Davis) Marrow, at the time or a little later residents of Harrison County, where they died. Of this marriage were born and by the parents reared: Thomas Albert, December 30, 1857; Rosa Byrd, July 12, 1859, and Belle A., June 6, 1865.

Further about the family:

Dr. S. B. Thompson married a Miss Ruffner, of the Kanawha County Ruffners, and settled in his practice on the Great Kanawha.

Dr. John Brown, after graduation, married Miss M. E. Vance, daughter of James Vance, of Spencer, and he devoted all his life to his practice in and about Spencer. They left a family: Joseph B., Irene, Druit, Homer, William, Bertrand and James B.

Mattie N., daughter of W. W. and Susan K. (Tomlin) Thompson, married Addison Austin Smith, of Spencer, December 4, 1866. Their children are Susie, wife of J. Adelbert Brown, of Parkersburg; Frederick, of Ravenswood; Walter, now of Clarksburg; Anna and Marvin, all born in Spencer.

Francis Marion Thompson, son of William W. and Susan K. (Tomlin) Thompson, served in the Confederate armies of the Civil War. On September 25, 1866, united in marriage with Miss Susan Daniel. See Daniel. They made their home on Vandal Fork of Upper Spring Creek, where to them were born and by them reared the following four sons:

Stephen Brown married Miss Ida McMillan. See McMillan, Chapter V., Smithfield District. He was twenty years cashier of Roane County Bank, of Spencer. See Chapter IX, this book. Other sons are Charles W.

Thompson and Homer Franklin, of Charleston, West Virginia, and Rossel Garrett Thompson, who married Miss Cammie Belt, April 24, 1900, his age 24, her age 21.

The marriage of the children of Squire William W. and Susan (Morrow) Thompson are as follows:

Thomas Albert, married Miss Martha M. Pursley, of Spencer District, daughter of Hudson Pursley, on September 10, 1882. He succeeded to the last home-farm on Charles Fork, and later became a merchant resident of Spencer. They reared several children.

Rosa Byrd married Joseph B. Vance, a cabinet maker of Spencer, on June 23, 1885. They rearer one son and two daughters. The name of the son, Harry B. Daughters: Ora, wife of Harry F. Hersman, and Zelma, wife of Thomas Frances O'Brien, now of Charleston.

Bella A., daughter of Wm. W. and Susan Thompson, married George F. Cunningham, July 4, 1887. He was a resident lawyer of Spencer, prosecuting attorney. Of this marriage a daughter was born, named Ethel. She married Holly Simmons, son of Millard Filmore Simmons, of Spencer. Ethel and Holly at this time reside in Point Pleasant, W. Va.

THORN: First of the name in Reedy Country.

Arthur Boreman Thorn, first in Roane County's corps of school teachers on establishment of the free schools of Roane, to establishing and popularizing of which he, by his successful work, contributed. Was a son of Zadoc and Mary Evalyn (Moody) Thorn, his wife, who settled on Main Reedy—in Wirt County—in the year 1852, near which time Arthur B. was born.

Arthur Boreman Thorn united in marriage with Miss Editha Morris, in Wirt County, about 1874, she a daughter of Isaac Morris and wife, one time residents of Left Fork of Reedy Creek. Their son, George Morris, being Clerk of the County Court of Wirt County at the time of the marriage of his sister, Editha, with Arthur B. Thorn.

Arthur B. Thorn was a popular and successful school teacher in the Reedy country for many years. He and his wife, Edith, within a year after marriage made their home on Middle Fork of Reedy, two and a half miles from the Town of Reedy, on a tract of forest lands which they made into a home by the usual labor and methods of true pioneers. This is still their home. He became a successful and accurate land surveyor in his later years, of which work he did much in all parts of the county. His name appears among the charter members of the lodge I. O. O. F. No. 101, of Spencer, year 1899.

Of the children born to Arthur B. and Editha, his wife, they have brought up and given to the citizenry the following named: O. E. "Burt," Mabel, Camden, Grover, Zadoc and Rienza.

O. E. Thorn is an ordained minister of the Gospel.

Mabel married William L. Santee, March 19, 1901, his age then 26, born in Green County, Pennsylvania; her age 24, born in Roane County.

THRASH: Of Reedy. First about 1880.

Cicero Columbus Thrash, the first of this family name to make a home in Roane County, was born near Petroleum, Ritchie County, Western Virginia, May 29, 1854, son of William and Lizzie(Marple) Thrash.

Ancestry and posterity so far as given the writer:

John Thrash and Prudie, his wife, were of the first settlers on Hughes River, in what is now Ritchie County, West Virginia. There they made out of the forest their farm and home and brought up the following named children: Richard, Mike, John, David, William and a son and a daughter whose names we do not have. Of these:

William Thrash united in marriage with Miss Lizzie Marple, both young persons near the same age. She having been born in Barbour County about the year 1820, and their marriage took place about the time of the foundation of Ritchie County, 1843.

William Thrash and Lizzie, his wife, made their home near what is now Petroleum in Ritchie County, and there brought up their family of four sons and one daughter. Their names: Bennett, John, Albert, Cicero Columbus, and Florence. This daughter, Florence, married Marion Hennon. They lived for some years on Staats Run of Middle Fork of Reedy.

Cicero C. Thrash, first mentioned, and son of William and Lizzie (Marple) Thrash, was born at Petroleum, Ritchie County, May 29, 1854. He first married Miss Elizabeth A. Howard, of Green County, Pennsylvania. Of this marriage one child, a daughter named Clara B., was born, January 31, 1875; married at 15, Lemley L. Anderson, 23, on September 6, 1891. The wife, Elizabeth A., having died, Cicero C. Thrash came to Middle Reedy about the year 1880, here united in marriage with Miss Mary Carminta Hardman, on June 10, 1881. She was born on Reedy August 17, 1861, daughter of John and Sarah (Romine) Hardman.

C. C. Thrash and his wife, Mary Carminta, acquired the Larkin Howell farm-home on Middle Fork, with other lands and these made their home and brought up a family of three sons and three daughters: Albert Lee, April 27, 1883; Allie Vera, August 17, 1884; Beulah Pauline, July 3, 1887; Fred Green, July 30, 1889; Cleopatra, May 30, 1897, and Harry Columbus, on April 17, 1900.

These all have become citizens of Roane, and each commenced his career, remained or gone away.

Albert Lee Thrash, of the above family, became a young school teacher of Roane, taught a few years; was elected and served one term as County Superintendent of Schools of Roane County—years 1911 to 1915. Afterward learned banking and has for some years served in one capacity or another in the First National Bank of Reedy, and is the present Cashier of that bank.

Fred Green Thrash, of above family, at age of 21, married Miss Ethel Belle Montgomery, 19, on December 25, 1910. She was born in Green County, Pennsylvania.

VICARS: Of Higby of Harper.

William L. Vickers was the first of this name in Roane. He was born in Scott County, Virginia, October 2, 1853, son of Joseph and Elizabeth (Hart) Vicars, one of the oldest families of Scott County. His father died when William L. was nine years old and his mother died when he was thirteen. He came to Roane County in the year 1863; on November 29, 1877, married Viola Virginia Shafer, born December 9, 1859, daughter of John W. and Mariah (Dobson) Shafer. This Dobson family is that of the Monongahela Valley, some of whose daughters were carried off by Indians. To William L. and Viola Vicars was born only one child, named John W. Vicars.

John W. Vicars was born on the farm on Higly in Harper District, September 6, 1878. He married Miss Minnie Stanley, January 2, 1904, his age 24, her age 18. He is now—1927—a resident of Higly and prominent in affairs of the district.

VINEYARD: Of Walton, Smithfield, Spencer.

Presley Vineyard, Sr., and his wife, Cynthia, daughter of William and Sarah (Ashley) Hammack, built the first mill and made the first farm worth mentioning on the upper Pocatalico, about 1830. To Presley and Cynthia (Hammack) Vineyard, there on Poca, were born ten children, as follows: William, Nancy, Margaret ("Polly"), Delana, Charity, John (never married)*, Cynthia, Rachel and Presley, Jr. These founded nine families, all in Roane County, as follows:

William Vineyard married Sarah, daughter of Robert and Catherine (Stover) Looney, July 28, 1840, and made their home on head of Poca— Vineyard's Run. The names of the seven children of William and Sarah Vineyard are: Elizabeth, who married .... Kelley; Robert; Rachel, wife of James Hall of head of Left Hand; Presley E. married Julia A. Combs, December 20, 1869, "Evidence of William Combs" means one or both uniting parties not then twenty-one years old, and made their home in Smithfield. They are the parents of Thomas Elbert Vineyard of City of Spencer. Fred Vineyard on the old home place in Smithfield, and Sallie Vineyard, wife of Frederick Wells; W. Brad Vineyard, son of William and Sarah, married Rebecca A., daughter of James Keen, of Geary District (see name KEEN), and lives yet on part of the old William Vineyard home farm. Of Samuel Vineyard we have no information.

Nancy, daughter of Presley, Sr., and Cynthia Vineyard, married John T. Reynolds.

*NOTE: On Kanawha County records is seen: "John Vineyard to Sarah Jane Shaver, April 12, 1851." Report signed Rev. Wm. Gillett.

Susanna married Alexander West, Jr., of Spring Creek, July 28, 1840

Polly Vineyard, daughter of Presley and Cynthia (Hammack) Vineyard, married John Paxton, settled near Walton.

Delana Vineyard, son of Presley, Sr., married .... Summerfield, to them were born four sons and one daughter, their names: William, of Charleston; Elihu "Mack" Vineyard, of Johnson Creek, who married Lona Bonnet, May 9, 1894, his age 32, her age 21; James M. Vineyard, of Upper Poca, married Cassa C. Helper, June 27, 1871; and Cynthia became the wife of John M. Looney, of mouth of Johnson Creek; George W. married Sarah Hively, November 9, 1877.

Charity, daughter of Presley, Sr., and Cynthia (Hammack) Vineyard, married Peter Looney, year 1844; John Vineyard never married, we have nothing further of him; Cynthia, daughter of Presley, Sr., and Cynthia (Hammack) Vineyard, married Henderson Sergeant, long deceased; Rachel married Henderson White; Presley Vineyard, son of Presley Sr., and Cynthia (Hammack) Vineyard, married Margaret M. Seabolt, September 15, 1856. Of this marriage one son survives, his name, Rufus Vineyard, resident of Upper Poca in Walton District.

WAREN: See Chapter VI, Smith and Chapter IX, City of Spencer.

Rev. William L. Waren, pioneer preacher of the Methodist Protestant branch of the Methodist church, with his wife, Elizabeth (Kearns), and several children, were the first of the name here in Roane.

The name Waren is often spelled "Warren," but is never pronounced by those who know, like the word has the double rr. The a is sounded as in baren.

Reverend William L. Waren should be given a place in the history of establishing the M. P. church in Roane, second only to that of Rev. Pery Lowther. I think it should be written Rev. Pery Lowther first, William L. Waren second, and Joseph Dunn third. See Chapter IX, Churches of Spencer, and the subject of churches in each of the chapters on the several magisterial districts.

Rev. William L. Waren and Elizabeth, his wife, may have been married in Greenbrier County. They lived there last before coming to head of Mill Creek, Reedy and Spring Creek, which coming and arrival was about the year 1850. Their older children must have been then well nigh grown.

The names of these in order of ages, as remembered by Ottie Waren, a grandson, were William, Jr., Daniel Fisher, Hettie, Nancy, Susan, and Ellen. Their marriages:

Of William and Hettie we do not know.

Susan married Elliot Stalnaker, of Reedy.

Ellen united in marriage with Elihu Runnion, of Spencer. They made their home here and reared a family of several children. The marriage of these several daughters took place either in what is now

Roane County while it was part of Jackson County, or in Jackson County soon after formation of Roane.

Daniel Bisher Waren, son of Rev. William L. and wife, followed the footsteps of his father and became an M. P. preacher of Roane and adjoining counties. He was twice married. First Miss Margaret Ann Runnion, daughter of Henry Runnion and wife, of "New California"— Spencer.

Their sons and daughters were: Elihu, Catherine, Elizabeth, Anthony Lee, Elijah S., Rose, Annie, Minnie and Ottie.

Further about these sons and daughters of Rev. Daniel B. Waren and Margaret Ann (Runnion), his wife:

Catherine married Vincent Tibble in Jackson County. They have left two children.

Elizabeth wedded Lee Anderson.

Of Elihu and Anthony L. we have no information.

Elijah married May Eaton, of Reedy Eatons.

Rose, we have nothing as to her.

Annie married Herbert Brock, Webb City, Missouri.

Minnie wedded John Luther in Spencer, November 6, 1901, her age then 20 years, his age 27. He was of McDowell County, and served as State Senator of the district, years 1917 and 1919. Lives there now 1927.

Ottie was born, 1882; married Miss Dora O'Dell Rowe, December 5, 1909; he then 27, she 23. His residence is near the old homestead. They have two sons and one daughter.

Daniel Bisher Waren, after death of Margaret Ann, married Lucy Pickens in Jackson Conuty. They brought up two sons and three daughters, whose names we do not have.

WARNER:

Only one family of this name has thus far contributed to the county homes and citizens:

Addison Warner and his wife, natives of Upshur County, each born about the year 1840, she a daughter of .... Roberts, an old family of that name, resident then in Upshur. To them were born two children: Asbury and Olive. They all came to and settled first on upper Left Reedy, in Curtis District.

Asbury Warner married Annie Jones, a daughter of Granville and Sarah J. (Settle) Jones, of Curtis District, therefore granddaughter of Abner Settle. We do not know whether or not a child was born of this marriage. Annie died within a year or so after her marriage. For a second wife Asbury M. Warner married, May 30, 1876, Florida Hickle, daughter of Benjamin and Ada (Boothe) Hickle, of Vandal Fork of Spring Creek. To Asbury M. and Florida Warner, were born some children, only two of whom reached adult ages, their names, Benjiman H., born in year 1881, and Iral L., born in 1885.

Benjiman H. Warner, son of Asbury M. and Florida Warner, married Flora B. Walters, April 29, 1900; his age 19, her age 19. They made their farm-home on Slate of Spencer District.

Ira L. Warner, son of Asbury M. and Florida, married Ocie F. Harrah, August 10, 1907; his age 22, her age 22. She was born in Nicholas County, West Virginia. He began early life as an enthusiastic school teacher. He has lived and taught in Kanawha County since the year 1920.

WATSON: Of Upper Spring Creek

William Watson, with his wife, Nancy (Nutter) Watson, whom he had married in Doddridge County, Western Virginia, with their five daughters and one son, all born in Doddridge, came to make their life's home in Roane County in the year 1875.

They purchased their farm of ample acreage and settled on it, most of it in the virgin forest, located some four miles above—south—of Spencer, on the road, Spencer to Walton.

Their industry and good judgment soon made it a desirable home, and the Watson family prominent in affairs of the county for many years.

The names and something further about the children of William and Nancy (Nutter) Watson we write, in order of their respective ages, as follows:

Malinda, first daughter, married twice, first William Crihfield, of which union three children were born; second, William Wyatt. No child born.

Sarah married Sylvester Smith, in Doddridge County.

Juliet married John Stephens, of Potacalico.

Mary married David Haught, of Doddridge County.

Jane married Samuel Louden, never lived here.

Frank Marion Watson, only son of William and Nancy, married Mary Jane Stalnaker, of same neighborhood, April 9; 1879. Frank Marion became owner of the old ancestral home and he, his wife and family have lived there many years. State Road No. 14, graded and concreted, passes near their door. He and his wife have reared three sons and five daughters. Since giving the writer the above information Frank Marion Watson has died.

WATTS: Of Reedy.

William Watts and his wife, Elizabeth (Burr), whom he had married in Greenbrier County, Western Virginia, with four of their first born children, came from that county and settled on the farm, first one on the eastern side of Reedy Creek below "Three Forks," in the year 1849.

This Watts place, and the family, were prominent there for twenty years. We have no information as to the ancestry of the Watts's prior to their residence in Greenbrier.

William and Elizabeth (Burr) Watts reared three sons and three daughters. Their names: William Granville, Littleton, Sallie Burr, Victoria, John T. and Margaret.

Further about these:

William Granville Watts, in his earliest manhood, became a clerk in a store in Ravenswood. Later a partner of the firm. Later an independent merchant. He then took in his brother, John T., as a partner. William G. married in Ravenswood, Mary Taylor Hoff. They spent their lives in that town and reared five children.

Sallie Burr married Harvey H. Rader. See name Rader.

Victoria and Littleton died childless.

John T. Watts married a Miss Florence Harwood. They have ever since made their home in Ravenswood, West Virginia, and have reared five children.

Margaret ("Maggie"), daughter of William and Elizabeth (Burr) Watts, married Edgar Hylbert, of Wirt County, near Reedy line, on August 7, 1884; her age 21, his age 20. They made their home near Reedy and have nine children.

WEBB: Of upper Henry's Fork.

John Fletcher Webb, son of John and Margaret (Ferguson) Webb, his wife, was born in Russell County, Virginia, year 1845; came to the country of the upper Henry's Fork about 1878. There, on July 10, 1879, united in marriage with Miss Lucretia King, about his own age, daughter of George W. King, pioneer.

John F. and Lucretia obtained a tract of virgin forest lands on Wolfe Run. On it made their home and there brought up eight sons and two daughters. Named here in order of respective births as given me by William O. Webb, are as follows:

Waide, George B., Rosco, Frank, Harry, Smith, William O., Homer, Clara and Ollie.

William O. Webb, of above family, was born March 10, 1895. Hê is a business man at this time—1927—of the City of Clarksburg, West Virginia.

WEBB: Of Rush Creek of Henrys Fork.

Milton and Elizabeth ("Bettie" Bays) Webb were the first of this name to settle in the forest here. They were Virginians and came here shortly before the Civil War (1861), from Russell County, in which county their four sons and two daughters that were brought with them had been born. The names of these, in order of their ages: Charles, John, Wesley, George W., Jane, Emily and William. Of these we are further told that:

John Wesley Webb married Nancy Greathouse, daughter of Samuel and Sidnie Greathouse. Their eldest child, whose name is Lora, married Isaac J. Nichols, of the same neighborhood. Others of their children are L. D. Webb, Samuel Webb, and a daughter, Rena Myrtle.

Charles Webb married Eliza McGlothlin.

Rev. George A. Webb is a son of Charles and Eliza. He now resides in the City of Spencer.

George W. Webb married Mahala, daughter of Neddie Greathouse, of the Spencer District family.

Jane Webb married Tunis Nichols.

William Webb, the youngest of this family, married Elizabeth, daughter of Samuel Greathouse.

Emily Webb married Zandue Drake, born in Russell County, Virginia.

Jonas Webb, son of John W. and Margaret (Ferguson) Webb, was born in Russell County, Virginia, and came to Roane County in the year 1850; married Elizabeth Moore of Calhoun County, West Virginia, To Jonas B. and Elizabeth were born, here, six sons and three daughters. Their names: John P., who married Alice Nichols, of Smithfield District; Roxie, Ben Ferguson, Samuel, Viola, Vincent, Floyd, Grover and Rosie.

WELCH:

This name occurs in the county boundary lines. Welch's Mill on Elk Fork of Mill Creek being the second object: "To the thirteenth mile stone on the Spencer and Ripley turnpike; thence to Welch's Mill." We have no information concerning the family except that he, John Welch, with his wife, who was Elizabeth Arnold, settled there about the year 1845, with one son, Isiah, and two daughters, one of whom married Major Henry Stump, built the water grist mill there, of the then usual type of which there were so many everywhere in western Virginïa—a dam across the stream, of logs, skilfully notched together with dovetailed anchors of heavy logs, about five feet high, all laid together in such a way that the weight of head water came on long logs, dovetailed anchors of the dam pressing its parts more firmly on each other. Here John Welch and his wife raised at least one child to maturity, that being Isiah Welch, who was a prominent young man of that part of the county about the close of the "Civil War." Another family of the upper Pocatalico country claims no blood relation with this family, and one member of this last, says that "this is the Isiah Welch who went to the southern part of West Virginia and founded the community center that soon became the county seat of McDowell County and perpetuates his name, "Welch."

WELCH: Of Upper Poca.

The first of these was James Welch—one member of the family spells it "Walch." James Welch and his wife, Sallie (Cox) Welch, from Harrison County, settled here in the year 1842, a very young man and wife, to whom were born on the farm they made there, eight sons and five daughters, named as follows: John, James Mac, Washington, William, Franklin, Jefferson and Patrick. The names of the daughters are Mary Jane, who married Carr Nichols, of Spencer District; Nancy, who married Monroe Shamblin; Sallie, who married John Keiffer, son of Henry Kieffer, of Rush Creek of Henry's Fork. We have no data as to the other two daughters of James and Sallie (Cox) Welch.

Of this Welch family, John and James Mac, when they grew to manhood, bought the little old water mill built some years before by Henry Shamblin, their brother-in-law's father, which had already brought to that neighborhood "Shamblin's Mill." It was a prosperous spot. John and James Mac improved the mill ,put in the French buhrs and added a saw mill equipment, the then up-and-down or sash saw. They sawed lumber several years and many substantial frame houses were built of lumber sawed on that mill.

This Shambling's Mill became the United States Postoffice, name and place soon after the "Civil War." Then it developed into the oil field, "Hammack," and the irreverent and facetious stranger dubbed it "String Town." James Mac Welch related the following:

"I was a youngster about ten years old at the time of the battle of Spencer and surrender of it to General Jenkins. In the night of the second day after the surrender, about thirty paroled Unionists came to our house—hungry?—yes! Mother and the girls were preparing supper for all of them. They each wore on his shoulder a piece of black crepe, or black calico, wide as my hand, the parole token. Father remarked to them—with his broad smile, he was Irish, you know, 'Boys, I expected you to return under the crape, but it never occurred to me you might be carrying of it each for himself, and need feeding.' "

WEST:

Alexander, Jr., first to lay off town lots later becoming City of Spencer.

WEST:

Jesse built the first Hotel "Tavern" on Main Street, Spencer.

WEST:

Granville W. West, farmer on Vandale Fork, 1890, was born in Lewis County, Western Virginia, near Weston, February 9, 1844, one of five sons of Edward and Julia Ann (Sleeth) West, natives, descendants of the Wests, early settlers of Hackers Creek. Edward being a son of John West, who was a son of Alexander West and .... Hughes, his wife, who was a sister of Jesse and Elias Hughes, of border warfare fame. The other brothers of Granville W. West, above mentioned, were: Mansfield, Warden, William and James Farnsworth West.

Granville W. West served as a volunteer soldier of the Union armies, 'through the Civil War and was a member of the Cleavenger G. A. R. Post of Spencer while he lived here. He married, year 1864, in Lewis County, Miss Nancy King, daughter of William King, at that time a resident of Lewis County. They lived in Lewis County until the year 1890, at which time they, with their family, moved to Roane County, settling on a tract of one hundred and twenty-five acres of forest lands on Vandel Fork of Spring Creek. There reared their family of five sons and one daughter, whose names and marriages are as follows: James Addison married Lydia Vanhorn; Lyda E. married Miss Ida

Cox, daughter of Washington Cox; Emory, born 1876, married Miss Vernia Boothe; Embury, twin brother of Emory, married Myrtle McKown; Annie married Mr. Estey Arnett, son of Thomas Arnett; Ernest, born 1882, youngest of the family, married Ora Arnett, daughter of Thomas and Isabell (Donaldson) Arnett.

James Farnsworth West, son of Edward and Julia Ann (Sleeth) West, above mentioned, was born in Lewis County, year 1845, married in Lewis County, 1869, Miss Sarah S. Brown. She was born in Lewis County, 1851, daughter of a family of Browns of Ohio, temporarily in Lewis County as turnpike contractors.

James F. and Sarah S., his wife, made their home in Lewis County, West Virginia but a short time, then in Gilmer County until the year 1890, when they, with their several children, moved to Roane, purchased a fine farm on upper Spring Creek three miles above Spencer, same through which State Concrete Road No. 14 now passes; made a stock farm of it. They later sold it and now live the easy life their ages and labor entitles them to, in the City of Spencer. The names and somewhat further of their five sons and one daughter are as follows: Howard M. married Byrd Cutright, April 14, 1901, his age 24, her's 20, she a daughter of Columbus Cutright of Roane; Homer E. married Catherine Dalton, October 16, 1892, his age 20, her's 22, she a daughter of Joseph Dalton of Roane; Elmer H. married Miss Nancy Elizabeth Regar, July 8, 1900, his age 22, her age 19, she born in Lewis County, daughter of Lowe Reger; Okey married Miss Ida Queen, March 25, 1908, his age 22, her age 21, she a daughter of Harper Queen of Upper Reedy; Hattie P. married in Spencer, Mr. Homer B. Scott, November 5, 1908, her age 22, his age 25, he was born in Bradford County, Pennsylvania.

Raymond, the youngest son, is yet unmarried, and at this time, 1927, is a teacher in one of the Business Schools of Charleston.

WEST: Of Spencer and East Spencer District.

Joseph Alexander West was born in Powhatan County, Virginia, September 26, 1820, son of John S. and Martha S. (Jones) West; John S., born in Caroline County, 1787, and Martha S., in 1784. He, Joseph A., graduated from Randolph-Macon College in the year 1843; was at once ordained a Methodist minister of the gospel; a member of that national conference and present when the Wesleyan church divided and one part became Methodist Episcopal, South; he adhered to this latter branch.

He filled pulpits regularly onward; found at work in Lewis County in the year 1853. In this last county he met and married Miss Elizabeth Hanger, August, 1854. She was born in 1834, daughter of George Hanger. To them were born George Tyree, May 24, 1855; Albert Kelley, November 1, 1857; Charles Fenton, August 26, 1860. The wife Elizabeth died September 9, 1860.

Joseph A. West now (February 4, 1864, in Roane County), married Margaret Ann, daughter of Abraham and Eve (Goff) Springston, widow of Andrew J. Showen; with three children, their names and

HISTORY OF ROANE COUNTY 695

year of births: Marcellus, 1854; John W., 1858, and James A. Showen, 1860. These three were reared by Joseph A., married, made homes in Roane County and reared families in Roane County, several of whom are yet here.

Of the marriage of Joseph A. West and Margaret Ann, above named, was born only one child, Joseph Sheppard West, born May 17, 1865, on a home farm at the head of Little Creek in Spencer District. Here Reverend Joseph A. West died. Sometime after middle-age, he was thrown from a horse; in the fall his head was injured in a way that at times caused inability to concentrate, and dimmed his confidence, so he had retired from the ministry some years before his death.

Further of this family:

George Tyree West, born May 24, 1855, married Miss Anna Rogers, near Spencer, March 30, 1875. He was a good carpenter and farmer. They made their life-time home a mile or so east of Spencer; reared several children, among whom is Benjamin West, dentist, at Lumber Port, Harrison County.

Albert Kelley West, born November 1, 1857, married three times: first in Roane County, Miss Nettie Riddle; the other wives we do not know. He reared and sent out two sons, Carey and Landon; and a daughter, Elizabeth. Some of these are prosperous in the far south, we are told.

Charles Fenton West, third son of Joseph A. and Elizabeth (Hanger) West, was born in Roane County, on the farm above mentioned, August 26, 1860; grew up there; acquired all the education doled out by the county free schools; taught school some terms, and became a farmer and general trader. On the first day of April, 1886, he united in marriage with Miss Florence Chenowith, born December 8, 1858, daughter of Robert James and Elizabeth Jane (Knotts) Chenowith, large farmers of Minnora, Clahoun County, West Virginia, both descendants of pioneer families of Virginia and westward. C. Fenton and his wife, Florence West, lived several years on a farm ,east of and not far from Spencer; but have had their residence in the Town of Spencer the last fifteen years or more, where he has conducted a grocery and general store business at one or more periods. Both are active church workers and, she especially, was one of the pioneer members and workers in the Anti-Saloon League or Temperance societies that condemned the use and sale of intoxicating liquors. They have reared no son or daughter of their own. But about the year 1914, adopted as their daughter, Edith Gladie Douglas, born in Calhoun County, West Virginia, August 26, 1915, daughter of Ballard and Flossie (Sharp) Douglass, his wife; Ballard having died in the year 1915.

Joseph Sheppard West, son of Joseph Alexander and Margaret Ann (Goff-Showen) West, was born on the farm above mentioned, May 17, 1865; was diligent at the district school of the neighborhood; a teacher of the county force at twenty years of age, has taught continually ever since.

On January 22, 1887, he united in marriage with Miss Amelia Belle Burgess, daughter of George W. and Mary (Rapp) Burgess, he then 22 years old ; she 21, born in Roane. George W. and Mary Burgess, his wife, having been born in Augusta County, Virginia. To Jos. Sheppard and Amelia Belle, his wife, have been born and by them brought up, four sons and four daughters. School teachers all, or most of them.

WESTFALL:

The name, one time written "Westfallen" which last is only the plural form of the same word, is the family name of pioneers of the Monongahela Valley. These of whom we are writing came to Poca country from Harrison or Lewis County, as early, possibly, as the year 1845. These were two brothers, the name of the first we do not have. The second was John H. Westfall, of whom and his family we will deal after dealing first with the family of the unknown brother and his wife who settled on upper Flat Fork, or Cox's Fork; their children being two daughters and a son; their names: (1) Barbara, who became the wife of Andrew Stewart, son of William Stewart, pioneer of Reedy, 1848 or 1850, where "Andy" and Barbara made their home, attended the mill and reared a large family. See name "Stewart." (2) Debora, who married Henderson Harper, of Poca; and (3) Noah Westfall, who for his fifth or sixth wife married Martha Rhodes, of lower Poca, year 1881.

John H. Westfall, first above meentioned, before coming here had married, in Lewis County, Western Virginia, Miss Miranda Green. To John H. and Miranda (Green) were born—most of them in Lewis County—the following named six sons and five daughters:

Anderson, who married Jane Clarkson, January 5, 1860; Clark, who married Matilda Clarkson, September 24, 1860; Nathan; Columbus; Epison; W. H. "Buck." Of the daughters of John H. and Miranda (Green) Westfall, we can name: Minerva, who married Mr. Ratcliff; Sarah Elizabeth, wife of Ransom Whited of Walton; Dorcas, wife of Thomas Allen of head of Mill Creek; Louisette, wife of I. S. Reed, of divide between Poca and Reedy; and Jane, who married G. R. Reed or Reid. These "Westfallen" men were distinguished for their large size, blond complexion and long beards. They have left numerous descendants here in Roane.

A. Henry Westfall married Nancy M. Eakin, November 21, 1870.

WHITED: Moses.

In the first part of the decade, 1850 to 1860, Moses Whited and Millie, his wife, of an old Virginia family of Whiteds, came from Russell County, Virginia, and purchased a large tract of land on Poca extending to within half mile of the place now Gandeeville, then the farms of the Gandees, lying down the creek and eastward.

With Moses and Millie came their four sons, Henderson, Robert Francis Clinton and John; all of whom had each his wife with him when he arrived or went back to Russell County and married one and brought her here. For some reason the name then was pronounced as

HISTORY OF ROANE COUNTY   697

if spelled "Whitehead." I have seen many of the second generation of these, and a few of the men of the first. They were all of a clean blond complexion and very light colored hair ,tall and athletic looking. This predominance of the light hair possibly accounted for the pronunciation of the name. We take up the sons of Moses and Millie and say further, that

Henderson's wife was Rebecca A., daughter of James Boothe, family of Russell County ,who settled on Big Creek of Pocatalico. To Henderson and Rebecca were born, Riben, Moses, John Jr. and Shouldis.

Robert's wife was of Russell County, Virginia, but we do not have her family name. To Robert and wife were born Charles, Jerome, Potter and Thomas.

Francis C., son of Moses and Millie Whited, married Jane Lyons in Russell County, Virginia. To them were born here, Ranson Doddridge and Henry Clinton. Of these two sons we say further, that

Ranson Doddridge Whited married Sarah E. Westfall, January 25, 1867.

Henry Clinton Whited, son of Francis Clinton ,third son of Moses and Millie Whited, was born in Roane County, West Virginia, year 1860, married Ruhama, daughter of Clark Westfall of near head waters of Mill Creek in Roane County, year 1881, and made their farm home on head of Mill Creek. To Henry C. and Ruhama were born four sons. She died; and for a second wife Henry C. married Elizabeth Kile of Flat Fork, Harper District. She was born in Harrison County, West Virginia, year 1863. Henry C. and Elizabeth (Kile) Westfall raised four daughters, two of whom are married and two are Misses yet, 1926, at home.

John Whited, son of Moses and Millie Whited, married Susan Lyons in Russell County, Virginia, about the year 1857, and they soon made their home first near Gandeeville, later purchased forest lands on head of Frozen Camp, made there a large home-farm and reared their family of four sons and four daughters, whose names are as follows: Crocket, Jerome B., Thomas, and Millie Ann, who married Jacob Hinzman; Emily, wife of James Carpenter; Margaret, oldest of the daughters married James Hickman; and Caroline, the youngest, married William D. Kelley, son of Blackburn Kelley. All these made homes in Roane County.

Riben Moses Whited, son of Henderson and Rebecca (Boothe) Whited, married Rebecca Boothe, December 22, 1858, she a daughter of James Boothe on Big Creek of Pocatalico. To Riben M. and Rebecca were born seven sons and two daughters, their names and marriages as follows:

William J. Whited, to Sarah S. Mahan, December 3, 1885; his age 21, her age 19; Isaac A. Whited, to Minnie V. Noel, March 18, 1894, his age 28, her age 19; Edward Riben Whited, to Eliza J. Canterbury, December 15, 1895, ages, his 24, her's 21; Albert A. Whited, to Eunice N. Taylor, August 19, 1894, his age 21, hers 21, she a daughter of Ira Taylor; John Julian Whited, born January 25, 1876, to Enie Tolley of Flat Fork, October 13, 1901, he then 24, she 17; Erastus Doddridge Whited to Emma Hively, March 17, 1901, his age 22, her's 27, she a daughter of Mathew Hively, of Pocatalico; Ezra Garfield Whited to Lelia Shouldis, December 17, 1899, his age 19, her's then 19.

The two daughters of Riben Moses Whited and his wife Rebecca, were oldest of the family; America Alice, married Perry S. Good, December 27, 1880; Nancy D. married Hannibal Ryan, August 9, 1888, her age then 21, his age 24, she born in Athens County, Ohio, the marriage records have it. Riben M. and wife resided there in Ohio a year or so next following the Civil War.

WHITNEY:

Silas Porter Whitney, long spoken of here as the Reverend S. P. Whitney, was the first of this family name in Roane County, settled here in 1874.

Rev. Silas P. Whitney was born in Saratoga County, New York, February 4, 1835, son of Solomon E. and Susan (Woodworth) Whitney; born in 1808, and 1811, respectively. Silas Porter Whitney became devoted to the tenets of the Adventist Christian Church; the western center of authority of that church called him to Chicago; next the Boston authority sent him to a point in Ohio. He was thirty-four years old at the time of coming west. From Ohio he was sent to the "Valley of the Great Kanawha;" from here he traveled into many counties of West Virginia.

In his biography in Hardesty's, Silas P. mentions two brothers, sons of Solomon and Susan Whitney, also born in New York; Seldon L. and George H. both soldiers in New York regiments of the Union Army of 1862-65, 22d and 72d regiments respectively; Seldon L. was killed in the battle of South Mountain.

While preaching, Silas Porter met and married Mollie M. Thomas, July 10, 1871, at the home of the bride's parents, George D. and Sarah (Jones) Thomas, at Sissonsville, where Mollie M. was born April 8, 1853. The next year, 1872, Rev. Silas and his wife came to Roane County, settling a short time on Rock Creek, thence came to Big Lick, where they finished their long and active lives. He was twenty years president of the Southern Ohio A. C. Conference.

To Silas Porter and Mollie M. (Thomas) Whitney were born and brought up the following children:

George Emmons, Benjamin Franklin, Matilda and Rebecca. Of these sons and daughters we have further to say:

George Emmons Whitney, son of Silas P. and Mollie M. (Thomas) Whitney, born in Roane County, April 25, 1872, married Miss Mattie Lou Taylor in North Alabama, in the year 1900. At once made their home in Walton District, Roane County. To them were born here, Silas Pembroke, Guy Emmons, Bassel Freeman, Violet, being a youth yet at home with her parents.

George Emmons Whitney was long a popular school teacher of the county, and was elected and served one term, four years, as a member

HISTORY OF ROANE COUNTY 699

of the county court and was an enthusiast for hard-surfaced roads, and supported a bond issued of Walton District to connect that district's main road with Spencer's; then came the State inter-county roads enactment and that road was taken over by the State, becoming State Road No. 14.

Benjamin Franklin, son of Silas P. and Mollie M. (Thomas) Whitney, born March 26, 1874, married Lou or Louisa Wamack in North Alabama, where they now (1926) reside; Benjamin F. being at this time U. S. District Collector of Internal Revenue, in office at Atlanta, Georgia.

Matilda, daughter of S. P. and Mollie M. Whitney married Diron Carroll, residents of South Charleston.

Rebecca, daughter of S. P. and Mollie M. Whitney, born April 16, 1881, married Coy Taylor of Roane, son of Albert Taylor of near Walton.

WILSON: Of upper Spring Creek, First.

William R. Wilson and his wife, Elizabeth (Wolfe, sister of Jos. B.) with their family of several children, all born on the Buckhannon of the Monongahela, came to, and settled on, upper right hand fork of Spring Creek, about the year 1854.

The names of those children were: Abram, Jacob, Albinus, Sylvester and Rachel V.

Of these we write further as follows:

Abram married Jane Shouldis of Jackson County, West Virginia, and went to the far west.

Jacob married Virginia Cox, January, 1860. See "Cox."

Albinus married, first P. M. Chidester, 1871. She died and he married Sarah Carpenter, April, 1879.

Sylvester married Sarah Conley, November 11, 1872. See "Conley."

Rachel V. married Washington Cox, February 24, 1859; settled on Rush Creek of Pocatalico.

Jacob Wilson and Virginia Cox, his wife, were parents of the following children: William Franklin, who married Columbia Radabaugh, daughter of James Radabaugh of Reedy; Kate, whose marriage we don't know; Joseph L., early a young business man of Spencer, now of Huntington, West Virginia; Cora married William Rhodes of Cottageville, West Virginia; Dexter P. and Sylvester, Jr., twins, though the marriage records make a difference of one year in their ages; Jeremiah, Mcle and Newton.

Of above, Sylvester A. Wilson married Margaret A. Marks, March 17, 1887; his age 21, her's 18.

Dexter P. Wilson married Martha Scyoc, March 23, 1893; his age 26, her's 18.

WINE:

A Travis Wine is mentioned in Hardesty's History as an early settler of Walton District; however, we find nothing substantiating the statement.

John Wine, son of a Wine family living on the Great Kanawha somewhere near Raymond City, appears to be the first of this name to settle in Roane. This John Wine came here when a young man and worked on the construction of the Glenville, Ripley and Ohio turnpike, about 1854. He married about the year 1846, Miss .... Miller, a daughter of the pioneer Samuel Miller, then residing above Spencer Town, formerly of Curtis. To John and (Miller), his wife, were born Charles Wine and Richard Wine.

Richard Wine married Nancy Miller. To him and his wife were born Angeline, Jerry, John, James, and a son known as "Bunk" Wine. Richard Wine long kept a hotel in Spencer.

Charles, son of John and (Miller) Wine, married.................................. To them were born, Thomas, who served as a Union soldier, married Mary E. Bower of near Spencer March 11, 1873.

Others of the family of Charley Wine and wife: Nancy Jane, Mary C., Leona, Josephine, Norman and Mathew "Mat" Wine and a Jas. M. Wine.

WITTEN: A. H., long of Spencer.

Albert and Arthur Witten were English, born and broughht up in London, where A. H. served as a clerk in his father's counting house.

Albert and Arthur are next found on the Ohio River about the year 1875. One of these brothers married and made his home about Point Pleasant, West Virginia; both were excellent house and sign painters.

A. H. Witten while working in Spencer woed and won for wife Miss Eliza Showen of the Curtis District family; their marriage being on November 10, 1880; A. H. and Eliza, his wife, thereafter made their home for many years in Spencer, where to them were born and by them brought up the following two daughters and one son: Jessie, Katie and Arthur.

Katie became the wife of Floyd Lee Linger, June 20, 1894; her age then 22, his 28; he was born in Lewis County, West Virginia.

The mother having died, A. H., Jessie and Arthur Jr., went to Akron, Ohio, where A. H. embarked in a grocery business which he conducted with such success as to leave some twenty thousand dollars as his estate on his death there a few years ago.

WHITE: Of upper Big Sandy.

Arthur and Rebecca (Miller) White are the first of this name to settle on a farm on upper Big Sandy; at or about the mouth of Simmons Run, where Uler postoffice now (1926) is. His grandson says he was of an old Virginia family last living in Tazwell County; a granddaughter, wife of Samuel B. Wright, is represented by her husband as giving Russell County as the place of Arthur White's last residence before coming to Big Sandy, and that she was born in Russell, in 1831, and married Samuel B. Wright here on Sanday, year 1851; so we are persuaded to place arrival of Arthur and Rebecca White here as about the year 1845.

Shortly after his arrived here, Arthur White purchased of Rev. Davidson Ross, eleven hundred acres of "wild lands" located as first mentioned, on upper Sandy. Here Arthur and Rebecca began one of those masterful careers of clearing lands and raising a large family. Married twice—Arthur became father of six children of the first wife, and seven of the second, their names as follows: John, Timothy, Benjamin, James, Rafe, Alexander. For a second wife Arthur married Margaret Harold. The children of this marriage are: Barbara, Annie, Mariah, Jackson, Michael, Robert and Ali.

Of the above sons of Arthur and Rebecca White we notice that Benjamin became the father of John White, a merchant of Newton, several years next before year 1915.

And that James, the fourth son of Arthur and Rebecca, married near Newton, Talitha, daughter of Isaac and Margaret (Peggy Bishop) Drake, and made their home on the old place on upper Sandy. Of this marriage ten children were born, their names as follows: Margaret, who became the wife of Phillip Justice of Left Hand; Lydia, wife of J. H. Hall; James Harvey (died); Hulda, who married Levi Smith and is now living in Charleston, West Virginia; Davidson W., "Double-u White," was born, year 1871; married, 1894, Georgia, daughter of H. F. and Harriette Reed, formerly of Craig County, Virginia. Of this marriage there are at this time, 1926, three sons and five daughters.

WOODYARD: Of City of Spencer, first here.

William Woodyard, merchant, real estate man, State Senator. Ancestry, marriage, career, children.

Among the pioneers of Wirt County, near the year 1800, was a family Woodyard. Of these was one Lewis Woodyard who united in marriage at "Beauchamps" Mills, now Elizabeth, on the Little Kanawha, when that part of the Little Kanawha Valley was part of Wood County, in records of which will be found the marriage of Lewis Woodyard and Catherine Wiseman; she a daughter of a pioneer family of Wisemans of that locality. They made their home on lands extending to the river and kept the ferry; there brought up their family of five sons and four daughters, as learned from George A. Roberts of City of Elizabeth, Wirt County historian.

The names of these sons and daughters of Lewis Woodyard and wife, are Caleb, Isaac, John, Frank, William, Annie, Harriett, Mary and Emma.

These all married and scattered each on his own.

William Woodyard, son of Lewis and Catherine (Wiseman) Woodyard was born in Wirt County, Western Virginia, year 1840; buried at Spencer, 1895.

He came to Spencer, possibly during the commotion of the Civil War. The town was garrisoned in 1862 by four regiments of Union troops under Col. John C. Rathbone, a native of Wirt County, as were many of his troops.

William Woodyard united in marriage with Miss Isabelle Chapman, February 24, 1866; she a daughter of Dr. Henry D. Chapman and wife; born 1848, died 1915.

To William and Isabelle (Chapman) Woodyard, were born and by them brought up, in Spencer, the following sons and daughters: Catherine, Harry Chapman, Ralph, Louise and Jeanette. Something further of these:

Katherine H. married Frank M. Baldwin, October 2, 1895; his age given 27, her's 25. Ralph died in Havana, never married. His body is buried in Spencer cemetery.

Helen Louise married Ernst Kaltenbach, June 6, 1894, his age 38, her age 19. They at once made their home in Detroit, Michigan.

Jeanette, youngest of the family, married Leonard S. Hall, of New Martinsville, W. Va.

Harry Chapman Woodyard, above mentioned, was born in Spencer, November 13, 1867; attended first the town schools, then "was sent away to school." His first work was that of station agent at Spencer depot of the R. S. & G. Railway. He united in marriage with Emma J. Douglass, born year 1868, daughter of Andrew and Ruhama (Dilworth) Douglass, of Romines Mills, Harrison County, at her parent's home; Emma J. having been married previously to a Mr. Kelley, who had died shortly after marriage.

Harry C. and Emma Woodyard began their united careers at Spencer. He was a shrewd investor, she a sagacious discerner. He was elected by the people and served as State Senator for the district of which Roane was a part for the twenty-fourth and twenty-fifth sessions, 1899-1901. He was elected and represented the Congressional District of which Roane is a part, in 1902, and thereafter to every term except one 1922-1924, his last term expiring March 3, 1927.

To Harry C. and Emma J. Woodyard, his wife, were born and by them brought up, three sons and no daughter: William, Jr., Edward Douglass and Henry Chapman.

These sons are all married and have businesses and homes in Spencer. They were mainly educated in the schools at Spencer, finished in Washington, D. C., and in some school or college in Pennsylvania. William was for some time part of the management of the Spencer Water and Ice Company; married, 1926, Miss Frances Huddleston, of Spencer.

Edward D. Woodyard is editor of the Times-Record; married a Miss Josephine Boynton, of Gloversville, N. Y., at Washington, D. C.

Henry C. is co-editor with Edward D., of the Times-Record. He married a Miss Ida L. Moore, of Charleston.

HISTORY OF ROANE COUNTY 703

WRIGHT: Of upper Geary District.
Samuel B. Wright was born in Nelson County, Virginia, October 16, 1818, son of Benjiman and Jane (Borden) Wright, each born in Amherst County, Virginia. Samuel came to Big Sandy some time in the decade beginning 1840. He was a blacksmith and carpenter by trade. On November 17, 1851 he married Jane Smith, on Sandy, she was born in Russell County, Virginia, December 15, 1831, daughter of Ali and Jane (King) Smith, who left Russell, lived a while in Pike County, Kentucky, from there came to Big Sandy somtime prior to the marriage of Jane with Samuel. To Samuel and Jane (Wright), his wife, were born, on Sandy, the following named children: Louisa, April 16, 1854; Nancy E., March 21, 1856; Albert, July 19, 1858; Samuel K., February 11, 1863; Daniel L., July 29, 1866; Maria J., August 4, 1860; George A., October 23, 1874. Samuel B. Wright served three years as a Confederate soldier, 14th Virginia Cavalry.

WRIGHT: Of Lower Flat Fork, Harper District.
John B. Wright, was born in Roanoke, Virginia, in the year 1869, arrived alone on Pocatalico some time prior to the year 1896. On being asked why he left the place of his birth, his reply was "to escape the tyranny of a step mother. I was only a small boy when I left; made my way here nad liked it." He became a substantial citizen. On September, 1896, John B. Wright and Esta M. Conley were married at the bride's home, her age 27, his age 27. She was a daughter of Jeremiah Conley. See the name "Conley."

YOUNG:
Squire Young, son of John H. and Catherine (Slack) Young, of a Pennsylvania family of the name Young, was born in Kanawha County, Western Virginia, January 11, 1831. About 1847 the family of John H. Young lived on head waters of Mill Creek which later became a part of Harper District. Two sons are remembered; their names Brigham and Squier.
Squier's first work was that of stake driver for surveyors and engineers at constructing the Glenville, Ripley and Ohio turnpike, 1850 to 1853.
Squier Young was twice married, each time to daughters of Roane County families. The first wife was Elizabeth, daughter of St. Clair Summers, of Jarrett's Ford. The children of this marriage were William M. Young, of Left Hand, on State Route No. 14 (1926). Catherine, who married John E. Hunt, son of the Hunts of Harper District, who was County Superintendent of Schools one term, 1885-1887. Henry F., son of Squier, married the daughter of Frank Taylor, of Kanawha County. James Perry "Pet" Young, married Emma E. Gibson, in Roane County, October 15, 1895. She being the daughter

of H. Frank Gibson, of near Walton, James Perry's age 27, her age
26. To them were born several children. Emma E., the wife of
J. P. Young, died about the year 1920. James ("Pet") Young became
the owner of the large cattle farm near Looneyville, known as the J. M.
Simmons farm. He lived there until his wife's death, though still
owning the farm he stays in Spencer much. Names of the children
of J. P. and Emma E. (Gibson) Young, given in the order of their
ages are Lawrence W., Mary E., Minnie, Mabel, George S. and Henry.

For a second wife Squier Young married Nancy E. Jennings, 1877.
To them were born two daughters, Cora E., who married Perry Moody
Marks, of Roane County, August 27, 1907, his age 28, her age 24;
Laura J. married Cyrus Dayton Hunt, June 29, 1899, his age 21, her
age 21.

Of descendants of Brigam Young, son of John H. and Catherine
(Slack) Young, two are known in Roane County. They being Samuel
Young, of Spencer, and Downtain Young, a farmer of Clay or Colhoun
County.

Squire Young gave the writer the above information in October, 1926,
and departed this life three or four months afterward.

www.ingramcontent.com/pod-product-compliance
Lightning Source LLC
Chambersburg PA
CBHW061437300426
44114CB00014B/1719